The Pilgrimage Chronicles
Book II

Embrace the Quest

with Tor and Siffy Torkildson

Introduction by Brandon Wilson

Sacred World Explorations
Alaska

First edition, Sacred World Explorations, 2017.

Published by Sacred World Explorations, Alaska, USA
Text © 2017 Tor Torkildson and authors
Cover art: Lorie Karnath
Maps: Siffy Torkildson
Page layout and design: Siffy Torkildson

ISBN 978-0-692-96788-1

Sacred World Explorations
Alaska

Dedication

We dedicate *The Pilgrimage Chronicles: Embrace the Quest* to the extraordinary explorers, Annie Peck, and Pat Morrow. In their unique and remarkable ways, they inspire us to live the life we imagined. They set the bar high, led by example, and we are trying our best to follow in their bootstraps. This is our quest.

Keep on Keeping On (KOKO)!
Tor y Siffy Torkildson

Pat Morrow   Annie Peck

Equator

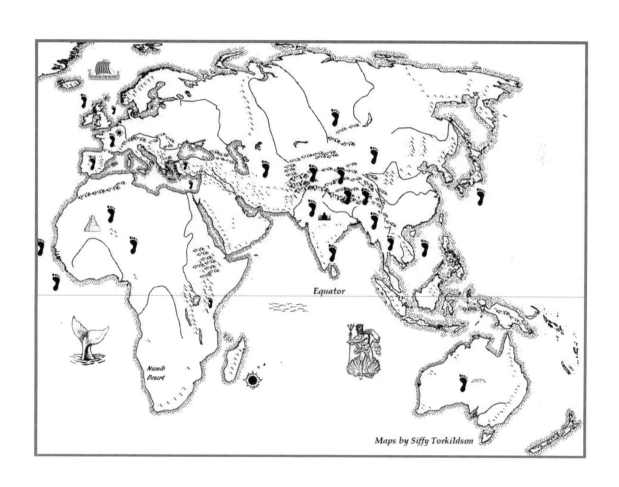

Equator

Namib
Desert

Maps by Siffy Torkildson

With Gratitude

We would like to give special tribute and our sincere gratitude to Edwin Bernbaum, Lorie Karnath, and Brandon Wilson for their unselfish willingness to espouse, *The Pilgrimage Chronicles: Embrace the Quest*, and their many contributions to the book's creation and originality.

We would like to express gratitude to Edwin Bernbaum for his dedication to sharing the myths, practices, and religious beliefs surrounding legendary holy peaks around the globe, providing a unique synthesis of natural history, environmental and cross-cultural studies, and in-depth religious scholarship. We are grateful to Edwin Bernbaum for sharing his vision of Shambala with the world and an excerpt from his seminal work, *Sacred Mountains of the World,* in *The Pilgrimage Chronicles*.

This book would not be as beautiful as it is without the cover painting by Lorie Karnath. We received a number of entries for our cover art contest, and Lorie's stood out. Lorie's consistent professional guidance, encourage- ment, essay, and cover art bring this book to life. Lorie is involved in so many projects to help humanity, and the environment, that we are honored and deeply thankful for her time and enthusiasm she brings to this project.

When we think about what it means to promote peace, and to be a pilgrim, the first person that comes to mind is Brandon Wilson. He is the real deal. As a peace pilgrim, he has walked from Lhasa to Kathmandu, England to Rome, and France to Jerusalem, and explored nearly 100 countries. Brandon so graciously wrote the introduction for *The Pilgrimage Chronicles* and shared his own experiences concerning his personal transition from being a traveler to becoming a pilgrim. Brandon Wilson inspires us to go out into the world and embrace our own quest.

We feel fortunate to have these three-exceptional human beings guiding us and inspiring the creation of this anthology. We consider them dear friends and look forward to partaking in many adventures together in the future. Thank you, Ed, Lorie, and Brandon, for all you do and your friendship.

Tor and Siffy

We'd like to give a special thank you to the Pilgrimage tribe. You know who you are.

Keep on Keeping on!

with Tor and Siffy Torkildson

The Art of Pilgrimage
By cover artist Lorie Karnath

A pilgrimage is not about a physical journey but rather represents a conduit towards a meaningful transference. Actual travel to reach a specific destination becomes peripheral to the intent. The pilgrim is present in the moment rather than to tangential surroundings, embodying a metaphysical process that fosters an awakening of perception, a deepening of awareness that can lead towards an expansion of consciousness.

Whether rendered in realistic or in abstract terms, the act of painting can often be a pilgrimage in itself. It proffers a response rather than a reactive undertaking representing the artist's unique experiences and observations which are melded into a singular present moment. Similar to pilgrimages involving physical displacement throughout the artist's journey, there is an ongoing process of orientation, a resonance with a specific body of knowledge, a balancing of both internal as well as external annotations and interpretations, these encompassed within a new format.

The cover for this book depicts a particular mountain, the majestic Mount Meru also referred to by many other names. While many mountains inspire both awe and reverence, Meru is considered by many to be the most magical and sacred place on earth, the apex of a "Cosmic Ocean" around which all the planets revolve. It has been described as the center of the world as well as its spiritual crown. Remotely situated in the northernmost portion of the Himalayas, it stretches resplendently, wreathed in clouds, towards the heavens, providing a backdrop for the spectra of the sun's light, seemingly beyond the scope of human realms. It spurs the imagination and embodies the concept of pilgrimage serving as an allegorical transition between the physical, metaphysical and spiritual spheres.

A pilgrimage, even when undertaken in the company of others, represents a mostly solitary pursuit. Like the process of painting, it often embodies trajectories of silent contemplation, allowing for the formation of an inner quiet providing a template where the breadth and texture of an individual's experience can flow unobstructed. The painting on the back of the book depicts a lone pilgrim, hardly discernible, an integration of the self, within the beauty and vastness of the natural world that envelops him. A blending of the mind, spirit and physical world.

Front cover painting title: The Promised Way.
Back cover painting title: The Wanderer.

Mount Kailash. *Photograph by Edwin Bernbaum.*

Edwin Bernbaum

Excerpt from *Sacred Mountains of the World*

*A*s the loftiest mountains on earth, the Himalayas have come to embody the highest ideals and aspirations. The sight of their sublime peaks, soaring high and clean above the dusty, congested plains of India, has for centuries inspired visions of transcendent splendor and spiritual liberation. Invoking such visions, the *Puranas*, ancient works of Hindu mythology, have this to say of Himachal, or the Himalayas:

In the space of a hundred ages of the gods, I could not describe to you the glories of Himachal [Himalaya] . . . that Himachal where Shiva dwells and where the Ganges falls like the tendril of a lotus from the foot of Vishnu . . . There are no other mountains like Himachal for there are found Mount Kailas and Lake Manasarovar. . . As the dew is dried up by the morning sun, so are the sins of humankind by the sight of Himachal.

Mount Kailas

One peak in the Himalayan region stands out above all others as the ultimate sacred mountain for more than a half a billion people in India, Tibet, Nepal, and Bhutan. Hidden behind the main range of the Himalayas at a high point of the Tibetan Plateau northwest of Nepal, Mount Kailas rises in isolated splendor near the sources of four major rivers of the Indian subcontinent—the Indus, the Brahmaputra, the Sutlej, and the Karnali. Hindus also regard it as the place where the divine form of the Ganges, the holiest river of all, cascading from heaven first touches the earth to course invisibly through the locks of Shiva's hair before spewing forth from a glacier 140 miles to the west. Not far from the foot of the peak itself, at nearly fifteen thousand feet above sea level, reflecting the light of its snows, repose the calm blue waters of the most sacred lake of Hindu religion and mythology—the holy Manasarovar, "Ocean of the Mind." The hardiest of Hindu pilgrims aspire to take the long and dangerous journey over high passes to bathe in its icy waters and cleanse their minds of the sins that threaten to condemn them to the suffering of rebirth. Buddhists know it as Anavatapta, the "Unheated One," a lake that the historical Buddha is said to have magically visited when he lived and taught in India during the fifth century B.C.

At only 22,028 feet Kailas is thousands of feet lower than Everest and many other Himalayan peaks. Its extraordinary setting and appearance, however, more than make up for its modest height. Situated in a high desert beyond the reach of monsoon rains, the peak rises in a bright and flawless sky, alone above a golden plain, unchallenged by the ranges of softly rounded hills that flank it on either side. Unlike Everest, which merges with other mountains to vanish behind them, Kailas retains its grandeur when viewed from a distance. More than any other peak in the Himalayas, it opens the mind to the cosmos around it, evoking a sense of infinite space that makes one aware of a vaster universe encompassing the limited world of ordinary experience.

Placed on a pedestal of striated rock, its dome of snow shining white in the sun, Kailas looks more like a piece of marble sculpture fashioned by the hands of the gods than a mountain created by the forces of nature. Indeed, Tibetans often compare the peak to the pagoda palace of a deity or the reliquary of a saint, and they treat it as such, prostrating themselves before it. It has also served as an inspiration for numerous Hindu temples and shrines in the distant plains of India. The mere sight of the peak has a powerful effect, bringing tears to the eyes of many who behold it, leaving them convinced that they have glimpsed the abode of the gods beyond the round of life and death.

Hindus view Mount Kailas as the divine dwelling place of the great god Shiva and his wife, the beautiful goddess Parvati. There, as the supreme yogi, naked and smeared with ashes, his matted hair coiled on top of his head, he sits on a tiger skin, steeped in the indescribable bliss of meditation. From his position of aloof splendor on the summit of Kailas, his third eye blazing with supernatural power and awareness, the Lord of the Mountain calmly surveys the joys and sorrows, the triumphs and tragedies, the entire play of illusion that makes up life in the world below. As one of the three forms of the supreme deity—Brahma and Vishnu being the other two—Shiva is the god of destruction and lord of the dance. The power of his meditation destroys the world of illusions that bind people to the painful cycle of death and rebirth. When he rises to dance, he takes on the functions of Brahma and Vishnu and creates and preserves the universe itself.

According to a well-known Hindu myth, Shiva was once meditating in the mountains near Kailas. The lesser gods learned that only a son born of his powerful semen could defeat the demons who were oppressing the earth. They therefore sent Parvati, the daughter of the mountain god Himalaya, to seduce the celibate Shiva. She spent thousands of years practising austerities and meditating in his presence until she caught his attention. At that point Kama, the god of love, shot one of his flowered arrows at Shiva, who seeing him at the last minute burned him to ashes with a glance of his flaming eye. But it was too late: the arrow hit its mark and Shiva fell in love with Parvati. They were married in a magnificent ceremony in the mountain palace of the god Himalaya and then went to dwell on Kailas, where they made love and had a supernatural son, Karttikeya, who grew up to defeat the demons and liberate the world from evil.[i]

Indian paintings often depict idyllic family scenes of Shiva and Parvati with Karttikeya and their other son, the delightful elephant-headed god, Ganesha, picnicking in beautiful meadows and forests on top of Mount Kailas. The opening lines of the *Tantra of the Great Liberation*, a major work of Hindu mysticism, describe this paradise:

The enchanting summit of the Lord of Mountains, resplendent with all its various jewels, clad with many a tree and many a creeper, melodious with the song of many a bird, scented with the fragrance of all the season's flowers, most beautiful, fanned by soft, cool, and perfumed breezes, shadowed by the still shade of stately trees; where cool groves resound with the sweet-voiced songs of troops of celestial nymphs. . .[ii]

As a sacred mountain of multi-faceted significance, Kailas encompasses the extremes of spiritual asceticism and material riches. The great epics of Indian literature, the *Mahabharata* and *Ramayana*, refer to the peak as the luxurious residence of Kubera, the god of wealth who lives in the far north. *The Cloud Messenger*, a poem composed in the fifth century by the Sanskrit poet and dramatist Kalidasa, the Indian equivalent of Shakespeare, relates the story of a love-lorn *yaksha*, a supernatural being of Hindu mythology, banished to southern India from his home in Alaka, the city of Kubera on the summit of Kailas. Consumed with longing for his lover back on the sacred mountain, he sends her a message with a passing cloud that he spies drifting north toward the Himalayas. In his instructions to this unusual messenger, he compares the heavenly qualities of the city to those of the cloud itself:

Its palaces resemble you in various ways: your lightning flashes in the brilliance of their beautiful women;
Colorful paintings on their walls match the hues of your rainbow;
The music of tambourines, beating in song and dance, echoes the soft rumble of your thunder;
Floors paved with jewels reflect the gleaming waters you carry within you;
While roofs reaching up to the sky equal you in your loftiness.[iii]

Like the sacred mountain it so beautifully describes, *The Cloud Messenger* represents a peak of perfection in the history of Indian literature.

Kailas also has great significance for the Buddhists of Tibet and figures prominently in one of the most beautiful and widely read works of Tibetan literature—*The Hundred Thousand Songs of Milarepa*. Like the Hindus of India, the Tibetans regard Kailas as the ultimate sacred mountain, the one that they dream of beholding at least once in their lifetimes, although few ever have the opportunity to do so. Situated in the high and wind-swept reaches of western Tibet, it lies far from the centers of population in the central and eastern parts of the country. Tibetans call Kailas by two different names: Tise and Kang Rimpoche, the "Precious One of Glacial Snow." The second name indicates the high esteem in which they hold it: Rimpoche is the title reserved for the very highest lamas or Buddhist priests, such as the Dalai Lama, the exiled ruler of Tibet, whom they view as incarnations of spiritual beings called Bodhisattvas.

Kailas is noted in Tibetan history and literature as the scene of a famous mountain climbing contest between Tibet's most beloved Yogi, Milarepa, and Naro Bhun Chon, a priest of the indigenous non-Buddhist religion of Bon. Milarepa, who roamed the high mountains in the twelfth century clad only in a cotton shirt and the warmth of his meditation, came to pay homage to Kailas and the sacred lake near its foot. When he arrived with his disciples, Naro Bhun Chon accosted him, saying that the area was the special preserve of the Bon religion and that he would have to take up its practices if he wished to stay. Milarepa refused, and a series of contests of supernatural power ensued to determine whose teachings would prevail—those of the Buddha, which had been recently introduced from India into Tibet, or those of Shenrab, the great teacher who had founded Bon in the vicinity of Kailas thousands of years before. After a succession of embarrassing losses in which he refused to concede defeat, Naro challenged Milarepa to a race that would settle the issue once and for all: the first to reach the summit of Kailas on the fifteenth day of the month would be acknowledged the spiritual master of the mountain.

While Milarepa relaxed and enjoyed the beautiful scenery, Naro went into spiritual training, strenuously praying to his deity for the power needed to make the ascent. On the appointed day, early in the morning, the Bon priest put on a green cloak and took off flying on his shaman's drum toward the summit of Kailas. Milarepa was still asleep. His anxious disciples woke him up to tell him that Naro had reached the waist of the mountain. Quite unconcerned, he made a gesture with his hand, and the Bon priest found himself circling around the peak, unable to go higher. Then, putting on a cloak for wings, Milarepa snapped his finger and with the first light of the sun flew in a second to the summit of Kailas—certainly the most elegant ascent in the history of mountaineering, and one of the earliest ever recorded.

When poor Naro looked up to see Milarepa sitting at ease on top of the mountain, he fell off in amazement, and his drum tumbled down the south face of Kailas, leaving a series of indentations that look like a line of steps ascending the peak. Whereas Tibetan Buddhists attribute these indentations to the fall of the Bon priest, Hindus view them as a stairway leading up to the heaven of Shiva on the summit itself. Neither they nor any Tibetans, however, would ever contemplate trying to climb this, the most sacred of mountains. Completely humbled, Naro finally acknowledged defeat, and Milarepa magnanimously allowed him to stay on a nearby peak where he might practice his religion and continue to gaze on Kailas, now indisputably

Buddhist. Milarepa's feelings about the mountain are lyrically expressed in the words of one of his many songs of spiritual accomplishment:

The prophecy of Buddha says most truly,
That this snow mountain is the navel of the world,
A place where the snow leopards dance.
The mountain top, the crystal-like pagoda,
Is the white and glistening palace of Demchog...
This is the great place of accomplished yogis;
Here one attains transcendent accomplishments.
There is no place more wonderful than this,
There is no place more marvelous than here.[iv]

Milarepa adds that the snow mountains encircling Kailas are the dwelling place of five hundred Buddhist saints who have attained Nirvana, the blessed state of transcendence free from suffering. According to legend, those who have gained spiritual acuity may sometimes hear the divine music of their chanting in the high clear atmosphere of the Tibetan Plateau.

In his song Milarepa refers to the palace of Demchog, the principal Buddhist deity of the sacred mountain. Of awesome appearance, blue like the sky, draped with garlands of skulls and embracing his female consort, Demchog, the "One of Supreme Bliss," dances in the ecstatic realization of ultimate reality on the summit of Kailas. An important tutelary deity of Tibetan Buddhism, he guides practitioners of meditation along the short and dangerous path leading to enlightenment in this life. Lay people and lamas alike travel for weeks and even months to his sacred mountain to experience a moment of power or revelation that will show them the way to transcend the passions and illusions of this world. They view Kailas with the invisible pagoda palace of the deity on its summit as the center of a *mandala* or sacred circle that represents the divine space of Demchog where they may come to know the power and wisdom that will set them free from the bondage of suffering. In the practice of meditation, Tibetan yogis will visualize and identify themselves with this deity and their surroundings with his domain in order to awaken to their own true nature and transform their experience of the world from a profane place of illusion into the sacred realm of ultimate reality.

Every peak and prominent feature surrounding Mount Kailas corresponds to the place of a particular deity dwelling in the *mandala* of Demchog. The Buddhas of the four directions, such as Amitabha, the Buddha of Boundless Light, and Ratnasambhava, the One Born of a Jewel, occupy valleys on each side of the mountain. They embody various aspects of the transcendent awareness awakened in the attainment of enlightenment, such as the wisdom of discrimination and the wisdom of equality. The highest pass on the pilgrimage route around the peak is called Drolma La, the Pass of the Savioress, the most important female deity in Tibet. Tibetans regard three hills near Kailas as the dwellings of Manjusri, Vajrapani, and Avalokiteshvara—the three principal Bodhisattvas, or Enlightenment Beings, who symbolize the wisdom, power, and compassion needed to attain the ultimate goal of Enlightenment for the sake of others.[v]

The *mandala* of Demchog on Kailas presents a vision of the world as the sacred realm of a deity. The pattern of such a *mandala* appears frequently in works of Tibetan art depicting the universe as a circle of mountains, oceans, and continents arrayed around a mythical mountain at the very center, shooting up from the depths of hell to the heights of heaven—and the great void that lies beyond. This mountain, called Meru by the Hindus and Sumeru by the Buddhists, plays a pivotal role in Hinduism and Buddhism as the divine axis of the cosmos. According to Hindu mythology, Brahma, the supreme deity in the form of the creator, lives on its summit, surrounded by lesser deities; in the Buddhist version, the king of the gods, Indra, the equivalent of Zeus in Greek mythology, resides in a glorious palace on its peak, thousands of miles above the earth. Our world appears in the latter version as a triangular continent shaped like India, situated in an ocean to the south of Meru, which rises far to the north, looming over seven rings of golden mountains, so high that the sun and moon must circle around its flanks.[vi]

Meru and Kailas appear as separate mountains in early texts of Buddhist and Hindu mythology, but later tradition has tended to bring them together and identify them as one and the same. Today many Indians and Tibetans view Kailas as the place where the invisible form of Meru breaks through to appear in the physical plane of existence. A pilgrimage to the mountain, therefore, represents for them a journey to the very center of the universe— the cosmic point where everything begins and ends, the divine source of all that exists and has significance. In circling the peak and paying homage to a vision of Shiva or Demchog on its shining summit, they make contact with something deep within themselves that links them to the supreme reality underlying and infusing the cosmos itself.

For most Hindus and Buddhists of India and Tibet, the journey to Kailas is, in fact, the ultimate pilgrimage, both in terms of the sanctity of its goal and the difficulty of the way. Pilgrims coming from the plains of India must first surmount the formidable ice barrier of the Himalayas, crossing passes more than 16,000 feet high, often clad in sandals and cotton clothes. After a difficult ascent through eerie gorges twisting between towering mountains lost in mist, they emerge from the monsoon clouds to behold a brilliant landscape of yellow, red, and purple plains stretching off toward distant peaks, shining beneath an intense blue sky. Until not long ago, they would have had to trust in the gods to protect them from bandits while crossing these plains to reach Mount Kailas on the other side. The Chinese, who took over Tibet in 1950 and only recently opened the mountain to foreign visitors, have eliminated the robbers, along with most of the shrines and monasteries in the area. Pilgrims from central and eastern Tibet do not have to contend with the steep ramparts of the Himalayas, but do have to travel for weeks and even months across the bleak and inhospitable Tibetan Plateau.

The routes of the two converge at the shores of Lake Manasarovar, where the Indians, to the astonishment of Tibetans, strip for a ritual immersion in its clear but icy waters. The circumambulation of the holy mountain, the ultimate goal of the pilgrimage, normally takes three days, with frequent stops at shrines and temples to recite prayers and perform rituals to the gods. Some Tibetan pilgrims, to increase the religious merit accruing from their efforts, take much longer, two to three weeks, making full-length body prostrations all the way around the mountain, unfazed by the streams, boulders, and glaciers they must cross. The high point of the pilgrimage comes at the Drolma La, a pass on the northeast side of Kailas at nearly 19,000 feet, festooned with prayer flags strung between cairns. Just before this pass, Tibetans leave part of themselves—a lock of hair or a tooth—symbolizing their own death and rebirth to a new and more spiritual life. On the far side of the Drolma La, a narrow crevice in the rocks through which Tibetan pilgrims must squeeze their bodies separates sinners destined for hell from those who will attain heaven—or the higher goal of Nirvana.

The hardy few who manage to reach Kailas and complete the circuit of the mountain—about 200 Indians and an indeterminate number of Nepalis and Tibetans a year—come back with a sublime vision of another, sacred realm of existence and a renewed determination to strive for the highest goals of spiritual accomplishment. Lama Anagarika Govinda, a European who became a Tibetan lama and made the pilgrimage to Kailas in 1948, had this to say of his fellow pilgrims:

They return to their country with shining eyes, enriched by an experience which all through their life will be a source of strength and inspiration, because they have been face to face with the Eternal, they have seen the Land of the Gods.[vii]

Lama Govinda was one of the very few Western travelers to reach Mount Kailas before the area around the mountain was officially opened to Westerners in 1984. The first Europeans to see the peak, two Jesuit missionaries named Ippolito Desideri and Manuel Freyre who passed by it on a journey from Kashmir to Lhasa in 1715, did not think much of it: "Close by is a mountain of excessive height and great circumference, always enveloped in cloud, covered with snow and ice, and most horrible, barren, steep and bitterly cold." The small group of explorers, military men, sportsmen, and other travelers who followed them had a very different impression of the mountain, and a number of them even fell under its spell.

Captain C. G. Rawling, a member of a British military expedition that invaded Tibet in 1903, had this to say of Kailas:

It is indeed difficult to place before the mental vision a true picture of this most beautiful mountain. In shape it resembles a vast cathedral, the roof of which, rising to a ridge in the centre, is otherwise regular in outline and covered with eternal snow.[viii]

During the nineteenth and twentieth centuries, a number of Westerners who did not have the advantage of travelling in official capacities had to sneak into Tibet to see the sacred peak. Most of them wore the same disguise, which they each prided themselves on so originally choosing: that of a deaf and dumb Indian pilgrim. One of these "pilgrims" was an Austrian geologist and mountaineer named Herbert Tichy who went to India in 1936 to do research, but with the primary intention of going to Kailas. He succeeded in reaching his goal, but almost blew his disguise by taking a picture at the wrong moment. On his return to India, he received a letter from the governor of the Punjab, congratulating him as a fellow pilgrim to Kailas and regretfully informing him that he would be arrested in a few days for illegally crossing the Tibetan border. Tichy took the kind hint and immediately left for Europe.[ix]

In 1988 I went to the sacred mountain. Late in the afternoon three of us climbed up a ridge for a view of the south face with its staircase leading to heaven. Polished to a smooth finish by wind and sun, the white dome of Kailas gleamed against the sky, amazingly pure in the simplicity of its form. The wind came up, ripping at our faces, and my companions decided to go down. It was autumn and very cold. I stayed alone to watch the mountain turn orange and red in the sunset. As shadows deepened behind the peak, I began to fear that I had lingered too long. But something kept me there to see the last ray of the sun flare gold on the summit. Then, no longer anxious, but strangely excited, I started down in the twilight, suspended in the sky over the darkening plain of Barkha with the waters of Lake Manasarovar and the snows of the Himalayas glimmering blue in the distance. I felt as I had twenty years before when I first went to Nepal and stayed alone, high on a ridge, to watch Mount Everest fade in the sunset—open and free. Whistling a song, I danced down the slopes of the mountain, filled with a wild feeling of laughter and joy.

Excerpt from *Sacred Mountains of the World* (University of California Press) by Edwin Bernbaum. ©1990, 1997.

Notes

[i] This myth is the subject of Kalidasa's famous poem <u>Kumarasambhava</u>, translated in Kalidasa, <u>The Origin of the Young God: Kalidasa's Kumarasambhava</u>, trans. Hank Heifetz (Berkeley and Los Angeles: University of California Press, 1985).

[ii] Arthur (Sir John Woodroffe) Avalon, trans., <u>Tantra of the Great Liberation (Mahanirvana Tantra</u> (1913; repr., New York: Dover Publications, 1972), p. 1. Woodroffe maintains that "the summit of the Lord of Mountains" refers to Shiva's paradise on Kailas, but it could refer to the realm of the god Himalaya, King of the Mountains.

[iii] <u>Meghaduta</u> 64, for another translation see Leonard Nathan trans, <u>The Transport of Love: The Meghaduta of Kalidasa</u> (Berkeley & Los Angeles: University of California Press, 1976), p. 59.

[iv] Garma C. C. Chang, trans., <u>The Hundred Thousand Songs of Milarepa</u>, 2 vols. (Boston: Shambhala Publications, 1977), 1:262. The story of Milarepa and Naro Bhun Chon appears in pp. 215-24.

[v] Demchog is the Tibetan name for the tantric deity whose name in Sanskrit is Chakrasamvara. Most Buddhas and Bodhisattvas in Tibetan Buddhism have both Tibetan and Sanskrit names. Demchog shares a number of characteristics with Shiva. Both wear tiger skins, and just as Shiva has Parvati, Demchog has a female consort named Dorje Phagmo. For a beautiful description of Kailas, its significance, the pilgrimage around it, and the <u>mandala</u> imposed on the region see Lama Anagarika Govinda, <u>The Way of the White Clouds</u> (Berkeley: Shambhala, 1962), pp. 197-219. More recent descriptions of the circumambulation appear in Stephen Batchelor, <u>The Tibet Guide</u> (London: Wisdom Publications, 1987), pp. 357-70, Hugh Swift, <u>Trekking in Nepal, West Tibet, and Bhutan</u> (San Francisco: Sierra Club Books, 1989), pp. 221-31, and Russell Johnson and Kerry Moran, <u>The Sacred Mountain of Tibet: On Pilgrimage to Mount Kailas</u> (Rochester, VT: Park Street Press, 1989)—the last illustrated with beautiful pictures.

[vi] The Hindu version of Meru rises in the center of our world, called Jambudvipa. Sumeru means "Good Meru." For more on Meru see the chapters on Central Asia and South and Southeast Asia in this book and I. W. Mabbett, "The Symbolism of Mount Meru," <u>History of Religions</u> 23, no. 1 (1983).

[vii] Govinda, <u>Way of the White Clouds</u>, p. 206. In recent years the Chinese have allowed eight groups of 25 Indian pilgrims a year to go to Kailas. More Tibetans and Nepalis visit the mountain on pilgrimage, but no figures are available. Because they can now come in trucks across the plateau, the number of Tibetan pilgrims has increased in recent years.

[viii] The quotes from Desideri and Rawling appear in John Snelling, <u>The Sacred Mountain</u> (London and the Hague: East West Publications, 1983), pp. 53 and 86. Snelling's book provides one of the most complete accounts in English of Kailas, its religious significance, and its history.

[ix] Snelling, <u>Sacred Mountain</u>, pp. 120-32, and Herbert Tichy, <u>Himalaya</u>, trans. R. Rickett and D. Streatfeild (New York: G. P. Putnam's Sons, 1970), pp. 35-45.

Introduction

by Brandon Wilson

*E*ver since our existence began on this tiny twirling sphere, humankind has waged a never-ending search for meaning. That curiosity has fueled our imagination and exploration in all fields, settings, and even dimensions. Our collective sense of wonder has led us to seek what's atop the world's highest mountains, at the bottom of a yawning ocean abyss, into the infinite mystery of deep space, or even to the other side of consciousness.

Pilgrims have especially been part of humanity's landscape. *Solvitur ambuland* or "It is solved by walking" was a phrase coined by Diogenes of Sinope and echoed by philosophers since. Whether monarchs, monks, philosophers or peasants in their everyday lives, they've all gone on pilgrimage to find peace, show devotion, search for truth, reconnect with the Universe, pay penance, or seek enlightenment. For many today, pilgrimage becomes something more: a quest, an undeniable clarion call we must follow.

The Pilgrimage Chronicles: Embrace the Quest is a unique anthology that brings together, at one exceptional moment in time, an extraordinary collection of modern pilgrims, explorers, scientists, writers, and adventurers who share their personal pilgrimages with us. These 33 essays include journeys of the soul on the Spain's well-trod Camino de Santiago and Japan's Shikoku Trails; exploring sacred Tibetan regions and Mount Kailash; walking in the footsteps of Gandhi; seeking the legendary Paradise in central Asia; chasing eclipses; stalking Viking ancestors; searching for the source of the Amazon; discovering an elusive and rare bird; fulfilling mountain quests in Bolivia, and hunting for life's meaning from Burma to Timbuktu.

However, wherever they journey, pilgrims ultimately discover certain transcendent truths:

> A pilgrimage is the act of deliberate travel; traveling outside while traveling within. It is a chance to reconnect with the earth, to listen, to face your inner self, to actively commune with a greater power.

> A pilgrimage is a refuge from the din and clutter of the outside world. It is a unique dimension to appreciate life's wonder and revel in its minutiae. It is the heady aroma drifting from fields of thyme, or the drone of bees in a sun-dappled forest. It is autumn frost blanketing a multi-hued trail, and the rough grain of your walking stick rubbing against your palm.

A pilgrimage is time devoted purely to the present. There is no past, no future, only now. Your world is your breath, a heartbeat reverberating in your ears, a Zen-like placing of each footstep along a well-trod path.

A pilgrimage is a trampoline for the mind, a purging of the soul. It is a thousand small moments. It is unexpected acts of kindness and fleeting revelations. It is surrendering to fate, spontaneity, absolute unknown, and small arrows that mark your way.

A pilgrimage is often a solitary journey. Yet as we traverse this portal between past and present, we pay homage to those who have gone this way before while leaving our essence for those who pass long after we are gone.

A pilgrimage is traveling lightly. Just as we leave most of our worldly belongings behind, on the trail there is a gentle unraveling of fears, emotions, desires and demons as we surrender unwanted psychic baggage to the universe.

A pilgrimage is letting go, then discovering, and in truth be found.

A pilgrimage is peace personified, one deliberate step at a time. When serenity is found within, how long can our world remain without?

Each pilgrim's journey is unique. It can never be repeated. Yet it continues long after we return home to distant shores. They are our passion, our reasons for being.

Join us and discover your own inspiration from this incomparable and very personal collection of pilgrims' journeys from around our wonderous planet.

Brandon Wilson, Chevalier, Sovereign Hospitaller Order of St. John of Jerusalem

Preface

By Tor Torkildson, Chronicles series editor

*D*efinition of *pilgrimage:*

1: A journey of a pilgrim; *especially:* one to a shrine or a sacred place.

2: The course of life on earth.

Definition of *quest:*

1: A jury of inquest: investigation.

2: An act or instance of seeking: pursuit, search: a chivalrous enterprise in medieval romance usually involving an adventurous journey.

In many regards, this book has become a pilgrimage and a quest. Within the pages of, *The Pilgrimage Chronicles: Embrace the Quest*, the reader will embark on journeys to sacred places, be involved in romance and grand adventures, investigate distant landscapes, and find themselves searching or making inquiries. Our destination is, in a sense, sacred, with the belief that certain voyages out, might become voyages in. Think of it as a sort of geo-poetic quest: the glint of an outer light reflected or inner light revealed. Through our memory maps, we will navigate the sacred world, creating a web of connections from everywhere to everywhere through this amazing group of authors and experiences.

It seems just yesterday that, *The Walkabout Chronicles: Epic Journeys by Foot*, was born from a dream. The book has been a resounding success. It has traveled around the world, and through the process of creating the book, Siffy and I have had the pleasure of making many new friends and becoming a part of something greater than ourselves.

In other words, the book brought meaning. We are now a part of a Tribe of seekers, explorers, and writers who embrace life to the fullest and cherish each moment to the best of our abilities. Something I recently read summed up this feeling perfectly for me:

The Bushman in the Kalahari Desert talk about the two "hungers." There is the Great Hunger and there is the Little Hunger. The Little Hunger wants food for the belly; but the Great Hunger, the greatest hunger of all, is the search for meaning...There is ultimately only one thing that makes human beings deeply and profoundly bitter, and that is to have thrust upon them a life without meaning. There is nothing wrong in searching for happiness. But of far more comfort to the soul is something greater than happiness or unhappiness, and that is meaning. Because meaning transfigures all. Once what you are doing has for you meaning, it is irrelevant whether you're happy or unhappy. You are content—you are not alone in your Spirit-you.

It seems only fitting that we carry on with this spirit that has embraced us; therefore, we have decided to keep the positive energy in motion with this book, *The Pilgrimage Chronicles: Embrace the Quest,* book two. A series is born. Once again, we have gathered an extraordinary collection of original and diverse essays from around the world. In this book, you will find traditional pilgrimages, personal quests, and far-flung journeys, all seeking to bring meaning to life.

The essays will take you to India, along the Camino, searching for paradise, into the Amazon jungle, along the sacred pathways of Japan, over the Himalaya, into the night sky, and deep into the soul of the seeker. They will make you laugh, cry, or grow thoughtful. We hope the book will encourage readers to seek out their own quests and live the life they imagined. We are honored and humbled by the writers who have so graciously shared their journey with us for this anthology. What a remarkable group of human beings. Siffy and I have found encouragement and hope through our interaction with this tribe. This book is a MODERN day WONDER voyage.

Endorsements for
The Pilgrimage Chronicles: Embrace the Quest

"This wonderful anthology will inspire you to pursue your own quest and seek the life you have always imagined."

~Wade Davis, author of *Light at the Edge of the World: A Journey Through the Realm of Vanishing Cultures.*

"If curiosity is your religion, and high adventure your cup of tea, this book is guaranteed to spin your prayer wheel and satiate your thirst."

~Pat Morrow, first to climb the Seven Summits (Cartstensz Pyramid variation).

"Alpinism is activity and storytelling. Without it it's sterile and empty. Tor Torkildson's collection is the proof of it."

~Reinhold Messner, first climber to ascend all fourteen peaks over 8,000 meters.

"'The Pilgrimage Chronicles: Embrace the Quest' brings together absorbing accounts of exceptional explorers from around the world. It is the kind of book that takes readers on journeys, physical and mental, that will stick in their minds for a long time to come. Only a year after their book 'The Walkabout Chronicles' appeared, the editors, Tor and Siffy, have managed to once again pull off an important publishing event."

~Johan Reinhard, Explorer-in-residence at the National Geographic Society.

Endorsements for
The Walkabout Chronicles: Epic Journeys by Foot

"This marvelous collection adds a new mile to the written way, a new stride to the literature of the leg."

~Robert Macfarlane, author of *Mountain's of the Mind*.

"It all changes, everything, and walking illustrates that elemental condition of our lives. Nothing else so completely clears our minds, or lays bare the soul of place. This monumental book full of graceful prose by writers and explorers, walks us through the familiar, the unfamiliar, and downright strange."

~Tim Cahill, author of *Hold the Englightenment*.

Monastery at Gyantse. Kham, Tibet. 2012.
Photograph by Karen McDiarmid.

"And while I stood there I saw more than I can tell and I understood more than I saw; for I was seeing in a sacred manner the shapes of all things in the spirit, and the shape of all shapes as they must live together like one being."
~Black Elk

Table of Contents

Mu Gompa, Nepal. *Photograph by Tor Torkildson.*

Jerusalem under siege. *Photograph by Brandon Wilson.*

Brandon Wilson

Often travelers of the road, and of life, are so anxious to get somewhere, that the getting there, the actual journey, takes a back seat to the reward at the end. That wasn't for us anymore. The ultimate beauty of walking, of "traveling deliberately" one foot in front of the other, was the opportunity to observe and wallow in the minute details of everyday life surrounding us. There was time to share a moment of peoples' lives, their hopes, their triumphs, their fears, and to truly live the path leading to the destination. It was a blessing. Our lives were reduced to raw essentials.
~from *Yak Butter Blues: A Tibetan Trek of Faith*, by Brandon Wilson

Metamorphosis: The Making of a Pilgrim

*P*ilgrimage is my passion, although it hasn't always been this way. Not so long ago, I'd never heard of modern "pilgrims."

Are there such people? And does REI have a special department handling buckled shoes and funny hats?

When I first set off on independent travel with a backpack and insatiable dream, like many, I was intent on seeing as much of the world as possible in as short a time as recommended by family doctors. It's impossible to fit much into a backpack—or a standard two-week American vacation. Cheryl, my winsome conspirator, and I were intent on inventing ways to capture more time away from work, even if it meant quitting "respectable" jobs and starting a new life once we either ran out of money or were too exhausted to catch another midnight train. With luck and sacrifice, we made great escapes several times as we checked off a mental list of the world's esoteric must-dos: exploring the lost-love opulence of the Taj Mahal, chanting in the Great Pyramid King's Chamber, exploring druids at Stonehenge, fending off pickpockets aboard Asian night trains, paying respects at Jim Morrison's grave, exploring monkey temples, discovering an entire chapel made of bones in Evora, Portugal, floating past ghats down the Ganges, hiking Ireland's Crough Patrick, investigating Sasquatch sightings, surviving drunken bacchanals on Greek nude beaches, bartering in Kathmandu back alleys and gnome hunting in the Alps, to name a few.

Travel became an addiction that led to harder options and we just couldn't say 'No.'

By the time we found ourselves in Eastern Europe, during the fall of the Berlin Wall, we were thrust into a new brand of travel improvisation— adventure travel. Nothing was set in stone. The rules changed from country to country and day to day as we traveled the way average locals did, drank pilsen and gobbled lard sandwiches where they ate, and dozed in falling-star hotels where they slept. They were wild days when a pack of Kent cigarettes could either get you a front seat in the Budapest opera or keep you from getting shot by an East German soldier as you poked your head through a newly chistled hole in the Berlin Wall.

Those were great times. That thrill of adventure travel only intensified as we prepared to set off to travel the length of Africa over seven months aboard a do-it-yourself overland safari.

However, as Mark Twain once wrote, "I have found out there ain't no surer way to find out whether you like people or hate them than to travel with them." No truer words were spoken. After Cheryl and I survived three months of misadventures, we resolved to leave the other twenty travelers half-way across the continent. We were on two different journeys. While we wanted to immerse ourselves in the intense and often quirky culture, our companions were content to play cards and down gin & tonics while Africa galloped past their windows.

By then, we'd already had a savory slurp of what indy travel might be like outside the protective chrysalis of the overland truck. And we ached for more and jumped at the chance. While our companions set up tables and prepared delicate little cucumber sandwiches in the midst of the Congolese jungle, Cheryl and I set off alone down the one muddy red road, seeking the face of the gritty, unsanitized Africa. And we were never disappointed. One day a fellow approached from nowhere and led us through dense undergrowth to proudly show us the boar head he'd recently mounted on a pike outside his mud house. On another day, a small group of us ended up spending the night with a pygmy tribe, hunting for dik-dik and then sharing their banquet and a bong as we boogied by firelight under the jungle's canopy.

Soon afterwards, we set off on our own across the continent. We climbed Kilimanjaro, white-water rafted down Victoria Falls' Class V Zambezi rapids and landed in South Africa just after Nelson Mandela was released from prison. It was life-changing, but the best was yet to come.

We became accidental pilgrims.

Shortly after returning to our so-called normal lives, Cheryl and I heard about an ancient 650-mile Buddhist pilgrimage trail that crossed Tibet from Lhasa to Kathmandu. It had been closed since the Chinese invasion in the 1950s and we immediately envisioned it as the ultimate adventure. We quickly devised a plan to take off. We'd hike from village to village and stay with locals to witness their modern struggles and share yak butter tea around their fires. But when we asked the Chinese Embassy permission to make our journey, they refused us visas and shot us a full page of reasons our mission was "impossible." Perhaps it's the obstinate Scot in me, but their rejection made it all the more enticing. We decided to re-apply for permission once we reached Kathmandu. If they refused, well, we'd just sneak in and rely on our wits and good luck to get us back home.

As luck would have it, the official Chinese policy changed just the day before we applied in Nepal. The border opened for the first time in decades and they approved a 60-day visa to complete our journey. Our only requirement was to take their five-day propaganda-laden tour in Lhasa and then we could set off for Kathmandu on our own. The trip was afoot.

On first glance, Lhasa was far different from what we'd imagined. Chinese soldiers lurked everywhere. Video cameras tracked every move. Spotting a Tibetan was like finding Waldo.

Are we too late to discover the real Tibet?

In search of answers we climbed to the Potala Palace rooftop. Surrounded by the snowy Himalayan panorama, the challenge ahead chilled us to the bone. Then, inexplicably, we were blanketed with a warm, reassuring feeling as though we would never be alone on our journey. Any doubts vanquished in the wind.

In light of Tibet's obvious cultural invasion, we sensed our trip had to mean something more than just a simple adventure and a couple facing the "impossibilities" of Tibet. It could also be a symbolic act—a quest. If two westerners could make the ancient journey without upsetting global politics, why not allow Tibetans to also make their pilgrimage, as they once had done by prostrating inchworm style to their holy sites in Lhasa and Kathmandu? With that goal, we bought a colorful strand of prayer flags from a vendor in the Barkhor, which we vowed to try to present to the King of Nepal when (and if) we were successful. With any luck, he'd fly them as a sign of solidarity with the Tibetan people.

Ever wary of the danger of facing blizzards atop 14,000+ foot Tibetan passes in November, we set off on our harrowing 1100-kilometer journey at breakneck speed—four-to-six kilometers an hour—less with a head-wind. Even after buying Sadhu, our Tibetan wanderhorse to carry our supplies, we were less than swift. Any western notion of forcing our will to find food, water, a place to roll out our sleeping bag, or to generally mold the trip to our expectations quickly vanished. Over the month, the one continual lesson we learned was to let go; to trust in the Universe to provide. And it did.

One evening, after a particularly harsh hike, we stopped at a roadside inn. Famished, Cheryl began to unpack and we soon discovered the fuel bottle with our only pump must have fallen off Sadhu somewhere on the scorched plain. Now, with its loss, there was no way to cook food for the rest of our journey. We couldn't even boil water to drink. Of all the things we could have lost, that hurt us the most. It was a blow at our very survival.

Wallowing in silent self-pity, we were suddenly jolted when there was a hesitant rap at the door. It swung open and the innkeeper's wife shuffled in—carrying a thermos of boiled water. Our luck, our lives, had become just that magical.

Little-by-little we persevered over a month, one step at a time, overcoming sandblasted natty-bits, blizzards, bullets, bitter thirst and all-too-real starvation. We faced the "impossible" head-on until we eventually returned to Kathmandu where it was our honor to finally present our prayer flags at the Royal Palace. We hope they'd make some small difference to people who'd suffered so much, yet shared even more with two strangers.

Looking back, that journey transformed how we perceived travel and its potential for personal growth. With each step, it'd inadvertently fired my fascination with pilgrimage.

Odysseys into the unknown continued in 1999, when I became a simple pilgrim on the newly popular Camino de Santiago across Spain. In preparation for the 732-km trek with a backpack (and no Sadhu), I followed a strict exercise regimen, something I'd never considered necessary before. It was my first time alone as a pilgrim and I vowed to be ready for anything. After pumping iron and working out for six months, I was in the best shape of my life.

Anxious to begin, and having to fit my pilgrimage into thirty days, I set a frantic pace out of Hawaii with a two-day flight to Barcelona, a night bus to Pamplona, and then hitched a ride to Roncesvalles near the French border. Time waits for no pilgrim. Instead of spending the night, I immediately began hiking west toward Santiago. Adrenaline was my cocktail and I was poured doubles—until my high-tech running shoes were ripped to shreds. Limping into the simple refugio in Zubiri that night, I gingerly took off my runners and wet socks to discover eight new blisters. Morning broke all too soon, along with my sores.

I was slowed to a slug's pace. In doing so, a Zen-like method of "deliberate walking" developed, unveiling a beautifully complex and tranquil world with every step. I wallowed in nature's abundance. Slowing down taught me that a pilgrimage is a "journey outside—while traveling within." Each day, after walking twenty-five kilometers, I'd arrive at a *refugio* or hostel where pilgrims or *peregrinos* from around the world spent the night together. We'd experience the same cold showers, aches, blisters, and then a *peregrino* plate and bottle of Rioja wine at a local café. As difficult as it was, there were no sweeter times.

My comrades were from throughout the world, each dealing with a life-changing event: loss of a loved one or a job, a divorce or disappointment, the onset of a disease or recent survival from one. All were looking for answers and meaning. All voluntarily left homes, families, jobs and outside life on this incredible journey. And as much the thousand-year-old trail immersed us in culture and cuisine, walking the Way of St. James also forced us to confront our own lives head-on: our hopes, fears, relationships, our life's work and choices. It was a portal to truth.

Each day became a gentle unraveling of life, as we peeled away the onion-like layers of walls and insecurities. We learned to trust our intuition again, to trust others, and celebrate the small victories along the way: the simple act of making it another day along the trail, finding water when it was so searingly hot your feet melted into asphalt, or having an "angel" on the trail surprise you with a cup of coffee, or simple *"Buen Camino."* Those small miracles made us appreciate the larger ones along the path—and in life.

Afterwards, my personal metamorphosis accelerated. Pilgrimage forces you to examine what's necessary and the Camino was a metaphor for life itself. We often carry the unnecessary with us like heavy, cumbersome backpacks. Along the way, I'd learned to let go of those things unneeded anymore. I quickly examined how I was living, left my business of fifteen years, and devoted myself to writing about adventure and pilgrim travel.

Today, when I'm not on pilgrimage, I'm dreaming of it. Long distance trekking, especially these time-forgotten paths, has become my sweet obsession. Given my new-found love of Spain, one autumn I wandered the Via de la Plata from Sevilla to Santiago. On another, Cheryl joined me for a pilgrimage on the Camino French Way, and yet another for a trek in 100-degree weather on the little-known Camino Catalan/Aragonés from outside Barcelona.

Even though Spain is renowned for its warm pilgrim welcome, after making these journeys to Santiago de Compostela, I longed for something different. Rome was the next obvious choice. I'd heard about the Via Francigena that leads 1850-km from Canterbury Cathedral in England across the length of France to Switzerland and then to Rome. Although it has a long history as a path for kings, traders, artists and armies, it was documented in an early diary by Sigeric, Archbishop of Canterbury, who returned via a similar path after visiting the Pope in 990 AD.

As a pioneer of the trail, I faced unique challenges. Directions were sketchy. There were no helpful yellow Camino arrows pointing the way. Even many of those living along the path had no idea of its pilgrimage connection. There was no assurance of a *refugio* or companionship at the end of each day. So, I risked walking alone in the sizzling heat for eight hours only to arrive at a church, present my pilgrim's passport to a weary priest and be told there was no place to sleep.

"The next village is *only* eight kilometres down the road," he'd claim with a shrug.

To a pilgrim, that was another exhausting two hours. Consequently, I spent a few nights curled up on someone's floor or outside on the church stoop, wearing everything in my backpack, waiting for the warmth of sunrise. It was one of many humbling lessons I've never forgotten.

My fondest memories were nightly sessions spent practicing my mangled Italian or French with villagers. They were surprised someone would choose to walk to Rome when they could simply drive. Even so, I was rewarded with their unexpected support: the fruit peddler who refused payment for his apple; the café owner who surprised me with a morning espresso; the village priest and his mother who treated me like royalty and wept when I left; the Sisters of San Guistiniana who took me in and fed me when I could walk no farther; the amiable WW II paratrooper who'd served with American Allies who bought me a glass of vino to toast his fallen comrades.

For all the small sacrifices, the Via Francigena was more than a spiritual pilgrimage. It opened my eyes to history and culture in an intimate way I'd missed as a budget traveller. It was a chance to stroll ancient Roman roads; to explore castles, frescoes, and holy relics sequestered in tiny chapels. It was an opportunity to discover Siena's magnificent marbled Duomo and the living medieval museum that is San Gimignano. It was a chance to experience local festivals, such as the annual wine harvest or *vendage* of the Champagne region. Certainly, no Italian or French sojourn would be complete without sampling an incredible variety of wines—and I did my best. To quote Dom Pérignon, "Brothers, I have tasted the stars!" Actually, an entire galaxy.

And as always, there was the solemn opportunity to take part in an honoured tradition of wandering the same path, in the same spirit, as thousands of pilgrims this past millennium.

Eventually arriving in Rome, I was deluged by an emotional avalanche. After my solitude, it seemed a hundred thousand devotees had arrived for the weekly Jubilee Celebration in St. Peter's Square. The faithful had come from around the world to listen to Pope John Paul II, but perhaps I was the only *pellegrino* who had walked there.

Today, there are pilgrimages in many locales, even in Norway and Sweden where you can retrace St. Olav's Way to Trondheim. For me, it offered an added bonus: a path to discover Viking roots.

The trail of St. Olav wends across fields of wheat, barley and rye, through primeval pine forests, past crystalline lakes to healing wells and mountaintops boasting eagle-view panoramas. You're surrounded by a profusion of wildlife from the tiniest tundra wildflower to enormous wild raspberries; from wayward sheep to deer, elk and even moose. Then there is the culture. This is the enchanted homeland of Peer Gynt where the sun barely sets all summer. Where else could you spend the night in a reconstructed 12th century farm and sleep on a medieval bed draped in reindeer hides? The most fascinating area was Dovrefjell where I trekked across a tundra-like landscape and forded swollen rivers, hopping from stone to stone.

Like every jump, another bit of transformation occurred with my every step. My simple walking meditation became a "trampoline" for my mind, heart and soul. There was a clarity and deep peace that continued long after the trail was finished.

Surely each pilgrimage is unique and transformative. Like Heraclitus the Greek philosopher once said, "You never step in the same river twice."

Over two decades, my most daunting and meaningful odyssey was a pilgrimage for peace I made with Émile, a 68-year-old French friend I'd met on that first Spanish Camino. Out of the blue, he asked if I'd be interested in joining him on a pilgrimage to Jerusalem.

Thrilled with the possibility, it took just twenty seconds to answer, *"Mais oui!"*

Then, I wondered, 'Pilgrims already have many routes to Santiago and Rome, but what about the Holy City? It's the ultimate pilgrimage destination for three major faiths. Maybe we could blaze a new trail and transform the route of the First Crusades, a trail of war, into an international path of peace.' The irony wasn't lost on me.

With just three months to prepare, I was plagued with uncertainties. Could we walk the daily equivalent of a marathon—and have the physical and mental stamina to do it again day after day for at least five months? What about languages? Visas? And how do you pack light, but still carry enough gear to be ready for rain or snow in Europe as well as the heat of the Middle East?

Although I like to plan to prevent problems in advance, I'd learned to not over-obsess to the point of talking myself out of another adventure. Besides, you have to have a certain amount of faith when you approach challenges and trust the Universe will provide.

We hit the trail from Émile's home in France in mid-April. Walking 25-55 kilometers daily, the two-continent, eleven-country trek led us from the canals of France to the Bavarian Black Forest where we met the source of the Danube River and *Donau Radweg*. The Danube bicycle path spans 1367-kilometers through four countries all the way to Budapest, Hungary. We walked alone eight to ten hours every day, slogging through the remains of snow and weeks of rain. However, it was far from torture and it swiftly restored my faith in humanity.

Spotting us soggy, famished and bedraggled, "angels" would invite us home for a bowl of soup or bottle of wine. After learning we were pilgrims, they'd offer us a free or discounted room. Or maybe direct us to the right path at a critical junction in the trail. Some days, it was almost too easy. However, all that would soon change.

Outside of Budapest, we became pioneers. The trail morphed into badly maintained two-lane roads. However, even in countries as impoverished as Serbia and Bulgaria, we were welcomed by folks nearly every day. Invariably their response was warm and emotional. Our message was their own. They'd suffered from wars for centuries. Even the media in larger cities was supportive and we reached millions with a message of peace.

Given their fervor, it was especially disheartening to hear that Israel and Hezbollah in Lebanon were bombing each other again. Some in Belgrade even went so far as to speculate it was the beginning of World War Three.

To risk it all and walk through a warzone in Syria and possibly Jordan seemed reckless—even for me. It ran contrary to my belief that it's better to take time to make good plans so we can live to tell the tale. Émile and I promised to re-evaluate our plans based on the situation when we reached Turkey in another month or so.

Well, by the time we reached Istanbul, my companion was clearly suffering from his diabetes and regrettably decided to return home. As for me, I continued alone across the high plains of Turkey. However, I struggled with a difficult decision.

If this is to be a path for future pilgrims, isn't the safest path best?

Literally standing at the crossroads in central Turkey, I made a choice. I'd head south to the coast, steering clear of conflict and a new Ebola-type virus in eastern Turkey. Besides, this route coincided with a Crusader trail to Cyprus and then across the sea to what was once Palestine.

Although I was initially apprehensive about Turkish Muslims' reaction to an American walking a pilgrimage, they were openhearted. They have their own strong pilgrimage tradition and required *haj* to Mecca. Nightly, they reassured me we are cousins, branches of the same tree of Abraham. Hardly a day passed when I wasn't taken under someone's wing. I couldn't leave a village without someone motioning to me crooning, "Chai, chai?" (Tea, tea?) as they stirred an invisible cup. Alanya's television station even insisted on shooting an interview on the beach before I caught the ferry to Northern Cyprus.

Truthfully, even this route was never guaranteed. The infamous Green Line between partitioned Cyprus had only just opened. So, I was greatly relieved to cross without a problem and trek another three days through drowsy mountain villages to Limassol on the southern coast. Then, hopping the weekly cargo ship, I caught the overnight crossing to recently shelled Haifa.

Over the months, I'd heard rumors about the new Israel National Trail transecting the country. Hiking this path turned out to be a welcome change, as it took me off-road into the ancient hills, along the beach to Tel Aviv, and then southeast toward Jerusalem. Although the country was still on high alert, more trail "angels" gave me a rare glimpse into Israeli life.

Finally, in late September after hiking 4217-kilometers over 137 days, I walked through historic Jaffa Gate into the Old City of Jerusalem. There was no fanfare, no welcoming committee. Only one solitary peace pilgrim grateful to all those who helped him realize a dream. If anything was accomplished beyond personal fulfillment, I hope we planted seeds along what I've called the Templar Trail, in honor of those first knights, along with Knights Hospitaller, who protected and cared for early pilgrims. We pray those seeds will take root and it will someday become a true international path for peace that all may walk in brotherhood and tolerance.

For as much as we pay lip service to peace, on this pilgrimage I learned firsthand that it comes from within—one person at a time. Once pilgrims walk, talk, eat and share together over the same table, we realize how much alike we are. A stranger's hopes and fears are so similar to our own. The simple act of walking together helps dispel fear and hatred, while allowing people to find a tranquil sanctuary within. Returning home, it's only natural to share our serenity with families, friends and co-workers.

For me, so much has transpired over the decades. I've changed from a wild adventurer pushing boundaries into a seeker and pilgrim savoring each moment of retrospection. Undoubtedly, the exploration has continued; only the setting has changed from the world-at-large to the universe within. Walking is a first step, but one everyone can take to find personal peace. See for yourself. And may your own be achieved one step-at-a-time—no matter where you wander.

Questions and Answers

1. What compelled you to set out on your pilgrimage?
After years of budget travel and then adventure travel, I was seeking something more than a smorgesbord of experiences to check off a bucket list. I was looking for an intense journey that allowed me to wallow in the minutiae of a different life; something more spiritual; something that brought more meaning to life. Fortunately, and quite accidentally, I discovered pilgrimage while on a trek across Tibet with my wife and our chestnut horse, Sadhu. It was the most intense experience one could imagine. Over forty days our journey evolved, as we connected with fervent prostrating pilgrims and often spent the night with former monks awaiting the Dalai Lama's return. Our simple adventure transformed into a quest.

2. Is there a book, song, poem, or movie that inspired your quest?
I've been inspired by the writings of Herman Hesse, Henry David Thoreau and the transendentalists, and to a lesser extent Hemingway and Jack Kerouac. For inspiration when exhausted and walking, I like to hum Beethoven's *Ode to Joy* or the old Shaker song, *Simple Gifts*.

> 'Tis the gift to be simple, 'tis the gift to be free
> 'Tis the gift to come down where we ought to be,
> And when we find ourselves in the place just right,
> 'Twill be in the valley of love and delight.

3. Where is your sacred place and why did you choose it?
I've strived to re-discover a hidden magic in the world; a connectedness with the Universe. I've sensed it in my very soul. This is the vision and power of the ancients, something misplaced in our Western rush for wealth and meaning. Fortunately, it still exists today.

There is no one sacred space. On each pilgrimage journey, I discover new ones: a bucolic lakeside in Norway; a Swiss mountaintop overlooking the Eiger, Jungfrau and Mönch; a field of sunflowers on the Camino de Santiago. A Bohemian forest becomes a cathedral where I don solitude like a comfortable cloak. Allowing introspection and quiet contemplation, they each remind me of an omnipresent magic in the world, a force of never-ending birth and death, creation and destruction. In quietude, these are revealed if only we listen.

4. How did your pilgrimage change your life or not?
They have added meaning and purpose to my life. They taught invaluable lessons. I've learned how to dim the endless cacophony of the outside world. To slow down. To savor the small victories. To reconnect with a Universal force. To await inspiration and respect intuition.

5. What is the most important piece of advice that you have received in your life? Do you have advice to share from your experiences?

"Lessons of the Trail"
Be trusting.
Have faith that the trail knows where it's going–even if you don't.
Be generous.
Travel lightly. All in life is a gift. What you don't need, give away.
Be kind.
On the trail, even the smallest word of encouragement makes a difference.
Be humble.
Walking on dirt is easier on the feet than walking on pavement, anyway.
Be human.
There is no harm in getting lost–only in staying lost.
Be a friend.
Folks on the trail impact your life, if just for a moment. All too soon they leave to follow their own path. Don't resent this. Bid them good journey. Thank them for their gift.
Be content.
Savor the small victories now, along the way.
Be grateful.
Even the smallest things on the trail are either a gift or lesson.
Be flexible.
Sometimes trails just vanish. That doesn't mean you were on the wrong path–there's just a better one now.
Be focused.
Never look back. *Sempre diretto!* (Straight ahead!)
Be courageous.
A mountain is always highest when you're climbing it.
Be hopeful.
Tomorrow is another day waiting with the possibility of success.
Be happy.
Laughter and song are nature's tonic for adversity.
Be aware.
It is the journey that ultimately matters, not the destination.
Above all else, love all living things on the trail. Love God, your fellow travelers, yourself.

Photograph courtesy of Brandon Wilson.

Biography

Brandon Wilson is peace pilgrim, long distance trekker, Lowell Thomas Gold Award-winning author/photographer and explorer. He has explored nearly 100 countries, including making an African transect from London to Cape Town. However, over decades, he's been especially passionate about hiking historic long-distance pilgrim trails. In 1992, Brandon and his wife Cheryl became the first Western couple to trek the 1100-kilometer trail from Lhasa, Tibet to Kathmandu. Then he focused on Europe, trekking the Camino de Santiago Francés (twice) across northern Spain, then the Via de la Plata from Seville, and the Camino Catalan and Camino Aragonés from Barcelona. Brandon was the first American to traverse the 1850-kilometer Via Francigena from Canterbury, England to Rome. In 2006, he hiked and founded the 4500-kilometer Templar Trail, recreating the route of the First Crusades as a path of peace from France to Jerusalem. Later, in 2009, Brandon and Cheryl trekked the Via Alpina along the backbone of the Alps across eight countries from Trieste to Monaco, climbing the equivalent of 12 Mt. Everests. In 2015, he hiked the ancient St. Olav's Way for the second time across Norway and Sweden on an Explorers Club Flag expedition. Most recently, he trekked the Alta Via 1 across the Italian Dolomites. Brandon is a Fellow of The Explorers Club and was recently knighted by the Sovereign Hospitaller Order of St. John of Jerusalem/Knights of Malta. He lives in the French Alps in the shadow of Mt. Blanc.

Website: pilgrimstales.com, and books available at: amazon.com/Brandon-Wilson. Facebook: Brandon Wilson Adventure Travel Author.

Photograph by Deb Halbot.

Sue Regan Kenney

There is no way to happiness. Happiness is the way.
~The Buddha

A Barefoot Pilgrimage to the Soul

*D*ecades ago I became disenchanted with the idea of belonging to a religious group of any sort. I was raised Roman Catholic, and my faith wavered during my adult life. It came to a halt when I discovered that Christmas day was originally a pagan celebration marking winter solstice; it was taken hostage by the Catholics and turned into the day Christ was born. My trust in the church collapsed. That revelation sent me walking—ultimately, on an inner journey back to my authentic self that I couldn't have designed more perfectly.

I was introduced to the Camino in 2001 after I had been suddenly downsized from my corporate telecom position as an account executive at Lucent Technologies. They escorted me out of the office and I was forbidden to return. It came as a shock to me and sent me on an urgent quest to make a decision about what to do next. It had become clear to me that without my corporate identity I didn't know what I was supposed to be doing on this earth. In order to understand this, I somehow sensed, I would have to connect with my authentic soul. This was definitely outside of my comfort zone!

Before all of this took place, I had seen a TV show about walking tours in Spain. It profiled the Camino in Spain as a medieval Roman Catholic pilgrimage route over one thousand years old. The pilgrim's destination was Santiago—which means St. James in Spanish—the place where he was buried. Because the pilgrims believed if they were closer to the remains of an apostle they would be closer to God, millions have walked the pilgrimage over the centuries.

Knowing I had to face things I'd been avoiding in my life, I wondered if a long walk was just the medicine I needed. I liked the idea of slowing down and simplifying my life to the act of walking and carrying all that I needed on my back, and I wasn't interested in having a religiously dogmatic experience. With that understanding, it took me about two minutes to decide that I was going to Spain to walk.

That afternoon I found someone to live with my daughter Meghan while I was away, someone to manage the house, and then I paid the bills and booked a plane ticket to Paris. The next day I bought a backpack and the best high-top Italian leather boots I could find; they boasted a thick one-inch sole and lots of ankle support. Right away I started walking every day in my neighborhood. Time passed quickly, and five weeks later I was in St. Jean Pied de Port, France, about to begin on this ancient path.

A few days into the walk, my body was stiff, my legs were tired and my feet were sore; however, this didn't stop me from getting up each day to walk another twenty-five to forty kilometres. What I loved about being on this pilgrimage route was the people and the conversations I had while walking on the path, eating meals, and spending my evenings at the pilgrim hostels. One such person was 'Dino the Greek,' whom I met the first day. Strangely, he liked to walk in his bare feet. The first time I saw him trudging along the dirt path I commented on his lack of boots or socks. He said, "I was in the army in Greece, and they used to make us go barefoot because it works all the small muscles in the feet, giving the larger ones a break." I'd never heard of that idea. Then he added, "It's like natural reflexology!" That made sense to me. It was my first introduction to the idea of walking barefoot at all, and I remember thinking Dino was a nut for doing it. Of course it never occurred to me that nine years later I would be following his bare-footsteps.

Over the next eight hundred kilometres I experienced every emotion I ever knew, every pain I ever felt, and every level of love, sadness and joy. What I didn't expect was how exhausting it was for my mind. There are many more stories that I would love to share with you, but this essay is focused on my barefoot journey, so I'd like to take you to the end of this Camino and how barefooting came into my life.

They say when the Camino ends, the journey is just beginning. Leaving Santiago, I was in a state of absolute peace, yet at the same time I was terrified to return home to face the next stage of my life. I arrived at the airport in Toronto and was thrilled to find my children all there to greet me along with my sister Joanne. Everything was unfolding the way I had imagined until Simone said, "Ew, didn't you shower? You smell." We all laughed together. It seems I had absorbed the scent of the Camino path into my skin, and I jokingly said, "I brought the Camino home with me." At that time, I didn't know that I had taken on the essence of the teachings, the energy of the pilgrims of the past and the love of the universe. I'd experienced numerous revelations and a certain clarity of vision that would be the foundation for a new perspective on life.

Back at home I struggled to fit in. My children told me they were concerned about who I had become. Using every ounce of wisdom received on the Camino, I replied, "I haven't changed. I'm just more of myself." That idea worked for a while, but, realistically, I had changed. With no interest in spending energy finding a 'real' job, I filled my time telling stories of my journey and I walked as much as I could. My daughters asked what they should tell people when they were asked what their mother did for a living. I said, "Tell them I'm a storyteller." In our society, the role of storyteller doesn't carry a level of status, and they weren't impressed. Eventually I wrote the book *My Camino* and then travelled all over North America doing book signings, walking paths and sharing stories of the incredible life lessons I had learned on the Camino.

There is a saying on the Camino that you should never walk past a pilgrim in need. If you do, then you have to go back to the beginning of your journey and walk that part all over again. When I think of the definition of a pilgrim as anyone who is on a journey with a destination in mind, then I know we are all pilgrims each on our own journey to find our way.

When I first started coaching people on walking the Camino, I tried to convince them to walk alone. I believed that was the only way they could experience all the joys and face their fears. Still, people insisted they wanted to walk in a group. It occurred to me that maybe they were pilgrims in need. What if they wanted to do the Camino but they couldn't do it alone? Who was I to decide what was right for them? I didn't want to walk past a pilgrim in need, so I booked a group.

The first time I took a group, I was pleasantly surprised at how the journey unfolded. We walked over two hundred kilometres, and while that distance didn't give us the same opportunity to meet our Camino family— the many other pilgrims who meet on the path and bond as a group—as those who walked eight hundred kilometres, we did have something special. Our group had already become a Camino family thanks to the conference calls we had had before we left. Everyone bonded prior to starting the physical journey, and this made it a more powerful experience.

In some ways walking in a group is better than walking alone. We are a community of pilgrims there to support and hold space for each other. For the next nine years, I was coaching and guiding groups to walk the Camino Frances, initially as a way to show my gratitude to the Camino for all she gave me. I was convinced my purpose in life was to inspire people to use walking as a way to find peace on their life journey. Through this work I was fulfilled spiritually, emotionally and mentally.

It was a cool August day in 2010 when my world shifted. I was in the forest. Early in the morning, I had decided it was a perfect day for a walk in the woods, and I went to my favourite place to walk which was a nearby trail, Kahshe Barrens in Muskoka, Canada. The ground was covered in a cushion of red and yellow leaves so thick I could feel it under the sole of my boot. It had rained the day before, so I was purposely avoiding the mud and slippery rocks.

Have you ever noticed—in the city or the forest—that when all noise comes to a halt, it leaves you suspended in a moment of absolute silence? It happened that day in the forest. I stopped walking and paused, realizing I was receiving a message from Mother Earth. It wasn't a voice or the sound of words I could hear, but rather it came as a knowing, as though she just dropped the message into my being. It was a clear, *'Guide them back to the forest.'* Immediately I knew exactly what I was supposed to do. She wanted me to guide people to reconnect with nature. That's all. Whether it was in their garden or backyard, near a tree, in a park or a true forest, I felt confident that she would be there to nurture them, guide them, heal them and ultimately love them as one.

Excited to get started, my first mission was to post on social media photos and videos of me walking the trail in Muskoka, showing viewers the trees, the ground, the streams and any nature I could find. They were fun to do and well received, but I felt like it wasn't quite what she was expecting from me. Each time I went to the forest, I paused and listened intently for more direction, but nothing presented itself.

Several weeks after that first message, I arrived back at my cottage on the lake after a walk in Muskoka. I was sitting on my favourite spot on the granite stone by the water's edge, in a state of mindfulness. There was a moment in my meditation where I was unusually distracted by the silence, and so I paused. Suddenly I received another directive from Mother Earth— a knowing—and this time the message was *"Be still."*

"Well, that's exactly what I was doing," I said out loud, as though she were listening to me. There was no response from her, so I sat as still as the rock I was sitting on, staring into the water. At some point in a state of timelessness, I was moved to take my shoes and socks off and put my bare feet on the granite. The moment my bare soles touched the cool rock, a surge of Kundalini energy went through my entire body, raising goosebumps on my arms and legs as the cellular vibration increased in intensity.

Then, as if I had been given instructions that didn't come in the form of lessons, spoken words or an ideology from a book I read, I knew what I was to do. To bring people back to the forest, I'd have to lead them in my bare feet so they could reconnect with her healing. It was simple. She didn't say how many people she wanted me to guide back to the forest; it could be one person or a worldwide movement. That was up to me.

The last year I walked the Camino in boots was 2010. I walked the reverse way, retracing the steps of my original journey by starting in Santiago and ending up in St. Jean Pied de Port, France. It's called walking *el contrario*— the contrary way. Walking in my hiking boots along the edge of a road beside a ditch, I lost my balance and fell, landing on my back. With all my strength I tried to roll to get up, but I couldn't because of my backpack. Feeling like a turtle on its back, I started laughing at the situation. Eventually I managed to roll over far enough to flip over onto my belly and clumsily get up. From that day onward, I was afraid of falling again, and I changed the way I walked to being extra cautious, which I found to be more stressful.

While researching barefooting, I found a "barefoot professor" by the name of Daniel Howell in the USA. He has written about the role of the neural pathways on our soles: they protect and keep us out of danger and adjust the muscles in our feet, legs and back. Most people don't know that we have between 100,000 and 200,000 sensory nerve receptors in our feet whose job is to inform the brain of the environment the body is living in. Those messages are received by the central nervous system, which makes adjustments to different parts of the body to respond and protect us.

Learning to walk barefoot again was a slow process. The skin on the soles of our feet is unique because it has the ability to adapt to different terrains and grip so we can avoid falling. When we've been in shoes for a long time, the skin is soft and ultra sensitive, so it takes time to adjust. (In my last Camino group, one lady, a yoga teacher for twenty years, took her shoes off in the Galician forest. As soon as she started walking barefoot, she announced excitedly, "My vision has improved!" It didn't surprise me at all, as I found there were improvements to my vision. In time, I felt like I had developed another set of eyes that were on the soles of my feet, committed to protecting me at all times. Over the years I have come to trust them with my life.)

Several Facebook groups were discussing how to overcome some of these challenges, and someone presented the idea that when we wear boots with a lot of support and thick heels, it has the same effect as keeping our feet in a soft cast. If you've ever broken a bone, you know that the muscles atrophy and it takes weeks, if not months, to gain their strength back. Now imagine what has happened to the muscles in your feet after a lifetime of wearing shoes thirty, forty, fifty or sixty years later! Or even after walking on the Camino twenty to forty kilometres a day over several days or weeks.

Throughout the years of wearing boots and shoes, my arches had fallen and the muscles in my feet were very weak. Because I loved the forest, it was natural for me to start walking there first. About eight months later I walked 225 kilometres on the Camino barefoot most of the way. People stared at me and some questioned why I wasn't wearing socks and boots. I was walking through the tiny village of Vega de Valcarce when three men walked past me speaking Portuguese. One of them yelled out, "What are your sins?" I guess he thought I was doing penance, but barefooting is the furthest thing from that. It doesn't hurt your feet once you've adapted to it. I would say wearing boots is more like penance! I called out to him, "I don't have any sins!" and kept walking. It was liberating and felt amazing to be connected to the earth through the soles of my feet. My feet got stronger, I became more flexible and I gained amazing balance. My fear of falling was gone.

In my bare feet I walk slower and look where I am going. From this place I am present and in the moment all the time. Like everyone, I was initially afraid of stepping on glass or cutting my foot, but there is a certain trust I've developed in the Mother Earth that calms me, allowing my inner child to be present. She is curious, naive, child-like and innocent in her approach to exploring the world around her. Lindsy, another of my group pilgrims, who always used to wear shoes even around the house, likes being connected, too. She said that it was barefooting on the Camino that forced her to slow down and smell the roses, and now she walks barefoot every chance she gets.

There are always some pilgrims who want to walk the Camino barefoot. In North America, shoes are not only a status symbol but, without them, you can be barred entry from stores and restaurants. Fortunately, it isn't a problem on the Camino, which gives my group of pilgrims the opportunity to try barefooting. For the last six years I have been walking barefoot with my groups, covering one-hundred—or two-hundred-kilometre routes, and my favourite place to be is in the forest in Galicia. I always encourage the pilgrims to walk barefoot on the Camino on a dirt path, or any natural environment, preferably with undulating terrain, so they will continue to strengthen the muscles in their feet and legs and adapt the skin on the soles so it becomes more resilient. One pilgrim, Sandy, said she loved walking there in the cool mud because it felt very therapeutic.

One of the problems I encountered when I took off my boots was the adjustment in the alignment as I transitioned from a heel to a zero drop. Starting off with a new approach to Camino footwear, I bought minimalist shoes with less support rather than more, and to slowly migrate into everyday shoes that don't have a heel. Once out of my heavy boots and shoes, I could feel the ground and reconnect with nature, presenting a more spiritual experience. One of the pilgrims, Cindy, who was in my last group, decided to wear only her bare feet or a pair of zero-drop minimalist shoes. Every time I saw her, it looked as though she were floating. She wrote to me and said, "Walking barefoot has been a transformative experience for me. I feel more connected to the earth, to those around me and ultimately to myself. It energized me in unexpected ways and opened aspects of myself long buried and lost." By the end of the Camino, if we are wearing heeled walking shoes or supportive boots, it's possible our muscles are actually weaker than when we started.

People always ask why I walk barefoot. The simple answer is because it's healthy for my body, an approach to Earthing, and it connects me with nature. Each time I walk the Camino or a trail in Ecuador or the forest in Muskoka, it is another chance for me to be connected to the universe. And I'm practicing mindfulness while in a state of absolute awareness about my surroundings. My sacred place has become the forest because it is there that all the answers to my questions come, where all the healing to my body happens, where I am at peace, and I am one with Mother Earth.

Life is distilled down to something that is so very simple on the Camino. Walking in my bare feet, I am free, without a worry in the world about getting a blister, stiff ankles, sore knees, tendonitis or other conditions from wearing boots or shoes. The common fears and judgements we have disappear, and, instead, I feel a natural survival process is in play.

Although my pilgrimage started with my first Camino in 2001, I believe I am still on that same quest. If I relate the Camino experience to my barefoot journey to the soul, it's clear to me it will never end. Each time I meet a pilgrim, in 'regular' life or on the Camino, I will tell them about Mother Earth's request for me to guide them to the forest and the importance of reconnecting their bare soles to nature.

My most sacred place in the world is the forest. It's the place where my soul is nourished, my body is healed, my mind is wiser, and my heart is held in the love of the universe. She is there for us—we have only to bare our soles to receive her gifts.

As I told my children that day I arrived at the airport, "I brought the Camino home with me." I now know that I did. Each moment in my life, each lesson that I learn, each experience I have, each time I return to Spain or to Muskoka to walk barefoot, I am on the same path on a journey back to my authentic self.

That day the Great Mother Earth asked me to guide people to the forest in my bare feet was a turning point in my life, when I began to truly understand what I was here to do in the world; connect sole to soul.

Questions and Answers

1. What compelled you to set out on your pilgrimage?
I was downsized from my corporate telecom career and decided to go for a long walk to figure things out.

2. Is there a book, song, poem, or movie that inspired your quest?
In 2001 there weren't any decent movies about the Camino but I did find Shirley MacLaine's book *The Camino* and it was the only book I read before I left. Because of her book, I thought about wild dogs attacking me all the time. I read a book *Earthing* just after I started walking barefoot and it inspired me to keep going and stay connected to the earth.

3. Where is your sacred place and why did you choose it?
My sacred place is the forest. There is a trail in Muskoka, Canada called Kahshe Barrens and it's my preferred place to be. I chose it because it is very quiet, few people walk the trails and the terrain is perfect for bare feet because it is undulating, mossy, there are soft leaves and pine needles, mud, and much more.

4. How did your pilgrimage change your life or not?
My first Camino changed my life because I learned to live more simply, walk slowly, carry everything I needed on my back and I came to a clear understanding of the aphorism to 'never walk past a pilgrim in need'. Walking the Camino barefoot changed my life because I found my inner child, the girl I had been looking for all my life.

5. What is the most important piece of advice that you have received in your life? Do you have advice to share from your experiences?
The most important piece of advice that I have received in my life is to get out of the way. To learn to trust I will be guided on my journey and I don't have to take control of everything. As the Buddha says, this too shall pass.

Doing yoga on the Camino.
Photograph courtesy of Sue Regan Kenney.

Biography

Sue is the author of the best-selling book *My Camino,* which is in development as a feature film. In it she shares stories of her spiritual journey walking five hundred miles across the north of Spain on an ancient medieval pilgrimage route that changed her life. Since that first pilgrimage she has returned to the path over twenty times as an expert pilgrim, coaching and guiding groups. Her second book is *Confessions of a Pilgrim* and tells the story of her pilgrimage on the Portuguese Route. She is an internationally acclaimed keynote speaker who has facilitated barefoot and Camino workshops worldwide. As the designer of the first-ever truly barefoot shoe, called Barebottoms, Sue pitched her business idea on the renowned reality show *Dragons' Den.* Her barefoot lifestyle is centered around nature at her lakeside cottage in Canada, and she can often be found walking, running or doing yoga in the forest. Her third and most recent book is called *How to Wear Bare Feet.*

www.suekenney.ca, Facebook: My Camino / Sue Regan Kenney, Instagram: @caminosue

Dravidian Temples. *Photograph by Jerry Auld.*

Jerry Auld

A Carnival of Sorts

*T*he thing was—we knew it would end. It had to end, it was *supposed* to. We enjoyed the beer and sun without much thought to responsibility or pace because that was all going to be decided for us very soon, and there was no telling exactly when. Pre-emptively, the eight others had decided to leave several times now, and we'd pursued the farewell parties in such earnest that they'd missed the Karnataka bus each time.

We'd swim in the mornings and climb out of the surf and pass the stalls selling cold drinks and knick-knacks and Seven-Seas. Jim said, "Know why Shiva has so many incarnations? So they can sell anything to anybody."

Jim was world-weary in his broader sense. I couldn't guess his age. Maybe 30. He looked much older, but he was gregarious in small things, always giving things to the young boys running up to practice their English. In the oppressive heat on the way back to the empty fishing village, Jim said, "This monsoon is a hoax: it's a way for the locals to get a break from the crowds."

"And look," I said. "We're ruining it for them."

Later he said, "I don't blame them: everyone wants their home to themselves once in a while." He dropped a card on the old cable spool we used as a table.

"And that's how it begins," said Karen, throwing down a matching pair. Karen of the brown eyes. She had a way of looking at things as if they were individually on a stage, a way of coaxing out their soliloquy. Deep languid depths, like a slow sweeping net that one could only wish might snag and stay.

The fan above us beat a wobbly gait that seemed exhausted, an endless chanting of metal hitches, the only reason it didn't careen off was that nobody cared.

"It's down to your good self, Jerry." Jim said. And that's how it is: one chance played upon another chance until it is no longer anything but fortune or fate. But I had no cards and now the tide was out. I folded and went for a walk to the old Portuguese fort whose red battlements crumbled high above the white beach and the thumping surf and the huge horizon that curved just slightly to let you know everything familiar was just out of reach.

"*Whatcha doing here, Jer?*" said the Voice.

Anyone that has travelled solo for an extensive time knows this voice. That annoying one that is always right but only bothers to make an appearance after the fact. Calls you *Jer* when no one else would be allowed. There are rules. Life rules. Rules that living things follow. The *Voice* doesn't follow rules. Physics, Time, all that. The Voice is never drunk, never tired, never mad. It is the voice of your thoughts, but deeper, calmer. Like a miniature alien at the soupy controls of this lumbering human machine.

Good question though. Waiting, I figured. For the rains that aren't coming.

"*You're wasting this,*" the Voice said.

I had come to that little fishing village because it was rated as the most inundated in all of India by the monsoon. Over a metre of rain in a month. I had come to experience what that actually meant. And India was a place of pilgrimages, a place that you could actually wander with just a cloth about your waist—an abundance of food, a cultural celebration of aesthetics, and the not freezing-to-death. You could take your time here. But the monsoon was now more than three weeks late, and in the afternoon, when the heat grew, the few of us left would cluster in my back room by the refrigerator and deal the cards.

It was there I heard of the Gol Gumbaz. And that's how that goes: a mention here, an anecdote there, a short story that paints a mere sketch in your imagination, but enough for the Voice to chew away at.

"It's one of the largest free-standing domes in the world, a third larger than St. Paul's," said someone. "Truth? Never heard of it," another. "It's just the next state over, Karnataka, on the interior plateau. There's a gallery that runs the inside of the dome. The acoustics are so perfect you can clap and hear seven distinct echoes—no more, no less. Someone can whisper and—if you sit exactly in the right place—you hear it like they're beside you. The whispering gallery, it is."

Or Hampi—another mythical place—an entire city of carved stone, spread across miles; apparently abandoned even before being inhabited. "Imagine being the astrologer there, just before the grand opening, after 20 years' hard labour. 'Nope, the stars are all wrong. Pack up, we can't stay here!'"

The mysteries of India were there on the surface to see, a pilgrimage that seemed to need nothing more than sitting on your doorstep. Some mysteries were small and universal, however:

"Why do all the face cards have two faces?" asked Karen, who seemed to not care for the games themselves. "Two faces looking separate directions? What is a 'Jack' anyway? Is it a knight?" There were guesses all around: A prince. The inbred nephew locked in the tower. A Jester. A Monk. "What is his purpose?" Karen queried under knotted brow. "He seems lost, redundant."

The cards seemed ridiculous then, as if seeing them for the first time as adults. And nature doesn't need people to understand in order to happen, so the monsoon did arrive and break over the town and flood the road and soak even through the sandy concrete walls of the house. And soon I really was the only one left. Alone.

Said the Voice, "*Not alone.*"

Weeks of rain, steel grey days, the mold, the unbreakable humidity, staring at the blue lightning like the flickering of a TV on the curvaceous ironwork of my dirty windows, the crossbars of the roof, the slanted palm's heads like wet cats leaning down, crisscrossing the road that was now a river.

At night, as the wind tore at me on the battlements, I could watch the low ceiling of heavy clouds being lit far out to sea, the lightning arching underneath and connecting them across their vast bellies in an instant; a flashing electronic message that kept signalling: *you missed your bus.*

And in the dark and damp the Voice said: "*What is a whispering gallery?*"

Buses are easy to board, it turns out. The driver puts it in gear and you wait for the future to pull up. Up through the winding muddy roads of the Western Ghats and into the Deccan plateau—the huge interior plain. There the bus rattled out from under the arch of cloud that marked the tail of the monsoon and the sky cleared. Cool dry air. Karnataka.

People who believe in reincarnation should not be allowed to drive public transport in India. The screeching, blaring macho staredown that were Indian roads required some respect for present life. Perhaps my former ceiling fan had made me soft to the karmic wheel, but I avoided the big roads. No bus should travel straight, anyway, lest it be called a train. And so I passed by Hampi and walked the empty spaces between huge boulders, and the empty squares, and the massive but still very empty elephant stables, and I boarded the bus again in silence.

And at Bijapur, I found the Gol Gumbaz, and handed a megaphone to the Voice. It was a squat mausoleum that, unlike the Taj Mahal's brilliant white marble and soaring lines, seemed to shroud itself in mundane greys.

Sitting there all alone with no one to play telephone with, a great dome arching before you, one tends to pause. But speaking here isn't mundane: your words are going to circle around to your very own ear. You go with the phrase that bubbles up.

Whatcha doing here?

And I couldn't tell if it was me or the Voice that was asking.

The reply came like a clap: *Waiting.*

Echoing perfectly seven times. *Still waiting.*

But then I whispered: *What are you waiting for*? And there was silence.

Humph. Some acoustics.

It was embarrassing to shout in a place that is designed to make you face the emptiness of your seeking. Outside, I passed, the forlorn kiosks selling handicrafts and cold drinks. Something odd caught my eye: a small sandalwood cube, carved like a cage, but with gaps bigger than anything it could imprison. The bars were exactly like those in the wrought-iron window of my late villa.

"What is it?" I asked, even as I was forgetting the response—surely some

27

esoteric symbol of Shiva or Vishnu or Brahma. Instead the woman smiled, shy and uncertain: "People want what they know, it is like this."

I realized it had been months since I had bought something superfluous, symbolic. A month in the south off-season since I'd seen another Westerner. Her son pushed the wooden cage into my hand, ran the prices. We both knew it was a game. Deflecting his grandiose claims, I said, "Know why Shiva has so many incarnations? So they can sell anything to anybody."

"Hahaha" said the boy. "OK, fourteen rupees. Just last day I heard the same story."

"Seven-Seas Jim!" I said, "Which way did they go?" He pointed down the road. East. The coast. Where? We all shrugged. Somewhere small, interesting. Surely.

Buses, it turns out, are easy to board. I jumped one to the next town, and another, and another. I rolled the sandalwood cube in my hand—a dry wood that never seemed to saturate—and wondered what it could possibly be used to contain. Night didn't fall in India so much as gather on the ground and rise like dust. On a platform, somewhere, I turned the small cage in my sweat like an empty sponge. I asked about buses to the coast: I must have been close now.

The ubiquitous boy, eager and insistent, tugged my hand towards one. He wore a necklace, a pendant, decidedly hand-made and Western: a two-faced man—one side happy, the other crying—the masks of the Western theater but angular, distorted by the sharp edge of the smooth grey indigenous stone. The Jack. I asked him where he got it.

"Mahali," he said. The stone-cutters' town on the sea. Where temple statues are made.

"And who gave that to you?"

He looked at me like there was another level of graft to be won. "Come," he said. "No bus." And led off down the soft streets under snarls of power lines and dust-hazy skies. Near the center rose the sharp outlines of Dravidian temples. I wasn't as far south as Maduri, I was sure, but here was the same structure: a steep layer-cake of colourful figurines rising into the dusk. I halted at the outside; being pulled into murky temples is a loaded deck of cards, and although it helps to be a relative giant compared to the inhabitants, the best play is as the foolhardy foreigner with no attention span. They can't pitch if you can't catch.

We entered through a small iron door into a pillared chamber stained by a millennium of incense. The sadhu, berobed and headdressed and shiny with oil or sweat or just firelit skin, was incomprehensible, and I shook my head as the boy watched. The sadhu raised his arms and intoned something dramatic, paused, saw no response, then leered at me and winked. He was an actor, like us all, seeking connection with his audience, trying to establish the game's rules. My heart wasn't in it. Acting was too much work. I found myself rolling the sandalwood cage in my palm.

The sadhu watched calmly, saw his opening. No point avoiding it, I opened my hand. He turned his head slightly, told me it's Shiva's thingamawidget, got sly and asked me what's inside. It was obvious it was empty. That was not the point of the contradiction-is-profound game. I dreamt up the biggest thing that wouldn't make sense: the universe, my soul, dark knowledge of human intention. All too easy. None of it felt right. I realized I was all too tired of the game.

I said, "It's empty." Contradiction clashed with cold reality in a cage match.

"Do you want to know what's really inside?"

I said I didn't want to know, and as I said it, I realised it was true. He said, "Open it."

I said, "There's nothing to release," but then I knew that was not just true but irrelevant. It was the container itself that was important, not the non-contents. That was the obviousness I'd been missing since pondering its purpose.

I held it in my hand like it was *I* that imprisoned *it*. It was for me to release and I couldn't.

The shiny sadhu glanced at the boy watching us and waved curiously, as if telling us to be gone.

I ducked back out the door, but it must have been a different door as it led to a narrow courtyard with no obvious exit. There waited the boy. He motioned to me. I groaned—the next pitch—and waved him off. But I had nowhere else to go and I felt like nothing could be taken from the man who had nothing inside.

"*Go. This is it,*" said the Voice.

The boy led through to a second sandy courtyard of plain stone, then into a shaded low hall that smelt of a dank well. On the polished steps that were once carved into lotus leaves was an old man in robes as worn as the steps. He smiled. No teeth. Waved me in with quick downward flaps of his wrist. The way you can fall in love at first sight—as if you know a face, as if it belongs to a small personal album that you've never seen but know intimately—so you can know holiness. It is a sense of certainty. Maybe one in a thousand in this land of actors. This one? This one, yes. The Voice was silent. Everything in me was watching. Holiness forces a calm, the fetters of respect, upon you.

The old man nodded—a quick bobbing, barely moving. "What is your good name?" he asked. "What is your good country?" The standard street fare conversation, but the impression I had was of him straining to turn both ears toward me, listening intently the way seasoned touts the world over can know the city of a stranger by the tiniest variances in their accent. But when he stopped his questions and looked full at me, he spoke in exactly the tone of the Voice.

My *Voice.*

"You"—he raised a knobby walking stick I hadn't seen from within the folds of his cloak and jabbed me in the belly—"are two."

I was silent. A strange humming feeling rose in the base of my skull where my ancient lizard brain still resided.

"You are two, Jack," he said again, tapping his stick on the stone flagging as if breaking my spell.

"I am two," I said, blowing my cheeks out. "Yeah. Too tired." A feeble defence. I was reeling, because the sensation was that he was speaking from within me, and there was no bartering with that.

"He knows you," I thought. The Voice was silent, as if impossible to hear both in the same room. "Traitor," I thought.

The old man smiled at me, "You feel lost, redundant. But you are two: one mind: two faces." He puffed up his tiny arms, mocking me. "You are the warrior. Strong, alone, needing no one. And. You are the priest, needing the crowd, for hearing and being heard. You are both."

How was it to hear words you know are truth? The humming feeling had expanded—I felt full of static, as if jammed between stations.

The old man said, "You know this already. You crave the crowd when you are alone, and crave silence when you are in a crowd. You will always be in motion from one to the other. You will never be content; always restless. You will never have a home."

Cutting through the inner white noise was a feeling of intense sadness: a view of the cold expanse of time like the curve of the ocean where everything was just over the horizon. At that moment the thing I wanted the most was a home.

"You've been searching and waiting to find the end of the search, but it is in your feet. It is not in the markings on the map, but in the act of drawing the map. Know this, find belonging."

His stick was out and tapping on my little sandalwood cage. "The bars only define the cage, not the space, like the lines on a map tell you where a mapmaker went, not all possibilities. Where you go is all down to your good self," the old one said, turning away.

The boy hung back, hiding behind a massive pillar, reminding me of the boy at the Gol Gumbaz, and the rumours of friends by the sea.

Buses are easy to board; like climbing into bed to the possibility of a dream.

It was late, so late, and I clattered along the secondary roads in a twisting path more like a crack working through plaster, but in the morning—a morning, a dawn—I looked up the aisle of a bus with twenty silent people, I being one of them, as the sun rose slowly through the haze of heat and salt. The golden hills of the Eastern Ghats rose to my right, as the sun haloed through the watery horizon on the left. The fresh smell of the sea and the clear washed-out blue of the sky seemed a wake up, and I was struck by an intense peace, a sense of belonging, to the twenty silent strangers in the other seats, to the villages through which we were creakily threading, to the light itself on the far hills. I could not move, but felt assured that if I extended my arm and flicked my fingers, that the horizon would vibrate. I was the creator and the destroyer in the great slow dance of life.

The sensation lasted for a time, perhaps until the sun was high and we slowed and stopped at the seaside town of Mahalibalipuram, home to the workers of stone. I walked the soft sand streets, listened to the tapping of a thousand chisels, saw the garish and intricate statues of the old gods in the native slate grey, and the old temples on the beach piled and worn like giant sand castles.

I found my friends, and new ones. Jim considered me as if something had changed, and Karen's eyes did not slip. The reunion parties took up several nights under the sweeping lighthouse beams and the Southern Cross. And that's how it was: there were mentions of Sri Lanka, of the Andaman Isles, of the Himalayas now coming into condition, and of the fishtailed peak of Machapuchare, a peak sacred to Shiva and thus forbidden to summit. The Swiss girl at the end of the table smiled back, dark tangles, familiar somehow. The Voice was all ears. "If it was meant to be, it was meant to be," she said.

I said, "The map doesn't draw itself, sometimes you have to hold the pen."

"You see what I have to work with," said the Voice.

In the bright mornings we stretched on the rooftops, listening to the chisels. Seven-Seas Jim said, "I've done nothing all week, so why do I feel so content?"

Pilgrimages tend to choose you. Sacred places can only send quiet invites. They are just a personal perspective, one that lets you look with wonder and appreciation. But live there? They are not a cage designed to hold your dreams, only to attract them. I knew then that it was time to go.

Buses are easy to board, it turns out, because pilgrimages don't really end, they just lead to the next one.

"What is a fishtail peak?" said the Voice.

Questions and Answers

1. What compelled you to set out on your pilgrimage?
I had a story I wanted to write and I needed an affordable, colourful, and surprising place to do that in, as usual, the pilgrimage I was really on ended up finding me.

2. Is there a book, song, poem, or movie that inspired your quest?
The Snow Leopard by Peter Matthiessen, and *Siddharta* by Hermann Hesse. The monochromatic lithographs or luminescent paintings of David Roberts and Maxfield Parrish—the smoky air, the vivid but discrete splash of colour, secrets buried under the drift of ages.

3. Where is your sacred place and why did you choose it?
Mahalabalapurum. It chose me. This is that story.

4. How did your pilgrimage change your life or not?
I've never felt such a sense of peace or connected-ness. It's curious: you can't easily sustain that feeling; but you can't forget it either.

5. What is the most important piece of advice that you have received in your life? Do you have advice to share from your experiences?
I was told that I would never be content. That I would always be restless. This has helped me be at peace with myself and use that energy to sharpen the focus on my craft. Knowing that nothing is permanent or lasts very long takes the pressure off. And knowing the stories are the way we transmit everything really important gives me meaning.

Photograph courtesy of Jerry Auld.

Biography

Jerry Auld writes fiction about wild places. His first novel *Hooker & Brown* (Brindle & Glass, 2009) was shortlisted for both the Boardman Tasker award for Mountain Literature, and the Banff Mountain Book Festival Literature award. His second book, *Short Peaks,* is a collection of really short stories about mountains around the world (Imaginary Mountain Surveyors, 2013). He lives and thrives in Canmore, Alberta.

jerryauld.com
www.facebook.com/jerry.auld

Arita in the Western Desert of Egypt. *Photograph by Barbara Hanlo.*

Arita Baaijens

Risk discomfort and solitude for understanding.
~Wade Davis

Looking for Paradise

*L*ate in the day the chill of the coming winter is palpable. A frigid air makes veins on the cheek burst and covers the marshy ponds after sunset with a brittle layer of ice. "Bad luck," says my Russian guide Misha Paltsyn, as he turns his horse toward the windswept plateau in the Siberian Altai, on the border of Russia and Mongolia. We search in vain for the Argali, mountain sheep with huge horns residing within inhospitable areas. They are shy and for indigenous peoples an important totem animal.

This trip is a diversion after two failed attempts to find Shambhala, a mythical kingdom where reside those who are pure of spirit. Attaining Shambhala is an idea which for Buddhists is the equivalent of achieving a high state of spiritual development. And according to some, this mysterious realm is also a reality, to be found in a hidden valley surrounded by icy peaks somewhere north of the Himalayas. Insiders claim that the Altai, a pristine mountain range in southern Siberia, is high on the list of potential locations and when I learned that, it made my heart race with joy. A search for an earthly paradise in a maze of mountain chasms and glaciers was exactly the challenge I was looking for.

Let me make something clear from the beginning. As a biologist and agnostic I do not believe in the existence of a mysterious realm where only the good prevails. My mission has a different purpose: to restore my purpose in life. The past twenty years I wandered much of the year with camels through the deserts of North Africa. For this, I gave up a comfortable career, old age pension and love relationships. It was a price I willingly paid. Roaming between sand and rocks, I was happier than I ever thought possible, but a few years ago, the unthinkable happened: the spell was broken. The desert was done with me, the flame of inspiration was extinguished. It was a disaster for me personally, and for me as a writer. How in the name of heaven should I continue without this feeling of purpose and sacred fire? Should I be one more egg in a crate, or should I stand up because the alarm goes off? If, during this period, I had been handed a potion that would have turned me into a stone or tree, I would have swallowed it without hesitation. After three somber years I only saw one way out and that was to find a new obsession. That is how I arrived in Siberia, where I first heard about that Shambhala might be found in the Altai Golden Mountains.

"Argali sheep, there!" Misha interrupts my thoughts. High above us our binoculars transform moving dots into rugged sheep with impressive, curling horns. We watch with great satisfaction as they step out of sight in a mass of rocks and stones. After our successful search, we nudge the horses and dash away across the swampy plain to our lodgings in a ramshackle shepherd's hut with a boarded up window at the edge of a mountain lake. The setting sun turns the plateau into a hall of mirrors: glistening waterholes and silver streams as far as the eye can see. By the time we reach the refuge the purple colored sky is no longer distinguishable from the dark earth below.

"To life," In the fire warmed cabin Misha lifts the glass. The vodka bottle is half empty before I dare to start relating my experiences about strange happenings during my search for Shambhala. Strange ideas, that is, for rational thinking beings, like Misha and me, for whom stories with no scientific explanation belong to the realm of fiction. There was this odd Russian girl with whom I went on horseback to Akem, a high mountain lake where Shambhala might be found. Halfway on the trail fog and heavy snow barred our path. Winter came in and to my chagrin it seemed Akem would remain inaccessible the rest of the year. The holy lake sometimes does not allow an approach, explained the girl, of our misfortune, while giggling like a moron. The next day she suddenly disappeared. Later I learned that she reached Akem, and who knows, perhaps Shambhala, on her own, leaving me with three horses and the expenses. Misha almost chokes with laughter. Encouraged, I start talking about the village of Kosh Agach. After years of drought, rain was much needed there. Villagers complained to the local shaman. After an elaborate ritual in which the entire village participated, the first downpours appeared; only a week later it was again dry.

Misha laughs no longer, but looks at me questioningly. Have I given way to humbugs? The Altai, cradle of shamanism, also attracts posers and spiritual charlatans. I do not belong to either category, I declare firmly. Science is my bible and I sail blindly to the songs of physicists to explain natural phenomena. "Yet there is something amiss," I hear myself protest. Not so long ago we thought someone's intelligence could be predicted by the size of his skull. And wasn't the universe a predictable machine until Einstein formulated the theory of relativity? Each theory is fated to be rewritten. What researchers do is interpret their observations of the facts as best as they can, which is different from claiming an absolute truth. The boundary between knowledge and acts of faith is therefore less distinct than I had previously considered.

The wood stove crackles, fist-sized mice play tag above the floor and our shadows dance against the wooden beams. "Truth is an agreement between the likeminded," I murmur.

"Mm," Misha replies. It sounds defensive.

Misha's hesitation is understandable. I too struggle with the question of how, in the absence of hard evidence or measurable data, one can distinguish fantasy from reality. I think of the visionaries who have crossed my path. They all had a 'direct line to the gods', saw visions or felt a slight tingling of their bodies in places of power. The only one to whom nothing special ever happened during rituals and spiritual sessions was myself. Even my dreams were disappointingly normal. "Your problem," said a seer with piercing eyes, "is a failure to surrender." Earlier on this man had given me a raw egg. The contents of which I must spread to all directions on a busy intersection in Amsterdam. Then, the self-proclaimed seer and healer had prophesied, everything would be just fine with me. My gaze turns from Misha to the red-hot stove and the steaming horse saddles. Even without a raw egg, hope glimmers. Especially when I hear that my guide and horseman promises to bring me to a sacred valley tomorrow. "Perhaps you will find there that which you're are searching for."

Later that evening the banja, a Russian sauna that makes the bitterly cold winters bearable, waits for me. The fire roars and water hisses on hot stones. Now, washed clean and bundled up, an hour later I step into the freezing cold. Nothing but emptiness and stillness. Cutting wind, tingling cheeks and stars above me cheerfully wink. There is an explosion in my head. Thinking is no longer possible. So I howl to the moon. I feel again the joy and gladness, and the ecstatic happiness that I recognize from my first years in the desert.

Karakol

With renewed energy I resume my search for Shambhala. After a long drive on bumpy roads and over mountain passes, biologist Misha Paltsyn drops me off at the opening to the sacred Karakol Valley, the spiritual heart of the Altai. The gently sloping valley is guarded at its northern end by the mountain Uch Enmek, which means three fontanels. Local taboo says that it is not allowed to look at the snow covered giant. And speaking the true name of the mountain is prohibited as well, out of respect for the master spirit, or *ee* of the mountain.

"This mountain and valley preserve the balance in the world," explains geologist Danil Mamyev. The custodian of the valley explains that everything in nature—mountains, trees, rocks, water—possesses a presence, or spiritual entity, *ee*, with which people can communicate. Mountains possess the most powerful ee and therefore people are careful not to raise their anger.

In the voice of this founder of the Uch Enmek Culture Park I detect no trace of irony. His muscular arms loosely crossed and his gaze focused on the clouds, Danil Mamyev explains the cosmology of the Altai. The earth possesses organs, just like humans. The mountain Uch Enmek is a fontanel, and receives information and energy from the cosmos.

Further on, a small hill acts as an umbilical cord and transmits information to the earth. Hence Karakol is locally known as the navel of the world.

Do fellow geologists not tap a finger against the head when they hear him talk? "Modern science has just appeared," comments this man of solid composure dryly, "And our traditional knowledge is thousands of years old." An academic training does not undermine or contradict his faith in traditional knowledge. If I believe Danil Mamyev, then he learned in college what his ancestors already knew, but in a more complex and persistent way. He points to downy white clouds that veil the face of Uch Enmek and also to an old weathered standing stone. Trees, stones, rivers, all contribute to knowledge, he says. Shamans pick up this information intuitively and share their interpreted knowledge. According to Danil there is nothing mysterious or strange about that. In the body of Altai thought, man is an organic part of a bigger picture. Invisible strings connect us to the moon, the wind, the grass. Good and evil exist, but the concept of sin is absent. One's destiny is determined at the time of birth, so it is not your fault if you have an aggressive disposition. Fortunately, there are sacred places where people can go for purification, and leave behind the accumulated negative forces.

A sudden gust of wind makes me shiver. Undoubtedly Danil sees a spectre, but I'm just cold. To understand and appreciate another culture requires an open and receptive mind, but my head is brainwashed by science and is yet unlocked. "You rely on research," Danil guesses my thoughts. "We respect and listen to the ways of the shaman."

We wade through the long meadow grass to a kurgan, an imposing tumulus dating from the time of the Scythians, a nomadic people of heroic legend who roamed the Altai region over two thousand years ago. The sun warms my face. A soft breeze plays with the grasses and rustles the tree leaves. Clouds drift lazily from here to there. The Altai remains almost untouched thanks to faith in an animate nature and thanks to an extensive system of protective rules and taboos. To trifle with nature disturbs the balance and make the spirits angry. Danil says that as a young boy his father would reprimand him for picking up a stone or picking a flower. Nature is to be left in peace, was a practice he learned at an early age. If you really are in need of something, such as firewood, cranberries, mushrooms, or nuts, you ask permission of the ee first and then take only what you need.

Danil Mamyev stops at a standing stone about the size of a man, which guards a mound of several meters in breath. The tomb of the ancient chief belongs to an extensive system of tumuli, rock carvings and hundreds of enigmatic stone structures which enrich this area. Recent physical geographical research in the valley gives a clue as to why for thousands of years the Karakol Valley has been venerated as a sacred space. The stones with which the kurgans are constructed, are strongly magnetic, they say. And they are so set that the graves together form a giant magnetic ring. This ring corresponds to an underground, naturally formed oval ring of a rock that is similarly magnetic. This puzzles the archaeologists but not the indigenous population. To these observers, science confirms the belief in the uniqueness and function of the Karakol Valley, where knowledge and energy from the cosmos are seeping into the earth. The kurgan complex creates a force field that attracts cosmic information, similar to the way a lightning rod attracts electricity. "The separation between earth and cosmos here is very thin," explains Danil; easy access to higher spheres. Then, gazing with a slightly provocative look: "Though not everyone can perceive the strong energy."

Is this magnetic ring a gateway to Shambhala? In the world of *Indiana Jones* and *Alice in Wonderland* it might just be that. And in the world of Danil Mamyev? It remains silent. A silence that leaves Danil in contemplation as he looks over the valley. It may be my imagination, but it is as if long tentacles search my brain to discover the intention of my question.

"We do not believe in a heavenly paradise," says Danil finally. "Our landscape offers everything the soul needs to develop completely." In the Altai there is no need for an irreconcilable god who sends people eternally to hell or rewards them with the jackpot. Humanity must find its happiness on earth and where to do so better than in the Altai, a word that means golden mountains, mother, god and heaven all together.

With a broad sweep, Danil Mamyev's strong arms gather heaven and earth. All biological and non-biological life on our planet is of cosmic origin. In the vast network of connections is reflected the big picture in the smallest particle. The big picture, we must imagine as a pulsating cosmic egg of giant proportions, Kangyj, from which everything originates. Souls, living beings, but also planets, stars and all kinds of energy. Listening to Danil Mamyev, the Altai seems a charming fairy tale, but the reality is less sweet. It can be a pretty mess, admits the geologist, and talks about the uproar that arose in the early nineties when he proposed a plan to protect the valley. It was the time of perestroika, when cooperatively owned land was being divided up and distributed to families in the valley. Danil Mamyev saw Russian developers, cunning and deceitful, who for a song bought up the most beautiful places in the Altai to build hotels and attract tourists. Karakol Valley had to be saved, and Danil's proposal was to ask for the status of cultural conservancy. Many did not agree. Never, screamed villagers, who under no circumstances would allow tourists in the sacred valley. A frightened look appears in Danil's eyes. He received death threats and feared for his life. But he also discovered at the height of the conflict, his true mission. Everything his life had taught him and that he had done led to this moment and this place. Therefore he fought on and preserved the valley.

The shaman

"You have luck," said Danil Mamyev as he brings me back to his camping area in the valley. The next day brings a modest music festival in honor of his friend Arzhan, who is a shaman from a neighboring village. Valley residents and friends perform on the stage to thank him and give support for his difficult task. To be a shaman is no fun. Often a shaman is a person with a troubled soul, who after experiencing a serious physical or spiritual trauma succumbs to the call to mediate between humans and spirits. For the shaman, constantly switching between two worlds is a demanding task. It is especially so if the shaman helps a lot of people.

I am surprised to recognize in Arzhan the burly musician who I met the year before in a forest after my nocturnal dip in an icy lake. I had heard misty shreds of music and followed the sounds to a high blazing fire. There I saw a man with a moon shaped face, entranced in the playing of his topshur, a stringed instrument. No, no, he dismissed my compliments. He was a just ordinary man and his music was nothing. Goose bumps on my arms told a different tale. Now, one year after the encounter in the moonlit forest, I am sharing a traditional hexagonal wooden house with him, his wife, and his closest friends. Someone picks up a guitar and strums it by the fire. Another pours vodka and tea. We talk, laugh, and nurture the spirit of the fire with delicacies and listen to Arzhan; he hears and sees so much more than us. There are asides about ghosts, and talk about significant events and dreams, I let all of it wash over me. The boundary between dream and reality fades, time seems left outdoors. In this pleasant and strange mood my mind empties like a car running out of fuel. The gauge slowly falls to zero.

"What can we learn from you?" Someone asks suddenly. According to the custom and logic of the Altai a stranger brings valuable insights and knowledge, the expectant glances make me uncomfortable as I shift on my stool. What was it that I brought except cynicism and disbelief? "Nothing," I say, to tell the truth.

I had come to learn.

"Tomorrow, get up before sunrise," concludes Arzhan. Any further explanation he considers unnecessary.

Frosted blades of grass crunch beneath my feet and clouds of vapor escape my lips as I emerge in the morning twilight to wait for what is coming. The shaman and Danil Mamyev make preparations for offerings beside a sacred birch with colored prayer ribbons. This afternoon the sun is directly above the equator and the length of the day anywhere on earth is more or less equal to that of the night. Autumn Equinox, traditionally the time when the harvest is celebrated and people take stock. What does one keep, what does one let go, what should change?

Danil beckons. Silently we stand around the altar, a simple stacked column of flat stones. Fog is dripping from the trees, mist hovers over the country and smoke circles from the sacred juniper smudges purify the clearing where we stand. The shaman lights a fire, sprinkles milk in all directions and honors the spirits with song. To a sacred place, Danil Mamyev had told me, you enter only with a pure heart and a head full of good thoughts. You do not ask for material things, you can show gratitude and leave an offering behind. What I will let go of? What I will leave at the altar is the desire that I've cherished so long, to find an obsession. Obsession belongs to the desert period, I realize, and that stage of my life is complete. The question is: whether I dare to go a step further. Do I dare to step outside the boundaries of my own culture and open myself to another model of reality to explore? I am not saying that I suddenly believe in spirits or in the existence of the kingdom of Shambhala, but now I know that the mind and the heart must act together. I take the leap. And so, when the first rays of the sun touch the altar, my focus on finding an obsession has passed into an exploration of new possibilities.

Questions and Answers

"There are no questions or answers in PARADISE."
Tor

Arita and her horse Gaziz on the Ukok Plateau, Altai Mountains, Siberia.
Photograph by Arita Baaijens.

Biography

Arita Baaijens grew up in Ede and studied biology in Amsterdam. After seven years working as an environmental biologist, she traded her job for a risky adventure in the Egyptian desert. She purchased camels, and as the only Western woman, traveled the Sahara alone. Not only did Arita learn to survive in the desert, her self-imposed solitude changed her outlook on life. The barren landscape of sand and rocks brought her back to a pure existence. Without time being filled with economic and cultural activities, one cannot help but become reflective. Although confrontation with vast emptiness can be frightening, solitude brings out one's strength. The desert taught Arita to turn her fear of the unknown into a positive force. After all, if there is no one to ask for help, you are forced to find your own solutions. A true master learns to make something from nothing.

After two decades of sand and camels, Siberia called. It was in the Altai Mountains that Arita began looking for the mythical Shambala, a legendary paradise tucked in a hidden valley, surrounded by icy mountain peaks. After searching for many years, paradise remained elusive, but it was through meetings with local shepherds and shamans that Arita became intrigued with their unshakable belief in nature spirits and nature as an animated being. She has received international recognition and awards for her writings and her research on the meaning of landscape. She is a fellow of the Royal Geographical Society, Wings and the Explorers Club.

www.aritabaaijens.nl

"Our stories come from our lives and from the playwright's pen, the mind of the actor, the roles we create, the artistry of life itself and the quest for peace."
~Maya Angelou

Man Digging in well. Photograph by Ariane Kirtley.

"Filthy water cannot be washed."
~African proverb

Viking chapel and cemetery, Wyre, Orkney. *Photograph by Keith A. Skinner.*

Keith Skinner

I take my journey back to seek my kindred,
Old founts dried up whose rivers run far on
Through you and me.
~Edwin Muir, *The Labyrinth*

Finding Margaret

A light rain began to fall as the ferry edged away from Mainland, Orkney's largest island, toward the neighboring island of Rousay. The handful of passengers were scattered around the small, dingy cabin where diesel fumes mingled with those of coal oil heaters and the damp morning chill.

A finger of land stretched out across the water in the distance. Typical for Orkney, there were no trees in sight along its surface. It was a landscape of vacant slopes in varying shades of green and brown, dotted with spiky tufts of straw-colored grass and sporadic clumps of wildflowers. I was uncertain if it was the island of Wyre but tried, nonetheless, to picture a young girl running across the horizon against the slate gray sky.

"What takes you to Wyre," the ferry agent had asked when I inquired about tickets.

"My grandmother."

"Your grandmother lives on Wyre?" He looked doubtful, as if he knew each resident on the island personally.

"My seventh great-grandmother. She was born and raised there."

I wasn't sure the clarification would make sense to him—it didn't to me just a month earlier—but I didn't explain it meant seven "greats" in front of "grandmother."

"We don't often get people going to Wyre." He smiled in a way that was both bemused and condescending. "Nothing there, you know."

I could have expounded further, but would he have understood that I wanted to walk the ground my grandmother had walked, occupy the place where she'd spent the first part of her unusual life? I just shrugged, content to be considered an eccentric American.

"Just so you understand you'll be out there four hours, and only with a special stop. We normally don't return until late afternoon."

Mainland, where the ferry had departed, was the sprawling heart of Orkney and its largest island. Wyre was home to only seventeen people and one of the smallest occupied islands in the archipelago.

The trip to Orkney had been planned for months when I learned my great-grandfather was included in the 1895 publication *The Erskine-Halcro Genealogy*. Among numerous surprises, the book revealed that the Halcro branch of my family had Norse and Danish origins and had occupied parts of Orkney for hundreds of years, perhaps even before it became part of Scotland. The Erskine branch, however, lived on the Scottish mainland, but a grisly scandal that befell one generation of Erskines brought the two families together. Margaret Halcro, the grandmother from Wyre, was a child of the conjoined families.

Margaret's grandmother was one of the disgraced Erskines, the only one to survive. She had conspired with her brother and two sisters to poison two young nephews in order to usurp their estate. The brother and two sisters were beheaded. Margaret's grandmother, having shown more remorse, was spared and banished to Orkney instead. The exile may have been worse than death for her. She was a Stewart, related to the royal family that included Mary, Queen of Scots. After arriving in Orkney, she married a man from the Halcro family and found herself on the island of Wyre, the wife of a modest tenant farmer. Their son, Margaret's father, also pursued a life of farming, which is where Margaret's story began.

I'd been drawn to Orkney by its fascinating early history. Evidence of Neolithic settlers, fierce Pictish tribes, and Viking raiders could still be seen throughout the islands and was often well-preserved. Discovering I had a personal connection to Orkney had made the trip even more compelling. Margaret's story, in particular, resonated with me. She was a native Orcadian raised on a remote island under the dark cloud of her grandmother's scandal. How had that shaped her life?

My wife Chris and I were the only remaining passengers as the ferry left Rousay and headed for Wyre, a journey of only five minutes. The ferry nuzzled into the stark landing without the usual bustle of passengers or vehicles starting their engines. All we could see from the cabin door was a simple concrete pier, two huts, and a single-track road leading up the hill. When the female deckhand sounded the all clear to debark, I asked her solemnly, "You're not going to forget us, are you?"

We headed up the deserted road that climbed inland then veered lengthwise across rolling pastureland. I'd tried to suppress any preconceptions about Wyre before arriving. I wanted to hear its sounds firsthand, smell its air and absorb the essence of the place as my grandmother had. Well the air was thick with the essence of sheep dung and the only sounds within earshot were bleating sheep and the loud thrum of a wind turbine spinning furiously in the wind. Wind was a constant in Orkney. Stripped of its timber centuries earlier, the Orcadian landscape was continually scoured by wanton winds. The sound of the turbine only amplified their presence.

The total area of Wyre was just over one square mile and we could see most of it from the crest of the road. Judging by the arrangement of buildings and the grid of stone walls and wire fences, there appeared to be six or seven farms, each with a long gravel lane leading to a distant family compound. Two cars passed us as we walked along the road but we saw no other signs of human activity.

The ferry agent had said there was nothing to see, but we soon came to the Wyre Heritage Center, a garage-sized structure at the island's core. The Center was unmanned but also unlocked. A table inside with tea-making supplies and instant soup let us know we were welcome to make ourselves at home. Maps, photos, and information about Wyre covered the walls. One table was stacked with binders containing more material. After looking around briefly, we agreed to return for lunch. By that time, we would welcome some respite from the wind and intermittent rain.

We followed a trail behind the Center across a pasture full of sheep to the remains of a twelfth century Viking chapel and cemetery. My pulse quickened as I swung open the ancient iron gate to enter. The chapel could have been the family church for some generation of Halcros. Margaret might have been baptized within its walls. Even if it was in ruins by her time, she would have explored its interior, looking out through the arched doorway and narrow window as I had done upon entering. We searched for evidence of Halcros buried in the small cemetery, but all the tombstones predating the nineteenth century had been scrubbed smooth by centuries of wind, rain, and snow.

Not far from the chapel, atop the island's highest point, stood other ruins, those of a fortress built about the same time as the chapel by a Viking chieftain named Kolbein Hrúga. Though there was little chance of finding any trace of Halcros, we climbed the hill to explore the ruins. Walking through the structure that was five feet high in places, I imagined the children of Wyre hiding within its stone chambers. The Halcros must have considered the fortress a treasured part of their Norse heritage. The fortress and its Viking lord were both mentioned in the Norse chronicle, the *Orkneyinga Saga*. And more than once during our stay, we'd heard Orcadians proudly proclaim that they weren't Scottish but rather of Viking blood. Surely Margaret's father, brimming with that same pride, would have filled Margaret's imagination with visions of longships in the harbors and Vikings roaming the islands. From the fortress, she would have had a clear view of all the surrounding islands. What did she imagine about herself from that stony perch?

Even with the company of other children and the millieu of Viking lore, life on the island must have been lonely much of the time. Trips across Pentland Firth for supplies or to visit friends and family would have required a considerable undertaking in the seventeenth century. Did Margaret feel small and marooned on Wyre? Or was the island something of a sanctuary for her?

I found some possible answers to those questions back in the Heritage

Center. After warming ourselves with tea and sandwiches, we studied the dozen or so binders we'd noticed earlier. Some had photos of more recent island residents and community events while others were devoted to the historically significant aspects of Wyre. An old map of the island's tenant farms revealed the distribution of land had remained almost unchanged over the centuries. There were stories about Kolbein Hrúga and the fortress as well as the odd history of the Heritage Center building, which had been a fishing shed on another island. The real find, however, was an article about the celebrated Scottish poet Edwin Muir, who had spent part of his childhood on Wyre. His family had lived on the Bu, the farm originally occupied by Kolbein Hrúga. Years later, when asked about his time on the island, he said it was the happiest part of his childhood.

I knew Margaret had left Wyre permanently when she was nineteen to move to the Scottish mainland. Her parish minister, concerned about the reception the granddaughter of a notorious murderess might receive, drafted a certificate of character that described Margaret as "free of all scandal, reproach, or blame." After settling in southern Scotland, she married an older man, an eminent minister from a family of well-heeled nobles. The two sons from that marriage became notable figures in Scottish history. Yet, the Center's binders made no mention of Margaret or any other Halcro. In fact, they covered very little ground prior to the nineteenth century.

Wading through a flock of marauding sheep, we returned to the ferry landing, still uncertain if a boat would meet us. But at 1:30 p.m. sharp, the ferry arrived as promised. As I watched Wyre disappear into the mist, I felt pangs of regret mixed with a sense of relief. I'd made the trip hoping to learn more about Margaret's childhood and family, something that would bring her more into focus as a person. Visiting the chapel and fortress had helped but not enough. At the same time, I was eager to leave Wyre's lonesome, windblown terrain and be among people again.

In admitting that to myself, it occurred to me that Margaret, glancing back at Wyre as she sailed for the Scottish mainland, would have experienced a similar conflict all those years ago. And in that moment, I realized that I had found the trace of Margaret I'd been seeking. That sensation of inner turmoil we shared, different though it may have been in the two us, provided an intimate glimpse of the flesh-and-blood Margaret. I'd come to Wyre expecting to find an isolated young girl burdened by a troubled family history. But the Margaret I'd found was a determined young woman, bracing herself as she ventured from a childhood refuge toward her destiny in the unknown world beyond.

Questions and Answers

We write to taste life twice, in the moment and in retrospect.
~Anaïs Nin

1. What compelled you to set out on your pilgrimage?
As I mention in the story, just before departing for Orkney on a trip that had been planned for months, I discovered I was related to a family that had occupied the islands for centuries, people of Norse heritage. My seventh great-grandmother grew up on one of the smaller islands, living a rather isolated, obscure life. Given my new-found interest in Orcadian history, I wanted to learn more about what type of person she was, more than I could learn from the internet or sparse printed information.

2. Is there a book, song, poem, or movie that inspired your quest?
The book where I learned about my grandmother and her family was the 1895 *Erskine-Halcro Genealogy*. It's an important document of early Scottish history. I also found several Edwin Muir poems that resonated with me, though after I'd been to Wyre. I used one in the epigraph for my story.

3. Where is your sacred place and why did you choose it?
I think one aspect of the journey was trying to determine if the island of Wyre, where the story takes place, was a sacred place for my ancestor. It was certainly a significant place in terms of history in its day but I was more interested in what it meant to my great-grandmother.

4. How did your pilgrimage change your life or not?
As is often the case when I take the time to understand a place's evolution over long periods of time, I was awed by the permanence and resilience of both the landscape and the antiquities on Wyre, the chapel and Viking fortress. I didn't mention it in the story, but there are several archeological sites on the island that include standing stones, among other things. Americans, perhaps more so than other cultures, tend to think of antiquities as something two or three centuries old. The buildings on Wyre were built in the twelfth century and other artifacts on the island date back to 2500 B.C. So it's stunning to think I saw and reacted to the same artifacts that my great-grandmother did in the seventeenth century, and as the first Vikings on the island did before her. Given Orkney's climate, which can be severe at times, it's surprising that anything could survive the ravages of time.

5. What is the most important piece of advice that you have received in your life? Do you have advice to share from your experiences?

I continue to appreciate the importance of connecting the dots in terms of place and time. Where does a place fit in relation to its neighbors? Why did people settle there or why did they leave? And how did that influence the people who live there now and the type of place it's become? Where did their customs come from? I used to do very little research before my trips. Now I spend a lot of time looking at migrations, wars, environmental factors, language, music, etc. The research helps me better understand the nuance of what I'm experiencing in the present day.

Photograph courtesy of Keith Skinner.

Biography

Keith Skinner is a writer and photographer from Berkeley, California focusing on history and culture. His nonfiction has appeared in *Travelers' Tales* anthologies, *The San Francisco Chronicle*, *Wild Musette*, and others. He is currently working on a historical novel set in 19th century California.

Website: keith-skinner.com, Twitter: @renegade_image, www.facebook.com/KeithSkinnerWriter

Deep well in Azawak. *Photograph by Ariane Kirtley.*

Ariane Alzhara Kirtley

I slept and dreamt that life was joy. I awoke and saw that life was service.
I acted and behold, service was joy.
~Rabindranath Tagore

A Quest for Water
(Based on actual events in the southern Sahara)

1. NO WATER WITHOUT RAIN

*S*adouan sat underneath a goat-hide tent, braiding her daughter Mouheini's hair. The air inside was stifling. It was early May, with temperatures soaring higher than 45 degrees Celsius. It was rare that Sadouan could get her fifteen-year-old to sit still, so she tried to ignore the heat. For over nine months it hadn't rained, and there was no water to bathe with. Skin infestations had become common yet again, as they did every year during the hot season. So, she took advantage of the moment to remove fleas and lice from her daughter's scalp.

"Mother, you are pulling too hard!" Mouheini complained. At the same time, a goat walked into the tent. Sadouan gently shooed it away, "I have nothing for you today, little one. We are nearly out of water."

"My darling, keep your voice down," Sadouan scolded Mouheini. "You'll wake up Tahir!" Mouheini glanced tenderly at her baby brother, asleep on a traditional bed made of woven mats and carved wooden posts. "The braids need to be tight so that they will hold until the Tabaski festival," Sadouan said. "You must look beautiful. I'm giving you the special festivity braids." She smiled and added teasingly "Abdoul will be here."

Abdoul was Sadouan's nephew. Mouheini and he had been betrothed since her birth. They were to be married the following September, after the rainy season had ended.

Thinking of her daughter's wedding reminded Sadouan of the day, sixteen years ago, when at age thirteen she had married her own cousin Alhassan. An arranged marriage to cousins was a centuries-old tradition for these Tuareg herders in the Azawak, a huge plain of sandy grasslands in northwestern Niger, on the southern rim of the Sahara Desert. Yet, Sadouan did have concerns. Would Abdoul be a good husband to her firstborn, she wondered? Would he be able to provide, so that her daughter and her unborn children would have food to eat every day? And most importantly, would they have water? A constant search for water had become an ever-increasing preoccupation in the Azawak over the past ten years.

"Mother, I wish you would not remind me about Abdoul. I do not want to marry him." Mouheini knew that in the end she would not have a choice. But she wanted her mother to know that the situation was not of her own volition. "My dear," responded Sadouan sympathetically, "I know you are not happy about it. But you are fifteen, and most girls have already gotten married by your age. Your aunt is starting to wonder if you will ever marry Abdoul. She and the entire family are becoming impatient."

Mouheini knew she could not convince her family to change their mind, so she changed the subject. "Anyway, Tabaski is a few days away, so why are you braiding my hair today?" She winced as Sadouan tightened a braid. "I do not want to sit here in the heat, I want to go with the other girls now. It's much cooler underneath the acacias. Please, Mother!" she begged.

Mouheini wanted to be out in the dry marshland, sitting under the shade of the acacia trees with her girlfriends, playing games, singing songs, or engaging in storytelling contests, which she often won. She loved recounting stories that Sadouan had told her, and making up some of her own. Already she had spent all morning doing chores.

"My darling daughter, I really do not know how you will be ready to marry and raise a family. You still have the heart of a child." Sadouan shook her head. "By the way, have you forgotten?" she asked. "Tomorrow it is your turn to fetch water for the community, together with Takat and Raichatou. I must braid your hair today, in case we don't have time before Tabaski." Mouheini moaned. "I have to fetch water *already*?!" At least, she told herself, she would be traveling with two of her favorite cousins.

Mouheini missed the rainy season, when the water chore amounted to frolicking in the wet marsh. She longed for the long baths in the water, and playing with clay statuettes that she molded out of the mud with her siblings and cousins. This year, the rainy season had only lasted five weeks, beginning in late July and ending in early September. After it had ended, the marsh water had evaporated, forcing her and her fellow water fetchers to dig in the mud, often for hours at a time, to reach rainwater reserves that had seeped below. Once this water had run dry, men came and dug shallow wells in the dry marsh. She had spent hours watching as the men chased the water, digging deeper and deeper into the pits of the earth. During a single day, they would move from one hand-dug water hole to the next, waiting for the water to pool back into the bottom. This water was turbid and polluted, hardly more than mud; drinking it meant that Mouheini and her siblings often suffered from diarrhea. They did not know that unclean water could cause illness, and drank the rare water they could get with relish.

Fetching water at these marsh pits was a trivial task compared to the hardship to come; now that they had run dry, she spent her water fetching days travelling to deep pulley-operated nomad wells, no less than half a day's journey away from home. Many times, her water quest would last several days; if the first well had run dry, she and her cousins had to look for another, even further away. During this time, Mouheini would worry about her little siblings at home. If she was gone for too long, one of them might become very sick, or even die from thirst.

This responsibility was heavy to bear, especially for a young teenager. However, it wasn't only the long walk that caused her anxiety. Added to the heat and fatigue was the risk of running into drug traffickers or jihadi rebels. In recent years, the attacks by armed men on civilians were increasingly frequent. She had even heard stories that they sometimes did terrible things to women and girls. She wondered how they justified their violence in the name of Allah. Her Allah was kind and good. How could Allah want people to hurt others?

Mouheini's thoughts were cut short by Tahir's crying. Her baby brother had just awoken from his nap, and wanted to breastfeed. "Tahir's diarrhea is getting worse and worse," Sadouan stated gravely, while offering her breast to her baby. She was truly concerned for his life. She had already lost one child due to complications linked to dehydration and diarrhea. She could not bear the thought of losing another.

While nursing Tahir, Sadouan's thoughts transported her back to when she was a little girl. During her youth, it rained often, even daily, from June to September. It had been a much easier time. In those days, she had herded her parents' goats, while her brothers and father cared for their cows and camels. But as time went on, the rains had become more and more infrequent. Why did it rain so little now, only filling the marshes for a few months after the rains ended? Without water, most of their animals had died. These changes deeply frightened her, and made her worry about her children's future.

2. THE WATER SEARCH BEGINS

At four in the morning, Mouheini felt a hand rocking her gently. "Wake up, my daughter, I've prepared your donkey." Her father, Alhassan, sat above her with a wistful regard, wishing he did not have to ask his daughter to undertake such an arduous, and possibly perilous journey. "Mother has prepared the *illiwa* for you." As Mouheini quietly sipped this millet porridge with a large wooden spoon, Alhassan sat with her to keep her company. He explained, "After the Tabaski festival I will be leaving toward the south with our camels and cows, to find water for them. Your brothers will be coming with me. So will Abdoul." Mouheini felt a sinking feeling in her heart. She didn't want her father to leave. Sadouan would be distraught about caring for the family alone. When he was away, times were always harder; they skipped many meals, sometimes living off of one small bowl of rice or millet a day. Sadouan often went begging from the other families; yet they too had little to eat. This pending reality frightened Mouheini.

"Daddy, do you really have to go?" asked Mouheini, committing *senti*, talking while eating, a Tuareg *faux pas*. "Don't worry, I will make sure that Abdoul and your brothers stay safe." Alhassan caressed his daughter's face, trying to reassure her. "I am not worried about Abdoul. It is you I care about," she responded firmly.

"Ok, my gazelle, it is time for you to leave now," Alhassan said. "Otherwise you will be caught in the worst of the heat before reaching the well."

"The well? Oh, no!" she groaned. Mouheini had almost forgotten her responsibility of the day... she sorely hoped that there would be water in the nearest well, which was around 25 kilometers away, so that she and her cousins would be home by that evening. If there was no water there, they would need to seek even further away; they might not be back until the next day... or even later. "We will be back tonight," she promised herself.

Alhassan checked the ropes holding the empty jerry cans attached to their donkeys. Sadouan wrapped a few pieces of dried goat meat in a cloth for her daughter's lunch, and handed it to Mouheini while whispering, "Please, darling, stay safe and return home quickly! I don't know how long our water will last... your siblings won't have anything to drink soon... and...," she continued, with a stammer, "I don't know how long Tahir will live if we run out of water." Mouheini knew that her mother meant well to remind her of her brothers and sisters, but it was a burden knowing that they relied on her to live from one day to the next. "Yes, Mother, I will not let you or Tahir down. By tonight, we will all have water, Allah willing!"

Takat and Raichatou, Mouheini's younger cousins and water-fetching companions, stood sleepily next to their donkeys, while their parents said goodbye to them. A small group of additional donkeys with jerry cans attached to their sides milled about nearby. All would undertake the water quest. The girls were tasked with fetching as much water as they could for the five families that made up their small nomadic community.

Takat and Raichatou also felt downhearted about their mission. They went water gathering at least once a week. Mouheini, as the oldest of the girls, was sent on almost every water quest. To her, it felt like each foray for water was more difficult than the last, and the idea of another day-long round-trip hike under the searing sun filled her with anxiety, especially since she could not be certain of what she would find at the well.

The girls finally left around 5 am. They were so accustomed to journeying at night, that they knew their home territory even in the dark. Until the day broke, they counted on the positions of the stars to guide them northwest beyond their home territory, toward the closest well. For the first few hours of the journey, the girls walked alongside their donkeys, not wanting to tire their animals before the heat set in. Already temperatures were over 38 degrees; by 7 am the heat would be nearly unbearable.

At first, the girls walked in silence. Takat was practically sleepwalking, until she tripped on a large stone. She fell to the ground, burying a long acacia thorn into her leg. Her shrieks of pain sent shivers through Mouheini's body; all three of them felt exhausted, even as the voyage was just beginning. Mouheini helped remove the thorn; as the eldest, it was her responsibility to care for the younger girls. She took Takat in her arms, "Now now, dear, we must continue on to the well," she said. "If we get there early enough, there will be more water, and we'll be able to get home faster." Seeing that this reassurance had little effect, she added, "I will tell you a story I learned about a genie, if you get up and walk." Takat nodded that she wanted to hear her cousin's story. Raichatou chimed in, "Yes, please tell us a story, otherwise I'm going to fall asleep!"

Mouheini, though she also felt the effects of too little sleep, took it upon herself to cheer up her little cousins. She told her stories until a halo of pink encircled the eastern horizon, announcing the rising sun. The splendor of first dawn brought extra joy to the girls, despite the bittersweet reality that the heat would also begin rising on the trail of the sun.

"Let's take a break to rest and eat before it gets too hot," Mouheini proposed. Takat and Raichatou both eagerly answered, "Yes!" They removed a plastic mat from one of the donkeys, laid it on the ground, and sat down. Mouheini pulled out her dried meat, Takat her gourd of fermented goat milk, and Raichatou unpeeled a cloth wrap that hid the traditional Tuareg *boule* of millet. They untied a small metal bowl, into which they scooped a portion of the millet which had been cooked into a paste and formed into a ball, and stirred in milk and a little water. United under the splendor of sunrise, the girls enjoyed their meager feast and forgot about the challenges of the morning so far, as well as those that might lay ahead.

After a short rest, they packed up their belongings onto their donkeys and continued their journey. The closer they got to the deep nomad well, the easier it became to ignore the constant flies and sweat trickling down their faces. They sang and giggled freely, while Mouheini became even more creative with her stories. They no longer felt defeated by their thirst and dehydration. Around an hour away from their destination, they shared their last few drops of water, trusting that they soon would fill their jerry cans and drink to their heart's content.

3. BURIED ALIVE!

The screeching of wood pulleys welcomed them from afar. As they approached the well, they saw three donkeys attached together, pulling ropes of interminable length on one side, while four others pulled together opposite them, heaving up large rubber water containers from 130 meters in the earth. Even ten donkeys on either end would not have sufficed to make the job less strenuous. One donkey tripped from exhaustion, bringing down the others with it. As the girls approached, they noticed a donkey lying almost lifeless on the ground near the well. They knew that the animal would be dead by the end of the day. It was often this way during the dry season.

Mouheini went up to one of the men to ask if they could fill up their jerry cans, pointing to her cousins and their donkeys. The man glanced over and shook his head. "You will have to wait a while," he said. "Many people and animals are already waiting, and there is hardly any water seeping through at the bottom of the well. Right now, we are only bringing up mud. We'll be sending in a boy soon to dig the well deeper. Maybe there'll be water afterward, Allah willing." Mouheini informed Takat and Raichatou. "This means we're going to be stuck here several hours!" Raichatou exclaimed, "maybe we should walk ahead to the next well?"

"There is no guarantee there'll be water there either," replied Mouheini. After considering their options, the girls decided to wait rather than look for another well. Takat found a shady spot beneath an acacia tree, where an elderly woman sat weaving a mat while she waited. After laying out their own mat, the girls distracted themselves by playing mancala and other traditional games with rocks in the sand.

They waited for hours, as more and more people and animals showed up at the well, hopeful to retrieve water. "I'm not so sure we made the right decision to stay," Raichatou opined. "We'd still be walking if we had gone," replied Takat. Mouheini, trying to keep the peace, reassured them, "It will be our turn soon."

Just at that moment, Mouheini looked up to see a woman walk by, hiding herself behind a mat. The old woman also observed the lady with her mat, and shook her head in disgust. She whispered to the girls: "This water problem is the root of all evil these days. Men are leaving our land to find jobs elsewhere, and when they return, they bring back crazy ideas. A woman hiding herself so that men do not see her?! Tuareg women used to show themselves proudly, and now they cower behind mats and veils. They say it is for Allah. It's just silliness, if you ask me. Those men are trying to keep their wives to themselves, as if a mat is going to stop a woman from finding another man!"

The old woman went back to her weaving. The girls looked at one another, not quite knowing what to think. The two younger ones giggled. Mouheini did not. Would Abdoul also insist that she cover herself with a mat whenever she was not among family members? She did not want to find out. She did not want to leave her parents and siblings to live with Abdoul's family. Thinking of her brothers and sisters brought her back to reality, to her water quest. She direly hoped they were okay, and that Tahir still had water to drink.

"I'm so thirsty," lamented Raichatou, "and hungry, too." Wanting to see if they would be able to get their water soon, and hoping to distract her cousin from discouragement, Mouheini proposed, "Let's find some water to drink."

Not far from the well sat a corroded aluminum trough from which a few cows drank muddy filth lying at the bottom. The girls scooped as much of the liquid as they could into their hands to assuage their thirst.

At the well, men were tying a teenage boy around Mouheini's age onto a rope. The girls drew nearer to watch as the boy was lowered into the bowels of the earth; he was being sent into the well to dig the bottom deeper, in the hope that more water would seep through. The process seemed interminable, and Mouheini felt badly for the boy. "If it's hot up here," she told herself, "I can only imagine what the heat must be like so deep into the earth!" Just the thought of it made her shudder. They watched and waited, but nothing happened for quite some time. So, they returned to their mat beside the acacia tree, to snack on their food.

After a while, the men holding the rope felt tugging from the bottom; it was a signal for them to lug the boy back up. Several men began pulling on the rope, when suddenly the one nearest the well yelled frantically, "Pull harder, pull harder, the rope is being dragged back in. Pull harder!" Five more men joined, but all were being drawn into the well. One man hollered "keep pulling!" while another screamed, "the well is caving in!" The girls watched this dreadful scene in horror.

Ten minutes later, the men were still desperately trying to retrieve the boy, but it was too late. The boy had been buried alive. "How could this be possible?" Mouheini asked herself. Less than a half hour earlier, the boy had been standing in front of them. He could not just be gone!

After much effort to heave the boy out of the well, the men finally accepted that the earth had won the battle. The only way of retrieving the boy now was to send another man in to recover his body. Cries of anguish rang out around them. Takat and Raichatou sobbed while Mouheini pulled them together into a group embrace. "It's ok, my little ones. It's ok. We must go so we can get to the next well before dark."

"The *next* well?" Raichatou asked, incredulous.

Mouheini asked the old woman if she knew of a well that might have water. "About 17 km north there is a well. I heard that it is still operating. You should try there." She explained as best she could the path to take, while the three girls listened intently but with increasing discouragement. On the other hand, this was not the first time that they would have traveled to several wells before finding water. It was, however, the first time that they had ever seen a boy die in a well.

Takat placed their mat back on her donkey, and the trio somberly headed north. Walking wordlessly, they had no heart to sing or tell stories. Mouheini could not get the image of the boy's face out of her mind. The thought of the dead boy repeatedly reminded her of baby Tahir. "Don't die little brother!" she prayed to herself.

4. A CLOSE CALL

Undertaking this trek beneath the torrid mid-afternoon sun was unbearable; Mouheini's entire body felt like it was baking. The girls had not been able to fill up their jerry cans, and were desperately thirsty. With each step, they felt like weights were being added to their feet, and their donkeys walked as if all the water cans were full rather than empty. Mouheini did not like flogging them, and so she resorted to pulling the weary beasts, while Takat and Raichatou helped by pushing from behind. During one of these efforts, one of Takat's flip-flops got caught on a protruding plant root, and she fell flat on her face. She ruefully examined her shoe, which had torn apart. From then on she winced at every step, because the earth burnt her foot. However, she dared not voice her pain; she did not want Raichatou and Mouheini to worry. What could they do for her anyway? Even the donkeys were too exhausted to carry her.

They stopped counting the dried marshlands that they walked through. On the one hand, these parched spaces of earth provided shade, thanks to the acacia trees that grew there. On the other hand, both the girls and the donkeys stepped on one long painful thorn after another. Along one of these marshland stretches, Raichatou yelled out, "I can't move, I can't move." Mouheini looked back to find her hobbling on one foot.

Both Takat and Mouheini rushed to the injured girl's side. Raichatou had been punctured by a particularly long thorn that had "nailed" her shoe to her foot. Mouheini, using all her strength, helped pull out the thorn while Takat held Raichatou's hand. The girl's whimpering brought everyone to a standstill. They looked at one another and began crying. "I cannot get that boy's face out of my head," Takat admitted, sobbing. "I know," Mouheini answered. "What a terrible way to die. He went in there to help us have water. And he died for it. Dear Allah, why oh why?" She quickly pulled her spirits together, "I know that this is difficult, as it always is getting water. But we've got to think ahead. Tahir is sick at home, and mom is waiting for us. I know aunties are waiting for you. We will find water, I promise you."

Looking at Raichatou, Mouheini asked, "Will you be able to walk?" Then, glancing at Takat, realizing only now that her cousin was walking with only one shoe: "What happened?" Takat reassured everyone with a grim smile: "It's not so hot anymore, and I've gotten good at avoiding the thorns." The girls walked on.

The sun began to set on the horizon as the trio neared the second well. Mouheini tried to improve the spirits of the younger two by recounting a story about a genie who fell in love with a human maiden. She was deep into detailing a love sequence, when suddenly, machine guns rang in the distance. Mouheini jumped. Confused, she looked around. She saw nothing strange. Again, they heard more gunshots, followed by men's angry screams. Suddenly, several pickups transporting dozens of men whizzed past, lifting up a huge cloud of dust in their wake. Dressed all in white, the men whooped and pumped their AK-47s into the air, as if in celebration. The girls fell to the ground, hiding behind their donkeys.

Mouheini grabbed onto Takat and held her tightly. More angry voices and screaming rang out from a distance, prompting Mouheini to pray, "Allah, protect us. Do not let these frightening men catch or hurt us." Lifting herself up behind her donkey, she peered over to see if the men were still in sight. It seemed as if they had not noticed the girls, and if they had, they had more pertinent business at hand. Nonetheless, remembering the stories of rape and violence she had heard about armed men from the West, and already traumatized by the long day's event, she yelled out at Takat and Raichatou to run away, ordering them to leave their donkeys behind. They ran and ran, until they collapsed on the ground from exhaustion.

"What will we do now?" Takat wailed, "I'm so scared. Where will we go tonight? How will we get water?" Fear and desperation finally won over Mouheini's ever strong and cheerful spirit, "I don't know, I just don't know," she cried.

"Psst, psst." The terrified girls did not hear the strange sound at first. "Pssssst", this time the summons was more insistent. They heard it clearly, coming from behind a giant termite hill. "Pssssst!!" There it was again, and out from behind the hill peaked the dark face of a turbaned boy. He waved them over. Mouheini motioned to the other two to stay back. "What do you want?" she demanded, tears streaming down her face. "I overheard you talking," said the boy, beckoning. "I can take you somewhere safe." He had an accent. Tamasheq, the Tuareg language, did not appear to be his native language.

Emotionally and physically drained, and desperately hungry and thirsty, Mouheini did not know whom to trust. Already so much calamity had befallen them during the day; her first impulse was to grab her cousins and run away again.

Still, the young adolescent looked friendly and reassuring. He stepped out from his hiding place and introduced himself, "My name is Fada." Mouheini saw that he was dressed in the typical garb of the Fulani nomads, including the large straw hat topped with a feather that he cradled next to his body. The Fulani and Tuareg, both traditionally nomadic pastoralists, lived harmoniously together throughout the Azawak. There were hardly ever any problems between them, so Mouheini did not think she should fear the boy, who appeared to be about her age.

"What are you doing here?" Mouheini asked.

"I had just filled my gourd at the well," Fada replied, "when I heard the pickups arrive, with the crazy men shooting in the air and yelling at everyone, demanding to have water and food. I didn't wait to see what happened next; I simply ran away as fast as I could." The boy took deep breaths, clearly traumatized by what he had undergone. "Anyway, I've been hiding here for a while, and then I heard all of you crying."

He paused, "I think it's safe now. If you want, you can come with me to my village. There you can get water and sleep tonight." Mouheini looked at him dubiously. Yet despite her suspicion, she wanted to believe in something. She was too tired to think of questions to ask. All she wanted was to drink some water and sleep. She looked at Takat and Raichatou, and called them over. "This boy... Fada... says he can help us."

Fada stepped up to them with a smile: "I live beyond those hills, not too far away. There is a well in my village. You could get water and spend the night there."

"Then why are you here?" Raichatou demanded. "Don't be so angry, I am only trying to help," Fada responded, trying to stay patient. "I am returning home after a few weeks away herding cows with my uncle. The well was on my way. Do you want to come with me or not? We could be there in less than two hours if we hurry. I know the way, even in the dark." He understood their fear and distrust. He too had been terrified by the armed men. He wondered what had happened to the village where the well had been attacked. He had heard stories of people being kidnapped during these types of raids, and then left stranded to die in the middle of the desert.

"Two hours! I don't know if I can go that far," wailed Raichatou. "I'm so hungry and thirsty." Mouheini sympathized with her, but then she thought of Tahir. "We don't have any choice," she declared. "We could die out here." Choking back tears, Raichatou and Takat nodded their assent.

Takat asked Fada if they could have a sip of his water. He handed over his plastic milk jug, and each took a swig. He then pulled out a few wild yellow berries from his sash. "Would you like some?" he offered. The girls took them gratefully, suddenly feeling more energized, thanks to the sustenance, and to Fada's generosity. Mouheini pulled out her last few pieces of dry meat, which she shared with everyone. "Before we head away, we must retrieve our donkeys," she declared. Fada offered to help her find the animals in order to allow Raichatou and Takat time to rest at the termite mound.

The four companions stayed clear of any vehicle tracks, fearing a return of the armed men, and hid in the shadows of the night. Fada asked a few questions in an attempt to converse with Mouheini. He explained that he lived in a village shared between Tuareg and Fulani, which was why he spoke some Tamasheq. He told them that Cheikh Almoustapha, a well-respected Tuareg religious leader from neighboring Mali, presided over their village. He felt sure the cheikh would be kind to the three water searchers.

After a long moment of silence, Mouheini recounted the story of the boy at the well, "He was about our age, Fada. I can't get his face out of my mind. I can't imagine what a terrible death that must be." Fada waited a moment before responding. "I've been sent down into a well to dig like that boy," he shared. "It's what I imagine hell being like. So dark and hot, and no air. And you know going in how dangerous it is. You just know. Any time dirt starts falling from above, you think that your time has come." Mouheini cringed at the idea of Fada deep in the well.

Fada changed the subject: "Aren't you old enough to be married?" he asked. Mouheini blushed and defensively retorted, "Aren't you?" Suddenly feeling uncomfortable, she added, "We really must hurry back home early tomorrow. My brother is sick and Mother needs water quickly. She fears he may die otherwise. The problem is, I have no idea where we are going and how far we are from home by now. I've never heard of your well."

Fada felt sorry for her. "I will help you get your water quickly," he said, "so that you can get back to your family. Your brother will be fine, I'm sure." Mouheini appreciated his compassion.

Fada continued, "Our well is new; it's been open since January. It was built by people from far far away, who called it a 'borehole.' You should have seen them when they came with their trucks and drilling rigs. Those machines looked like gigantic monsters eating away at the earth. And when the drilling was done, I'd never seen so much water pour out of the ground. I didn't even know so much water existed!"

Mouheini listened in awe. She couldn't comprehend most of what Fada was saying, but his excitement was contagious. "What is a borehole, and what is a rig?" she asked naively. Of course, she could not possibly know what all these things were—how could she? The only reason he knew himself was that he had seen the magic with his own eyes. Trying to simplify his description, he said, "A borehole is dug by a rig, and run by a pump that brings water to the surface. Not like a normal well, where donkeys have to pull water out with long ropes."

"Ahhh," Mouheini nodded her head, though she still did not understand what he meant. "The best thing," Fada continued, "is that the water comes out clean. It won't make you sick. I didn't know before that marsh and well water could give you diarrhea. But the people explained to us that the water that we used to drink could kill people. This water gives health instead!"

Mouheini hung on to Fada's every word. Even though they were unfamiliar, they were magical coming out of his mouth. She grew impatient to see this very special well. She was also enjoying listening to Fada in his imperfect yet melodious Tamasheq.

Despite not wanting to alarm her, Fada voiced his innermost concern: "I hope that my village hasn't been attacked." Sensing Mouheini's sudden tenseness, he quickly reassured her: "No one dares hurt Cheikh Almoustapha, so I think it will be safe." Mouheini prayed that he was right.

By this time, Raichatou and Takat had mounted onto their donkeys and fallen asleep. The animals walked slowly, but did not balk. They seemed to understand that better times were close ahead. Mouheini hummed to herself. Fada joined in, thinking to himself that she had the voice of an angel. He had not yet seen her in the light of day, but she looked very beautiful to him, even in the dark. He sensed in her a purity that he had never seen before. As he followed the stars homeward, he felt proud to help her and her cousins.

After a while, Mouheini stopped thinking about her brother and the boy in the well, or the possibility of running into additional danger at Fada's village. She even stopped questioning the confusing feelings that Fada's presence provoked in her. She had lost herself in a walking, humming trance.

Fada's voice brought her back to reality. "Look over there," he exclaimed. "Do you see the light in the distance?" It took a few moments for her eyes to adjust, but she did see firelight ahead, atop what seemed to be a hill. "Do you think that it could be dangerous people?" she asked fearfully. "No," Fada reassured her. "That's my village. We are almost there." Mouheini sighed with relief. She dreamt of curling up on her mat and sleeping, restfully and peacefully.

5. WELCOMED LIKE PRINCESSES

"Who goes there?" A looming voice bellowed, before the children reached the hill. The voice belonged to Wasselkou, Cheikh Almoustapha's right-hand man. "Wasselkou, it is Fada, with friends." Wasselkou beamed a flashlight toward Fada and the girls. "Ah, it IS you, Fada! Come quickly. It is a dangerous night. There have been attacks nearby. We are patrolling the area to protect the village. Come quickly." Fada guided the girls toward the cheikh's home. "Assalamualaikum," he said, announcing himself before entering: "Peace be with you!" From inside came the customary response "Bismillah", meaning, "By the grace of God!"

Fada promised Mouheini that he would personally introduce the girls to the cheikh before heading home, and added, "I wish you could stay with me, but I think the cheikh will prefer to keep you in his concession." Mouheini felt tempted to insist on staying with him, but was too shy to do so. She had also hoped to see Fada's magical well, but realized that this wish would have to wait until the morning. Fada went inside the adobe house, while the girls sat waiting outside. A teenage girl brought them a bowl filled with delicious crystal-clear water and a plate topped with dates, both of which they consumed ravenously, though Mouheini set some dates aside for Fada.

A few moments later, a magnificent tall man wrapped in an indigo turban, and holding a kerosene lantern, stepped out of the home. He beckoned the girls to him, ushering them inside: "Come, children, Fada has informed me that you are looking for shelter and water. He says you have had many misadventures. I will help you as best I can. Come tell me your story."

The trio followed Cheikh Almoustapha into his home, where the light from his lantern illuminated a room adorned with wool mats on the ground and traditional Tuareg camel bags and other decorations on the wall. The girls hesitated to talk. They felt shy in front of such a mighty man. The cheikh called a young teenage girl over to his side. "I understand, you do not want to speak with me directly," he said. "You may talk to me through my daughter Housseina." Relieved, Mouheini recounted their day's misfortunes.

The cheikh listened with great empathy, while pretending to be otherwise occupied. When Mouheini had finished, he turned around, "Alhamdulillah, you are safe now. Thanks be to God that the armed men did not get a hold of you." Turning to Housseina, he said, "Please bring our guests water for their bath, and food to dine on. Tomorrow, we will fill their jerry cans with water from our borehole."

Mouheini turned to Housseina: "Fada also mentioned something called a borehole. I still don't understand what this is."

"It's a special type of well," the girl replied, "that makes water easy to get from the ground. You will see for yourselves in the morning." She handed each girl a long candle.

Despite their weariness, the cousins washed themselves with the warm water, pre-heated outside in the sun during the day. It was the first bath that they had enjoyed in many months; in fact, they had forgotten what clean skin felt like. They had never been so clean, because their prior baths had all taken place in the marshes. Housseina laid out colorful clean clothes for them to wear; clothes that she had sewn for herself and her younger sisters. She also brought out a dish of millet laden with goat meat and vegetable sauce, which the girls ate ravenously.

"Where is Fada?" Mouheini asked Housseina, hoping to thank him and wish him a good night. Longing for the familiarity of his presence, she would have preferred to spend the night at his home. "He has gone to be with his family. You will see him in the morning," responded the cheikh's daughter. "Eat and rest now. Your bed has been laid out over there." Housseina pointed to a mattress lying outside of the home, near the mattresses of other children and women who had already fallen asleep. It was much too hot to sleep indoors. Raichatou turned toward Takat, declaring, "We will sleep well tonight." Both of them smiled.

Mouheini also wanted to smile. But she had a longing she did not understand, to talk more with someone she hardly knew. And she could not help but go over the day's events: their near escape from the armed men, the boy in the well, and baby Tahir at home. She picked at her food while the younger girls feasted. Takat, committing *senti*, exclaimed, "we have been welcomed here as if we were princesses!" The other two girls giggled.

Finally, the trio lay their weary heads to rest; Mouheini slept in the middle, ever-protective of her little cousins. She lay awake looking at the stars, pondering many things. She could not help but think of her imminent wedding with Abdoul. She knew she had no right to question her parent's choice, but why must she marry Abdoul? Why?

In the middle of the night, Takat woke up screaming from a nightmare about the face of the boy who had died in the well. Mouheini held her tight, caressed her hair, and sang her back to sleep.

6. A FOUNTAIN OF LIQUID SILVER

Completely worn out by the previous day, the girls slept until mid-morning, when the sun, already high in the sky, seared their skin. Other than a few goats, the concession was empty. Next to their mattress sat a covered bowl filled with *illiwa* porridge. They ate eagerly before heading out to look for their hosts. Hearing a great deal of commotion behind the concession wall, they decided to take a look. Mouheini was particularly eager to find Fada; she still could not explain to herself why she cared so much. She also kept reminding herself of Tahir—they must find water quickly, and begin their journey back home this morning. If they arrived there before evening, he might still have a chance. After all, Sadouan did have a little water remaining when the girls took off on their quest.

When the girls stepped out of the concession, an inexplicable vision stopped them in their tracks. A large metallic tower loomed above numerous people and animals, all lined up near strange metal things out of which flowed clear gushing water. The liquid, its clarity and quantity, looked to them like magical flowing silver. The girls had never seen faucets before, nor a water tower. More importantly, they had never in all their lives seen so much water; and never ever had they seen such happiness-inducing beauty and purity. They had entered water paradise.

Fada spotted the girls, and knowingly observed their giddy expressions of joy; he had experienced the same sense of awe not so long ago, when the borehole was first built. Approaching them, he exclaimed, "I've been waiting for you to wake up for hours! Cheikh asked me to fill up your jerry cans, which I did. You are all set to head home, as soon as your donkeys finish drinking. They already ate, and I think they'll be fit to carry you!"

Even though Fada did not really want them to leave, he was proud to be of help to Mouheini. He felt that she was truly angelic, and was deeply attracted to her combination of innocence and strength. "Cheikh even gave you some additional jerry cans," he added. "Look!" They peered over to where several jerry cans stood, theirs and others, on the ground, near the foot of the borehole. It all seemed so extraordinary. Mouheini could not take her eyes off the boy. He exuded luminous kindness, which accentuated his handsome features. This type of staring was uncustomary; when she realized that her gaze had been transfixed upon Fada, she regained her composure, and looked away.

"Come over here," Fada beckoned them. Raichatou and Takat ran over to the faucets and splashed water over their faces, hands and feet. Near the faucets were six troughs; each filled with the same miraculously crystalline water. Drinking contentedly at these troughs, their donkeys stood in the midst of cows, sheep and goats. Mouheini would have happily jumped into one of the troughs to take a bath. Instead, she became mesmerized by the magical scene of her cousins and Fada playing in the water fountains. Filled with an overwhelming sense of amazement, she wondered why she had never heard of the existence of this very special well, or this village, before now. She could not have imagined such a perfect scene in her wildest dreams. This village and its "borehole" would provide material for future stories, that was for sure!!

Mouheini's reveries were interrupted by the cheikh, who appeared from beyond the hill, trailing behind him a herd of sheep. As he came nearer, he waived the girls towards him, "Come now, young ladies. Did you rest well?" he asked. They nodded, respectfully looking downward. "You should begin your journey home quickly," he said. "Tomorrow is the Tabaski festival. Your parents will want you near them. And they will also want their water."

"How can we ever repay you?" asked Mouheini. "You need not repay me," he replied. "Water is a gift from God. This borehole was a gift from God. Come here whenever you need water. Be safe and careful, and always remember to thank Allah! Now, follow me." Mouheini did not want to leave Fada, so she waved for him to follow. He did, but kept at a distance. He too was confused about his feelings; why was he so sad knowing that the girls would be leaving soon?

Cheikh Almoustapha guided the three cousins to Housseina, who gently handed a parcel of food to Mouheini, "Be safe, my friends," she said, "I pray that you arrive before dark, so that you can be with your families for the festivities tomorrow!"

"Before you leave, take these," the cheikh handed over three sheep, one for each girl. "It is my gift to you for the Tabaski. Many villages were attacked last night. The genies of protection must have followed you into our village. May Allah protect you as you protected us."

"Leave in peace," he added. "I have decided to send Fada to accompany you home. Fada knows how to get just about anywhere in all of the Azawak, so I know you will be in good hands. Wasselkou is explaining the shortest route to him as we speak." Mouheini's heart skipped a beat upon hearing this news. She glanced back to Fada and Wasselkou, and smiled.

"What is going on with Mouheini?" Raichatou asked Takat. "I'm going to tell Aunt Sadouan how they look at each other, and she won't be happy." Takat snapped, "Just keep quiet, you have no idea what's going on. Leave Mouheini alone, she'll be fine without your help!"

7. SAYING GOODBYE

Fada and Mouheini gathered the donkeys together so that Wasselkou could help tie the jerry cans onto their backs. The load was heavy, but the donkeys felt revived thanks to the water and food that they had been given, so they did not seem to mind. The girls all gazed one last time in wonderment at the miraculous fountain of life. It was one of the most beautiful sights that they had ever seen. If only this well were not so far from home, they would return often.

Fada and the girls waved an animated farewell to Cheikh Almoustapha, Housseina, and the other villagers. Raichatou and Takat mounted their donkeys, but Mouheini did not. She preferred to walk near Fada. She justified this choice to herself with the thought that the donkeys were already carrying enough weight—she would just slow them down if they were to carry her.

Takat and Raichatou chatted merrily and sang songs; for the longest time, Fada and Mouheini advanced side by side in silence. Finally, Mouheini said, "yesterday, you mentioned that neither of us is married. Indeed, I am still a girl. But after the rains, I am set to marry my cousin Abdoul. It has been arranged by my parents, as is customary."

Fada took a while before asking, "Does he make you feel like I do?"

"What do you mean?" asked Mouheini.

"Do you look at him the way you look at me? Does he make you feel good when you see him?" responded Fada.

Mouheini blushed. "I still do not know what you mean," she said, falteringly.

Fada responded, almost a whisper, "Sure you do." Again, both went silent.

Moments later, a jerry can started slipping off a donkey; it had not been tied on tightly enough. Fada and Mouheini ran in unison to catch it. As they tied it back on, helping one another weave the rope, their hands touched several times. Every time, Mouheini felt feelings she had never felt before. Fada did not hesitate to look at her, and he caressed her hand purposefully. She glanced away. Part of her wanted to run away. She could not allow herself think of him in this way. In a few months, she would be marrying Abdoul; besides, never before had a Tuareg and a Fulani married each other in her community. Cross-ethnic marriages were simply unheard of.

No, she could not let herself think such thoughts. She avoided Fada much of the way home, ignoring her impulse to spend as much time as she could with him, and despite his efforts to speak with her. Instead, she edged closer to the younger girls to tell them stories. Fada finally kept his distance, all the while listening to Mouheini's enchanting voice. He did not understand why he yearned to be near this Tuareg girl; he had never before had such feelings, despite the many girls he had met during Gerewol festivals; these celebrations were held after the rains began, so that young Fulani men and women would meet and elope.

After many long hours under the unforgiving sun, and a few breaks to share the food that Housseina had wrapped in their parcel, the landscape became familiar. Mouheini recognized the acacia trees and dry marshland that belonged to her home territory, and rejoiced at the idea that they would all arrive before dinner. And yet the thought also made her sad. Part of her did not want the walk to end so soon; she guessed that Fada would not stay long. At this thought, she moved to his side again. "I am sorry, Fada," she said. "I didn't mean to ignore you. But things are confusing to me. I do not know you. My parents do not know you. I like you but I cannot go against my custom."

Fada looked down, happy to be near her again, yet sad knowing that she spoke the truth. "I understand," he replied. "Do not be downcast. Rejoice now. You are almost home. Your family will be pleased to have you home, and so happy to have water and the sheep..."

"And so will that man you are to marry. Abdoul. He is very lucky," he concluded. They both continued walking in silence.

The sun began to dip behind the horizon. Takat and Raichatou jumped off their donkeys; they were so eager to get home that they sang songs and chased one another, in order to pass the time. Raichatou looked back at Mouheini and Fada occasionally, unhappy that Mouheini had allowed herself to become so close to this boy. Takat, on the other hand, felt intrigued by their friendship.

Fada and the girls began crossing one of the dry marshlands near their camp, when suddenly they heard men's voices beyond the acacia trees. Before they went much further, they saw men riding atop camels. Mouheini ordered everyone to be quiet, whispering that they might have to run. "These men might be dangerous," she warned.

As the men came closer, Mouheini recognized the loving, familiar face of her father, and bounded joyously towards him. He got off of his camel as fast as he could, and welcomed her into his arms. "My dearest gazelle, we were so worried," he declared. "Abdoul arrived late this afternoon, informing us that armed men had attacked villages and kidnapped people. Alhamdulillah, you are safe, my beautiful child!"

She held on to her father tightly. "How is Tahir, Father?" she asked. "I tried to come back as quickly as possible... I hope I am not too late." She began crying, allowing all her pent-up apprehension to flow out of her in the safety of her father's arms. Alhassan held her even tighter. "Come home and see for yourself my child," he said softly.

Mouheini introduced Fada to Alhassan and Abdoul. As they all began walking home, she told them about the boy who had been asphyxiated in the well, the armed men at the second well, and described at length how Fada had helped them. She also recounted the cheikh's generosity and described the borehole of clean flowing water.

Looking at Fada, Alhassan said, "Thank you so much for providing safety to our children, and for bringing them home to us. How can we ever repay you?" Fada knew the answer he wanted to give, but a single glance at Abdoul reminded him that he had no chance to win Mouheini's hand. "Please, it's nothing," he replied. "It is I who would like to repay you for this opportunity. Look, the cheikh has sent his gift of gratitude, to help you celebrate the Tabaski feast tomorrow."

Fada was uneasy. He did not want to return home, but he also could not bear seeing Mouheini alongside Abdoul. Hastily, he announced, "I must return home now, so that I too can be with my family for the festivities." Mouheini whipped around, facing Fada to protest, "No, you cannot leave now," she exclaimed indignantly. "It will be dark soon. Come home with us please. Spend the night with our family. You can leave early tomorrow morning!" Abdoul looked at Mouheini incredulously. What could explain this strange and inappropriate outburst? He decided he did not like the attention she gave to this Fulani boy.

Alhassan would not allow such an honored guest to return home in the middle of the night. He too objected, along with his daughter: "No, you must stay with us tonight and return tomorrow. We will feed you and share our mats."

"Dear Father," Fada responded respectfully, "you forget, I am a Fulani. Walking is my second nature, and I really do prefer to be home before morning, so that I can be with my mother during the festivities."

"But it isn't safe!" Mouheini challenged him. "What if the armed men are still around? No, father..." Fada gently cut off Mouheini's words, "Thank you, kind Mouheini, for your concern. I promise I will be fine. I will leave now, and rest in a few hours under the stars."

Alhassan insisted some more, "I do not want to let you leave like this. You saved the life of my daughter and nieces. Might you at least have dinner with us?" Abdoul stood observing this interaction, and secretly hoped Fada would say no and leave.

Fada looked over at Mouheini; their eyes caught, and both noticed the other tearing up. He looked away, determined that he needed to leave as soon as possible. He felt such anguish in his heart that he feared he would not be able to control his crying. "Again, thank you," he said, "but I have enough food for my journey home. I will leave now. Please do come often to Cheikh Almoustapha's village. You will always find plenty of water and a friendly welcome there!"

After filling up his plastic milk container from one of the jerry cans, he approached Mouheini and whispered, "Never forget me. Come see me whenever you can." She handed over the food that was left in the parcel given to them by Housseina, and whispered back, "Allah willing!" not truly believing she ever would. She looked back at him until his silhouette could no longer be distinguished from the acacia trees in the advancing twilight.

8. BITTERSWEET REJOICING

Hearing the camels and donkeys arrive, Sadouan stepped out of her tent, holding baby Tahir in her arms. Her heart leapt for joy at seeing her daughter riding alongside her husband, along with her nieces Raichatou and Takat. "You are safe my child, you are safe!" she cried out, folding her daughter into her arms. "When I heard of the attacks," she exclaimed, "I was so worried. And you hardly ever have been away this long. Praise Allah for your return!"

Mouheini hugged her mother tightly, and then swept Tahir into her arms, kissing his little face over and over. "Tahir is safe!" she told herself, her body trembling.

"Let's get you some water young man!" she murmured lovingly to him.

Sadouan and the other women looked in wonderment at all the full jerry cans and the three braying sheep the cheikh had offered to them. They praised Allah and prayed for the cheikh. "We will have a wonderful feast tomorrow!" they told each other gleefully. Everyone was mesmerized at the liquid's transparent color. After tasting it, Halima, Mouheini's four-year old sister, spat it out: "It's no good," she declared with a grimace. "I like marsh water better, at least it tastes like something."

Mouheini laughed at her little sister. She then recalled that Fada had explained to her that clean water meant healthy water. Should she tell them this new information, she wondered? Or would they disbelieve it, coming as it did from outside their culture? Mouheini's head was spinning. Fada had just left and all she wanted was to tell her parents to call him back, so he could explain—why clean water was best and why he wanted to spend so much time with her.

She suddenly realized how much she had changed over the course of a day and a half. Before she left yesterday morning, she was a simple Tuareg girl in a simplistic world of fetching water to survive. She was going to get married in the long-established universe of a desert nomad.

Today, nothing seemed so simple. She had seen a boy die, and grown men who might kill others. She had discovered that some people, not that far from where she lived, not only drank clean water but had it in abundance— while she and her family more often than not drank mud. She had benefitted from the great kindness of strangers, and yet she was not permitted to think of marrying the kindest of them all. And she had felt her first heartbreak, as she watched Fada depart into the desert.

As she stood there, laughing at her sister, she made a decision; she would learn lessons from all these things. Her world view had shifted; how could she now accept everything she had been taught after everything she had experienced? She didn't know the answer, but she decided one thing. As her first order of business, she would lead water-gathering expeditions to Fada's borehole, so her family could drink more healthily. Of course, she also realized that it would be a good pretext to visit her newfound friend.

That was as far as her thinking got that day, because her family decided to start Tabaski festivities early. Alhassan slaughtered one of the sheep to welcome the three girls home, and to celebrate the joyous gift of the crystalline water. Mouheini, Raichatou, and Takat were offered the most prized pieces of meat—the entrails. Mouheini, holding tight to Tahir, distributed her share among her six brothers and sisters. The smaller children were also given the brain, as tradition would have it. Mouheini made sure that Tahir had plenty of water to drink.

While she sat eating her meat, she did not commit *senti*. Yet her mind did wander to a paradise where liquid silver flowed, and to a trail lost in the desert, where a captivating, luminous soul was heading on his trek homeward. She prayed Allah for his safety.

Questions and Answers

1. What compelled you to set out on your pilgrimage?
The pilgrimage that I have chosen to share is not my own. It is a reenactment of the quest for water and survival undertaken on daily basis by the girls of the Azawak region of Niger. I used my dear friend, a young girl named Mouheini, as the model for the heroine of this pilgrimage. When I first traveled to the Azawak in 2005, I lived with her parents, Sadouan and Alhassan. They offered me everything they had despite having and owning very little. Like Mouheini in my story, the real Mouheini was often sent out on a perilous quest for water, as were many other girls like her. Every aspect of my story is based on tales I heard about Mouheini and her brave peers. Moreover, learning about their punishing walks to find water, often more than 35 kilometers away in unbearable heat, inspired me to undertake my own life's quest; to help the half a million people of the Azawak gain access to clean and abundant water every single day.

2. Is there a book, song, poem, or movie that inspired your quest?
Mouheini—her purity, her smile, her joy in the face of hardship—is the inspiration for my story. It is her quest and that of many other girls in the Azawak that I felt deserved to be recounted; it is one that has never been told before.

3. Where is your sacred place and why did you choose it?
Within the context of *The Pilgrimage Chronicles*, the Florida-sized Azawak region of Niger is my sacred place. I did not choose it. It chose me. As with Paul on the road to Tarsus, it was a calling from above that I couldn't refuse. While I originally travelled there intentionally to conduct my Fulbright research, I had no idea I was embarking on my life quest. My fate since the day my feet touched its soil has become my life's daily story. Over the past eleven years Niger is constantly in my thoughts, and I work daily with the people so that they may have access to basic services, and that their children may have hopes and dreams beyond simple survival.

4. How did your pilgrimage change your life or not?
My pilgrimage has been an existential quest as much as a developmental or physical one. While I did travel across Europe and West Africa to finally arrive in the drought-plagued Azawak region of Niger, my choice to dedicate my life to its people was a spiritual decision that completely changed my life path. I could not have imagined that 13 years later, through the organization I founded, Amman Imman: Water is Life, that I would have helped more than 100,000 people gain access to water and other life-enhancing services. Today, many girls like Mouheini, Takat, and Raichatou no longer endure

such perilous journeys to seek life-giving water; they have it in their village. They also have access to free medical services and have time to attend school. My external and internal pilgrimages have therefore not only changed my life plan (or helped me accomplish it), but they have also changed the lives of many people living in the Azawak.

5. What is the most important piece of advice that you have received in your life? Do you have advice to share from your experiences?
"Fear nothing but fear itself." My footsteps of life have been guided by this phrase. I would encourage others to live boldly, generously, and authentically; to follow their dreams, always allowing kindness to guide their decisions, and to share their dream-making accomplishments with as many as they can.

Ariane and her children with Fati's family. *Photograph courtesy of Ariane Kirtley.*

Biography

My name tells my story: Ariane Alzhara Kirtley. Like Ariane in Greek mythology, I lead others to safety. Like Alzhara flowers, I blossomed in the wondrous Saharan wastelands. And in the footsteps of my family Kirtley—"over those hills" in Old Gaelic—I am driven by a compulsion to walk, seeking new adventures, discoveries and meaning. After obtaining a Bachelor Degree in Anthropology and a Master of Public Health from Yale, I founded *Amman Imman: Water is Life* to help Africa's indigenous populations. I am also the mother of Fassely (9), Soriya (5), and Indima (2). Similarly to how my parents raised my brother and me, we travel the globe as a family.

https://www.arianekirtley.com
Amman Imman: Water is Life: https://www.ammanimman.org
Instagram: https://www.instagram.com/alzharawalking
Facebook: https://www.facebook.com/akirtley

Photograph by Carolyn Affleck Youngs.

Carolyn Affleck Youngs

You do not even have to believe in yourself or your work. You have to keep yourself open and aware to the urges that motivate you. Keep the channel open.
~Martha Graham

One Step at a Time

*P*retty big shoes to fill, I thought.

My husband died suddenly in 2011. He'd walked for 25 years, 25,000 km, through 25 countries. Or at least that's my estimate. Derek was a pilgrim, known to many as the Peacewalker. He had said, very early on in our acquaintance, "Maybe you'll follow in my footsteps."

Derek actually did have big shoes. Size 12. People often asked him, "How many pairs have you worn through in all your travels?" He had no idea nor did he care. The more interesting question was, "Why do you walk?"

At first, Derek had a clear goal when he started walking in 1986 on the Great Peace March for Global Nuclear Disarmament. He hoped to change the world. Nine months later, having trekked from Los Angeles to Washington, DC, he realized that he hadn't changed the world, and couldn't expect to. But he had changed himself. And he had done something he had never imagined possible—cross a whole country one step at a time. After that, nothing stopped him. Derek kept walking, and over the course of 25 years, his peace manifesto turned into a mantra.

It was walking that brought us together. I had always loved walking for the sense of calm invigoration it gave me, the intimacy with ever-changing landscape, and the time it afforded for reflection. When I embarked on the Camino pilgrimage in Spain after my father died and my relationship broke up, it was solace I sought, and perhaps a new start. I got more than I bargained for.

Derek had been leading small groups of pilgrims on the Camino for years, and I joined his group in May of 2004. Our third day on the trail, he and I connected in a profound moment I can only explain by using the phrase soul mates. He was happily married, and 25 years older than I. To me he was a father figure for certain, and a mentor. To him, I was a protégée. But the tutelage went both ways.

In the relationship that evolved after we both returned home to Canada, I showed him how to use a camera, taught him about classical music, and read to him from my books on philosophy. Derek shared life lessons from his days on the road when he often didn't have food or a place to sleep for the night. He taught me that it was OK to not know. He helped me to trust in myself and the inherent goodness of the universe. Those lessons beat reading any day.

When we became a couple, Derek took me to many of the countries he had walked through. I helped him see these places differently, through a photographer's eyes. Every day was an adventure for us, surrounded by beauty, and our soundtrack was the peal of our own joyous laughter.

But then, everything changes. I am a widow. And as the reality of my loss sinks in, I find myself staying close to home, in my small quiet neighborhood. I feel raw. Overwhelmed at times. Every day I experience moments of intense sorrow but—I am buoyed up continually by something wonderful. I identify this something as the circle of love that my husband and I had created together. This bubble feels warm and fuzzy and safe, and my tender edges are soothed in the comfort of the echoes of our shared life: our green cushy couch, our Japanese garden with the small Buddha statue that sits gazing in at me peacefully from the patio, our favorite music on the stereo. Venturing out into the world is not easy. Everything is too loud, too bright, too fast, too hard. Friends, wanting to be helpful and trying to be sensitive, sometimes are just the opposite. It's easier to be alone. Fortunately, the bubble of love follows me when I take my daily hike alone up the mountain behind our house.

It is on one of these hikes that I realize a certain date is approaching. The thought fills me with both excitement and trepidation. I have a pilgrimage to undertake.

Somehow, a few months later, I am on the Camino. Thanks to the practical and emotional support of a friend in Europe, I am walking that familiar path with her, feeling the cool air on my skin, and watching the green valley fall away from us as we climb into the hills. She and I had met through Derek, and had been on the Camino together three times, so we feel at home on the trail and with each other. Nothing has to be said; she is grieving too. The circle of love now surrounds us both.

We bathe in the beauty, and relish the silence. We lose our way and then find it again, laughing as we remember Derek saying that getting lost and found is an integral part of any pilgrimage. And then, we arrive. How surreal it feels to stand on that cliff's edge, head in the clouds, as I throw a handful of ashes into the breeze. How could it be that not so long ago Derek and I had stood on that very spot and exchanged vows?

"I love you, darlin'," I can hear him whisper. Goosebumps race up my arms. I know that he's there with me now, on our wedding anniversary, May 3rd. I cry tears of grief, but of gratitude as well, for the precious time we had together. So full. So rich. What a beautiful end to my pilgrimage, I think. Little do I understand it has just begun.

After returning home I am tired, but pleasantly so. I allow myself a summer of nothing—a luxury I rarely give myself. I pay attention to the shifts in my grieving process. I never stifle my copious tears, and begin to notice myself laughing more. I start accepting social engagements, one friend at a time. My comfort zone slowly expands. Then, in early September, bereaved for six months, I am ready to try being around more people, so I choose a nurturing setting, a "spiritual" retreat just a few hours from home, at a beautiful facility nestled amongst the trees by the ocean's edge. The other guests are friendly, but I am far more lonely there than alone at home. When a couple of health issues crop up during my stay, a massive panic attack ensues, the first of my life, which marks the beginning of what some would call PTSD. Where is my big safety bubble of love?

The next months are hell. I am a mess. What had been chronic yet mild dysfunction in my spine has turned acute and debilitating. Lying on the floor offers the only total relief. My body needs exercise though, so I head out to walk, but sometimes, minutes after leaving the house I am seized by panic, dizzy, my heart racing, my hands shaking and my head feeling pierced by an iron rod. I stop hiking and go out in public as infrequently as possible. I can't bear other people's company or even maintain eye contact with the grocery store cashier.

I don't understand. My grieving journey had been progressing slowly but surely in the right direction, or so I'd thought. I cry out to Derek sometimes, asking, "Where are you? What's going to happen to me? What did I do wrong? Did I take too big a step?"

Derek's words ring in my head. "You'll get through this. Remember, if you get lost, you also get found. Just keep taking one little step at a time."

So I do, even though some weeks see little improvement. My thoughts race, anxiety simmering beneath the surface. I can't predict what will trigger it, like a sudden change in the TV's volume, or even just the spinning feeling when I turn my head too quickly. Faintness can turn to panic and then escalate into fears that I am losing my sanity.

Derek's words, though, continue to soothe and strengthen me. And I do a lot of work, on my own and with a counselor. Eventually in November it's time again to take more steps outside the comfort zone. I am afraid, but I have an airplane ticket—to Japan. Back in April, not long after my husband's death, before the panic attacks, I planned this trip for my birthday, accepting an invitation from friends outside Tokyo. The pilgrimage continues.

Japan had been important to Derek. Not long after the Great Peace March, he heard the story of Sadako and the thousand cranes. It's a true account of a little girl in Hiroshima who died as the result of the atomic bomb blast that rocked the world in 1945, killing over 140,000 people. Sadako, while dying in the hospital, had a visit from a friend who shared an old legend about wishes being granted if a thousand origami cranes were folded. Sadako began folding cranes, and although she died, the origami crane has become a potent symbol of peace. Wherever Derek went he retold this story and folded cranes, and all the steps he took from then on were towards Japan. He always said that because walking to Japan was his dream and not a literal goal, he had a lifetime to get there and the whole world to walk through.

A year into our friendship, we traveled to Hiroshima together to mark the 60th anniversary of the 1945 bombing. Although of course we had not walked on water to get there, his dream had come true. And it would continue to, in a different form. It was after returning from that trip that we began working on his memoir, which was to be called *Walking to Japan*.

Now, I would take a peace crane to Sadako's monument and spread more of Derek's ashes. Although I knew some people would be shocked to hear his ashes weren't kept or disposed of in one place, neither of us were hung up on convention, and my covert scatterings would have amused him greatly. As serious as Derek was about peace, he never took anything else too seriously, especially himself. He was always willing to let go—of notions or habits, things or relationships, if they were not moving him forward.

I want to be that flexible and willing. But Japan is far from home and I am frightened. With my departure date on the near horizon, I am full of doubt, not to mention pain. How can I do this, given my state? I worry. Once again, I hear Derek's voice in my ear. "Let go, trust, and just take that first step. The path will unfold before you. Sometimes the hardest part is just opening the door." This is a principle that Derek had believed and lived. I am trying to live it myself, and though the idea is simple, the practice is not easy. But I am determined not to give my power away to fear and be rendered too anxiety-stricken to follow through on my plans. This trip is crucial to the rest of my life.

Putting my faith in myself, my knowledge and skills, I build myself a support system. Once again, generous and kind friends help me with travel arrangements. Then, I arm myself with all manner of comfort and safety devices, including a notecard for my pocket that explains, in Japanese, to any stranger who might find me wandering lost or lying unconscious on the street, how to care for me and where to deliver me.

I take one step at a time. I board the plane and survive. I get off the plane in Tokyo and am fine. I get on a train and off a train and so it goes.

A pal accompanies me to Hiroshima. On the night of our arrival we craft a paper lantern in Derek's memory, and take it down to the river, setting it adrift just as a gentle rain begins to fall. In the distance we hear the song, "Give Peace a Chance" by John Lennon—one of Derek's favourites. I feel a tingle down my spine.

The next morning I walk from the guest house alone to Sadako's monument and leave a paper crane there. Tears stream down my cheeks, but then a huge smile spreads across my face as I hear a voice in my head. "You did it, babe," said Derek. I can see him beaming.

After a few weeks in Japan as a tourist on my own, I return home feeling significantly healed, emotionally if not physically. I begin to fall into a happy routine, returning to choral singing and I join a walking group for widows. I make it through the one-year anniversary of Derek's death by going for a long hike, rewarding myself with fish & chips just as he would have done. I get through our wedding anniversary in the same way. I am no longer experiencing severe panic attacks. Soon, I know I will face the project that I had been avoiding for over a year: *Walking to Japan*.

I had been unable to so much as glance at the manuscript since his death. The project felt like both a gift and a burden. Derek had left such a legacy, and it was so important to me to pass it on. But he'd conceived it as a collection of tales from the road, when now I knew it had potential to be so much more, which meant I had my work cut out for me. Could I rise to the occasion? Could I do him justice? I was not yet ready to find out. Another part of my pilgrimage was waiting to be walked.

My husband was born in 1940 in a small coastal town in Yorkshire called Redcar. It was World War II when his mother gave birth to him alone during an air raid. Years later a friend remarked to him, "No wonder you chose to dedicate your life to peace."

I invite a dear friend, Cynthia, to accompany me to England. We walk for a few days on the Cleveland Way, a path along the Yorkshire Coast. Derek had walked it in 1987, on a pilgrimage to his birthplace. There, he'd experienced a chance meeting with long-lost relatives, he'd stood in the very house where he was born, and he'd also found the unmarked burial plot of his father. I want to tread in his footsteps and take some ashes back to the sea where he had played as a child.

Breathtaking scenery unfurls under our feet, but so do challenges. I had thought the clifftop traverse would be flat, but it involves rough terrain as we climb down and up through ravines the whole way. I recall the story Derek told about his trek along that cliff's edge, when summer weather suddenly turned cold, wet and blustery and he feared being blown out to sea. But he persevered, and so do we. Fortunately we are blessed by good weather.

On June 16th we arrive in Redcar on what would have been Derek's 72nd birthday. The sun warms our faces, the waves crash at our feet, and fossils reveal themselves from under the sand. I watch a handful of ashes waft out over the sea. Derek has returned home. A rainbow appears, spanning the ocean.

I feel joy and relief that I couldn't have imagined. It is a completion. But, later, I sense a gentle prodding from Derek that I can't explain. Something small, unfinished. I trust that this will come clear if and when it needs to.

Cynthia and I sit planning our route back through London in the rental car, deciding on where to spend a few hours for lunch and a rest. Consulting the map, we notice Coventry. The only association I have with this name is a favorite Christmas song, "Coventry Carol," but goosebumps on my arm tell me that I have to go there.

The city's centerpiece is its cathedral. Arriving there, suddenly Derek's nudging makes sense. The stark modern structure sits amidst rubble. On various plaques around the site, I read about the history of Coventry and the building itself. In November, 1940, this industrial city was devastated by bombing and the cathedral was reduced to a shell. After the war, as in Hiroshima, a decision was made not to clear away the debris and forget the painful past, but instead to preserve the bomb site and incorporate it into a new structure, as a memorial, an act of faith and symbol of hope for the future. The new cathedral was completed in 1962. And one of my favorite musical works, Benjamin Britten's profound *War Requiem* was composed for its consecration.

What had once been the inside of the old church is now an outside space, and modern sculptures depicting the effects of war are set against the old stone and brick. Noticing a cross constructed from charred roof beams, I begin to weep. For several minutes, all I can do is stand and just take it all in, as I had done in Hiroshima when confronted with such blunt and poignant reminders of our terrifying human urge to destroy.

Cynthia and I are eager to see the interior of the church. At the main door a sign directs tourists to a side entrance where admission is charged. Only those who came to pray or worship can enter through the front. I can be stingy sometimes, and I do feel slightly reluctant to pay, but I realize, suddenly, when asked, that we are first and foremost there to pray.

We enter the space and are at once awestruck by the tranquility within. Cavernous and austere, the church's interior with its simple, arching lines, also possess a warmth and humanity in the small details of the lighting and the tapestry.

We sit, close our eyes, and meditate silently. I think of all those on earth who are in pain or poverty, suffering violence or illness or hunger. I call on Derek, I call on Gandhi, and I call on John Lennon—two of Derek's heroes. As we sit, organ music fills the huge space around us. I don't even know if the organist is performing a composed work, or merely testing out the keys and stops, but it doesn't matter. I am transported. Ecstatic. I can't remember ever feeling so moved and edified by such a total wall of sound.

In the silence that follows, gradually we open our eyes. The music echoes on in the shards of color that stream through the windows, the stained glass somehow both subtly reflecting the past and evoking the highest of humanity's potential—love, peace, truth and beauty.

We rise to leave, and while walking slowly toward the exit we notice a small chapel. Peering in, we are delighted by the sight of long strings of peace cranes hanging above the altar. Of course I have my origami paper with me, and, just as I had done with Derek hundreds of times, Cynthia and I fold cranes and each leave one as our grateful offering.

Rendered speechless in that sacred space, we find it difficult to rejoin the noisy world of people and traffic. But onward we go, driving in the silence of our rental car down the M40.

Our trip continues through southern England, and then Cynthia returns home. I spend a few days in London alone, enjoying sights and activities. I prepare to go home, but it returns to me, the sense of not being quite complete. Then, I remember, and feel a shiver down my neck.

In Battersea Park there sits a Peace Pagoda, built by Japanese Buddhist peace-walking monks in 1985. They are some of the very same monks Derek had met on the Great Peace March and then walked with in Europe. In the '90s, Derek reconnected with the sole monk living nearby. It was their last meeting.

The pagoda sits on the edge of the River Thames, a small elegant tower ringed with gold carvings of the Buddha on its smooth white sides. When you glimpse it through the trees it draws you in but asks you somehow to slow your approach. Solid and grounded, it seems to touch the clouds with its delicate stupa, connecting earth and sky. It exudes peace. I sit on its steps for some time, looking out at the river, then pull a sheet of paper out of my pack and make a crane.

Next, I find the monk's residence and knock on the door, but nobody answers. I don't even know if the same monk is still living there. My heart sinks, but I take comfort in the thought that perhaps he is off on a peace walk somewhere in the world. I leave my peace crane at the door, and suppose then that my pilgrimage is complete. But of course it isn't. While meandering along the winding streets of the old city later that day, a sudden thought lights up my consciousness. I could live here! I feel a shiver down my neck. And I know that my new dream, to live in London, will inform how my life now unfolds.

At home in Canada weeks later, I begin to tackle writing *Walking to Japan*, picking up where Derek and I had left off. It's a daunting task but I am motivated. I want to get back to London. The creative process brings up grief, but it's also a link to my husband. The lessons that he shares from his life are ones that I myself encounter, and he is guiding me through them.

I often find it difficult to keep my eyes off the goal, wondering, When, when? Why I am I not finished? But I forge ahead, working in fits and starts and taking long breaks. London is one of those long breaks when I return to live there for six months in 2013 after completing the first draft of the book.

Not long after my arrival I return to the Peace Pagoda, and knock on the door of the monk's dwelling. This time, the door opens, and a slim Japanese man in orange robes bows and ushers me in. I explain who I am, and hear an audible intake of air. He is shocked to learn the news of Derek's death. I sit, exchanging stories with this gentle soul and I know that I have made a friend. Every Wednesday for the duration of my stay in London I volunteer on the pagoda's grounds. Every time I walk there, I take my time, crossing the Thames on the Chelsea Bridge and threading my way through the park, anticipation growing with every step. Each sight of the gold-topped pagoda makes my heart swell.

Returning from London on New Year's Eve that year, I resume working on Derek's memoir with a new vigor. There are more ups and downs as I face self-doubt, anxiety and hopelessness, but I have to keep trusting in myself and the process. And somehow—a book gets published.

So here I am. I arrived at this destination much more at peace, more self-aware, and perhaps wiser than when I set out. I realize now that the only shoes I have to fill are my own. And Derek's dream, *Walking to Japan*, has become my own, and is taking me places I would never have imagined.

A pilgrimage, like any long journey, can come to its conclusion in a moment of elation when we stop, look back, and think, how on earth did I get here? That is exactly what I ask myself now. The answer, as always, is: one step at a time.

Nice and tidy.

Questions and Answers

1. What compelled you to set out on your pilgrimage?
Healing, a quest for more, and ultimately—love.

2. Is there a book, song, poem, or movie that inspired your quest?
A book, yes. The one my late husband starting writing and I finished.

3. Where is your sacred place and why did you choose it?
A little spot on a hilltop on the Camino pilgrimage in northern Spain. To make a long story short, it's where my husband and I got married.

4. How did your pilgrimage change your life or not?
My first pilgrimage was an introduction to my husband, and my current pilgrimage is in his honour. I can't imagine what my life would look like if I hadn't met him.

5. What is the most important piece of advice that you have received in your life? Do you have advice to share from your experiences?
Take one small step at a time.

Photograph courtesy of Carolyn Affleck Youngs.

Biography

Carolyn Affleck Youngs, born in 1965, currently lives in Victoria, Canada, and tries to balance her time between walking, choral singing, photography, blogging, editing, writing musical spoofs and practicing ventriloquism. She describes herself as an accidental author. Her pilgrimages include the Camino de Santiago in Spain, and the 88 Temples in Japan. She has walked all the city streets of Vancouver Canada, and dreams of walking across the country one day. *Walking to Japan* is her first book, co-written with husband Derek Youngs (1940-2011).

www.walkingtojapan.com
www.carolynaffleck.com

Walking to Japan. *Photograph by Carolyn Affleck Youngs.*

Walking India. *Photograph courtesy of Olie Hunter Smart.*

Olie Hunter Smart

Live life as if you were to die tomorrow. Learn as if you were to live forever.
~Mahatma Gandhi

A Paidal Yatra* through India
A search for personal stories of India's Independence 70 years on
(* a 'walking journey' in Hindi)

*B*ritain was once one of the most powerful countries in the world. At its height in the early 1920s the British Empire ruled over almost 460 million people, 25% of the global population, and covered a staggering 25% of the earth's land mass. It was famously known as 'the empire on which the sun never sets'. But us British don't like to talk about our colonial past, particularly all the atrocities, plunder and gory detail of how we ruled. We exclude it from our school curriculums, preferring to focus on periods when we fought and were victorious in battle, including, of course, the first and second world wars. It's as if we are trying to bury the past as generations pass, something that Sahshi Tharoor, Indian MP and author, terms as 'historical amnesia'. Colonialism is an incredibly important part of not only *our* history, but that of *all* commonwealth nations, many looking back in innumerable instances with appreciation and even fondness.

Two-hundred and fifty years after the East India Company arrived to trade and rule in India in 1612, power transferred to the British Crown in 1858, and now 2017 marks the 70th anniversary of Indian Independence from Britain. However, securing Independence wasn't easy. Ram Singh has been credited as the pioneer of the freedom movement and was the first to use non-cooperation against the British in the mid-19th Century. The Great Uprising of 1857 is regarded as India's first war of Independence, and despite gaining support from people of all sections of society, it was unsuccessful in its aim. These struggles continued into the 20th Century as younger visionaries picked up the mantle of these campaigns. 'Father of the Nation' Mahatma Gandhi was one such leader and fought for freedom for a vast part of his lifetime. However, in March 1930, there was one event that united the country in a way that would change it forever—The Salt Satyagraha. It was a 241 mile (385km) peaceful protest initiated and led by Gandhi against the British salt tax that forbade Indians to make their own salt. Gandhi's plan was to spend just over three weeks marching from his ashram in Ahmedabad to Dandi on the coast where he would break the law by harvesting salt from the shore. He had carefully selected the people that would join him on the route; people that had an influence within their community to gain support for this protest, but that would not overshadow him from gaining the media coverage he was after. This was to be yet another one of his coups against British rule; a pilgrimage in its own right. The march created tremendous enthusiasm and support throughout the country, formalising the movement of freedom that would lead to India shaking off 335 years of British rule, finally gaining Independence in 1947, and ultimately the collapse of the British Empire.

I decided to travel to India to retrace Gandhi's footsteps along this historic route. I prepared for my journey by watching Richard Attenborough's film *Gandhi* and reading Louis Fischer's *The Life of Mahatma Gandhi* both of which provide a good summary and by all accounts are an accurate and fair representation of the great man's life. But in order to better understand Gandhi and his motivations, I had to do more research on the British Raj. I read about the last Viceroy, Lord Mountbatten's time in India, and watched Gurinder Chadha's *The Viceroy's House*, yet the more I researched, the more I felt these provided a very one-sided, perhaps western view of the past. What did the *real* people of India experience during that period of history? How were they directly affected? What was it like to be forced to flee from one area that you lived in and resettle in another? What were their feelings towards the British at that time? All of these were questions that the films and books didn't really answer. So, the best way to find out was to travel through India and find answers to those questions myself. I wanted to hear real stories from those who experienced one of the most significant events of the 20th Century. It being 70 years since Independence, I'd have to act fast if I wanted to find people who could share their experiences with me. Many wouldn't live to see another notable anniversary. In order to speak to the older generations, I needed to travel slowly through the country to meet as many people as possible from all walks of life, and what better way than on foot. Plus, it's how Gandhi would have chosen to travel.

With a few more months' research and planning I had mapped out a 4,500 km route that would see me travel the full length of the country from the most northerly point in India to the southern-most tip, with significant Gandhi or Independence related points of interest to stop at along the way. Although Gandhi didn't visit many areas in the extreme north and south, his influence reached every part of the country and by walking the entire length of it, I would be able to understand and appreciate India's incredible diversity of people and the environment they live in, from Himalayan mountains to sandy deserts. I had made contacts on the ground that would not only help me navigate the trickier parts of the country, but also be able to introduce me to people of interest that I could speak to. I quit my London-based advertising job, packed my backpack, and set off for Leh, Ladakh in April 2017, not really knowing what my paidal yatra had in store for me.

Leh in April was warm in the day but bitterly cold at night, hitting -10° C. I'd arrived before the tourist season kicked off, and although much of the snow had melted, most of the guest houses, restaurants and souvenir shops (not that I needed souvenirs) remained closed. The area was just waking up after the winter, and with the roads to the rest of the country still closed, fresh supplies of fruit and vegetables were yet to make it to the region. But I did manage to find a piece of cake to celebrate my birthday! I spent a few days acclimatising to the altitude, staring at the mountains, visiting Buddhist monasteries where I circulated around the huge and elaborately decorated prayer wheels, spinning each three times clockwise to bring me luck, and preparing myself mentally for the epic walk I was about to undertake. This would be no ordinary pilgrimage.

My chosen start point was Turtuk, a small, peaceful village that sits on the Line of Control, the disputed border between India and Pakistan in the Nubra Valley. Ever since Partition took place whereby a line was drawn across a map to create a separate country for the Muslims, the two countries have been at war. Aside from the numerous military bases that Namgyal, my guide and I passed on route, you wouldn't be able to tell you were in an active war zone, the most recent battle being in 1999. Shina-Sen Khan, a young villager, showed me around explaining that his village used to lie in Pakistan territory until conflict in 1971 resulted in India gaining control. "We're proud to be Indian" he tells me. The continued military presence in the valley acts as a deterrent to possible invasion and provides support to maintain and develop the infrastructure of the area by building schools, maintaining roads and delivering food supplies in the harshest of winters. "They really help us out where we lack resources or expertise," he explained.

But how was this area impacted by Independence back in 1947? "Not that much" according to Sonam Safel, a guest house owner in Diskit with whom I stayed. "The British didn't really spend any time in the Ladakh region so when they left, the area continued to operate as it always had done. But Jawaharlal Nehru [India's first Prime Minister] did come and visit the region shortly after Independence."

In order to leave the Nubra Valley, Namgyal and I had to wind our way up and over Khardung-La, one of the highest motorable roads in the world at over 5,300 meters. Conditions were fair but as we reached the snow line they deteriorated; the wind picking up as the clouds rolled in—we needed to get up and over the mountain fast. Icy road conditions and minor altitude sickness in the form of uncontrollable legs didn't help as I skidded my way, almost drunkenly, up the road. Six hours later we made it to the top, and what an incredible feeling it was looking back at the jet-black road snaking its way through the white landscape.

From there we headed south through Leh and Lamayuru where I waved goodbye to Namgyal and met up with my new guide, Sangay, who would take me along an ancient trade route through the Zanskar Valley. As he handed me a pair of crampons, it suddenly dawned on me that this leg of the journey was going to be seriously challenging.

We spent the next 16 days trekking over four 5,000 meters-plus passes, thick snow covering each of them. We'd get up early each morning aiming to conquer the highest parts before the warm sun began to melt the top layers of snow. By mid-morning I'd find myself sinking knee-deep into slushy powder, struggling to keep pace with Sangay who was somewhat lighter than me, especially given my 25-kilogram backpack. At points, we'd have to cross fast flowing rivers of meltwater, unable to find where the washed-out bridges or trails used to lie. Well before dark we'd find a spot to set up camp, some nights next to a stream which would freeze overnight, other nights in a small village disconnected from the rest of the world for the majority of the year. They would welcome us in and give us a cup of butter tea, a warm mix of watery tea, soured butter and salt—an acquired taste if ever there was one. After each sip, my cup would be topped up, making it impossible to decline more of their favourite hot beverage. The generosity I was shown was incomparable to anywhere else I've been, possibly something to do with the harshness of the environment they live in and the lack of visitors travelling through. Spending time with villagers gave me the opportunity to find out some of their views and experiences of the British time and Independence. Tunduk Dorje, a 76 year old who has lived in Stayangs village all his life explained that he'd heard stories from other people, but in his mind there was very little impact given the remoteness of the region. I couldn't dispute this since there was only a trail into and out of his village. Sangay and I continued through beautiful and remote valleys, over the barren, rocky mountains, crossing unstable bridges and scrambling our way down small glaciers to Darcha. We were incredibly fortunate to travel successfully the full length of this mountainous trek so early in the season, though it left Sangay with the challenge of getting himself back home before the roads had opened up.

In Darcha I met up with my third and final guide, Tenzin, a young student who spoke English well. The region reminded me of alpine Switzerland or France, a comment he said many European tourists make. In one village we walked through, I spoke with Tsering Dorje, an 82 year old author who happily remembered the British times as a child in the Punjab Himalayas as it used to be known. "They gave us sweets, clothes and sometimes a little money," he recalled. But then on a more serious note, he told me "We were very pleased when we gained Independence. We could form our own government and do things for ourselves in our own country. [...] But the impact of Partition created miserable conditions. Refugees came to Kullu, something that we blame the British for."

Back on the road again, Tenzin and I followed the relatively quiet route to the top of the Rohtang Pass, finding narrow trails to cut as much of the winding road off as possible. We reached the top in just under a week, but as we drew closer to the summit I became overwhelmed by the sheer volume of people. Indian tourists dressed head to toe in snow-suits, complete with gloves and hats played in the snow, many for the first time in their lives. Yet I was wearing a thin pair of trousers and shirt with the sleeves rolled up! It being the first time I'd encountered many people, I told them about some of my journey. The surprised looks I got when I explained I'd come from Leh via the mountain trails, followed by the sheer look of disbelief when I told them I was walking the whole length of India, made me even more determined to continue this journey of discovery.

Within the space of a day it felt like I'd gone from winter to summer; cold winds and alpine landscapes were replaced by warm air, trees and flowers, quite a novelty to look at. I parted with Tenzin who headed back to his village in the Lahaul Valley. I'd finally reached the famed hill stations, the summertime destination for the ruling British escaping the Delhi heat, and I could see why. A similar climate to the UK and surrounded by mountains— what was not to like? Each hill station has an air of imperialism about it, particularly in terms of town layout and British architecture. Government offices have largely remained in the same buildings as British times, while churches, bridges and other baronial-style structures remain the focus of the towns. Upon reaching Shimla, the British summertime capital of India, I met up with Raaja Bhasin, a local historian who explained that "Shimla, or Simla as it was pronounced and spelt back then, could be described as the grandest outpost of Empire [...] a mock fairytale, small English town created miles away from its setting with a lifestyle that was enviable to anybody anywhere in the world." Exploring Shimla myself I got a sense that it has tried to maintain that way of life, becoming an overwhelmingly middle-class town that remains incredibly clean by Indian standards—plastic bags are banned as well as smoking in all public spaces. Perhaps these are things we should look to adopt in the UK? However, Raaja was quick to point out that the lifestyle maintained by the British back then was "sustained on the back of payments [taxes] which India made."

It took me two months from the start of my journey to reach the foothills of the Himalayas. As enjoyable and stunning as the mountains had been, they'd taken their toll on me. My feet developed new blisters as they expanded with the rising temperatures; one particular day I took my socks off to find a blister under my big toenail had separated the nail from the nail bed, while another toe had turned completely black. My 1960s canvas rucksack was also showing signs of strain—the original stitching holding the leather shoulder straps in place had given up, meaning I'd had to make a temporary repair with some paracord. We were ready for a change of scenery...some flatter routes for me and some judicious mending by a man with a sewing machine!

Reaching Chandigarh was a big milestone. Not only had I completed the high Himalaya section of my journey, and reached the flat plains of northern

India, but I had also arrived in the first city planned post-Independence. Built in the early 1950s, its grid system layout proved somewhat of a challenge for me to get my head around. Every sector has its own housing, school, parks, shops, medical centre and so on, each divided by a dual carriageway. Here I spoke to Inderjeet who explained that Chandigarh is one of the most modern and forward thinking cities in India. Men and women generally have more equality here; many women wear western dress, drive cars and take well paid jobs, and this was evident as I walked through the city.

Leaving Chandigarh, I chose to follow one of the most frequently mentioned legacies of the British—the railway. Not only would it keep me off the main national highway that leads to Delhi, but it would also take me through the agricultural areas of Punjab and Haryana. Tractors ploughed the fields while blaring Punjabi beat across the vast openness, workers constructed raised banks in preparation for flooding, and fields were planted with fast-growing crops such as rice or millet. Here I was invited to stay with a Sikh farming family that migrated from Lahore (placed in the newly formed Pakistan during partition). "My grandmother handed the keys of our house to a neighbour, asking them to keep an eye on the place for a few weeks until they came back," Mansimar Sethi explained. "They viewed Partition as a temporary thing similar to many of the riots and fights that had taken place before." Hearing about this heart-breaking experience somewhat took me by surprise, but goes to demonstrate just how little people knew about what was going on at the time. It's hard to imagine what you'd do if you were in that situation yourself.

As I approached Delhi I had no option but to move onto the main highway. Fortunately, a pavement/covered drain ran alongside the road ensuring my safety. I joined the teeming masses of people living in the city, passing through part of Delhi's sprawling suburbia, two vast temples and one of the city's phenomenal 'trash mountains'. As I neared the centre, the old British architecture became more evident—Connaught Place's Georgian architecture replicating Bath's Royal Crescent, the India Gate built as a memorial to the Indians that gave up their lives in the First World War, and the Secretariat Building housing government offices. However, none was quite as impressive as Rashtrapati Bhavan, formerly known as the Viceroy's House from where the British ruled the Indian sub-continent. But I was too tired for exploring just yet.

Tributes to Gandhi are dotted all over the city. Himanshu Dube, a business consultant with a keen interest in the great man, took the time to show me some of them. We visited Gandhi Smriti, formerly Birla House, which contains an in-depth museum on his life and work, but where he also spent his last 144 days before he was assassinated in January, 1948. Himanshu shared his inspiration for retracing the Salt March pilgrimage in 2015. "Gandhi was 61 years old when he undertook the march. Most companions were in their 20s, so it was an arduous trip to undertake when you are at retirement age. [...] Salt was a commodity that generated vast amounts of money for the British. Gandhi, representing all Indians, decided he would break the law [...] something anyone could join in with at home, on the coast, next to a lake. Disobedience against this law was recognition that this naturally occurring element is ours, a god given right and therefore it was a worthy pilgrimage for me." He also took me to visit the multiple statues that represent the Salt March across the city. These have proved enough of an inspiration for me to make Ahmedabad, the start of the Salt March, the next stop in my own pilgrimage.

After a much-needed rest in Delhi, I've reflected on the first three months of my journey of discovery. British times are looked back upon very fondly by most Indians I've met. We're credited with creating a united India, bringing together all 562 states and kingdoms that used to make up the sub-continent. The railway system is often highlighted as one of the greatest legacies despite it originally being used to aid the British in their exploitation of the country. They appreciate the solid foundations of administration, governance and education systems that were implemented, as well as having a single, uniting language that has opened up global opportunities over the years. However, there are some negative aspects of the British rule that are always brought up. Partition is the obvious one that tore the country into two (or three counting East Pakistan as it was at Partition, Bangladesh as it is now). But Colonel Dyer's actions and the atrocities of the Amritsar massacre, whereby he ordered British troops to open fire on an unarmed peaceful protest killing and wounding thousands, is frequently referred to as well. The general plundering of India's resources also comes up time and again, and I've even been asked a couple of times whether the Queen could return the Koh-i-Noor, a large diamond that was supposedly stolen during the conquest of Punjab in 1849. Sadly, I think that's a little beyond my capabilities!

The people I meet every day continue to impact my views on this period of history. Only this morning I was talking to a gentleman whose grandfather was heavily involved in the Indian Independence Movement, and well respected by the British. Yet when the British tried to give him 50 acres of land just outside of Delhi, he flat out refused to accept it, highlighting that it was not British soil to give away. That very point struck a deep chord with me, something that demonstrates quite how serious the people were about fighting for their freedom and the Independence of their homeland. Yet did India really gain her freedom during Independence, or was it just a transfer of power? If the constitution of India that was drawn up, and the system of governance was a replication of the British systems, why was all that pain and strife inflicted on the people of India? Was Partition really the right solution to give India back her freedom, and was creating the largest mass migration of humans in history, an estimated 14 million people, really a worthwhile price to pay for that freedom? Was it even a British created problem, or did the leaders of those newly Independent countries play a large part in forcing it through? Gandhi certainly was against a divided India. With each turn I seem to open up more questions than find answers.

I've covered 1,400 km through India so far and have at least another 3,000 km to go, so my pilgrimage to uncover these untold stories and experiences of Partition and Independence is very much still in progress. I hope I continue to meet incredible people with fascinating stories to share with me. From Delhi, I'll continue my quest for these stories and begin to learn more of Gandhi's role, heading out through Jaipur to Ahmedabad where I will visit the ashram that he set up. I will retrace his footsteps of the 385 km Salt March route to Dandi, progressing down the coast to Mumbai, a key trading post for the British and where the National Congress Party was based. I then head inland to Pune where Gandhi was imprisoned for his general troublemaking, along with other members of the Independence movement. I will walk the Western Ghats all the way to the southern tip where Gandhi's ashes were finally scattered after being taken to all corners of India following his death. And once I reach Kanyakumari, the end point of my life-changing trek, sitting in the temple there on the edge of the continent, looking out at the Indian Ocean, I will reflect on what a wise man once said, "Live life as if you were to die tomorrow. Learn as if you were to live forever" ~Mahatma Gandhi.

Further reading:

Attenborough, Richard; *Gandhi*; 1982.

Chadha, Gurinder; *The Viceroy's House*; 2017.

Fischer, Louis; *The Life of Mahatma Gandhi*, Harper Collins; 1950.

Mountbatten, Pamela; *India Remembered: A personal account of the Mountbattens during the transfer of power*; Pavilion Books; 2007.

Tharoor, Shashi; Interview with Jon Snow, Channel 4 News; On Youtube. 8th March 2017.

Questions and Answers

1. What compelled you to set out on your pilgrimage?
Having initially read about Gandhi's Salt March, I was doing a little more research into why he undertook the journey and the impact it had on the nation. However, I realised a lot of the sources for my research were British (or western); British authors, directors, film makers, etc. Where were the views of the Indian people; the *real* people that experienced this period of history? I could find very few sources, so I thought the best way to find out was to travel through India and find answers to those questions myself. I realised that I needed to act quickly if I wanted to hear these experiences and views given it was 70 years since Partition took place—those people wouldn't be around much longer. And so I set about planning my pilgrimage.

2. Is there a book, song, poem, or movie that inspired your quest?
The original inspiration for my quest actually came from an article about protests in *Shortlist Magazine* in 2015. It covered the most impactful protests throughout history including the March on Washington and Tiananmen Square, but the one that stood out to me was Gandhi's Salt March, a non-violent protest against the British salt tax. It briefly explained what it was and the impact it had on the nation. I thought it would be fun to re-trace Gandhi's 240 mile route, something that could be done in a few weeks. However, as I started researching the event, I realised there was a much bigger opportunity at stake. And it snowballed from there.

3. Where is your sacred place and why did you choose it?
India. It has fascinated me since I was a child. It's colour, vibrancy and cultural heritage entwined with Britain for over 350 years. It's the world's largest democracy, a place where 1.3 billion people from different classes and castes, and from many different religions live in harmony. It's a place where things work by defying logic. And I wanted to experience it. However, I have never found a real reason to make it to India, until now.

4. How did your pilgrimage change your life or not?
This journey has already had a huge impact on me and I'm less than half way through it! I came to India with a set of questions I wanted to answer and a rough idea about what I would find, however nothing has prepared me for some of the stories and experiences that I have heard—stories of migration, separation, violence and fear. I've been left speechless too many times to mention, and have found that it has opened up more questions than ones I came to answer. And I am sure it will continue to do so as I progress south. I feel compelled to share the stories that I've heard and the

experiences I've had to ensure that future generations learn about the *real* impact of one of the most significant historical events of the 20ᵗʰ century. I want to ensure my pilgrimage has an impact on other people, not just me.

5. What is the most important piece of advice that you have received in your life? Do you have advice to share from your experiences?
I was backpacking through Asia in 2013 when someone reminded me that every now and again I should look back at what was behind me. So often when we travel we just look forward and see the thing that is in front of us, the thing we have come to see. However, if we take the time to look behind ourselves, we get a different perspective. I thought about this further and realised that perhaps they weren't just talking about physically looking back to appreciate the view, but perhaps metaphorically—where I'd come in life. This made a lot of sense given my purpose for travelling at the time had been to escape a job I was no longer enjoying, and to re-consider my career options. Since then I've travelled extensively having many different experiences and encounters. I've been in situations that have excited and scared me, yet each and every time I look back and think where I would be had I not made the decision to put myself there. So, my one piece of advice would be to look back behind you, not only in the moment, but also in life.

Biography

Olie was born in the south of England, spending much of his youth messing about in boats. At the age of 18 he spent six months in Belize working on a conservation project to rebuild a remote ranger station and teaching in a local school. The experience gave him an appetite for adventure, travel, to see the world and to understand more about different people and cultures. Since then, Olie has worked in the London advertising industry, taking every opportunity to travel and see more of the world. In 2013 he backpacked his way from Russia, through Asia, Australasia and across South America. In 2015 Olie became one of only a handful of people to travel the length of the Amazon River on foot and by kayak. The year 2017 sees him take on a new challenge, to walk the length of India to uncover untold stories of India's struggle for Independence.

www.oliehuntersmart.com, Facebook, Twitter and Instagram.

Ascetic (yogi) who has spent a minimum of three years of meditation in isolation, visits Lhasa during Sagadawa (which celebrates the birth, enlightenment and death of the Buddha), Tibet . 1997.
Photograph by Pat Morrow.

"An encounter with your angel in real life appears to be virtually impossible. But that is far from the truth. All that is necessary is to recall that this encounter can take place in extreme circumstances, and especially at critical moments in a person's life. And it is within your powers to create the situation for such an encounter."
~Ilya Kabakov, l'étrange cité

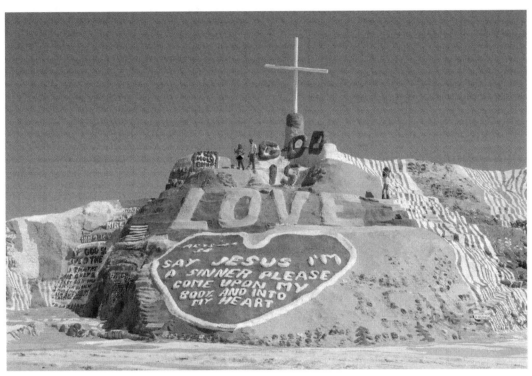

Photograph by James Dorsey.

James Dorsey

Travel leaves you speechless and turns you into a storyteller.
~Ibn Battuda

A Voice Crying in the Wilderness

*E*ach of us answers a different call. It comes from a mystical place deep inside that tells us where we must go next. There is no logic to it, only surrender. Our species was born to wander. Were this not true, the earth would not have been populated before domesticated animals or the wheel.

We wander to seek what we do not know; to satisfy questions that have no answers, and to find our own place in the great cosmic puzzle. We wander because we have no choice, and when we do this with an open heart, the word 'pilgrimage' becomes an appropriate title.

Salvation Mountain is simple enough; a manmade pile of adobe and paint that squats on a sun baked plain in the California desert, southeast of the great Salton Sea. It's not so much a mountain per se, but rather, an idea that has become larger than the sum of its parts.

It shares the hereditary land of the Coahuila people, whose mystical cosmology is part of its allure, and it's remote location aside, it draws seekers of all faiths like moths to a flame. It is the life work of a hermit named Leonard Knight, and while it looks much like an oversized birthday cake that someone sat on, for many, it is a sanctuary, a church, and a last outpost for hope.

At first sight, it may seem unremarkable and certainly not qualified to be called a mountain. Some laugh before taking a selfie and disappearing into their air conditioned car for the three hour trip back to civilization, never knowing what they have missed. But many more fall to their knees in prayer; others weep, while some approach prostrate with unworthiness. To those unfamiliar with the mountain's history, this might seem like gross theatrics, but, just as many more famous shrines began as token monuments, Salvation Mountain has become what its visitors have always wanted it to be.

Leonard Knight was born, unceremoniously, in Vermont in 1931, and spent his early years drifting, until his wanderings deposited him in the low Colorado Desert of Southern California. There, he claimed to have had a religious epiphany that carried with it the obligation to share his newfound zeal with the world. At first, Leonard wanted to hand-make a giant hot-air balloon with the message, "God is love" but after numerous technical failures, he switched tactics. Leonard said that Jesus came into him in that desert, and Christ had once wandered in a desert for 40 days, so what could be a more appropriate place to create a living prayer? Leonard gave up on his balloon and started to build a mountain.

In 1980, he began the glacially slow process of adding clay and paint to the terminus of a low flat mesa, using only a shovel and his bare hands. To anyone witnessing those early days, it must have seemed sheer madness, the ravings of a sun-stroked desert rat, hand making a mountain. But, as with all people of vision, Leonard's idea was also a quest. His mountain, growing a mere handful of earth at a time, would praise the Lord 24/7.

He probably would have scoffed at being labeled a pilgrim. As a simple and uneducated man he may not have even known the word, and yet, that is what he was. For Leonard, every handful of dirt added to his creation was a step closer to his Maker.

For almost three decades, Leonard worked from light till dark, where temperatures routinely topped 100 degrees Fahrenheit, adding a few feet of clay each day, and painting prayers whenever he finished a section. While he was offered a room in town, he chose to live in a rusted out truck, and on the handouts of visitors who came to see the crazy hermit. He never wavered, and in time, after many months, his mountain began to grow and take shape, eventually making sense to those who had laughed at it. Comparisons between Leonard Knight and John the Baptist are inevitable when you realize both of them were, "A voice crying out in the wilderness." (John: 1-23).

The town of Niland is the closest civilization to the mountain at six miles distance, but it is only a collection of disintegrating mobile homes that have not been mobile in decades, with a gas station, and a general store thrown in. Niland is home to more Jack rabbits and coyotes than people. There is only one road through town, and once on it, you feel the isolation. At first sight, the mountain appears to be melting, like a giant ice cream cone lying on its side. From the terminus of the dirt road, Leonard's mountain sweeps the eye upward from a tilted flat desert floor. This is where he painted his "Sea of Galilee," a 100 foot expanse of blue and white that simulates ocean waves lapping at the foot of the mountain. Your eye is drawn up to the massive red heart that has been called a valentine, but is filled with "The Sinner's Prayer." Further up on the sloping face, six foot letters proclaim, "God is love," and all of this is topped by a towering white cross that points heavenward, gleaming in the desert sun like a great bony finger. On both sides of this, from an unseen lake on the summit, cascading streams of blue and white paint simulate waterfalls that encircle the face of the mountain and return your eyes to the giant red heart, the main icon, as intended by Leonard. At this point, the mountains aura begins to draw you in.

Standing 100 feet tall, the face of the mountain seems insignificant in the vast open desert, but as you climb the yellow painted path to its summit, the bright primary colors captivate and unleash the need to touch. Touch is a physical manifestation of curiosity and a starting point for exploration. As a visitor, you must touch the mountain, to enter it, to understand it, to feel it, because, as Leonard said, "It is alive." Since every square inch is covered with paint, it is slick to the touch, and it glistens under the noonday sun. It is this tactile invitation that one cannot refuse, like feeling a statue in a museum; you just have to do it. Those who live nearby talk freely of the earth breathing in and out, especially on nights of the full moon. Others say whispered voices, carried by the wind are the essence of Leonard's prayers.

As I climb the path, I find one of Leonard's hand prints, in smeared paint. I try to imagine the incident: Leonard slips while painting, and puts out his hand for balance, leaving a perfect paw print there in the cerulean blue. I place my own hand over his, seeking even a minor physical connection to his essence, hoping for the tiniest insight to this creative act, and for the briefest moment, I understand what he has done as only another believer can. In such places, a visitor can never truly understand what is before them. They can only catch fleeting moments of enlightenment, but that is all most of us are after in the first place. When I reach the base of the cross, I am crying from emotions I cannot explain. Though that limited journey was but a few steps, it carried me for miles.

I sit with my back to the cross and imagine Leonard at work under a twirling sun that Van Gogh would have been proud to paint. A wave of serenity comes to me on the breeze along with the certainty that I belong here. I am the wanderer at one more shrine, content in the arms of gorgeous desolation. The summit offers a grand panoramic view. The towering mountains of the Anza-Borrego desert sit afar, turning purple in the afternoon light, while tumbleweeds race each other to nowhere. I feel the mountain breathing.

Below me, decaying vehicles circle us like Indians attacking a wagon train. Each rusting hulk covered with prayers, each one a silent witness to the epic struggle that took place here, each with a story to tell but no way to tell it. From above it might resemble the carnage of a battlefield. They are silent witnesses that have become home to the countless resident critters that share the mountain. It has been said that Leonard could talk to the animals, and did so often as they watched him work. Perhaps three decades of living among them provided that ability. More than once he has been compared to the Christian mystic, Francis of Assisi, who carried the same gift.

The path continues down, past a surreal forest of undulating trees and flowers of unknown origin, taking you to the "Hogan," a beehive shaped room filled with artifacts and fetishes that are the tools of a shaman, and Leonard's homage to the indigenous people. There is a local tale of a Mexican brujo who befriended Leonard and used the Hogan to conduct "vision quests," but such stories are always imbedded in legends with no access to their veracity. Across from the Hogan is "The maze" where fantastically twisted clay trees dance while reaching their Day-Glo branches skyward. It is a series of dead end rooms, and stairs that go nowhere, while glass windows give a view of nothing but the next wall, and where every possible space is filled with painted prayers. His personal mantra, repeated over and over is, "God is Love." Leonard liked to say that these dead ends were man's search for answers, and when nothing was found, they returned him back to God, where he started.

Viewed as art, Salvation Mountain is more folk than fine. It does not contain the overpowering grandeur of Michelangelo's Sistine, or Gaudy's, Sagrada familia, or even the Watts Towers of Simon Rodia, and yet, it stands equally alongside each of them as a monumental life work of a solo artist. Each of these epic creations began with an idea that invited curiosity, and once investigated, took the creator deeper, until eventually; it became an obsession, the engine of which can only be known to the few who have had that insatiable inner drive. Fortunately for most of us, those who retreat from the world to pursue their epic visions, usually leave them behind for the rest us to enjoy.

So what took me to Salvation Mountain? As a writer, I am always looking for stories, and my search for them has taken me around the world, usually to the most remote places. Writing is a lonely profession, a solitary blood sport, and we who secret ourselves in tiny rooms to pour out our hearts on paper or screens, understand the agony of creation in all its forms. My work is not epic like those mentioned above, it is quiet and personal, but it is a private daily struggle for truth and perfection. Leonard found his truth. I am close, but the search continues.

Just like Leonard I get up each day to work, all the while questioning the quality of what I am doing. While I cannot speak for others, I know how hopeless I would feel without some faith in something larger than myself. It took me many years to realize that my search for stories has always been a search within myself, for reasons and answers that are probably unattainable for a mere mortal, but the journey shares equal status with the destination. That is why I seek out places like the Mountain. That is why I am drawn to men like Leonard. That is why, without giving a name to it, I have always been a pilgrim, and each journey to a place like Salvation Mountain takes me a step closer to my own answers.

Leonard's physical journey ceased in 2011, when he was diagnosed with dementia. He spent his final days being cared for in a public ward, receiving visitors who wanted to meet him, but not knowing why. He died in 2014, never having returned to his mountain. One person, close to him, said his final words were, "God is Love." Local people will tell you they have seen Leonard, walking over his mountain in the moon light, having conversations with coyotes. This traveler admits that after a day on the mountain, I had questions, should I meet a talking coyote. Some say he sleeps each night in his old rusted out truck, shape shifting in the morning into a desert critter in order to listen to the visitors on his mountain. Being a folk tale, legend, or outright fabrication, time seems to merge all three until the final tale becomes accepted fact.

The mountain is open to everyone, and even in the summer heat, receives over 100 visitors a day. There are no fences or admission fees; no opening or closing hours. There are no security guards, or even docents. There are a few local people, some who live on site, in makeshift homes or Air Streams that watch over the mountain. While they have no authority over visitors, no one seems to challenge them when being yelled at for straying off the path or climbing on sections newly re-painted. They are true guardians of the dream, and seek nothing in return. No one will ask for money, but they will ask that you bring paint for the non-stop maintenance a living desert prayer requires. In that sense, the mountain continues to grow, and anyone can participate in that process. You may even meet a talking coyote who knew Leonard.

Whether you go as a tourist, volunteer, folk art lover, or religious seeker, Salvation Mountain will be what you need it to be.

I did not know what I needed until the mountain told me.

Questions and Answers

1. What compelled you to set out on your pilgrimage?
It took me many years to realize that every time I leave for a new destination I am doing so in hopes of it being a pilgrimage. In the case of this story, I was asked to write about a destination and it captured my soul once I arrived there.

2. Is there a book, song, poem, or movie that inspired your quest?
Salvation Mountain has been in several movies and mentioned in literary works and I had read a lot about it due to this publicity.

3. Where is your sacred place and why did you choose it?
It is in the Desert of Southern California just southeast of the great Salton Sea.

4. How did your pilgrimage change your life or not?
The only change is that I know there are many more such places that I wish to visit.

5. What is the most important piece of advice that you have received in your life? Do you have advice to share from your experiences?
The journey is more important than the destination. Our entire life is a journey with destination unknown.

Photograph courtesy of James Dorsey.

Biography

James Michael Dorsey is an explorer, award winning author, photographer, and lecturer who has traveled extensively in 48 countries. His main pursuit of the last 15 years has been visiting remote cultures, mostly in Asia and Africa.

His articles for mainstream publication strive to enlighten and entertain travelers about remote places they have never been while his literary endeavors are personal narratives about unique journeys and the people encountered along the way.

He is a fellow of the Explorers Club and a former director of the Adventurers Club. He is a former contributing editor at *Transitions Abroad* and a travel consultant to Brown&Hudson of London. James is a throwback to a bygone era of exploration and his stories and photos take the reader along with him.

www.jamesdorsey.com, Twitter: @ aging Explorer, Facebook

The Camino. *Photograph by Kendra Seignoret.*

Kendra Seignoret

It is the mark of an educated mind to be able to entertain
a thought without accepting it.
~Aristotle

Life's a Journey

*I*t was my last day on the Camino. I had four and a half hours to complete 20 km, and nothing was going to stop me. I was determined to complete my 38-day trek across Spain at the Santiago de Compostela Cathedral in time for Pilgrim's Mass. When I finally arrived, in under four hours no less, it went a little something like this:

Me: Excuse me! Did I reach? Is this the Cathedral?

Two older ladies: Yes! This is it!

Me: ...Really?

As I contemplated the lichen-encrusted façade of the large cathedral, I didn't even know what I was supposed to feel. But as I stood amongst the throng of excited pilgrims, I did know that this place was *not* why I was here. After snapping a quick photo, I left it behind in search of the Pilgrim's Office to get my *compostela*, the traditional Latin certificate of completion issued to pilgrims. But even that felt more like an anti-climactic formality rather than the culmination of a sweaty 800 km trek.

At the Pilgrim's Mass, I was lucky enough that the *botafumeiro* swung during that service. It's a tradition that dates back to the 12th-century, whereby the giant censer emits cleansing incense as it swings on a 65-metre long arched trajectory across the cathedral. I'll admit, seeing it baptize hundreds of enraptured pilgrims, even I had moisture in my eyes for a few moments. Or maybe it was just the smoke...yes, let's go with that.

I know I was very fortunate to have had this opportunity to participate in a tradition that has been around for more than a millennia, to be a part of something greater than myself. But that day, I wasn't able to shake a nagging feeling of incompletion. As I explored the city in the days that followed, I still did not feel like I had accomplished something. Nor did I find "the answer" that so many others say they learn along The Way. What was I missing? Did I do something wrong? What did it all mean?

Fast forward four years and I'm still processing my experience. What I've come to realize is that the journey, not the destination, is the key (and that clichés exist for a reason). When I'd arrived in Santiago in May 2013, I'd been focusing on the wrong thing that day: arriving in time for the Pilgrim's Mass. Changing my focus away from "start to finish" and instead, studying the journey itself, I've realized *that* was where my satisfaction lay, not in achieving the goal itself. After I embraced that point of view, I also realized that my Camino did not begin and end during that spring. It started long before then and still continues today.

In the spring of 2006, one year after university, I went to France, ostensibly to study French. But while that was true, it was also an opportunity to travel and to connect with a part of my roots. I stayed with my uncles in a small market town near Toulouse. One day, on one of my many walks around the area, a strange sight stopped me in my tracks. It was a large yellow symbol painted in the middle of a quiet country road. I was curious so I snapped a photo to remember it. Little did I know, that was the exact moment my pilgrimage began.

The painted yellow shape turned out to be a shell, one of the ubiquitous symbols of the Camino de Santiago. Seeing that large shell boldly sprawling across the road, it was as if my eyes were now open to it. Throughout that summer, I saw evidence of it all over the French Tarn region, including actual pilgrims in Moissac and Toulouse. As I learned more about the Camino, the more I was fascinated. Not by the religious side to it as I was not a Roman Catholic (in fact, I was barely a practicing Christian). But rather, I was intrigued by the whole concept of the Camino being a pilgrimage: a long journey to or a search for something of significance.

I think most of us are looking for something, and that something is different for everyone. Some people find it in faith. Others find it in purpose. Some searches are quick, while other journeys are longer with many twists and turns. I grew up within the Protestant Christian faith; it never satisfied me, something I found hard to admit during my twenties. As for purpose, I still hadn't figured out what I wanted to be as an adult so I was very frustrated. Therefore, at the time I discovered the Camino, I was wrestling with religious expectations for myself versus ditching a way of life that was all I have ever known. I had recently graduated university from a program I hated and was stressed about finding my next steps. On top of that, I was dealing with the aftermath of a not-quite-amicable divorce between my parents, after we all lived a life projecting "perfection" to others. Struggling to stay afloat, it was no wonder I found the concept of going on a long solo walk so appealing!

I returned home to Canada in the late fall 2006. I travelled some more, I worked, and eventually I found a secure and stable job which allowed me to finally move out on my own for the first time. I did all that I was "supposed" to do, but the Camino was always in the back of my mind. Every once in a while, I'd take it out, toy with it, and then tuck it away again.

My secure and stable job was in a cubicle and involved running a program that impacted thousands of employees across the country. While it was important work, I had very little interest in what I was doing. As the years dragged on, I felt more and more of my brain cells screaming, "Help me!" in squeaky little voices before *poof!* they died. In an attempt to combat this, I did things such as teach English to new immigrants to Canada and volunteered for three months in Guyana. While both were fantastic experiences, they were "safe" adventures helping others. It was time I did something for me, too, something (I thought) that had absolutely no practical value whatsoever, something that would solve my problems and add excitement to my every day. Seven years after the first time I saw that yellow painted shell on a French country lane, I was finally ready to walk the Camino de Santiago.

It was easy to believe that the Camino would be my "journey to something of significance", that something being the Cathedral. Having read all the different stories about the Camino experience, I had thought it would somehow provide me with what I was looking for. I had hoped it would help me figure out my life, find answers, maybe make a connection to faith, and perhaps find the answer to world peace while I was at it. But in the end, it didn't do any of that. But what it did do was teach me a series of lessons, some of which I'm still unpacking today.

As the train pulled into the station at St. Jean-Pied-du-Port, I realized I'd forgotten to take note of the address to my lodgings. It was not a good start to my Camino. But I decided to *make* it a good start by testing the Camino adage "the Camino provides". I threw myself into the throng of pilgrims heading into town, trusting that the flow would carry me by my *auberge*. And it did. Over the next 37 days in Spain, there were times when my lodgings of choice did not have space for my tired carcass—but the Camino always provided. There would always be space somewhere. Times when I thought I was lost, and just before I freaked out, I would finally find a painted Camino symbol to point the way. By the time I reached Santiago, I'd started to understand the first lesson of the Camino: to trust when I put myself out there, life will provide me with what I need.

When doing my research on the Camino, I kept coming across this concept of a "Camino Family"—a group with whom people ended up walking for days, if not weeks. I've always been an introvert and a loner so I dismissed this idea completely. The Camino had other ideas, however. As I contemplated the steep Pyrenees Mountains I had to conquer on my first day, I met an amazing woman with whom I walked for the next ten days. We had to part ways when she unfortunately broke her arm and had to return home. Over the next two weeks, I walked alone, sometimes meeting people and other times just enjoying the solitude. But when I started thinking that I was right, that the Camino Family was not for me, I fell into a new group with whom I walked off and on right through the end. We laughed together, we shared together, and we struggled together. By the end of my Camino, I realized the beauty that can exist in simple human interaction. I learned that even an introverted loner like me can enjoy conversations with random strangers. The second lesson of the Camino, therefore, was about finding the right balance between meeting my needs for solitude and interacting with the wider world around me.

Walking 800 km while carrying my own backpack meant that I quickly became appreciative of the concept of "minimalism". At the end of five weeks of walking, I realized just how little one needs to enjoy life. It was an eye opener, comparing my 20-pound backpack to my apartment full of stuff back home. I didn't realize until the Camino how "stuff" mentally weighs me down without me even noticing. I was reminded that the simple things are what bring me pleasure, that having fewer belongings to worry about brings freedom, and that experiences are where I need to look in order to find happiness. This third Camino lesson, therefore, was about figuring out what minimalism means to me and determining how I would want to apply it to my life in general.

The interesting thing with the Camino is that, rain or shine, pilgrims are outside for a good chunk of the day. It was a huge change for me as I had been a typical cubicle dweller back at home. But week after week of being outside and not using any form of transportation besides my feet for five weeks, I came to fully realize what a disservice my cubicle had been to me. To this day, I still remember the precise moment when I realized just how happy I was to be outside: I was on a quiet lane in the bucolic countryside, the sun was shining and no one on this planet knew where I was. It was liberating. It also emphasized the fourth Camino lesson: if I don't enjoy a certain aspect of my life, that does not mean life sucks. It just means I have to work harder to find joy and ways to be true to myself. I have to find ways to embrace a cubicle escape artist lifestyle.

The funny thing is that while walking the Camino has led me to these lessons, I did not recognize them *on* the Camino but rather during subsequent years. I still struggle with my Camino lessons on a daily basis, figuring out how to integrate them into my life. This is why I believe that my pilgrimage continues to this day. I remind myself to trust that when I put myself out there, life will provide me with what I need. I strive toward a balance between connecting with people and seeking my solitude. I continue to pursue an understanding of minimalism and how it can apply to my life. And finally, my drive towards being a cubicle escape artist remains strong and I continue to pursue a life filled with adventure.

The fact that I am still learning these lessons emphasizes that walking the Camino itself was not my pilgrimage. I still have not found "the answers" to my life nor did I end up making a connection to faith. And I certainly did not find the answer to world peace. However, I did have an experience that has had a profound impact on me and the way I approach life. It has encouraged me to see life itself as a pilgrimage, where I strive to remain in the moment and to be open to learning. I know that one day, my journey in life will bring me to the answers that I seek. And if it doesn't, well what a ride it would have been!

Questions and Answers

1. What compelled you to set out on your pilgrimage?
In the spring of 2006, near a small market town in the Tarn Region of France, I stumbled across a painted Camino shell splayed across a country road. I began researching the Camino and the more I learned about it, the more I was fascinated. I was intrigued by the whole concept of a pilgrimage, of a long journey to or a search for something of significance. However, as described in my essay, after a culmination of things, it was several years before I finally felt it was time for me to become a pilgrim myself.

2. Is there a book, song, poem, or movie that inspired your quest?
No—I deliberately did not read any books or watch any films about the Camino before I went. However, I did peruse a number of online forums and blogs for "practical" information to help with the planning. I tried not to focus on people's experiences as I did not want them to give me any preconceived notions. While I was on The Way, I met a number of people who had been inspired by the film!

3. Where is your sacred place and why did you choose it?
Places that particularly speak to me tend to have one of three qualities: solitude, sea air, or a view. So many places in nature make me smile, be it in the midst of a forest or on a mountain top. But if it is a place that manages to combine all three, such as a quiet spot on a cliff overlooking the ocean, well that is perfection!

4. How did your pilgrimage change your life or not?
As described in my essay, my Camino had an important impact on my life as it taught me four important lessons. I am still working through these lessons, four years after walking it, but that is okay. I'm still on my pilgrimage!

5. What is the most important piece of advice that you have received in your life? Do you have advice to share from your experiences?
Always be open to learning. You never know what different perspective or experience will unexpectedly resonate with you!

Photograph by Kimberly Ing.

Biography

Kendra Seignoret considers herself to be a cubicle escape artist: she tries to find ways to keep her job while also trying to escape it as often as possible. When she travels, she's generally that solo female with a camera firmly clutched to her face as she wanders around, narrowly avoiding being hit by some form of local transportation.

www.rustytraveltrunk.com

"Trust and start walking. We are not alone in the dark, our path will unfold as we move forward."
~Paulo Coelho

Llama fetuses. *Photograph by Julian Cook.*

Julian Cook

Oscillations

*S*trong oscillations of fever and chills are swinging me hard and fast on the sixth floor of the Hotel Milton. The effects of the sun get worse the higher you rise from sea level, and La Paz, Bolivia, is the world's highest capital at 13,000 feet. Consumed by the heat, I throw off the covers and in the next few moments I'm suffering teeth chattering chills as the sweat drenched sheets cool down. The ambivalence of hot and cold makes this illness twice as bad. Origins of this sickness were a mystery, but I had a relatively strong suspicion that it came from the street food I ate on Calle Illampu a couple of days before. Street food is the best stuff you can eat or so I thought. It's a long standing travel theory of mine that street food is generally safe because these folks are in the business of feeding their neighbors. It's hard to play fast and loose with food preparation when your customers aren't anonymous. I just hoped that when my friends Terry and Steven returned and found my body that they would agree on a Hemingway-esque story about how I died, preferably one that left out the punchline of "Yeah, he shit himself to death." Maybe they could even embellish some details.... I would have liked that. My pilgrimage wouldn't have been a complete loss.

* * *

Bolivia had long been on my list to visit, but first I needed to get there. The central municipality of La Paz makes its home at 13,000 feet, but the airport is even higher at nearly 16,000 feet. Being transplanted from environs closer to sea level, to half the height of cruising airliners, made staying vertical in the Bolivian Customs and Immigration line a genuinely monolithic struggle. The government officials were, as one might expect in a third world country, fulfilling their duties at a glacial pace. Two hours ticked by from the time we landed, until our visas were stamped, allowing us to legally enter South America's most impoverished country, and into a taxi where we continued to gasp for air. It was 4:30 a.m.

Descending from the thin heights of El Alto to the thick, inky depths of the city proper was an astonishing experience in night gazing. It was as dark as coal with an immaculate, star filled sky and no discernible delineation of the heaven and earth. Where land should have been on the horizon there was only more perfect darkness punctuated by the occasional, solitary bright light from buildings perched on the sides of completely invisible mountains. It was nearly 360 degrees of stars and I could make up my own temporary constellations in those star-filled mountains and they might have even had interesting names if only my brain weren't so addled. Thankfully, as we lost altitude, we gained oxygen. Sweet oxygen that was full, rich and satisfying to the lungs, satiating to my brain and the rest of my tired body. Only then was I confident that I wasn't malfunctioning in some way.

After securing rooms at the Hotel Milton, we slowly marched up the stairs, to lapse forward into well-deserved sleep. I woke up after a few hours to a gorgeous detonation of color and hue. On the street below, blankets were spread out and the locals were selling oranges, lemons, handicrafts and housewares.

Saturday is a market day in La Paz and the next couple of hours were spent strolling by women wearing traditional, highland indigenous fashions hawking their wares. "Hawking" might be a charitable description since these women were generally placid and just waiting for customers to walk up and buy. It was a nice change from most of my travels in the developing world where the autumn color of my skin subjects me to infinite, optimistic assertions of "I make you good deal!"

Yeah, I bet you will buddy.

Once again my friend Steven Newman was with me as well as another friend, and fellow software engineer, named Terry Knowlton. Whereas I get really weary of the constant wails of locals trying to chat me up in order to part the fool from his money, Steven always has a smile and is ready for conversation. He isn't afraid to look like an idiot, something I admire greatly. Terry has a sterling resemblance to Hunter S. Thompson when accessorized with the right hat, sunglasses and brandishing a Cohiba—that alone was an interesting spectacle. I wasn't sure where he was in this street scene, and as it turned out later it didn't matter because, as we later discovered, Terry possesses the navigation qualities of a spring Capistrano swallow. Steven was easy to find: a gentle, red-headed giant making conversation with a cross-legged indigenous vendor who was smiling and nodding her head because she was either agreeing with his witty banter or, more likely, was just nodding her head affirmatively at babble she didn't understand, which is the default mode of street sellers worldwide. It was a nice scene and I was reminded that success only comes when you're open to others. I simultaneously resented and admired his cheerfulness, something that happens often when we travel together.

Steven and I turned a corner and witnessed a beautiful sight. It was a beautiful, bubbling stockpot with fresh chicken, potatoes, carrots and local spices all rolling in a boil and we only got hungrier the more we looked at it. The elderly lady only asked three bolivianos a bowl and it was the best tasting 43 cents I have ever spent. The three bolivianos turned into six which later turned into nine.

Lost in our ecstasy of soup neither of us noticed Terry until he said "Hey guys." He had, not surprisingly, found us. I expected him to say "We can't stop here, this is bat country." Again, the resemblance was impeccable.

* * *

It's 8:00 a.m. Where is Jesus? You know? Son of God?

I've never been this high without some sort of fuselage around me. Le Cumbre sits at a lung sapping five kilometers above sea level, and light headed is about the last feeling I want at this moment. Jesus is here somewhere in the form of a statue with outstretched arms and I'd be happy to hug him back if I could only find him. I'm not generally a religious man, but a word with Jesus might be a good idea before I go screaming down, and hopefully not off of, the Yungas Road on my bicycle. The Yungas Road is better known as El Camino de la Muerte; the Road of Death.

It is not a marketing ploy, friend.

Before alternatives, it was estimated that 200–300 people a year died on the single track road that's only about 50 miles long. In one year alone, 25 vehicles plunged off the road and into the arms of their savior. That's one every two weeks. It's easy to see why the Inter-American Development Bank christened it the world's most dangerous road back in 1995.

There we stood on top of Le Cumbre Pass, astride our bicycles with the snow coming down and Jesus was nowhere to be seen. Time to call out the celestial understudy: Pachamama, the goddess revered by the Andean people. With a touch of the pure grain alcohol to our lips and a little spilled on our tires, as is the custom when invoking Pachamama's blessing, it was time to go.

We followed each other single file down the wet, frozen highway and for the first ten minutes everything was fine.

And then the sleet started.

I was hoping that the descent out of the snow would be quick, but conditions turned treacherous as I pulled down my goggles, which were fogging up, and the ice started pelting my corneas (ouch!, ouch!, ouch!).

Was this ever a mistake.

No way was I was going to risk a catastrophe by trying to put my goggles back on, so the regular process was to look ahead, endure the hideous sting of the ice pellets hitting my eyeballs and look away, hopefully not to wreck in the process. Descending down into the coca country, that's how it went until we reached the police checkpoint where it would be quickly confirmed that we weren't carrying drugs. Our collective gloves had small holes in them which rendered our hands to a solid, frozen state and it was hard to even know when I was successfully pushing the brakes hard enough to stop. Snow and ice by this time were melting on us, and in cahoots with the water spray from the road, we were saturated to our cores. Terry pushed his hands into his pants to warm up to which the tour guide, a quick witty Aussie name Marcos, smiled and said, "Now's not the time to be playing with yourself mate!" It got a pretty good laugh, but Terry was really feeling the pain of numbness, as we all were.

Only the first 14 kilometers of the road is paved, and by the time we had descended that far the precipitation had stopped, but we were still sodden. The heavy, saturated coveralls were a heavy and uncomfortable liability and they had to come off. That felt countless tons better, but we were still waterlogged. Thankfully we would dry out during our ride relatively quickly all except for one part: our feet. The capillary action of our socks managed to bring the water all the way down into our shoes, resulting in our feet becoming, and remaining nearly, 100% soaked until the end of the ride with every pedal downstroke, emphasizing an uncomfortable squish.

A few kilometers more of squishing along and at the top of the road we stopped. Before us lay the challenge. It was a thin brown line stretching into the distance, hugging the green mountainside. It's the longest and trickiest part of the road, a skinny dirt track of a road, about eight feet wide, with a 90 degree (sometimes less) cliff on your right and drop-offs to your left with no guard rails. Sheer drop offs that measure over 2000 feet. I was mostly confident in my brakes at this point and had the ride started here, I might have been more apprehensive. Regarding the Yungas Road, I understand the "why," as this was the only link between La Paz and Coroico for many years, but it's the "how" that intrigued me.

* * *

Google "List of Bolivian military victories" and you don't get much if anything. Bolivians are the Bad News Bears of the Latin American military league. With the exception of the war to gain independence from Spain (which they wouldn't have won without the help of Colombian and Peruvian forces), Bolivia has been a naively optimistic country when it comes to military battles. Bolivia's record is 1-4 on the battlefield and the last war was the most bloody.

The Chaco war between Bolivia and Paraguay was fought from 1932 to 1935 and the whole thing was about, and I know this will surprise you, oil. Bolivia and Paraguay have one thing in common, they are the only landlocked countries in South America, and that made getting arms something of a hardship since both countries depended on the goodwill of their neighbors' access to the ocean. Both had previously had access to the water and both lost their access due to military conflict. Bolivia had a relatively lucrative mining industry and certainly a much bigger army than Paraguay so you might think that this would be a fairly easy walk in the park.

Nope.

External oil interests were convinced that there were oil deposits in the sparsely populated, hot and semi-arid lowlands of Gran Chaco, as area extending into both Bolivia and Paraguay. Echoing what is a modern routine, international corporations jumped into the fray and financially backed their dogs in the fight: Royal Dutch Shell funded Paraguay, and Standard Oil stood behind Bolivia. That tended to level the playing field a bit, but there were two reasons why Paraguay would ultimately win the war. One, they were just plain better fighters. Two, having lost nearly half of its territory to Brazil and Argentina in the Paraguayan War, it viewed dominance of the Chaco as its last viable economic source and in no way could they allow that to fall to Bolivia. Paraguay was hungry.

And it didn't fall to Bolivia, but it was a bloody war; the bloodiest of all South American conflicts with some estimates placing the dead at 130,000.

That brings us to the Yungas Road; Bolivia used the captured Paraguayan prisoners of war to construct it, and it claimed hundreds of Paraguayan lives, but the lives being lost now are overwhelmingly Bolivian and they number in the thousands. Here's hoping that it doesn't claim a few American ones, and we took off hoping to appreciate their sacrifice.

This was certainly a much trickier ride because the beginning of the road was quite muddy and momentary panics set in as I hit my brakes and still managed to slide a bit. It was a short lived stretch of road to my relief, and it turned more into a gripping and gravelly roadway.

Over 2500 feet, nearly half a mile, is how far down the chasm plunged, and I got queasy just looking over the edge. That doesn't compare to what happened to some political prisoners though back in the 1980s. Latin America is full of political brutality and Bolivia is no exception. We were at a pass known as Martyrs of Democracy and it was here where several members of the opposition party met their end. They were simply thrown off the cliff to plunge to their deaths.

Yes. Just like that.

That's the way brutality works in Latin America. During the Guatemalan civil war, opponents were often taken up in helicopters and dropped into either volcanoes or into the open ocean.

Really? Does it have to be THAT bad?

Latin American conflicts remind us that sometimes fictional people are more real than actual humans who live and breathe.

For as big balled and hairy chested as "cycling down the road of death" sounds, you'd have to be pretty inept to plunge off the side, at least as far as bicycles are concerned, yet it has happened on a few occasions. Where motorized transportation is concerned is where it gets a little complicated. You drive on the left when coming down the road. This allows drivers to get a better handle on whether or not they are getting too close to the edge of the road. If you happen to be the driver descending the Yungas when coming upon an ascending vehicle, there is an added complication: you have to back up to a spot where the other vehicle may pass. Count me out on this. Even if you manage to stay on the road, there is a good chance that the road will crumble beneath you if you are too close to the edge, putting you on St. Peter's roll call. Drivers with years of experience have taken themselves and passengers to their deaths underestimating this.

When writing about the descent, it's hard to come up with adjectives to convey the whole experience. It was indeed, an excellent ride and one that I highly recommend if you are willing to take the chance. At the end of it all there's a nonstop spaghetti buffet at the monkey preserve. If cycling 40 miles of this doesn't do enough for you.....well.....

My first ziplining experience was in the Peten Jungle of Guatemala and that was at a comparatively kindergarten sized 120 feet above the jungle floor and because you can't see down to the actual floor, you don't really get a sense of how high up you happen to be. The Flying Fox completely dwarfed that experience by a factor of ten. You fly from peak to peak, above the valley floor at a height of 120 STORIES. Speeds reach up to 60 mph and unlike the jungle zipline you can see

all

the

way

down.

There's also another experience you get with the Flying Fox that catapults you from the ranks of merely crazy to the clinically insane: the superman harness. It's a full body harness where your back gets strapped to the rollers that speed you down the wires. It's as close to bird-like flying as the bi-pedaled get, and if you find yourself in a suitably and mentally impaired state as I did apparently, and are comfortable with the possibility of lavishly wetting yourself with fear, excitement (or something else), I highly recommend it.

Adrenaline flush adventures like skydiving and bungee jumping are not options for me now that I only have one kidney. It's another essay as to why I don't have my left kidney any longer but old "lefty" was remembered and fondly thought of on this trip. Bolivia was country number 48 in my travels, and it was bittersweet getting my buzz on without lefty cheering me on and filtering the impurities in my system. I say that with all seriousness because while some people collect spoons and Christmas ornaments wherever they go, I get drunk. I can see the eye rolls now but this is harder than it sounds. I have been completely hammered in the bone dry Sahara in the Islamic republic of Mauritania and that is not an easy thing to do.

We survived the road of death again, this time going up as bus passengers and, of course, hammered. No, sledge-hammered.

***

At four a.m. Steven banged on my door. "I don't have an alarm and I thought I'd see if you were up," he said, smiling, chipper and ready to go. I had been up for about two hours when I felt a heaviness in my stomach as dense as a neutron star. A heaviness that progressed to diarrhea and if that wasn't bad enough, the worst projectile vomiting I'd ever endured. We were supposed to start the three day, arduous Choro Trek through Bolivia's Andean Cordillera Real and I wasn't sure I was going to make it if this kept up. When I first started feeling ill I sent an email to my local friend Paul Osborne asking if he could get me Cipro, and apparently something was lost in translation as he showed up with charcoal tablets. I quickly popped a couple.

We were supposed to begin at La Cumbre again and maybe if I had spoken with Jesus or Pachamama I would have made it. Sadly it was not to be.

In the taxi, Paul was sitting in the passenger seat and I was behind the driver, Steven was in the middle and Terry was by the other window. I would occasionally have to roll the window down and lurch, but one time too many I was not fast enough and managed to soak the car door, my arm and the back of the driver's seat. Obviously, I could not go through with the trek in this condition, and when we got to La Cumbre I gave the guys my part of the expedition gear. I kept thinking "I could have made it," as I watched them walk away, but in retrospect, it would have been a terrible idea.

The taxi driver didn't seem at all upset that I ruined his taxi and he shuttled me back to the Hotel Milton free of charge.

I slowly plodded my way up to the sixth floor, and the bed was so very hot from the high sun baking it all morning. It felt unbelievably nice, and I collapsed into a deep sleep but woke up feeling even worse.

The problem with having one kidney is that you can't just take every drug someone hands you, NSAIDS like aspirin, are a definite no no. In hindsight, my desperate request to Paul to bring me Cipro was a terrible idea. I didn't even know if I could take it, so I emailed my nephrologist at Johns Hopkins.

And waited...

And waited...

And waited...

The waiting went on for a day and a half and my sickness only grew. By this time I would drift off to sleep, have a weird hallucinatory dream and wake up either frozen or incinerated. While I don't remember precisely if my mother was riding a camel or a pterodactyl, the dream's vivid nature is something I'll never forget. As far as sicknesses go in my travels, and I've had many, this one was a doozy.

My nephrologist's email had great news, Cipro was fine and I wasted no time asking the front desk where I could find a Pharmacia. Través de la Carretera; across the road. The cost for a one week treatment was $1.75, and the effect was near immediate. Finally rest, finally no strange dreams. After a day of treatment, I was feeling well enough to go out into La Paz proper.

While screaming down Death Road, and screaming even louder via the zipline, was a blast, it was a pilgrimage largely unfulfilled. I never made it to the Cordillera Real to go trekking so I'll always have an excuse to go back.

Questions and Answers

1. What compelled you to set out on your pilgrimage?
Bolivia was just one of many countries I have had the pleasure to visit. I visited many more before Bolivia and several after. What made this a pilgrimage was the vast, sweeping images of the Cordillera Real that just called out to me, and not being able to trek through them rips me up every time I think about it.

2. Is there a book, song, poem, or movie that inspired your quest?
Not singularly. When I was a child growing up in rural Kentucky, I always had an interest in every place that was not Kentucky. Mostly that grew from listening to hours of shortwave radio and hearing strange news and viewpoints that I hadn't heard before. During the summer months, when I was out of high school, I used to watch episodes of the *Love Boat* and I made my decision that as soon as I could, I was going to leave, and I did, at the age of 17 into my lifelong pursuit of adventure.

3. Where is your sacred place and why did you choose it?
So far, that would be Nepal and while I have tried to write an essay about it numerous times, I always fail a few paragraphs into it. It's just hard to capture the magic and the impact. I started following the Buddhist path in 1997 after my father died and I just felt the call to visit Nepal. The most impactful moment of that visit happened when I climbed onto a rooftop in Nagarkot on the rim of the Kathmandu Valley and saw the sun rise from behind the Langtag Range. I immediately knew my place in the universe and it was the realization that nothing I was fixating on mattered. None of it.

4. How did your pilgrimage change your life or not?
Nepal most definitely did. Buddhism, and years of meditation, encourage deliberate mindful-awareness of situations, and I find now when I travel that I am much more aware of the beauty of a place. I just pay attention more. I have had Nagarkot-like realizations in Thailand, Morocco and, most recently, when I climbed Mount Kilimanjaro.

5. What is the most important piece of advice that you have received in your life? Do you have advice to share from your experiences?
That would be from my friend Mary Wright who, when I contemplated leaving a job after several years to take a long trip, said to me "you can always get a job." Someone, somewhere, also mentioned that on your deathbed you never regret not working more, it's always experiences you never had, or time with your family that you wish you had more of. As I get

older, I see this more and more. When I mention to friends how many places I have been, they wonder how I have done it, but in fact, all you need to do is ..... well ...... just do it. You find it gets easier. It's a big world out there, so get busy.

.

Photograph courtesy of Julian Cook.

Biography

Youngest of ten children, originally from Shepherdsville, Kentucky, he is the only family member to have travelled outside of the United States. An accomplished artist with works in the homes of the famous and infamous, his greatest job is being a parent to his two children.

Sahara. *Photograph by Tor Torkildson.*

Photograph courtesy of Janet Hulstrand.

Janet Hulstrand

...And the end of all our exploring
Will be to arrive where we started
And know the place for the first time...
~T. S. Eliot

Back to Bonair

I'm ashamed to admit it now, but I never really liked my grandmother very much when she was alive.

More precisely, I had figured out at about the age of 10 that she didn't like *me*, and had done the only thing I could think of in retaliation, which was to not like her back.

This was a sad secret I kept to myself, never daring or even wanting to share it with anyone who might've cared—my mother, my sister, or the pack of girl cousins I had grown up with, seven of us close in age, six cousins almost as close as sisters, all of whom had adored her.

She often gave us matching birthday presents. One year she made us all gingham skirts, hand-embroidered in a cross-stitch pattern, in various colors. (Mine was the violet one, and I loved it.) But it was the present she had given me when I was 9 or 10 that convinced me deep down in my heart that she really didn't like me.

That was the year she gave us the ceramic figurines: they were marked on the bottom with the words "Little Homemaker" and MADE IN JAPAN. Each of the Little Homemakers had a different task: one of them was holding a piece of cake out toward an imaginary guest; another was wiping dishes: a third held a broom; one was stirring something in a mixing bowl, and another was sewing. *They* were all doing something useful: *my* little homemaker was talking on the phone and gazing into the distance. And that is where I got the idea that Grandma thought I talked too much.

She was a rather stern woman, disinclined to tolerate "nonsense" and "sassiness," and I was a lively, imaginative, sometimes willful child with plenty of both sass and nonsense in me, nonsense and sass that frequently spilled out. So the girl on the telephone was only the final bit of evidence I needed to confirm a suspicion I'd harbored for years: she really *didn't* like me.

Shortly after my Mom died, as I began to go through her things, I found a few tiny notebook pages, carefully stored in a drawer. The pages held entries from a journal my grandmother had written in 1931, when my mother and her brothers were small children. I opened the pages carefully, heart racing for some reason I didn't understand. Then I read:

My babies are growing up. I must write down some of their sayings and doings to help me remember on a lonesome day...We got 100 marbles for 5 cents tonight, and had lots of fun playing marbles after we got home from town. A new phonograph record for Elmer, "The Little Things of Life," and a big bag of overripe bananas to fill up on.

As I read these words I was transported, with a pang I felt in my chest, to those days during the Depression when my mother was a little girl in a poor, but happy, family. My grandmother was then a young mother in love with her children, wise enough to know that "a lonesome day" would come, hopeful that capturing the memory of happier times might help her when it did. For the first time I felt the hardness in my heart where she was concerned begin to melt. And I wanted to read more.

I knew there was more, much more. My mother's house was full of boxes of old letters, journals, and other assorted mementos that she had saved. And I remembered that my grandmother had always kept a tiny notebook tucked into her apron pocket, and that she would jot things in it in spare moments between doing her household tasks. I knew that if any of those little notebooks had survived, the most likely place they would be stored was in my mother's house, somewhere in the overwhelming piles of stuff.

I set out immediately on a passionate quest to find my grandmother's journals, a quest that lasted several years and involved many hours of discouraging and tedious work, sifting through piles of old papers. I hoped to find many years' worth of diaries; in the end, all I found was a few composition books she had written in as a schoolgirl. But those few pieces of writing fueled and guided me in my search for the grandmother I had never really known.

Back to Iowa.

If we were approaching Bonair from the east and we were about a mile away the first thing we should see would be the top of the elevator and the church steeple. As we come nearer we should see the houses and the white schoolhouse standing apart from the rest of the town...

So began the description my grandmother had written about her hometown in 1907. Fifteen years old at the time, she had gone on to describe the main street of her little town in careful and loving detail, building by building, ending her first entry with a description of the depot of the Chicago, Milwaukee and St. Paul Railway (*A low and rather small building...painted yellow, with brown trimmings...in one corner of the room there is usually a bright fire...Four maps are on the walls and a candy and gum slot machine is in one corner...Throughout the whole building everything will be found neat and in order.*)

I first read these words—in old-fashioned handwriting, in fading ink—eighty-five years after they were written, sitting in the unfinished attic of the brownstone in Brooklyn where I was living. As I read I felt a sudden rush of connection across the miles and the years—and a growing, and painful, confused sense of closeness I had never before felt with my grandmother.

As I turned the fragile pages slowly and carefully, I discovered a side of her I had never known. To my surprise, I also found evidence that the mischievous streak I had always felt she had disapproved of in me was not entirely foreign to her own character, as revealed in one of the sample letters she had written, apparently as an assigned exercise for school:

Dear papa,
Now you know very well, my dear, that I am a very economical girl, but it would certainly cost at the very least one dollar (small sum, indeed) to attend a county fair, and I beg of you to allow me to call your attention to the fact that it would injure my health to remain at home on that notable day when the fair is to be held, so you may observe what an economical turn of mind I have, for doctor bills would certainly amount to more than the named sum. Please forward the required amount at once.
From your dutiful daughter, Effie.

As I read on, I began to develop a desire, as amorphous and inchoate as it was strong, to follow the backward trail of my grandmother's life. It was clear from the descriptions in her notebook that Bonair had been a very small town. I didn't know if it even existed anymore, but if it did I wanted to find it, and see what it was like now. Most of all I wanted to learn more about the girl who had become my grandmother.

That summer I had the opportunity to visit Bonair. At first it had seemed that it probably did not exist any longer: this was before Google searches, and Bonair was not on most maps. But I kept looking, and finally I found it: it was near Cresco, in the northeastern corner of the state. Not too great a detour on the road from Minneapolis, where we would be visiting my Dad, to suburban Chicago, where we would be going to see my husband's parents on our way back east. So when we left my Dad's house in early August, instead of heading southeast from Minneapolis and across Wisconsin on the interstate, we dropped straight south and drove on smaller highways, into Iowa.

The Mississippi River valley in northeastern Iowa is wonderfully hilly, with forested river banks and high bluffs. The highway, U.S. 52, curves and dips along through these hills, and it is quiet, peaceful, and beautiful. As we neared Decorah and began to move in a more westerly direction, the land flattened out and we were driving through fields of corn and soybeans. We found our way to Cresco and from there got directions to Bonair.

Finally the magic moment arrived, when we were able to slowly drive down the main street of what was left of Bonair in 1992, a hundred years after my grandmother was born there.

We approached Bonair from the west, the opposite direction from the one my grandmother had described in her notebook. But no matter which way you came from, there was no church steeple, and no grain elevator. There was no train depot. There was a building on the north side of the street that looked as if it might have been a general store at one time. There were a few other homes, some old, some new, a couple of mobile homes. At the east end of town, where the Methodist church had once stood, in a vacant lot overgrown with weeds there was a church bell mounted on a brick foundation, and a brass plaque that read: "On this site stood the Bonair United Methodist Church. After fulfilling its purpose since 1890, closed with a farewell sermon, June 14, 1987."

The church, too, had been lovingly and painstakingly described in detail by my grandmother. Now it was gone, and there was nothing to see there but an empty churchyard returned to prairie, a weathered outhouse, the brick front steps of the church, a silent bell mounted on them, and the brass plaque. We turned back toward the center of town, and made our way to the building that looked like it might have been a general store.

If I had been alone, that probably would have been the end of the day's exploration; I would have been inclined to savor the experience privately, to mull and read, and think and wonder, before returning. But my husband is a more outgoing person than I am, and also had the good sense to see that it was silly to have come this far and not take it one step farther. So he knocked on the door, and we introduced ourselves to the woman who answered. What felt like a close and personal secret to me at the time, something I felt irrationally should not be spoken of in anything louder than a whisper was, to my husband, exciting news to share: I was in possession of my grandmother's journals! She had written all about this town! She had lived in this very building! His enthusiasm was irresistible: the woman invited us inside, and showed us the part of her home that had indeed once been a general store. I told her I was interested in finding out more about the history of the town, and wondered if she knew anything about what Bonair was like long ago. "Oh," she said with a sigh, "No, I don't know much. I come here when everything was gone." She directed us to a neighbor's house, and told us that the man who lived there had been here all his life. Perhaps he could tell us something more about the town.

We followed her directions, and a few minutes later were met at the door by the man's wife, who looked at us warily. She warmed up a little when I explained my mission, but told me that her husband was very sick and couldn't see anyone. I apologized for disturbing them, thanked her, and was turning to leave when she said, "You know, if you want to know about the history of this area, you really ought to go on over to Lime Springs, and talk to Anna May Davis. She's in her 80's, but she's as peppy as anything, and she knows absolutely everything." The woman added that she herself had grown up in Lime Springs, where her father had owned a mill, and that she had moved to Bonair in the 1930s when she married. "I can remember driving through Bonair when I was a girl, and getting quite a thrill," she said. "But by the time I got here most everything was gone." That was the second time in less than an hour that I had heard almost the exact same words: a refrain of loss.

We drove the seven miles to Lime Springs and found Ms. Davis listed in the local telephone directory. I called her and explained my interest: she invited us to come to her house immediately. As we sat in her living room and I explained what I was interested in learning about, I mentioned that my cousins were all busy creating and raising the next generation of our family, and that it seemed to have fallen to me to research the past. A vital, vibrant woman, indeed "peppy as anything," she went straight to the point. "You have a lot of work to do," she told me, "And there's no time to waste. There are people here you should talk to, but they'll soon be dying!"

A few months later, a major event occurred in our lives: the baby we had been wanting for some years was conceived. I continued to work on uncovering the story of my grandmother and her early life for as long as I could, at long distance, until shortly before his birth: I wrote letters to my mother's cousins, telling them what I was trying to do. I received pictures and letters from them, and from Anna May Davis, pictures that would help me in my search. I carefully filed it all, I kept notes, and I began to write.

Then finally, fourteen years later, with the blessing of my husband and our two boys, now 13 and 10, I returned to Bonair.

I had come to Bonair in the fall of 2006 without a fixed plan. In fact my going there at all had far more to do with the clear need for my husband and me to spend some time apart, than my having a clear sense of purpose about my writing. I had been invited to use the home of a friend who lived in a lovely river valley in southeastern Minnesota as a place of retreat anytime I wanted. It seemed like a good time to retreat, so I made a plan to be away for ten days, and bought my plane ticket.

My original thought had been to spend the time I was there reading the old letters I had found stored away in my parents' home when I was hunting for my grandmother's journals, and writing. But I was so close to Bonair. So I decided I would take a drive there, with a couple of questions to research, and see where they might lead. I knew, for example, how my grandparents had met (at a box-lunch social), but where was the social held, and when? I knew that my grandmother had grown up in Bonair, and my grandfather somewhere in Iowa, but I had no idea where. I felt sure that by asking a few questions of this nature, and either finding or not finding the answers, a path of further inquiry would open up before me, and I would follow it. It was a method that worked very well.

Cresco, Iowa, the county seat of Howard County, struck me as being a model small town. Everything a person could need was there: a clothing store, a grocery store, a gift shop, a Radio Shack, a hardware store, a furniture store. An Italian restaurant, a bakery, a diner. Good public and private schools, a well-equipped and up-to-date library, a local historical society, a community college. Doctors, a dentist, a pharmacy, a veterinarian. A bank, a law office, a post office. There was even a Curves exercise center, where you could work off the pounds gained in eating the caramel rolls they sell in the diner and the bakery. And of course there were quite a few churches.

There were also a couple of things that were noticeably absent: a McDonald's was one of them. Cresco was certainly a large enough community to support such franchises: the fact that none had been built there had to have been due to a decision, whether publicly argued or not. Though I was pretty sure local teenagers would not agree, I felt this was a salutary omission, and surely a large part of the reason that downtown Cresco was thriving.

It had been a beautiful drive there from the place I was staying, near Winona. The road led, at first windingly through the voluptuous bluffs and hills of the river valley, then onto a high plateau, where open sky and fields invited both contemplation and the all too rare opportunity to simply let my mind be still. In an e-mail I sent to my husband that night I attempted to describe it as he, a painter, might see it: "Iowa is beautiful. The drive here was full of gently rolling hills and curving roads, and the palette is of soft, earthy colors and rich textures: green hills, silvery gray sky, rich brown earth turned up in the fields, and the tawny color of dried corn stalks."

I had arrived in Cresco early in the morning, intending to stay only for the day, since I scarcely knew what I was doing there in the first place. I parked the car, and went into the county courthouse, where the volunteer head of the local genealogical society had offered to meet me and show me how to search the public records. Afterward, she led me across the street to the Cresco Public Library, housed in a classic old Carnegie structure dedicated in 1915, a building in which surely my grandmother, an avid reader, had spent a fair amount of time as a young woman, after she and her family had moved to Cresco.

On a weekday morning in autumn the library was well-used but quiet, and conducive to work. The librarian showed me where the newspaper archives were stored and how to use the microfilm machines. Then he left me alone, letting me know he was there to help me if I needed it.

As soon as I began reading, I found that there was a wealth of information about daily life in the area during the 1890s and the first decades of the twentieth century. Biweekly columns tracked the social life of the town in detail—trips by locals to nearby towns, by auto or rail, were often noted, as were visits from out-of-town friends and family, bridal showers and anniversaries, picnics and other special events. As the pile of photocopied pages beside me grew higher, I could see that there was plenty of information available even on just my own family, and right away I learned some new and interesting things about them. (I learned, for example, that the "somewhere in Iowa" my grandfather was from was Kendallville, another hamlet within Cresco's orbit.) And after combing through several years' worth of archives I managed to figure out more or less when he and my grandmother had met, though not exactly where.

Still, putting together the pieces of the puzzle that would convey the details and nuances of my grandmother's early life was not easy. I started with a few basic, and rather thin, pieces of information. For example, I knew that she had adored her older sister, Ini, who was ten years her senior. Ini had been a milliner in Lime Springs, and several pictures of her and my grandmother together show them wearing some very fine hats.

I knew that Ini had died young, leaving behind a husband and a four-year-old daughter. I knew that the daughter had gone to live with my grandparents shortly after Ini's death, and had stayed with them until her father remarried several years later. Why had she not stayed with her father the whole time? I wondered. And I wondered even more about Ini and her story as the pile of clips continued to grow.

Before her marriage, Ini had been a rather colorful figure in the social life of Lime Springs and the surrounding area. Ahead of her time, she was a successful businesswoman who went on regular trips by train to Minneapolis, Milwaukee, and Chicago, to purchase materials for her shop, often taking my grandmother with her.

She apparently knew how to create a popular local business. In March of 1911, shortly after she and Evan Griffith, the owner of a livery business in Lime Springs, had eloped, Ini threw a bash for the ladies of Bonair. "A company of ladies went to Lime Springs last Friday to attend Mrs. Griffith's spring millinery opening," the paper reported. "The parlors were tastefully decorated and many pretty things in the line of ladies' head-gear were displayed. At 6:00, in company with Mrs. Griffith, all repaired to the Howland Hotel, where a bounteous repast was served and which all enjoyed. The ladies departed on the 9:20 train, thanking the kind hostess who had entertained them so pleasantly."

I knew from reading the newspaper reports that sometime in 1912 Ini Griffith had given birth to her first child. But there was no further mention of the child, not even a name, and I was puzzled when I could find neither a birth certificate nor a death certificate on file in the county courthouse.

Around the same time the tone and the nature of the newspaper reports concerning Ini changed. It may be that her marriage was happy and her new life fulfilling. But I wondered. There were many reports of Ini spending time at her parents' home in Cresco with her little girl, often for days at a time. About a year before her death, an ad in the local paper announced an auction liquidating the stock of her husband's business, and the social column noted that he had gone to South Dakota in search of work. "Mrs. Griffith and Marjorie will follow afterward," the report added. But they never made it there. What happened?

I didn't know. And it was partly my growing curiosity about Ini that reminded me there was a world outside to explore as well as the fascinating journey into the past that the newspaper archives were drawing me into. The morning was gone. Reluctantly I pulled myself away from the microfilm machine. I decided to drive out to Bonair again, and on to Lime Springs.

It was a beautiful autumn day, brisk and sunny, with the warm, rich, low-slanting light characteristic of that time of year. As I drove out of Cresco toward Bonair, enjoying the colors of the sky and the rich texture of empty fields recently tilled, my mind emptied and I felt that particular kind of peace that is so hard to achieve in the crowded rush of the day to day, and so easy to at least momentarily achieve when one is released from it, driving on an open road through God's beautiful creation. As I neared Bonair, the radio station I was listening to began to play Mozart's *Laudate Dominum*, and despite all the things I was worried about on the home front, despite the heavy place in my heart whenever I thought about my faltering marriage, I was filled with an overwhelming sense of happiness and gratitude that I could be here, in this moment, approaching this town that held such meaning and interest for me, hearing this music. "Life is measured in moments," I had once said to Steve, trying to comfort him as he was grappling with his unhappiness over the general direction his life was taking. Here was a moment to be enjoyed, and I enjoyed it.

Bonair was no more filled with activity on that October day than it had been on a warm evening in August when Steve and I had been there together fourteen years earlier. In fact it was even quieter this time, with most children at school and most adults at work. I didn't see anyone. I drove slowly through the town, stopped at the church steps, read the plaque next to the silent church bell again, and was struck again with how sad the words on it were. I went to the end of the town near the deserted railroad tracks, and took some pictures. Then I drove on to Lime Springs, for lunch.

In the second decade of the twentieth century, when my great-aunt Ini Sanborn had lived there, Lime Springs was a bustling little town full of thriving businesses. It wasn't bustling anymore, and yet it was still a pretty little town, and an amazingly well-equipped one for its size. There was a public library open six days a week. There were a couple of restaurants. There was a post office, and an elementary school. I drove slowly around the downtown area, admiring the turn-of-the-century commercial buildings, and wondered if the one that had housed Ini's millinery shop was still standing. I had lunch in a restaurant in a converted industrial building with beautiful stamped-tin ceilings. Then I went to the post office, to ask where Anna May Davis was living.

I had inquired about her in Cresco, and had been surprised to learn that she was still alive—and had recently celebrated her 100th birthday. Some said she was still "doing fine." Others said she "wasn't herself" anymore. (Both were probably right.) I assumed she was in a retirement community or nursing home somewhere.

The young man working in the post office said, "She's right up the street, second house on the left." "You mean she's still living in her *house*?" I asked, incredulous. He smiled a half-smile, and nodded. "By *herself?*" I persisted. He nodded again. "She needs a little help now and then," he said. "And you have to knock hard. She doesn't hear very well."

I drove up the street, parked my car across from her house, and went to the door. I knocked—hard, and loud—and then waited for what seemed like a very long time. Finally the door opened, tentatively. There was a Styrofoam container of what appeared to be a delivery of hot food on the porch; very possibly it was because she was looking for her lunch that she had happened to come to the door, and not because she had heard my knock. I picked up the container and handed it to her. Before I could introduce myself, she asked me who I was representing. "I am representing myself," I said. "I am a writer. You helped me get started on a story I'm writing about my grandmother and I'm back, working on it again." I promised her I wouldn't take much of her time, said I would like to show her some pictures, wondered if she might know any of the people in them. She opened the door for me, and I stepped inside.

But it was not going to work. Her sight wasn't much better than her hearing. I tried writing out on my notepad what I wanted, tried to describe who I was and why I was there, but communication was desperately difficult and frustrating for both of us. I quickly decided a simple message was best.

"You helped me get started on a story I'm writing about my grandmother," I nearly shouted in her ear. And simultaneously scribbled, in big block letters I AM A WRITER. YOU HELPED ME. She smiled, and shook her head. "I can't imagine I helped you very much," she demurred. YOU HELPED A LOT. THANK YOU I wrote again.

Then I let myself out, feeling vaguely guilty about being there. Hoping that whoever it was that she had told me she was expecting would not arrive as I was leaving, and think that I was taking advantage of a vulnerable old woman, invading her privacy, no doubt bringing dangerous germs into the house at the beginning of flu season.

I went back to my car, sighed a deep sigh, and sat there for a while. Then I drove to the graveyard on the edge of town, where Anna May Davis's gravestone was already carved and installed in her family plot, waiting for the chiseling of the missing date. And there I found the graves of little baby Hugh Griffith, born in 1912, and his mother, my Great-Aunt Ini.

As I stood there reading their names, wondering about Ini's life, looking eastward at the beautiful big sky, the clouds filled with dramatic patterns of shadow and light, I felt the hint of a small, stealthy, but sure sense of peace begin to creep into my soul.

I still didn't know where I was going with my writing; and there were a ton of things I would have liked to know about both Ini and my grandmother that I knew I might not ever be able to find out. My relationship with my husband was in bad shape, and seemed to be getting worse, not better. There were so many problems, big ones, connected to that fact, that I had no idea how to solve. But I knew that coming here had been very important, somehow; and I felt that in doing so I would find the courage and wisdom I needed to move forward not only with my work but with the rest of my life.

I also knew that this place, where I had never lived and had hardly ever even visited was, in a very important sense, home.

Questions and Answers

1. What compelled you to set out on your pilgrimage?
Back to Bonair is about the beginning of my quest to uncover the story of my grandmother's inner life, and to acknowledge the debt I owe to both her and my mother for having instilled in me the passion for reading and writing that has defined my life's journey.

2. Is there a book, song, poem, or movie that inspired your quest?
It was the chance discovery of a few tiny pages of my grandmother's journals that led to a reversal in the way I had seen her for most of my life: and also to my telling the story of my search to learn more about who she really was in the memoir I am writing, A *Long Way from Iowa: Living the Dream Deferred.*

3. Where is your sacred place and why did you choose it?
I just ran across a quote by Aristotle, "Happiness is the settling of the soul into its most appropriate spot." That describes perfectly the happiness I felt when I decided to live in Essoyes, the little village in Champagne where I am living now. There are only three places on Earth where I feel completely and totally "at home." But for a variety of reasons, Essoyes is the most perfect place for me, the place I feel the happiest and most complete. I feel like I did not so much choose it, as surrender to a kind of inexorable pull toward it. I feel very lucky to be able to be here.

4. How did your pilgrimage change your life or not?
It's a continuing journey, so I'm not sure how to answer that. Except to say that I think it is continuing to change my life, in small ways that are hard to detect on a day-to-day basis. But nonetheless important.

5. What is the most important piece of advice that you have received in your life? Do you have advice to share from your experiences?
Probably the most valuable piece of advice I ever received was from my Uncle Lewey, who always said, "Worry less, pray more." These words always come to me in moments when I am tempted to panic: and since panicking never helps, no matter what the situation, they have become for me a lifesaving mantra.

Biography

Janet Hulstrand is a writer, editor, writing coach, and teacher of writing and literature who grew up in Minnesota, and lived for many years in New York City and Washington D.C. She now spends most of her time in Essoyes, a village in the Champagne region of France, where she leads "Writing from the Heart" workshops. She writes frequently for *Bonjour Paris, France Revisited*, and for her blog, *Writing from the Heart, Reading for the Road.*

https://wingedword.wordpress.com
http://www.theessoyesschool.com

"If you reject the food, ignore the customs, fear the religion and avoid the people, you might better stay at home."
~ James A. Michener

Photograph by Lorie Karnath.

Lorie Karnath

Pilgrimage to the Temple atop the Hermit's Head

*I*n Burma, the natural and the mystical often intersect. There is a special magic, a transient beauty that permeates its landscapes and which produces a willing suspension of the known in favour of the unfamiliar. Intertwined amidst its myriad of whimsical panoramas can be found the chronicle of many influences, a mingling of history, religion, superstition and tribal customs, this interlaced tapestry the country's true treasure. It is within this captivating template of both the natural and the mystical that each derives their respective narrative, outlining paths to venture upon and maxims to live by. Within this context, it is not difficult to encounter prospects for pilgrimage within Burma. Among these, the journey to an otherworldly sphere known as the "Golden Rock temple" atop Kyaiktiyo Mountain is considered one of Burma's most venerated of holy sites. The name Kyaiktiyo helps to further collaborate the spiritual source of the site, derived from Kyaik Eisi Yo as found in the ancient Burmese scriptures and which in the Mon language translates as "the pagoda upon the hermit's head." For many that undertake this journey there can be no sense of completeness until they have had the chance to worship at this sacred location.

On its own, the temple's small and unassuming structure appears suspect to conjure such devotion; however, it is its resting place that assuredly corroborates its divinity. The diminutive stupa dwells atop an enormous golden boulder that overhangs a vacuous abyss, this prevaricating at the edge of a cliff with the bulk of the stone shadowing the valley below. Seemingly only the faintest of overlap exists between the rock and the stone perch on which it balances. The shimmering golden orb pierces the cloud line, glowing incandescently above a canopy of dense verdant fauna, this eventually yielding to grasslands that ripple in wind choreographed patterns before converging with the unchecked rocky shoreline that stretches along itinerate seas below. Above the churning waters, the rock hovers ephemerally on its precarious perch, seemingly more inclined towards the heavens exempt from the banalities of earth's gravitational pull.

This luminous shimmer irradiating the Paung-Laung Ridge of the Eastern Yoma Mountains inevitably ensnares the imagination and propels the faithful. The unearthly gleam that emanates from the structure is the result of the layers upon layers of gold leaf applied over the centuries in testament to the sanctity of the site by those who come to worship here. To reach the pagoda by foot requires a concerted effort, yet the fervent belief in the sacredness of the location entices thousands of pilgrims to willingly undertake the journey each year. The trajectory offered by the pagoda's unusual setting provides opportunity for immersion amidst natural surroundings adding to the overall meditative aspect of the pilgrimage process. Most of the mountain is wrapped by a deep red, rich soil from which dense woodlands abundantly sprout, and these must first be negotiated to reach the shrine. The stifling heat further impedes the strenuous mountain ascent serving to emphasize the constraints of earthly physical limitations while the promise of the ethereal sparkles above. This, an ongoing reference for prospects of a higher state of being devoid of corporeal limitation. The experience of tangible exertion becomes integral to the pilgrimage, inspiring reflection amidst the quest for the metaphysical. For those of Buddhist belief, it offers a source for the accumulation of additional merit. The trek not only adds to one's overall perceptual awareness of the process, the terrain that one traverses provides the actual parameters for the legend that led to the temple's founding. The story behind this is a complex one but within its nuances can be drawn inspiration while the narrative unveils the particular significance of the site.

Having traversed the thick of the forest, one reaches the crest of the hill where a large tiled platform soon comes into view. The platform which leads to the Golden Rock functions as a place where the daily hoard of pilgrims can lay out mats and blankets to rest and pray. Interspersed amongst the worshippers are a number of additional shrines of which several are dedicated to the various protagonists that play a role in the many-faceted tale of the small pagoda atop the boulder. Each of these reliquaries offer moral instruction or proffer help to those seeking guidance.

The story is said to have first unfolded a very long time ago, at a time that was even before the first recorded Buddha had attained enlightenment and when the fabled Mon Kingdom of Thuwunnabhumi, also referred to these days as Thaton, existed. It was said that a pair of brothers lived as hermits in the thick of a mountainous forest that was so impenetrable that only occasionally would the sun's filtered light permeate the many-layered leaves of its canopy. This bounteous woodland canopy as described in this early chronicle is still very much in evidence, serving to shelter pilgrims from the sun's direct glare as they travel on their way to and from worshiping. From within this deep green enclave, the brothers managed to survive, foraging each day for food, mainly subsisting on whatever they could find in way of roots and forest fruits. Although it was not an easy existence, this was the life that the pair had purposely chosen for themselves and the brothers took great solace from the natural beauty of the nature that surrounded them. The forest provided them the serenity required to pursue their desire to meditate. The brothers had reportedly been born as princes and had grown up within the splendours of their parents' Royal Palace; however, had willingly forsaken all luxuries in order to pursue lives of purity and prayer, devoid of earthly pleasures. This was their choosing despite their father the

King's pleas to dissuade them.

As is often the case in Burmese legends, the start of one narrative begets a complex layering of intertwined stories and accounts, and it seems that in this instance around a similar timeframe a more secular scenario was also taking place within the very forests where the hermits had made their home. Unbeknownst to the brothers, a young and handsome alchemist happened to be wandering the woods close by. The Burmese forests are well-known to provide sanctuary to a host of creatures representing a wide spectrum of flora and fauna and other creatures which straddle the natural world, as well as originate from a multitude of places beyond the earth's spectral boundaries. As such it is not considered unusual that a female dragon chanced to be in the area and came upon the attractive alchemist. Finding the toned physique of the nomad to her liking, the dragon formulated a devious plan to meet the unsuspecting magic man. Conscious that her cascade of flashing green scales and large talons would frighten the alchemist away, the dragon assumed the guise of a human female of exceptional loveliness to entice him. Such was her newly fashioned exquisiteness that it did not take long for the man to fall deeply in love with this unexpected beauty discovered amongst the trees. The attraction between the pair moved swiftly and before much time had passed the dragon fell pregnant. However, when the time of birth came, the dragon's deception was exposed. Rather than a newly born baby, two large eggs were delivered amidst the soft mossy folds that lined the forest floor. Realizing that his love was falsely forged, the alchemist fled the forest in anguish. As there was no longer any reason for subterfuge, the dragon abandoned her human manifestation and soon returned to her lair.

Not long after this, some villagers from the region happened across the two exceptionally sizable eggs littered along the forest floor. When the villagers spotted one of the hermit brothers out in search of his quotidian fare, they pointed the eggs out to him. It was clear by their substantial dimensions that the eggs were of no ordinary provenance. The hermit gently gathered these and carefully carried the unusual find to his humble dwelling secreted well within the forest. One of the eggs he gifted to his brother and the other he kept for himself. The brothers tended to these with special care anticipating that one day whatever lay within would emerge. After quite some time had passed, the shells finally began to show the first traces of cracks. The brothers watched as little by little the eggs' outer casing gave way, eventually hatching, revealing two babes of human form, both male.

So now the brothers were tasked with seeking out ways to nourish and bring up the new-borns, not an easy undertaking in the middle of the forest with few amenities. Yet despite the lack of comforts that might help ensure the wellbeing of an infant, the brothers did their best to make up for the absence, in the form of affection that they dedicated to the diminutive beings under their care. Over time the dedicated and constant attention provided by the brothers overcame the limitations of their primitive habitat, as the two babies developed to be healthy toddlers and eventually strong and striking young boys.

As their adopted sons grew, the hermit brothers taught them all manner and means of survival in the forest. The boys learned to discern the direction and feel of the wind, hear the sounds, and smell the scent of an animal's passage, the crush of lichens underfoot or the blossoming of a new flower, all observances that would help reveal and predict the tenor of the forest at each moment. The two fathers and their sons enjoyed this uniquely intimate companionship within the cradle of nature for quite a number of years, until tragically one of the boys died. This tremendous heartbreak, however, was not to represent the end of their sorrows. While still reeling from the passing of the child, the brothers learned that their father the King had also perished. This unwelcome news came in the form of a delegation of ministers from the capital, who had laboriously travelled through the unknown terrain combing its remote regions in search of the brother's well-concealed refuge. The minister's intent was to return to the palace with the elder brother, who was the next in line of succession.

Despite the ministers' ardent pleas, the elder brother remained resolute not to take on the duties and trappings of kingship. The hardships he had undergone pursuing the life of a hermit had not dimmed his determination to pursue a life of piety. The ministers sought to prevail over the elder brother's resolve emphasizing the precarious nature of a kingdom without a ruler and his responsibility to his subjects. To placate the ministers, the brother offered his adopted son to return with the delegation to be crowned as the new ruler. Realizing that the elder brother was not to be persuaded, the ministers accepted the compromise and set out once again on the long journey through the forest back to the capital with the young boy who upon arrival was crowned the new King. Now the Kingdom of Thuwunnabhumi was a very special place that would eventually become known as the center of Theradava Buddhism. This is among the reasons that the Temple of Golden Rock holds such particular importance for the faithful. Theradava Buddhism incorporates the Hindu belief in reincarnation known as "Samsara" or the cycle of rebirth, based on a spiritual cause and effect represented by the laws of "karma," or "kamma" as it is called in Burma. It is these that govern one's Samsara outcome. Those of good conduct in both intent and action harvest good karma while those of bad conduct will yield bad karma.

This helps to explain why the adopted son, who despite his abrupt death, was far from precluded from the story following his demise. The boy when he died was pure both of heart and intent having enjoyed a wholesome life in the midst of nature's bounty and had therefore accumulated much good karma despite his young age. This had resulted in his being reborn within a relatively short time as a son to a wealthy man in the ancient country known as Mithila. In this new life, the boy would continue to follow a devout and virtuous path. Longing for permission to become a monk once he had attained manhood, he sought out the Lord Buddha Gutama, a greatly revered sage of the time. The Lord Buddha graciously granted the reincarnated boy's request to devote the remainder of his existence as a monk. Such was the man's devotion to worship and meditation he eventually attained the venerated rank of arahat and became known as Ashin Gawunpati, a living reference to the earth, "gawun" meaning laterite, referring to the ruddy sub-soils that cover much of Burma's equatorial forests.

Only those that are well advanced along the path of Enlightenment can be referred to as "arahat." Those accorded this tribute are considered as "perfected" having cleansed themselves of the human vanities and poisons of desire, hatred and ignorance. It is believed that an individual who has succeeded to fully expunge these mortal conceits and venoms can transcend the sorrows and sufferings of existence, and as such is released from the powers and controls of karma and along with these, the cycle of birth and death. Once fully purged of the poisons of humankind a person no longer is reborn, having attained Enlightenment or Nirvana. This, once achieved, allows one to persist in a transcendent state devoid of self, immune from the fetters of suffering or yearnings.

One day while in deep meditation, Ashin Gawunpati's reflections wandered to his earlier life rekindling fond reminiscences of his days as a youth roaming the forests of Thuwunnabhumi under the watchful care of his foster father and his brother. The vivid imageries of this time brought forth a deep appreciation for all that they had done for him. The recollection spurred a desire to visit the hermit brothers and convey his gratitude towards them. Setting out from Mithila, the undertaking was lengthy and strenuous, but when he finally arrived at the forest border he found that his senses, which in his former life had been honed to detect directional cues, had not deserted him, enabling an easy navigation of the dense woodland landscape. Negotiating the thick brush, the arahat was able to pick out the route to his former home. Upon arrival, he explained to the brothers that he was the boy that they had raised in the forest, now reborn. The brothers were overjoyed to learn of his fate and exalted at the elevated holy state that the young boy had reached in this next life. They listened enthralled as he told of the virtuous route he had chosen and how when he believed that he was ready to pursue this course had sought out the learned Lord Buddha. He spoke of how in the meantime the Lord Buddha himself had attained enlightenment and was now tirelessly sharing his learning to devotees in the region of his homeland. The brothers could hardly contain themselves such was their excitement of this news.

They entreated Ashin Gawunpati to appeal to the Lord Buddha asking that he come and visit them in the Thuwunnabhumi forest. The hermit brothers fervently wished to meet the holy teacher and hear first-hand his preaching, for it was to be upon these lessons that the precepts of Buddhism were to be founded. And so after a bit more discussion, Ashin took leave of the brothers and undertook the lengthy trek back towards his homeland. When he once again had the chance to encounter the Lord Buddha, Ashin Gawunpati dutifully conveyed the request as posed by the brother hermits. The Lord Buddha agreed to visit the brothers, and it is said that he set out with a large cortege of followers towards the far away land of Thuwunnabhumi spreading the word of the new faith as he journeyed.

One can imagine the eager anticipation of the brothers once they learned of the impending visit, and that all possible manner of reverential preparations were made to suitably welcome within the forest confines this most holy teacher. The Lord Buddha and his retinue were greeted by the hermit brothers along with their adoptive son, now the well-respected ruler of Thuwunnabhumi. In addition to the King, the brothers had invited another hermit living nearby within the forest. Although the forest gathering was a small one, the Lord Buddha spoke at great length proving his profound wisdom and abilities to disseminate his desire for universal love and peace. Nearing the end of the stay, as the Lord Buddha and his entourage made ready to depart, the three hermits deferentially implored him to bequeath them a remembrance of the special visit, a vestige that they could worship and which would serve to hold close the learned thoughts that he had conveyed to them. The Lord Buddha agreed to their entreaty and imparted to each of the brothers as well as to their forest neighbour strands of his own hair.

Such a precious relic required great care and proper tending to and so the younger of the brothers together with the neighbour hermit constructed a pagoda into which they inserted a small golden coffer to house the hairs that the great teacher had bestowed upon them. The elder brother settled on keeping the Buddha's gift close by, entwining the strands amongst the topknot of his own hair, this proximity enabling frequent worship of the treasure. For years after the Buddha's visit, the three hermits continued their unassuming and devout existence in the forest without incident. Over time both the younger brother Theiharaza and the neighbour Kelathaya died, leaving only Theikthadharma who although aged and failing still stowed the Buddha's hairs atop his person.

Though evident that his demise was drawing near, Theikthadharma seemingly neglected to make further provisions to ensure continued care of the Enlightened One's relic. This circumstance prompted the anxiety of the king of the nats, known as Thagyamin. Thagyamin is unique as the only one among the "Great Nats" not to have suffered an abrupt and brutal expiration, allowing for a more palatable alliance with Buddhism as he is not the direct result of a violent aftermath. Thagyamin is often depicted holding a conch shell representing a horn, a proclamation of strength, authority and dominion. The instrument's song was thought to expel evil as well as deter disaster and devastation. He is also often represented riding a three-headed white elephant, a reference to the most elevated of the heavenly places in Buddhism that still sustains a bond with the corporeal world.

Such was Thagyamin's concern over the fate of the holy relic that he undertook a special trip to earth and sought an audience with the judicious King of Thuwunnabhumi. For Thagyamin to request such a meeting clearly indicated a subject of great import. In his presence, Thagyamin spoke to the King about the inevitable approaching demise of his foster parent and the importance of safeguarding the precious Buddha hair. In agreement of the importance of assuring proper quarters to protect these, the two Kings, one representing the celestial realm inhabited by the nats, the other an earthly domain, set out through the forest. Arriving at their destination, the old hermit surprised by the regal visitors, queried the motive for their call. The Nat King clarified that the visit's purpose was motivated by the desire to build a pagoda over the Holy One's hairs, ensuring that others could worship before these once the hermit had passed on. It was only with great reluctance that the hermit finally acquiesced to the two King's desires and his agreement carried a challenging provision. This required that a rock should be found in his likeness before he would relinquish the hairs. Once found, a hollow could be dug within the boulder that would serve as the repository for the relic over which the pagoda could be constructed.

Although for many such a stipulation may have seemed daunting, nats are known to be especially resourceful and the King Nat perhaps most of all. Intent on ascertaining the sacred relic's well-being, Thagyamin did not hesitate to set out in search of a suitable rock that mirrored the contours of the hermit's thickset cranium. His journey took him far and wide, and while scouring the seashore, it is said that he propitiously found an enormous boulder at the bottom of the ocean that remarkably resembled the hermit. Such a massive structure required colossal reinforcements to transport. A boat, believed to have served in the conveyance of the rock, is said to have turned to stone following the delivery of the boulder to the place that Thagyamin had selected along its precipice high atop a hill. For those that make the journey the fossilized craft still can be seen within a few hundred feet of the hermit rock. Once Thagyamin had managed to secure the boulder, he returned to the hermit's dwelling to inform him that a most appropriate rock had been found and had already been positioned awaiting his approval. Thagyamin then guided the hermit and the King to the spectacular mountaintop setting. Upon seeing the remarkable likeness so dramatically perched at the edge of the cliff, the hermit could not help but express delight at the result of the King of the Nat's efforts. Such was his satisfaction that at his insistence the carving of a cavity within the boulder to house the relic began immediately. Upon completion, the hermit assiduously untwined the Buddha's hair from his own and reverently placed the holy strands in the newly created receptacle. Following this, at the crest of the boulder just above where the sacred hairs rest securely nestled in the rock's hollow, the pagoda was raised.

Only then, his mission completed, did Thagyamin return to his ethereal dominion with the knowledge that the Buddha's gift had been preserved for worshippers to follow. The hermit peaceably drew his last breath at the base of the pagoda amidst the shadow of his own profile. It is believed that it is the strength of the Buddha's hair that seemingly defies gravity enabling the massive boulder to maintain its precarious positioning along the slender mountain rim rather than plummet towards the breach of the precipice below. It is this credence that draws pilgrims from around the world, to witness for themselves this radiant wonder that tests the balancing edge of reality.

Although for centuries the only means of attaining the mountain's pinnacle was via the strenuous climb through the forest, in modern times a road representing a fairly perilous journey on its own has been constructed. This to allow for even the very old as well as the very young the opportunity to worship at the temple's site. Open bed trucks with a number of wood planks to serve as seating careen up and down the mountainside transporting would be pilgrims. Squeezed shoulder to shoulder any independent mobility is constrained, and the passengers sway back and forth as a unit while the trucks negotiate each hairpin turn. The cramped proximity ensures a fairly uncomfortable journey especially as the uncovered vehicles expose the occupants to the gruelling sun. The tight arrangements, however, do serve to mitigate the chance of being flung from the vehicle as it climbs or descends the hazardous route. For those who opt for this route and who are not ambulatory, litters are on hand to provide transportation from the vehicle drop off point to the pagoda platform. Very young children are oftentimes carried in large woven baskets, you can see them peering wide-eyed through bamboo thatch-work as the baskets swing back and forth to the cadence of the porter.

The searing heat of the day renders the tiles that cover the wide expanse of the platform leading to the temple barely traversable, and as shoes are not permitted in the sacred areas, all must cautiously pick their way across the platform surface that scorch our bare feet, to stake out positions amongst the congested assembly who have made the trip via the forest route or vehicle to worship. Some pray and make offerings to the other devotional sites that are strewn across the platform. Depending on the deity, the pilgrims may be seeking good health, luck in love, good fortune and probably of immediate importance; a safe journey on the perilous journey down the mountain. Others make their way to the golden rock itself where only men are allowed to touch the structure and add more gold leaf. As is the case for most of the Burmese holy sites the quest for spirituality is interspersed with a convivial sense of community.

As the evening falls, many settle into their chosen spaces. Even in the depth of night the rock smoulders, tendering a soft pacifying luminosity that envelops the large platform adjacent to the stupa littered with pilgrims, some in prayer, while others rest. There is a low underlying hum that persists throughout the nocturnal hours which only intensifies as morning approaches. As the early sun breaks across the valley intensifying in brilliance, the reflective light causes shifts in the golden boulder's contours. Oftentimes one can discern among these the attributes of an old man's face, the likeness as described by the shrine's legend.

Questions and Answers

1. What compelled you to set out on your pilgrimage?
For over two decades now I have been following the stories, the oral chronicles of Burma. From the first time that I stepped on Burmese soil I found myself mesmerized by this magical country. It was in the early 1990's at a time when Burma had little interface with the outside world. However, for those very few who succeeded in venturing to Burma, they were rewarded with a matchless experience, a breadth of spellbinding beauty. It was an encounter with an ancient country that had in many aspects been suspended in time, a complex tapestry of centuries interwoven with spirituality, history and cultural tradition.

Already, on descent towards the Yangon airport one could sense that Burma was somehow different from other places. The sky seen through the plane window was infused with a faint ruddy residue, causing the landscape below to appear as though through a filter, the coloring similar to that of an early sepia print.

One of the few existing vehicles at this time had been designated for our arrival, and soon we were cautiously navigating the uneven stone-strewn dirt pathways that served as the road towards the city center, adding to the sepia cloud as the vehicle's tires spun across the pounded red clay. By this time, the sun had begun to set and the arrival of evening heralded a relative cool, causing a hazy silver shimmer that hovered just above land level. This ethereal sheen served to further enhance the overall dreamlike character of the scenery providing a sense of otherworldly dimension. I would soon learn that throughout Burma one often encounters landscapes of considerable spectral context. Within these inspirational parameters, it becomes easily apparent just how Burma's fantastical trove of legends and other parables may have generated and flourished throughout the centuries.

My first journey to Burma only touched the outer layers of this mystical country, stirring an even greater curiosity to further uncover the mysteries of this unique land. Now, more than two decades later, my fascination remains undiminished. I have traveled to Burma on many occasions, visiting its most remote regions, often reaching these via river, foot, on the back of motorcycles and at times horse or oxen cart. Although today numerous roads have been newly completed or are under construction, until very recently these were not options. Primarily it has been Burma's labyrinth of rivers which has served as the core of the country's natural logistical system. These have enabled accessibility as well as provided means of separation amongst Burma's multitude of ethnic regions. Without easy access, many tribal groups have lived in relative seclusion, maintaining their beliefs, mores, and rituals just as they have for centuries. Spending time in a number of these areas, I have had the chance to witness countless traditional ceremonies unique to the widely varying communities, and perhaps even more importantly listen to their tales.

It is oftentimes through the country's legends and fables that one can best understand Burma as it came to be. These mostly verbal accounts serve to intertwine the country's religion, history, feats of nature and superstition in a manner that its written history never could. These stories have been passed from generation to generation, functioning throughout the ages as cause and effect guides to understanding the penchants of the natural world as well as contemplate the potentially numerous realms beyond this. The narratives range from those of the highest calling, seeking to instill a way of life, a moral code and pathway, to those of more common considerations, providing recipes for daily activities and concerns.

2. Is there a book, song, poem, or movie that inspired your quest?
My quest in chronicling Burma's oral histories was inspired by the beauty of the place and the people themselves. Within each landscape and tribal community one could discover a uniqueness, retained in many aspects due to isolation and historical circumstance. Now as modernization is creeping into even the more remote regions of the country, many of the country's tribal customs and traditions are rapidly disappearing. I wished to record as many of the stories that are distinct to each region and ethnic background before these too dissolve. In this case, a pilgrimage to Golden Rock, the chronicles that served to inspire me were the *Legend of Kyaiktiyo Pagoda, The Dragon, The Alchemist and the Eggs in the Forest,* and the tragic love story of King Teikthadharma Thiriraza and Nan Kyar Hae.

3. Where is your sacred place and why did you choose it?
Kyaiktiyo hill upon which the Golden Rock temple, also referred to as Kyaiktiyo pagoda, balances, is located in Burma's Mon State along the northern portion of the Tenasserim coast. The temple itself is situated at an elevation of approximately 1,100 m above sea level, resting along the Paung-Laung Ridge of the Eastern Yoma Mountains. It lies at a distance of 210 kilometres from Yangon and 140 kilometers north of Mawlamvine which is the capital of Mon State. I chose this spot as part of a series of stories which led me to there, this among Burma's most sacred places.

The surrounding regions and the rock itself, emphasizing our connections with the natural world, are crucial to the journey and the experience. As the Burmese cityscape and rural communities continue to rapidly evolve, among the most difficult of transitions for many is how to balance a profound reverence for nature together with the promises generated by economic prosperity, tempered by the resolutely ingrained fears of reprisal for interfering with nature's course. The Burmese maintain close ties to the planet itself as well as a multitude of beings that they believe co-inhabit the earth, inspired by both religious as well as animist sources. Many Burmese believe that any infringement against nature's way without proper permission, protocol and reparation could lead to significant retaliation. Buddha's doctrines emphasize the importance of remaining in harmony in nature, while other spirits are believed to inhabit, oversee and protect every aspect of the natural world. These philosophies and beliefs are integral to the pilgrimage experience to the temple and its gravity defying, natural setting.

4. How did your pilgrimage change your life or not?
For me this pilgrimage started more than two decades ago and continues through today changing my life on a regular basis. While these days the trip from the airport towards Yangon along hard topped roadways, and flyways plagued with traffic jams, represents a commute that is very different from my experiences in earlier times and might cause one to surmise the Burmese natural world and its spirit beings are not happy with the changes underway. Now there are literally millions of foreigners streaming towards Burma. Numerous taxis, and buses alongside a plethora of other forms of motorized vehicles crowd outside Yangon's modernized air-terminal, lined with aircraft from around the world. Even so, despite the country's newly acquired veneer, the Burma I first encountered can still be found, lingering beneath this shiny newness, entwined amidst its many tales.

5. What is the most important piece of advice that you have received in your life? Do you have advice to share from your experiences?
Do not seek to eschew the challenges that you encounter. These often open the doors to the greatest splendors and discoveries on offer, ones that will remain out of reach for those who do not embrace all that life brings.

Photograph courtesy of Lorie Karnath.

Biography

Lorie Karnath is an explorer, author, artist and educator. She is the Jason-Learning Explorer-at-Large, a science learning curriculum built around real-world phenomenon and practicing scientists. She is the managing editor of the *Molecular Frontiers Journal*, a global open-source science publication. She is also a founding member of the Molecular Frontiers Foundation, an organization dedicated to helping foster the promise of science. She served as the former president of the Explorers Club and is a fellow of this organization as well as the Royal Canadian Geographical Society and the Royal Geographical Society. She was a founding member of the RGS Hong Kong.

She has travelled to many of the planet's most elusive regions. For more than two decades she has been active in Burma, helping to bring medical and educational supplies to remote villages, most of these only accessible by river. She has spent time among many of the different tribal communities in Burma observing rituals and traditions unlikely to have been previously observed by Western eyes, or even anyone outside of these communities, as this country has been until recently restricted and closed off to outsiders. Lorie has written numerous articles and has lectured extensively on Burma observing the changes as the country unfolds and gains greater access to the outside world. She has studied Burma's turbulent history and wrote the book *Architecture in Burma; Moments in Time*, that considers the country's history through its architecture, published by Hatje Cantz. She also collaborated with the author Jan-Philipp Sendker on a book that chronicles Burma's tribal oral histories, in the form of fables and legends, by Blessing-Random House. http://explorersmuseum.org

Photograph by Brandon Wilson.

"That which we are, we are;
One equal temper of heroic hearts,
Made weak by time and fate, but strong in will
To strive, to seek, to find, and not to yield."
~Alfred Tennyson

Kumari. *Photograph courtesy of Tor Torkildson.*

Tor Torkildson

Every day is a journey, and the journey itself is home.
~Matsuo Basho

From Here to Timbuktu:
Becoming a Traveler

*I*t is a clear spring day and I feel cloud ridden. I have just graduated from the University of Minnesota with a degree in Asian Studies and have no plan, job, or quest to pursue. I drift down to my grandfather's saloon by the Mississippi River to have a beer and muse on my dilemma. My rotund grandfather stands behind the long wooden bar like a tank about to hit the battlefield. There are a few regulars scattered about and the room is thick with cigarette smoke. He looks surprised to see me.

"Uffda. What brings you down here this time of day, lose your job or something?" My grandfather has no idea that I have been attending university for the last four years and must think that I am working in a factory or something.

"No, I finished up my degree today and thought I'd have a few cold beers and decide what to do next."

"What to do next, what the hell does that mean? Jeepers mahn! Work, what else is there?"

I am comfortable with his gruffness and smile back. He walks to the end of the bar, reaches into the cooler, and slides a cold beer my way. The shift at the local moccasin factory has just ended and his regulars begin to pour in. Everyone likes my grandfather, everyone. He could care less.

The next day I stop by to talk to my friend Pierre Delattre, a visiting professor in the English department, hoping to receive advice. Pierre is a well-traveled hipster and had played a key role in the Beat era out in San Francisco with Jack Kerouac and Neal Cassidy. Fueled by my passion for the Beats, I had crashed his graduate level class and he had befriended me on the spot. If anyone knows what I should do with my life, I am sure it is Pierre.

"Robi Dass, good to see you, come on in and pull up a chair." Minutes after meeting me, Pierre had dubbed me Robi Dass, after Ram Dass I assumed.

Pierre wears a black beret, has long blond hair, and dancing aqua-marine colored eyes. When he grows excited, he seems to speak with multiple accents and waives his arms around like a Sicilian. I share my situation with him as honestly as possible.

"Frankly, I am lost and have no idea what to do with my life."

My university years had been one long bacchanalian party. I read a lot of books. Pierre remains silent for what seems like an eternity. Suddenly, he jumps up and does a little jig dance and says:

"Go to Timbuktu, Istanbul, Kathmandu, find the Living Goddess Kumari. Live man, live! Go see Ken at University Travel, get an around-the-world ticket, and set out Robi Dass. Go!"

I leave Pierre's office stunned and with a quest. Yes, I will go to Timbuktu and find the Living Goddess Kumari. First, I need to find out where Timbuktu is, and then I will purchase my ticket and fly away. My first stop is Dinkytown and the Biermaiers Bookstore, to snork around for used books to research my journey. For a week, I pore over a stack of travelogues and world atlases. I have found my calling and the excitement builds.

Ken sits behind his desk like a well-ornamented Pasha. He is Indian and has flowing black hair, a sing-song voice, wild eyes, and his fingers are adorned with gold rings with gem insets. He sparkles and projects electric energy my way.

"So, tell me, young man, where would you like to travel?" I take a deep breath.

"Timbuktu, Istanbul, Kathmandu." Ken leans back in his large leather chair and smiles.

"The old hippy route. It has been some time since I heard the name of those magical cities. Back in the late 60's everyone came in here asking to travel the Trail of Discovery. May I ask why you have chosen this route?"

"I want to live life and I need to find the Living Goddess Kumari?" I naively answer.

"Did you say Kumari?" Ken's eyes moisten and seem to glow; I wonder if he is in some sort of trance.

While Ken pounds away at this keyboard, looking for my tickets, my mind drifts to the journey and what I had read about Timbuktu.

The city was once the greatest center of learning, a salt caravan destination, a place steeped in mythical history and a never-never land. One day I heard a guy in my grandfather's saloon say:

"He's gone to Timbuktu, one step ahead of the law." Which brought the reply from another bar fly:

"He left his family in debt and disappeared." It all seemed like an antipodean mirage to me.

I leave Ken's with a one year, round-the-world open ticket, costing one thousand dollars. I sing Bob Seger's song, *Katmandu*, and dance my way down to my grandfather's saloon. I am ready for the pupil dilating experience ahead. I think about Pierre's advice to me concerning my writing:

"Always use the five senses, zoom in and out of the quest, like a camera lens. Describe your surroundings in detail, use dialogue, and keep coming back to the theme, the quest." I plan to write a book about my journey and

Kumari, so I had listened intently.

My grandfather is asleep in a back booth with a Louis L'Amour western in his lap. I order a double Windsor and spend an hour looking at myself in the large mirror across the bar from me. I wonder who I really am. I can see the long, wavy brown hair, blue-green eyes, gap teeth, but what is inside? I have spent twenty-two years avoiding this side of myself. The whiskey warms my chest and introspective thoughts flow at random across my brain.

"I told you to never drink whiskey kid." My grandfather is in my face and looks angry.

"I won't make a habit of it, like you, just celebrating my upcoming trip." He doesn't seem happy with my answer.

"Where you going?" He pours me another Windsor.

"Timbuktu, Istanbul, Kathmandu." I have never seen my grandfather's face turn so red.

"Jesus Christ mahn, don't you have any friends here?"

I say goodbye, grab my worn copy of, *On the Road*, and set out.

"The only people for me are the mad ones, the ones who are mad to live, mad to talk, mad to be saved, desirous of everything at the same time, the ones who never yawn or say a commonplace thing, but burn, burn, burn like fabulous yellow roman candles exploding like spiders across the stars and in the middle you see the blue centerlight pop and everybody goes 'Awww!'"

Timbuktu

When I board the plane to Paris I have the distinct feeling that I will never be going back. I am now officially a Traveler. My first stop is the Latin Quarter to meet George Whitman at the Shakespeare and Company bookstore.

"Be not inhospitable to strangers, lest they be angels in disguise" by W.B. Yeats, greets me as I walk into the bohemian English bookstore.

Later that night, I watch George cutting his hair with a candle and instantly grow fond of his unique character. Like my grandfather, he can be gruff, but there is an angel inside, and a warm heart. I spend several weeks sleeping amongst the books, writing poetry, stacking books, sweeping up, wandering Paris, enjoying the scene, and eating George's spaghetti dinners washed down with cheap red wine. I read: A *Moveable Feast, Tropic of Cancer, The Adventures and Misadventures of Maqrol, Dan Yak,* and the poetry of Baudelaire and Gregory Corso. When I tell George, I am leaving for Timbuktu, he hands me a thick book about the fabled city, and asks me to return with a head full of stories to share with the gang at the Tumbleweed Hotel, as he liked to call the store.

I briefly stop in Morocco to meet the writer Paul Bowles. I had been deeply moved by his book, *The Sheltering Sky,* and the haunting words written by Bowles:

"How many more times will you remember a certain afternoon of your childhood, some afternoon that's so deeply a part of your being that you can't even conceive of your life without it? Perhaps four or five times more. Perhaps not even that. How many more times will you watch the full moon rise? Perhaps twenty. And yet it all seems limitless."

I find Mr. Bowles an 'old world' gentleman, frail, with a head full of white hair, polished skin, and sharply dressed.

In his sparse apartment, there are no chairs and we sit on large Moroccan pillows. His eyes are blue and watery and strike me as world-weary. We sip mint tea and I watch him fiddle with his cigarette holder. I half expect him to pull out a pinch of kif. I ask him about William Burroughs and Allen Ginsberg. He answers all my questions slowly and intelligently. He harbors a wide breadth of knowledge and insight. In his presence I feel the sublime revealed. When I tell him that I am on a quest to reach Timbuktu, his eyes light up, and he shares the details of a trip that he took out into the desert to record the music of indigenous tribes. His eyes seem to drift far away as the story deepens.

On the plane to Bamako, Mali, I read about Timbuktu's fabled history:

Timbuktu was a center of Islamic scholarship under various African empires, home to a 25,000-student university and other madrasahs that served as wellsprings for the expansion of Islam throughout Africa from the 13th to 16th centuries. Sacred Muslim texts, in bound editions, traveled great distances to Timbuktu for the use of eminent scholars from Cairo, Baghdad, Persia, and elsewhere who were in residence in the city. The great teachings of Islam, from astronomy and mathematics to medicine and law, were collected and produced here in several hundred thousand manuscripts. Many of them remain, though in precarious condition, to form a priceless written record of African history. Timbuktu sits near the Niger River, where North Africa's savannas disappear into the sands of the Sahara, and part of its romantic image is being a camel caravan trade route. Timbuktu has become a metaphor for the exotic and unreachable.

I land in the sprawling city of Bamako, which stretches away from the Niger River, out to the great void of the Sahara. I am a white dot in a sea of blackness. My senses nearly explode with the smell and sounds of Africa. Vintage scooters weave in and out like schools of fish, amidst donkeys pulling carts piled high with fruit and rubbish; paper fires and plastic shelters line the road. African women in glorious fruit-bowl colored boubous, balance trays of fresh Nile perch on their heads, young boys roll bicycle rims, groups of men sit under trees smoking and watching the world go by, and I have never felt so alive. Children yell when they see me:

"Hey touba!" Slang for white person.

I catch a mini-bus to Se'gou and so begins my school of hard knocks in becoming a traveler. The Malian music is comforting to me when my world seems to be unraveling. I learn to look the hawkers in the eye and say no. I watch everything and try to use all my senses to capture the journey. I am traveling alone, but I never feel lonely. I feel I am on the cusp of something profound and brilliant.

The wide-open savannah on the way to Djenne surprises me with its massive baobab trees, which are often used as coffins, and can live longer than a thousand years. I see my first banco mosque constructed from mud, chaff, and water. The nights are coal black and cool. I seek counsel in the stars. From Mopti, I catch a ride on a canoe-like pinasse for a 3-day float down the murky brown Niger River. I watch for hippos. Fisherman pole their pirogues through thick hippo grass thickets as if stuck in time. We feast on perch and plantains. Bozo are the people of the river.

"If there is magic on this planet," wrote anthropologist Loren Eisely, "it is contained in water." Soon I will be leaving the river behind and venturing into the bent heat of the Sahel. My mind drifts to Major Gordon Laing and his epic journey to Timbuktu.

Major Laing was the first European explorer to reach the fabled city. It was a staggering feat, and the ultimate prize for adventurers in the early nineteenth century was to find the 'lost city' and the source of the Niger. The city was said to be built of gold and precious jewels. We will never know the full horror of what Laing experienced on his trek across the Sahara from Tripoli. His private journal was lost. Several letters speak of a hunger plagued, thirst-ridden, violent journey across the brain-boiling desert. In a brutal attack by Tuaregs in the wasteland of Wadi Ahnet he was abandoned and left to die. Laing suffered twenty-four injuries in the attack; eighteen were severe. Somehow, the tough Scot carried on and entered the walls of Timbuktu on, 13 August 1826. It took him three hundred and ninety-nine days to get there. Laing left the city thirty-five days later and was attacked again, this time having his head cut off. The story makes me paranoid, and I have to take several deep breaths to stay calm. I push myself to my limits of what I can withstand without going mad.

When I enter the mud brick walls of Timbuktu, I shed a layer of my former self, and embrace the armor of a real traveler. I have cut my teeth and arrived. There will be no looking back now, only the journey in the moment, the vast horizons ahead.

A caravan of camels laden with massive white salt slabs moves across the scene. Children run wild in rags and barefoot. A huge black man wanders past with milky eyes and a flowing white boubou. It is a city made of mud bricks and is slowly being buried by the Saharan sands. I check into Hotel Bouctou, after fighting my way through a throng of guides, artisans, and aggressive hustlers who seem ready to pounce on me. I collapse for fourteen hours. When I wake I feel disoriented, not by my surroundings, rather in the wisdom that I will never return home the same person that I was when I left. I may never see my grandfather or Pierre again. I will make new friends and find new families. Where there is wisdom to be found I will travel there.

I have been told the views from the roof of the Grand Marche are excellent and that it is a good place to pick up supplies and have a meal. I try to imagine the market during Leo Africanus's visit in 1526.

In his book *The History and Description of Africa and the Notable Thing Therein* he describes markets overflowing with goods from around the world and an overabundance of gold. Unfortunately, the great caravans have mostly disappeared, and have been replaced by motorized vehicles. The infinite vastness before me gives way to a clarity of thought. Looking out from the roof there is just the sand and horizon.

"Would you like to see the ancient books, Mister?" A teenage boy whispers.

"I certainly would; it is one of the reasons I have traveled so far." Like the greatest traveler of the medieval world, Ibn Battuta, I yearn to gaze upon the treasures of wisdom rumored to be hidden in the city. A Sudanese proverb says: "Salt comes from the north, gold from the south, and silver from the country of the white man, but the word of God and true wisdom are only found in Timbuctoo." Ibn Battuta left his home in Morocco as a young man, traveled 75,000 miles, to forty countries, and returned home twenty-four years later. I wonder when I will return home, if ever. In Ibn Battuta's words:

"Traveling—it leaves you speechless, then turns you into a storyteller."

The young boy takes my hand and leads me down a narrow alleyway. We duck into a house smelling of incense and mint tea. Payment is negotiated.

When Ibn Battuta arrived in Timbuktu in 1353, it was a major center of Islamic learning in black Africa. The city drew many Muslim scholars and became a center of book making.

Scholars came from around the world to study mathematics, science, astrology, jurisprudence, Arabic, and the Koran. It was a golden age of scholarship and the love of wisdom.

"Salaam Aleikum," comes a voice from the shadows. An old man in traditional robes motions for me to follow him into another room. I feel like the German explorer, Heinrich Barth, discovering the historic library of Timbuktu in 1853. Ancient manuscripts and books are passed before me. Despite not having the knowledge to understand the true importance of what I am experiencing, a chill runs up my arm, and my heart beats wildly.

Had Ibn Battuta held these very books in his hands? Before leaving the city, I visit the three sacred mosques and vow to return one day, via the northern salt caravan route. (Years later, I would leave by camel caravan from southern Morocco bound for Timbuktu. Eleven days into the journey, I suffered extreme burns on my legs and had to retreat for medical attention.)

Like the French explorer, Rene Caille, the first person to reach Timbuktu and return alive, I plan my departure. There will be no beheading. When Rene returned to France in 1828, he was awarded a 10,000-franc prize for his accomplishment by the Société de Geographies. I admire the simple way that Rene Caille traveled, how he took the time to learn the local customs and language, that he traveled like a common Muslim.

Istanbul

I set my sights on Istanbul.

The night train from Athens to Istanbul travels slowly across the dark landscape. I sip from my bottle of ouzo and reflect on the journey ahead. Suddenly, a wild looking Asian man enters my compartment with a huge grin and no front teeth. I offer him a swig from my bottle.

"Arigato." He is Japanese, and I ask him how he is in his own language.

"Ogenki desuka?"

"French bread very hard. Ahh ha! ha!" He points to his mouth.

"Robbed in Paris. Still got visa ahh ha! ha!" He takes another swig of ouzo. I take in his long leather coat with a sheep-skin liner and bed roll slung over his shoulder. I flash back to my favorite television show as a teenager, *Kung Fu*.

"Where are you going?" I ask.

"Awound the world. I was an architect all my life in Japan, never go nowhere, never see great buildings. I tell my wife I am old man, give her half the money, and go traveling so see." He curls up and goes to sleep.

I spend the night reading, *Zorba the Greek*, by Nikos Kazant Zakis. I muse on Zorba's words:

"I'm a man, and is man not stupid, so I married. Wife, children, house, everything. The full catastrophe."

Several days later, in Istanbul, I am visiting the Hagia Sophia Mosque and I run into the Japanese traveler again. He is wrapped in his coat and sleeping in the park next to the mosque. He is a modern-day Basho.

I am amazed that this elderly man is traveling rough and living his dream. Not wanting to interrupt his rest I let him be and carry on with my walkabout. Two years later, I will receive postcards from Cairo and Kathmandu sent by the Japanese traveler. They both say, "Very happy. Arigato."

The Pudding Shop sits in the Sultanahmet neighborhood close to the Blue Mosque and Hagia Sophia. It was popular in the 60's as a meeting place for the Beatniks and hippies traveling overland between Europe and Asia on the "hippie trail" that my travel agent Ken had mentioned. It was also popular because of the large selection of puddings and for being in the film, *Midnight Express*.

Their specialty is tavak gogsu, a rare pudding made from pounded chicken breast, rice flour, milk, and sugar topped with cinnamon. I am determined to try it and dig this cult-like establishment. Inside there is a long counter with many dishes on display, a myriad of colors, and heady aromas. I choose eggplant stuffed with dolmas and fish, lamb kababs, caramelized onion, and bell pepper filled borak, rice and chick peas, and the mouth-watering honey baklava. There are several notice boards spread around the restaurant for travelers to share information from the road. I am excited to cross the Bosporus River, where I will transition from Europe into Asia.

At night, I head to the Galata Bridge that spans the Golden Horn for a beer and fried fish. Old men and small boys fish from the bridge that shakes from the traffic above and smells of coal fires. A group of Turkish men gather around me asking questions. They seem happy when I tell them I am American, and argue with each other over who will buy my next round of Mamara beer. In fact, their enthusiasm for my beer drinking leaves me staggering drunk back to my traveler's hostel on a side street behind the Blue Mosque.

At 3:38 a.m. I am awakened by the call to prayer. A strange feeling deep inside me stirs, something ancient, and otherworldly. Known as ezan, I listen carefully to the bellowing of the muezzin:

Allahu Ekber	*God is Great*
Eşhedû en lâ ilâhe	*There is no god but*
illallah	*God*
Eşhedû enne	*Muhammed is the*
Muhammeden	*Prophet of God*
resulullah	*Come to prayer*
Hayya ale-salah	*Come to salvation*
Hayya alel-felah	*God is Great*
Allahu Ekber	*There is no god but*
Lâ ilahe illallah	*God*

I fall back asleep and dream of Ibn Battuta. At 5:42 a.m. the muezzin resumes, as it will six times a day. For a long time I lie in bed imagining the long history of this grand city, which has always bridged the gap between East and West. I dream of Alexander the Great passing through the city on his way to Asia, Marco Polo, and the Viking Varangian soldiers who waged battles here. There was the Byzantine era when the city was called Constantinople, the Muslim conquest in 1453, the beginning of the Ottoman Empire, the war between Turkey and Greece, and the forming of the Republic in 1923. Before leaving, I visit the Grand Bazaar, the largest covered market in the world. I pay homage to Rumi in Konya.

"When you are everywhere, you are nowhere. When you are somewhere, you are everywhere."

Kathmandu

"Timbuktu, Istanbul, Kathmandu...find the Living Goddess Kumari," settles in my brain like a melody. I am over halfway there. On the way, I take a train from Karachi to the Indus River with a local family of redheads who have green eyes, visit the ghats in Varanasi to ponder reincarnation as bodies burn, meditate in a Zen garden in Kyoto, visit with Vietnamese poets, sit under the Bodhi tree in Bodhgaya, ride a rickshaw over the Hooghly River in Calcutta, sip fine teas in Darjeeling, visit remote monasteries in Ladakh, before arriving by long-distance bus in Kathmandu. I check into the Kathmandu Guest House and head to KC's for a bite to eat. I order a steak sizzler and a piece of their otherworldly apple pie. I meet a Kiwi named Andy. He is a little pudgy guy and likes his weed.

"Hey, I am heading out tomorrow to hike the Annapurna circuit, want to join me, I have everything arranged and it will be a cheap adventure." He asks.

"Mountains, cheap, adventure, I'm in brother." Came my quick reply.

"Great, we need to get down to Durbar Square and meet my Sherpa Kalam, he is waiting for me."

Durbar Square is like walking into a Medieval movie set. Next to a great stupa I see a beat-up double-decker bus parked. There is a long-haired guy looking into the engine compartment. I walk up to him and ask where he came from.

"Drove this beast down from London mate." I spend some time chatting with the man about his adventures crossing Iran and Afghanistan. Andy approaches with a chubby and round-faced Kalam.

"Everything is set Tor, we will bus up to Pokhara, and from there set out on the Annapurna circuit with Kalam, two porters, and a cook. We leave in the morning." Kalam doesn't fit my idea of what a Sherpa should look like, but I keep my thoughts to myself, and delight in the idea of going into the high Himalaya.

On the way back to the hotel, I swing into a used bookstore and pick up a copy of Peter Matthiessen's, *The Snow Leopard*, and spend the night mesmerized by the book and the adventure that it portrays.

Sections of the book stir my soul.

The sun is roaring, it fills to bursting each crystal of snow. I flush with feeling, moved beyond my comprehension, and once again, the warm tears freeze upon my face. These rocks and mountains, all this matter, the snow itself, the air—the earth is ringing. All is moving, full of power, full of light.

It is the eighth day of our trek and I am wiped out, mind, body, and soul. Thorung La Pass looms above us at 5,461m. Andy and Kalam, both overweight little guys, seem to be in fine shape; this annoys me and drives me onward. My feet are covered in blisters and bleeding. My head aches. I find refuge in the surrounding mountain landscape, village life, and *The Snow Leopard*. We live on dahl bat and salted butter tea.

As we slowly work our way up the pass, it begins to snow lightly, a flurry at first. I question our sanity in going on, yet remain silent. This is the highest I have ever been. "We must keep going, no stopping, dangerous." Kalam finally speaks. We are now in a full-on blizzard and I have gone into survival mode. It is a life or death situation. In our world of whiteness, time stops and the raging winds seem to blow us forward. Seven days later we stumble into Kali Gandaki Gorge. I have two black toes and feel like I have survived a war zone. In some unexplainable way, the experience has made me older, maybe wiser, certainly thankful for every minute of life. The blizzard has rattled my worldview for good. I shall never forget the Annapurna Massif, Dhaulagiri, and Machhapuchhre 'Fishtale' mountains.

I spend a week recovering at the Kathmandu Guest House. Slowly I begin to wander the ancient streets and squares of Kathmandu. I engage merchants and Sadhus alike. Mandalas mesmerize me for hours at a time. Tibetan momos, pies, banana shakes, and sweets sustain me. I let myself go in the kaleidoscope of the city and drift about like a lost leaf, careless and lighthearted, no goal in mind.

"Timbuktu, Istanbul, Kathmandu," no longer rings like a church bell in my head.

One day while strolling across Durbar Square on my way to Freak Street, a dwarf calls me over.

"Psss...psss. I have something to show you Baba." Strangely enough, I follow the dwarf through a low doorway into a small courtyard. In the middle of the yard is a stone lingam. The wooden building surrounding me is ornately carved, with shutters above, and enclaves for holy men on my street level.

"Put an offering on the stone Baba."

I hear a pair of shutters open. Above me, a young girl is dressed in resplendent red and gold, bedecked in a golden tiara and sesh naag around her neck. She looks down at me. On her forehead, there is a third eye painted in vermilion on a backdrop of mustard oil and soot. I feel her 'divine eye' looking into my soul. The shutters are quickly closed and I am left with a sense of awe.

What just happened, who was that? I ask the dwarf.

"She is the Living Goddess Kumari. I felt you should meet her. Kumari is the manifestation of the divine female energy. The power of Kumari is so strong that even a glimpse of her is believed to bring good fortune."

I left Kathmandu knowing that I would return one day to unravel the mysteries of the little girl they call Kumari. But that would have to wait. I was young and yearning to see everything, go everywhere, feel and smell it all, talk to gurus and monks, revel in the great works of art, live in temples, bushwhack through jungles, ride camels across deserts, climb peaks, and travel within myself until I had exhausted my well of curiosity. I had become a Traveler.

It has been a strange and long journey.

Questions and Answers

1. What compelled you to set out on your pilgrimage?

My entire life I have had an untethered curiosity and a deep yearning for knowledge. As a boy, I used to look out over Lake Superior and drift away emotionally across the lake's infinite horizon. Ships would pass by and disappear to imaginary and exotic locations. I wanted to be like one of those ships or at least sailing on one. That, and the fact that I read thousands of books which transported me around the world metaphysically, and encouraged me to live life to the fullest.

2. Is there a book, song, poem, or movie that inspired your quest?

When I was thirteen, I read Jack Kerouac's, *On the Road*, and it had a profound influence on me. I read the book in one night and took off hitchhiking the very next day. Before long I found myself in Mexico. My family thought I was running away, when actually, I was running toward adventure like some Huck Finn character. Through my high school years, I did a lot of hitchhiking and riding the rails, back and forth across America, trying hard to emulate the Beats and the free-spirited hippies. Life on the road was a wonderful adventure and prepared me for a life as a traveler. Reading, *A Moveable Feast*, by Hemingway steered me toward Paris early on and once I made my way through, *The Adventures and Misadventures of Maqrol* by Alvaro Mutis, I became obsessed with seeing the world. I was also deeply influenced by the book, *This is It*, by Alan Watts, which in-turn led me to the Taoist and Buddhist monks like Li Po and Ikkyu "Crazy Cloud." Creedence Clear Water Revival rocked my world musically. Seeing the film, *Zorba the Greek*, instilled in me the feeling that life could be a song and dance; it made me want to live life to the fullest. So you see, I really wanted to be a mix of Jack Kerouac, Ikkyu, Hemingway, and Zorba the Greek. In many ways, I suppose I am a Sailor-Poet-Mountain Monk.

3. Where is your sacred place and why did you choose it?

The first time I went to Japan I intuitively knew that I had been there before. This all seemed a bit strange to me. I certainly do not look Japanese, grew up in a very un-Japanese environment, yet I had just spent four years studying Japanese history and language at university. The defining moment came, just after completing a shugyo retreat in the mountains with the Yamabushi monks, when I visited Enryaku-ji monastery on Mount Hiei near Kyoto. My intent was to introduce myself to the Marathon Monks. When I entered the inner chambers of the temple, I felt as if I were walking through a portal and into another realm. Monks chanted deeply, the air was saturated with incense, cymbals and bells rang out, and suddenly I had the very distinct emotion that I had been a practicing monk there in another life. Chills ran up my spine, and I felt a great confusion in my spirit.

4. How did your pilgrimage change your life or not?
In a sense, I became a homeless person, a traveler, and one destined to live a wandering existence.

5. What is the most important piece of advice that you have received in your life? Do you have advice to share from your experiences?
Swirl with the swirl and whirl with the whirl and no bones shall break. My advice to others is to, Keep on keeping on.

"If curiosity is your religion, and high adventure your cup of tea, this book is guaranteed to spin your prayer wheel and satiate your thirst." Pat Morrow.
Photograph by Siffy Torkildson.

Biography

Peripatetic traveler, Rob 'Tor' Torkildson, is a lifelong seeker and explorer who has worked and lived around the world for the last 30 years. Torkildson has tramped through the Amazon, over the Himalaya, and across the Sahara in his quest to experience sacred landscapes in over 120 countries. He has worked as a diver, commercial fisherman, ship navigator, customs and immigration expert, writer and publisher, a fixer in Africa, and as a vintner and owner of The Wild Hare Winery in San't Alfio, Sicily. Torkildson has published three travel memoirs, a novella, and in such magazines as the *Kyoto Journal, Beat Scene, Ripcord Adventure Journal, Canadian Mountain Journal*, and has won a Solas Award–Gold Medal from *Travelers' Tales*. Torkildson has degrees in Asian History and Psychology. He is a international fellow of the Explorers Club.

Sacredworldexplorations.com, and Sacredworld Explorations on Facebook.

Solar eclipse viewing, Reims, France. *Photograph by Siffy Torkildson.*

Siffy Torkildson

...At once this disk of sky slid over the sun like a lid. The sky snapped over the sun like a lens cover. The hatch in the brain slammed. Abruptly it was dark night, on the land and in the sky. In the night sky was a tiny ring of light. The hole where the sun belongs is very small. A thin ring of light marked its place. There was no sound. The eyes dried, the arteries drained, the lungs hushed. There was no world. We were the world's dead people rotating and orbiting around and around, embedded in the planet's crust, while the Earth rolled down. Our minds were light-years distant, forgetful of almost everything. Only an extraordinary act of will could recall to us our former, living selves and our contexts in matter and time. We had, it seems, loved the planet and loved our lives, but could no longer remember the way of them. We got the light wrong. In the sky was something that should not be there. In the black sky was a ring of light. It was a thin ring, an old, thin silver wedding band, an old, worn ring. It was an old wedding band in the sky, or a morsel of bone. There were stars. It was all over.
~Ann Dillard

Eclipse Pilgrimages

A lone bald eagle soars above me in the crisp, clear sky. The brilliant, snow-capped Kachemak Bay Mountains rise across the bay. I am in Alaska, standing on the Homer Spit, a natural feature that reminds me of a human-made jetty. The ice crunches and grinds against the boats and docks in the port; it is ten degrees Fahrenheit in mid-March. I sigh in relieve as I rejoice in the splendid, sunny day and my decision to return home. I had driven down from Anchorage, my temporary residence for the past several weeks, to clear my head. I made an ecliptic decision and booked my flight home to Germany to coincide with a partial solar eclipse. I'm soaring in relief and will be soon leaving my flea-bag hotel.

From a young age, I have been enamored with the stars since looking at pictures in the *Golden Guide to the Stars*. I have religiously read *Sky and Telescope Magazine* beginning at age twelve. Every time there was an article about a solar eclipse I dreamed of seeing one. I was also fascinated by maps. *National Geographic* lit my desire to travel, and I became a geographer. Seeing an eclipse would tie these two passions together.

Unlike a lunar eclipse which is observable from the side of Earth facing it, a solar eclipse is only viewable at totality from a narrow strip of land across approximately a third of the Earth, but only up to 170 miles across. A partial solar eclipse is visible over a larger area, but to see totality, one needs to be on the center line.

When I was 26 years old, I read that the 'the big one' was coming. It would be the longest solar eclipse during the 20th century; almost seven minutes—the longest possible being 7 minutes 31 seconds. Baja would be at the heart of the eclipse path, and being in the desert, the sky would likely be cloud-free. This was my first travel adventure, a road trip from far northern California to Cabo San Lucas.

Heading south from Ensenada into desolation, I ate raw clams and lobster in tiny villages. The dormant volcanoes of San Quintin rose mythically across the bay on the Pacific side of the peninsula. The salt flats of Guerro Negro glowed in the bright Baja sun. Inland, the desert heat of July was a drastic change from the cool, foggy Humboldt County coast where I lived, and I felt as if I were in an oven. Cardon cactuses, the tallest in the world, some over 60 feet, and boulder fields, covered the scorching high desert.

The humidity hit like a tsunami as we passed to the east side of the peninsula. Swimming in the Gulf of Baja felt like a warm bath but was an escape from the heat and mosquitoes. La Paz, with the colonial buildings, a tree-lined plaza, and locals going about their business was a contrast to the quiet desert.

Instead of going to the advertised place for eclipse viewing near the tourist-crazed town of Cabo San Lucas, I headed into the mountains above the surfer village of Todo Santos on the Pacific Ocean. I had studied the maps and determined this was the spot where the eclipse would be closest to maximum. Up a curvy dirt track I found a hill with a 365-degree view above a farm. The Moon's shadow would be coming across the ocean from the west.

I brought eclipse glasses made of Mylar that protects one's eyes from the harmful radiation of the Sun's photosphere. At first contact, when the first nip in the Sun appeared, I looked on and off through my glasses as I watched the Sun slowly eaten by the Moon. It takes over an hour for the Moon to nibble away at the Sun until totality.

Tiny crescents appeared on the ground through gaps between the leaves of the desert shrubs which served as pinholes—nature's projector. The temperature dropped. Two minutes before totality, I looked at my white sheet I had set out and saw the elusive shadow bands—like ripples on the bottom of a pool. They are caused by the motion of the Earth's atmosphere, and the thin crescent of the Sun sending the last few rays of light.

"Look, there is the shadow on the ocean! It is moving so fast and heading right toward us!" I enthusiastically tell my two companions.

The dry landscape dimmed as if it were twilight. Suddenly, the Moon devoured the Sun high in the sky. Venus, Mars, Jupiter and Mercury were all visible, as well as the star Regulus in the plum heavens. Confused roosters crowed, and dogs howled at the nearby farm. A pink twilight encircled the horizon. I thought of the myths surrounding eclipses.

Some cultures saw the eclipse as a battle between the Sun and the Moon. The Chinese believed a dragon was eating the Sun; while the Scandinavians thought it was Sköll, a giant wolf; in Vietnam a toad; for the Cherokee a frog, and in Egypt a serpent. The way to bring the Sun back was to scare the creature away by banging pots and drums, shouting and screaming.

The word eclipse comes from a Greek word meaning "abandonment." The Sun was abandoning the Earth.

". . . and the Sun has perished out of heaven, and an evil mist hovers over all."

-Homer, the Odyssey

When an eclipse is total, the blinding photosphere is not visible, and you can look directly at the Sun. This is the moment that brings eclipse chasers from all over the world, sometimes just to see a few seconds of totality. By a fortuitous coincidence, the Sun is 400 times larger than the Moon, but also 400 times further away, which gives the illusion that they are the same size in the sky. If the Sun or Moon were even a little different, we would not see the chromosphere or corona (the Sun's outer layers) during a total eclipse. No other moon/planet in our solar system has these unique conditions.

As I stared at the eclipse, the Sun's corona (meaning crown in Latin) surged several diameters further than the Sun on opposite sides. The corona is constantly changing, and this eclipse had two uncommonly long streamers. The six minutes and 40 seconds flew by, and then the land became sweltering again as I watched the shadow bands and crescents appear in reverse, while the out-of-place twilight disappeared. I felt as if I was coming off of a narcotic. The only way to alleviate the withdrawal was to make a pilgrimage to another eclipse. I had become an 'eclipse chaser.'

Several years later I finally had the time and money to plan another trip— I'd missed a few total eclipses, from South America to Asia. I was on my way to France and my first overseas trip. I could see the North American landscape disappear out the airplane window in the many hours of sunlight. The view below of the glaciers, mountains, blue lakes and icebergs of Greenland lit my imagination. I thought of the adventurers that walked and sailed across these lands, such as Louise Arner Boyd who led seven scientific expeditions by sea to the region around Greenland between 1926 and 1941. She participated in the 1928 international search for Roald Amundson, and a section of Greenland is named for her, Louise Boyd Land.

The Eiffel Tower sprung from the earth as I landed in Paris. I felt like I was in a dream. Thirty years of imagining visiting Paris and France; finally I was there. I took the train to the prearranged hotel my sister had booked. She had lived and studied in Paris and had flown in a few days earlier from San Francisco. I emerged from the Metro near the luxuriant Luxembourg Gardens. A sweet, elderly Parisian man greeted me at the front desk of our historic hotel.

"Bonjour puis-je vous aider?"

"Je cherche ma soeur. Elle est arrivée plus tôt aujourd'hui."

"Bien sur! laissez-moi voir, voici la clé."

"Merci beaucoup, Monsieur!"

He pointed the way to our room. It was thrilling to speak French in Paris after all my labors to learn the language.

My sister and I leisurely wandered the city visiting sites from the Louvre and Sacré-Cœur to Jim Morrison's grave. Languorous evenings were spent sitting along the Seine listening to a saxophone, watching the boats float by, and groups of young people enjoying the ambiance. I indulged in escargot, rabbit, and Bordeaux. Thunder crashed as we were caught in a rainstorm bicycling through the colorful gardens of Versailles, but it didn't matter.

On eclipse day we took a two-hour train ride to the center line at Reims, in the Champagne region of France. The train was overflowing with people due to the eclipse, and we sat on large suitcases near the bathrooms. The bucolic countryside of green hills, farmer's fields and vineyards passed by on the dismal, gray day.

We arrived to a flurry of activity. Men had set up telescopes of all sizes in the city parks, and the streets were crowded. We glanced at the Sun through our solar glasses, awaiting the eclipse near the imposing Notre Dame Cathedral, covered in angels and gargoyles. Joan of Arc, as she had seen in her visions, liberated France from the English in Reims in 1429, and Charles VII was crowned king in the cathedral. The cathedral had been the site of French coronations for centuries. An orchestra played in front of Notre Dame, and a weather balloon struggled to get off the ground to take measurements.

Sometimes eclipses were good omens. During a war in 585 BC, between the Lydians and Medes in Turkey, Herodotus recorded there was an eclipse during the battle. The warring factions, at war for six years, took this as a sign to make peace. The Batammaliba of Togo/Benin believed that the only way to stop the Sun and Moon from 'fighting' during an eclipse was to stop battling on Earth. In Italy flowers planted during an eclipse are thought to grow better.

Totality approached, and there were patches of blue sky as the clouds moved swiftly, while the crescent Sun revealed itself through the thin clouds in my eclipse glasses. The sky darkened about ten minutes before totality, even with cloud cover. City buses in Reims were still in service, and they turned their lights on.

All of a sudden there was a break in the clouds at third contact—when the Sun starts totality. Everyone cheered. Fire red prominences and Baily's beads (named for an English astronomer from the 19th century) glowed brightly around the edge of the Moon.

"What is the red?" My sister asked.

"Each bead is a point of light from the photosphere peeking through a lunar valley. Prominences are loops of gas that shoot off of the Sun thousands of miles from the chromosphere (the upper atmosphere of the Sun)."

"Wow! This is amazing and totally unexpected!" My sister commented.

Unlike in Baja, the corona streamers were hidden in the clouds, but the spire of the Gothic church near the eclipse made up for that. I imagined I was Jean of Arc leading her people into battle against the English beneath an eclipse.

"A day without night and a night without day." The old Christian monk tells Navarre in the movie *Ladyhawke*. Navarre is turned into a wolf at night while his love is a hawk during the day and thus they can never see each other because of a curse. Of course, the monk's meaning is a total eclipse, and the movie ends with the spell broken.

It is said an eclipse marked the wizard Merlin's and Jesus's deaths, as well as Mohammed's birth. An eclipse coincided with the death of the English King Henry I in AD 1133 and led to a struggle for power that brought civil war.

In the direction of the Moon's shadow, the clouds turned pink, like sunset. The diamond ring (when the first bit of sunlight appears from behind the Moon) was visible for a couple of seconds, and then the clouds covered the Sun as totality ended two minutes later. How fortunate we were. I hadn't noticed any drop in temperature on this 60 degree Fahrenheit day, although I read later that it dropped ten degrees. We had a glass of champagne in celebration.

My next eclipse pilgrimage happened to be in Madagascar, where I was living. In the Peace Corps, I had been assigned to work with Park Masoala in the rainforest of northeast Madagascar, but the center line would be going through the desert of the southwest.

Several days later, and 800 miles to the south, I arrived in Ihosy. The bus from the capital city of Tana in the center of the country, south along the central plateau to Fianar was the longest haul. Rolling brown hills reminded me of northern California in the summer. The bus radio was broken and everyone was quiet. On the coast where I lived the people would be singing and the children playing and making noise.

We stopped for lunch and to fix the radio in Antsirabe. I reveled in the scene. Hawkers selling oranges, French stores, an ornate Catholic church, a large bookstore, a few beggars, outdoor markets, French-style government buildings, pousse pousse drivers running barefoot looking for passengers, a hat salesman wearing a stack of hats, the imposing colonial Hotel des Thermas, and signs to the thermal baths. A warm day, men chatted in the shade of a taxi-brusse garage near a stand selling chunks of goat meat, including the head and hooves. Piles of shoes, dishware, bike parts and honey were set up along the road for sale. A few scrubby trees lined the streets.

With Bob Marley blaring on the fixed radio, we traveled through denuded mountains along a river, past recently planted rice fields, and then into the mountains. The driver often swerved for no apparent reason; he'd obviously had a few drinks on lunch break. The bus arrived in Fianar around midnight, and I met my friends who would accompany me to Ihosy. They were the only married couple in my Peace Corps group, and had been teaching their villagers how to make bread, as there was no bread in their village.

The next morning we passed the wineries in the mountains; the French, who had colonized the island, had discovered grapes grow well in this area. As we headed southwest, with fake grapes dangling from the front window of the bus, the landscape became more desolate and reminded me of Wyoming. Cacti and small baobabs dotted the landscape. Corn hung like pinecones on dead trees to dry. Unlike most of Madagascar, where rice is the staple, in the south it is corn.

Ihosy was hopping with Malagasy and Europeans. Government officials had flown in and were giving speeches at the town center, followed by musicians singing about the eclipse. Like the area around Tana, manioc fields, eucalyptus, and mud houses were in abundance. The people were darker, and there was more open space and fewer trees than in the northeast. The zebu (cows) that pulled the two-person carts had larger humps on their backs than the northern zebu.

In the morning, the local Peace Corp volunteer took a group of us for a drive to visit the Bara people. The Bara are of Bantu (African) descent, semi-nomadic, tall, thin and known to be quite fierce. After bouncing all over the road, we finally reached a village, where the women wore elaborate, colorful necklaces. We had a beer and chatted with the mayor; not to check in with the mayor anywhere in Madagascar is considered rude, and it helps with relations to the people. At the school, children marched in circles outside and then gathered around us while one of the volunteers entertained them by playing a flute.

In Ihosy, I noticed the hill above my friends' campsite near town looked like a perfect place to view the eclipse. A tall cross and a few graves sat on the apex of the desolate hill. Three German women and several Malagasy shared our viewing spot. The sky was partly cloudy, and the Sun was low in the sky to the northwest for this 430 pm eclipse on June 21, the winter solstice.

Some cultures believed the Sun was being stolen during a total eclipse; the Koreans thought dogs were trying to steal the Sun. A bear took a bite out of the Sun to pick a fight for the Pomo Indians of the Northwest. The Greeks presumed the gods were angry and would bring about their wrath. The Hindu god, Rahu, was beheaded by the other gods for drinking the gods' nectar. His head flew into the sky where he swallowed the Sun. Another myth from India was that food was poisoned by an eclipse, so people fasted.

In many cultures, it was prophesized to be dangerous to be outside during an eclipse, especially for pregnant women. For the Aymara Indians, their soul could be altered forever by an eclipse. Unfortunately, some Malagasy diviners told the people to stay inside, despite the government promoting safe viewing with eclipse glasses. Even when I was in France, some media channels told people to stay inside.

"All who live under the sky are woven together like one big mat." Malagasy proverb.

We watched with our eclipse glasses as the Moon slowly took a piece out of the Sun. Finally, totality! We removed our glasses and saw the Moon was blue-tinted and the corona streamers were perfectly symmetrical. Our little group cheered.

"Wow, this is unbelievable!" My friend exclaimed.

"It looks like twilight; see the pink all around the horizon!"

For the 2.5 minutes of totality, time seemed to stand still. Venus shone brightly to the west of the Sun. Slowly the landscape became brighter, then five minutes after totality the ominous, narrow dark cloud we had been nervous about, enveloped the Sun.

"We sure were lucky!"

I heard later that the cloud covered the eclipse at the party and concert, several miles west of Ihosy, where the majority of people went.

I have missed many eclipses because life gets in the way. Historically it was often a major expedition to see an eclipse, but the world has become much smaller and quicker.

While viewing a solar eclipse, Hipparchus, in 130 BC, determined the Moon's distance to the earth and was only off by 11 percent. Liu Hsiang, of China, in 28 BC was one of the first people to understand that the Moon is covering the Sun. The Greeks discovered that the Moon, which is tilted five degrees to the plane of the Earth's orbit, has a 19-year pattern: the Saros cycle.

The element helium (Helios means Sun in Greek) was discovered by a French astronomer, Jules Janssen, in 1868 while observing a solar eclipse in India, for the first time with a spectrograph which determines elements in stars. The 1919 eclipse on the island of Principe near Africa is where Sir Arthur Eddington confirmed Einstein's theory of relativity by photographing stars near the Sun during totality and seeing how light was bent by the Sun as predicted by Einstein.

The solar eclipse visible from Medina in 632 coincided with the death of Mohammad's son. But the Prophet stated, "Eclipses are not bad omens, but are cosmic spectacles that demonstrate the might and knowledge of Allah the Great." Today Muslims have a special eclipse prayer. The Navajo also view an eclipse as part of nature's law, and reflect on the order of the universe during a solar eclipse.

Eclipses represented transformations and new beginnings in some cultures, such as the Crow Nation. As the Sun 'dies' it is reborn after the eclipse, bringing better tidings as the Sun (male) and Moon (female) mate and give birth to a new universe. Many native cultures could predict eclipses.

My next pilgrimage was to see an annular eclipse. An annular eclipse refers to the annulus, or ring, around the Moon. The Moon varies in its distance from Earth; when it is closer to Earth, it looks bigger and covers the entire Sun during a total eclipse. During an annular eclipse, the Moon is further away, and it looks smaller from Earth. This leaves a space between the Moon and the Sun's edge. Some sunlight seeps out around the ring during an annular eclipse. The size of the 'ring of fire' can range depending on the distance of the Moon. The sky does not turn completely dark as during a total eclipse, and you can't stare directly at the Sun because the photosphere is not completely covered.

Panama City initially struck me as a mix of modern and old world decay, like orchids covered in rubbish. Skyscrapers soared across the city, while threadbare laundry dried, strung across rusted balconies, and psychedelic colored buses honked their horns on the busy, hot streets. I inhaled the scent of the jungle nearby as I relished in the afternoon rain showers with bowls of bouillabaisse, grilled octopus, and rum drinks. In Panama, I could smell the intrigue of a thousand untold stories.

The Panama Canal boat tour started on the Atlantic side of the Continental Divide, and passed through the Gaillard Cut, with giant, shelf-like steps leading up from the canal. I marveled at the engineering and labor involved in cutting through the mountain divide; the canal opened in 1914 after years of construction and setbacks. The boat slowly sunk as the gates were closed behind us in each lock, then the gates opened on the other side and we continued. A Swedish transport ship passed by and it seemed unbelievable it would fit, as the locks seemed so narrow. The locks have since been expanded to accommodate the larger ships of today. Pelicans and a pod of dolphins greeted us as we reached the Pacific Ocean.

My partner and I arrived by local bus on the day of the eclipse to Penonomé, two hours southwest of Panama City, where the Panamanian Astronomy Club had set up a viewing area on the airstrip. The airfield, surrounded by a dry grassy area with mountains in the distance, was bustling with 300 people including many groups. Tour buses and rows of vehicles were parked along the airstrip. Spanish, English, German and Japanese were all being spoken—eclipses bring people of all nations together. A few 'the big one' T-shirts and hats, as well as T-shirts from the African eclipse (which I saw in Madagascar) were worn proudly by eclipse chasers. Telescopes, cameras and tripods were scattered across the airfield. Teenage girls sold T-shirts and cold drinks at the Panamanian astronomy booth.

The Sun was straight above me being so near the equator and mid-afternoon. I had brought binoculars with solar filters—this would be my first venture using optical aid for an eclipse. A slight breeze relieved the heat, as did the somewhat hazy, thin clouds, yet one was thickening up. It was too much for one group, and they loaded back on their private bus to try to find a clearer location.

This was a rare hybrid eclipse, where the Moon is almost the same size as the Sun, so it is annular on some parts of the eclipse path, but total on other regions of the path—in this case in the middle of the South Pacific.

I noticed a sunspot through my binoculars opposite of the nibble in the Sun. Near totality around 4 pm it started to cool, and a thicker cloud covered the Sun. I wasn't sure if it was the Sun or the cloud that reduced the temperature. At 515 p.m. the Sun was total! Everyone cheered. Through my filtered binoculars, I briefly saw the red Baily's beads peering through the lunar valleys. Twenty-one seconds later annularity was over; this was a short eclipse.

"It is not quite as dramatic as a solar eclipse. And the landscape did not get as dark." I tell my companion. Everyone watched for another twenty minutes as the Moon started to move back across the Sun, and the crowds dispersed.

My next eclipse, another annular, was to occur near Las Vegas, Nevada where I was living. By coincidence it happened to be during the time my boyfriend Tor (husband now) would be visiting me from Germany where he lived.

Tor and I sat on a hill at 6,300 feet while the desolate brown landscape dimmed, as if at sunset, but it wasn't sunset yet; it was still more than an hour away. The hill reminded me of Madagascar, as there was also a cross at the top of a hill, and a small group. Tor and I had walked up from the 100-year-old Overland Hotel in the heart of the tiny town of Pioche, on center line, three hours by road northeast of Las Vegas.

This historic, silver mining town was notorious in the 1860s when it boasted a population of 10,000 people with seventy saloons. The main street was the site of numerous gun fights, and the settlement became known as one of the roughest mining camps in the west. Silver was discovered when a Paiute Indian led a Mormon missionary to the ore. Later, lead and zinc were extracted. The mines have been closed since the 1970s, but many relics remain, including a rusted tram on a nearby hill.

As we hiked up the trail, an old man and several teenagers headed straight up the hill and beat us to the top. The group was from Panaca, a Mormon ranching town a few miles away near the Utah border.

"Would you like some Mylar eclipse viewing glasses?" I asked the group.

"Yes, please. Can I use them for the Venus transit coming up?" A girl asked.

"Of course." I was impressed she knew about the transit, never to be seen again in our lifetime, where Venus is between the Earth and the Sun, and looks like a black dot on the Sun through a solar filter.

I watched first contact at 521 p.m. through my solar-filter covered binoculars. While waiting for totality we enjoyed a bottle of wine with our picnic dinner. By 610 p.m. the landscape became dimmer and at 630 p.m. was second contact, when the last bit of the Moon covered the Sun, and the eclipse formed the ring of fire! The Moon slowly came from the top left and then departed on the bottom right of the Sun.

Through my binoculars the Moon spun around onto the Sun, making speckled reddish tinges along the edge—Bailey's beads—as the Moon twirled onto the Sun, and then there was a perfect ring around the Moon. Before third contact, when the Moon left the Sun to end totality, I gave the binoculars to Tor. He watched as the Moon left the Sun, and the swirling of the Moon around the Sun again, something I hadn't seen during other eclipses.

"It looks like an Enso! The Zen circle is a representation of enlightenment. It also means we are all part of something greater, as there is a break in the Enso, opening into the universe, as I see for a moment now. It is said that those who gaze upon the Enso see different things." Tor exclaimed.

We both made wishes. The annular eclipse lasted 4.5 minutes and the Moon covered 94 percent of the Sun. The path was 8500 miles long and took 3.5 hours to traverse the Earth. The Sun, with a bite still in it, set over a mountain. Just as the Sun set, we saw the ever elusive green flash!

I had hoped to see the total eclipse in Svalbard, but I took a job in Anchorage, Alaska. Tor was not having any luck getting transferred to Alaska, and I was living in a seedy motel in Anchorage. I was doubting whether I should have moved to Alaska. I gave notice at my job and found a flight home which would coincide with the eclipse in Svalbard. As one travels further from center line, an eclipse gets smaller and smaller until there is no eclipse. Although I wasn't going to Svalbard, 68 percent of the Sun would be covered in Munich.

The taxi driver picks me up at 330 a.m. at my motel in Anchorage. The Ethiopian-born driver apologizes profusely for the loud beep that won't go away in his car. I had arrived in Alaska to a high pitched whine in my room, and now I was leaving with the same thing in my taxi! Maybe the universe is telling me that I am off kilter from where I should be.

"When I worked for a mapping company I made a map of Ethiopia. Although I have not been there, I want to visit the source of the Blue Nile, drink coffee in the country it came from, and visit a Coptic church." I tell him.

His eyes light up and he expounds on religion and politics.

"Everyone thinks I am Muslim, but the majority of Ethiopians are Christian."

"The colonial legacy of Africa has made Africans selfish."

"Why do Muslim terrorists want 1000 virgins when they die? What are they going to do with that many women? One is enough trouble! Maybe it is their punishment." He giggles.

"Anchorage is diverse; everyone gets along, even the rich and the poor. One time I talked to the mayor in a bar, who was slightly tipsy. I told him the main problem for homeless people is that they don't sleep."

In Seattle, I board my plane bound for Germany. I smile as I hear German spoken around me. I think of my flight to Alaska. When I had handed my backpack to the German customs agent; he noticed my tag, "Alaska! Jesus, man!"

Indeed. Was I crazy to leave my husband behind and try to make it in Alaska alone? We have worked so hard to come together. Love is more important than money I learned.

"Have my binoculars and solar filters ready when I land. Mid-eclipse is five minutes after I land." I tell my husband on the phone.

As the plane is landing during the eclipse, I feel everything has finally come together, and the landscape out my window seems darker than normal. Maybe the ancients and mystics were right; eclipses are magical.

I see Tor beaming at me in the airport.

"Come on, let's go! It is happening right now!" He tells me. We dash out of the airport into the parking lot.

Tor hands me the binoculars. The Sun looks like a crescent Moon. I have the distinct feeling that Tor isn't the only one happy to see me. My old friends, the Sun and Moon, also embrace me with yet another beautiful eclipse; this one full of love. My last eclipse pilgrimage is home. Who knows where the next one will lead me?

Questions and Answers

If you smile at the world, it smiles back.
~Peace Pilgrim

1. What compelled you to set out on your pilgrimage?
My first eclipse in Baja, 'the big one' would be the longest eclipse in my lifetime, and driving the entire length of Baja sounded like an adventure—I'd never been out of the U.S., except to Alberta. I chose France because I have French heritage, and having studied the French language for years, I dreamed of going there. The wildlife and canal of Panama interested me, and I was curious to see how an annular eclipse was different than a total eclipse. My eclipse pilgrimages helped get me out to see the world.

2. Is there a book, song, poem, or movie that inspired your quest?
As a young girl, *Star Trek* was an influence; the crew was exploring new planets like I wanted to explore the world and the heavens. *Star Wars* enchanted me as a teenager. My favorite scene is when Luke is looking across the desert from his home dreaming of far-away lands. He was stuck on the farm and couldn't wait to see the galaxy. As a child I dreamt of getting out of Minnesota, seeing the world, and living in Australia. *Sky and Telescope Magazine* has been an inspiration over the years for all things astronomical, including the photographs and stories of eclipse journeys.

3. Where is your sacred place and why did you choose it?
Dark skies are one of my sacred places; the darkest skies I have experienced have been in the Great Basin of Nevada; the mountains of northern California; northern Minnesota, Michigan and Montana; Madagascar and on Mount Kilimanjaro. One-third of humanity cannot see the Milky Way at night due to light pollution, according to the *New World Atlas of Artificial Night Sky Brightness*. Dark sky parks and dark sky preservation are needed more than ever.

Despite blocking the view of the stars, trees and forests are also my sacred place. As a child, it was a tall, straight oak tree in the woods by my house. One morning I sat in the sunbeams at its base, and I felt oneness with the universe. In Minneapolis, I stopped to hug two big cottonwoods on my jogging route. Several groves of redwoods in northern California were my places of contemplation. In Nevada, I talked to a family of three majestic ponderosa pines on my favorite trail in the Spring Mountains. In Madagascar, I sat under an endangered rosewood tree beside a bubbling stream, amidst the abundant greenery, as an escape from my *maraseka* (busy, crazy) village life where everyone was curious about the foreigner. Currently, my sacred tree is a linden tree that sits in a little valley all by itself

SIFFY TORKILDSON

near my home, where I practice qigong with my Bernese mountain dog at my side.

4. How did your pilgrimage change your life or not?
Through my lifelong pursuit of eclipses, I have traveled, as I dreamed of from a young age. Seeing eclipses has shown me how amazing the universe is and that humanity can still have a sense of awe. The eclipses gave me hope for humanity. And I am hooked on eclipse chasing!

"Awe is astronomy's core emotion," and a total eclipse is the apex of that. "Awe leads to a sense of small self, more prosocial tendencies, generosity and caring," says psychologist Paul Piff (University of California, Irvine). If we encourage awe, we will not only invite children to a lifelong passion to investigate the universe but encourage them to embrace kinder, more caring communities on Earth." Excerpted from William Sheehan's article, the Importance of Awe, in *Sky and Telescope*, March 2016.

5. What is the most important piece of advice that you have received in your life? Do you have advice to share from your experiences?
"Just do it."

It began with my horseback riding instructor yelling at me as a child, "No, don't try! Do!" Then in high school, Yoda said, "Do. Or do not. There is no try!" in the movie *The Empire Strikes Back*. Later, my Kwan Um Zen school's motto was also, "Just do it."

I often think of the quote from Princess Leia in Star Wars, "He has to follow his own path, no one can choose it for him." My advice to others is never give up, and change your situation if it is not working for you, no matter how difficult. This is the motto I have lived by.

Observing the Nevada eclipse. *Photograph by Tor Torkildson.*

Biography

Caroline 'Siffy' Torkildson is a geographer, cartographer, life-long star gazer, author, and book designer for Sacred World Explorations. She has worked at two science museums, an international mapping firm, as a researcher for the U.S. Forest Service and U.S. Environmental Protection Agency, and taught an introduction to the history of women explorers at Southern Oregon College, as well as astronomy at the Eisenhower Observatory in Minnesota. She has published a travel guide book, as well as a travel-memoir and is working on a book that follows in the footsteps of the adventurer, Annie Smith Peck. She has published in *Ripcord Adventure Journal* and has won a *Travelers' Tales* Solas Award. Torkildson has B.A. and M.A. degrees in geography from Humboldt State University in California, as well as a M.S. in geographic information science from St. Mary's University of Minnesota. She is a member of the Society of Woman Geographers, as well as the International Dark Sky Association. In her search for sacred landscapes and dark skies, Siffy has explored the Himalaya, Sahara, Europe, Alaska, Patagonia, and lived in Madagascar where she served in the Peace Corps.

Sacredworldexplorations.com, and Sacredworld Explorations on Facebook.

Gorée Island, Senegal. *Photograph by Oumar Dieng.*

Oumar Dieng

The illiterate of the 21st century will not be those who cannot read and write, but those who cannot learn, unlearn, and relearn.
~Alvin Toffler

A Wondrous Ocean

*I*t was always the same exact ritual. After my suitcase was packed, Mom went through her mystical checklist, making sure that I followed the steps as instructed. She would grab the very same aluminum cup she used for my siblings, fill it with water and verbalize all the incantations and prayers she could muster in several languages. Her native Pular first, then she'd throw in some Wolof, Arabic then back to her trusted Pular. She would pray for protection before sending me off to travel to the Gambia.

Mom would walk in front of me, moving from the bedroom door to the front door of the house. She'd dip her hand in the new holy water and spread droplets in front of her. If there were some water left over, she would clumsily spray it beside my feet. Without fail, I would instinctively jump out of the way for fear of getting my shoes wet. This symbolized that the road ahead and all its dangers and evils were cleansed on my behalf.

Mom has always been superstitious, but after Dad suddenly passed away from a heart attack, she was adamant about protecting us from the evils of the world, even if we didn't appreciate it. To her, every trip was perilous and may as well have been the same thing as taking a pilgrimage to Mecca in ancient times. So, for an added layer of mystical maraboutism, she would ask for protection from the ancestors. "Just in case," she would say while strongly urging me to do as I was told, despite my objections.

Every summer, as soon as school was out, I would take the day-long journey to the Gambia to visit my uncles. I was in my teens at the time. Although I felt perfectly capable of taking the 172-mile trip from Dakar to Banjul, Mom felt uneasy letting her youngest son go "into the wild" on his own. For five years, she insisted on traveling to the Gambia with me to show me the pitfalls and intricacies of travel in West Africa. She was overly cautious of everything and everyone, the exact opposite of Dad who welcomed hitchhikers and, on occasion, the homeless into our home.

A few days before the trip, she would visit a local marabou who would create a custom-fit talisman for me to put around my waist. This meant I had to visit the marabou in order to measure my waist for the gris-gris. I hated going because the marabou lived as a hermit in a poorly lit room filled with an overwhelming odor of thick incense. Every time we visited, I could barely breathe. At times I wondered if he would live until our next visit, given the amount of smoke constantly surrounding him. When I came up with an excuse to get out of going to see the marabou, Mom always found a way to get what she needed. She would tear a thin strip of cloth from her traditional loincloth, and wrap it around my waist as a way of getting a rough measurement. A few days before our trip she had me try on the new leather talisman.

"Here. Put this on!"

"What is it?" I asked.

"What do you think? It's for protection!"

The gris-gris was often bulky and uncomfortable to wear. I took the talisman without arguing, but later I removed it, once I was away from Mom's prying eyes. This ritual continued almost every year I visited my uncles.

While I did not enjoy Mom's overzealous fervor in protecting us, I understood it. Furthermore, I did enjoy my trips to the Gambia. Every stage of the trip had a certain mystery to it. Sometimes we encountered wild animals on the road and had to slow the car down to avoid hitting them. At other times, we were dodging ten-ton peanut trucks that were so overloaded with bags that they were tilted sideways from the crushing weight. There were so many other wonderful things to see along the way. Some were certainly dangerous but there were also the simple things: the young girls selling mangoes for pennies, the smiling faces of young children flocking to our packed seven-passenger car. It wasn't unusual to be sitting next to a woman transporting a small chicken cage, a crying baby or a sleepy passenger who claimed the right to one of my shoulders as a napping pillow. I always felt that the people, the fauna, and the flora were in harmonious communion.

There was something about these trips that appeased and calmed me. It was about the journey and the lessons nature taught me; a pilgrimage of sort.

One summer, my mother decided to join me on a trip to the Gambia. To get to the Gambia, from Senegal, you had to take a very unpleasant eight-hour road trip to get to the southern border. Once at the border, you take a ferry across the two-mile stretch of ocean to get to the Gambian shore. Because we arrived later than expected, we missed the last ferry of the day. Faced with the prospect of spending the night under an open sky, we decided to take a fishing boat (pirogue). A pirogue is basically a hole carved out of a tree trunk and painted in an abundance of green, yellow and red paint that is supposed to keep the wood waterproof. These fishing boats were certainly not designed for the high seas or windy days.

"The name 'pee-rogue' should have been a dead giveaway!" I thought.

Mom argued with the fishermen over the "outrageous prices they were charging"—one dollar, but she finally settled on a boat. The pirogue smelled like fish and had no life jackets or any safety devices. The boat was designed for twenty people, but the fishermen managed to pack more than one-hundred souls into it. It took ten men to push us into the tumultuous waves of the ocean, and immediately the boat started to tilt on its side. The fishermen quickly shuffled bodies to strategic places to balance the load. The apprentice fisherman was skimping around the outside edge of the boat carelessly, which made me realize that he was the only one who could swim. The older men and women passengers were dressed in loose clothing not suitable for swimming. The fisherman yelled out:

"Nobody move. Please, stay in your seated position for the entire duration of the trip!"

I imagined that he had a conversation with another fisherman that went like this:

"Do you think it will float?"

"Meh, just make sure everyone pays in full before they get onboard!"

The forward momentum of the boat, propelled by a rusty single-engine Yamaha motor was the only thing keeping us afloat. The water was within half an inch of the boat's edge. The ocean was particularly rough that evening and it had just stopped raining. I could feel the kinetic power of the Atlantic Ocean all around us. The thundering roar of the waves travelled through my feet and exploded in my chest. The ocean was shrouded in an ominous green which was probably caused by the stirred-up algae and plankton that had dissolved into a giant elixir which we were on top of.

About a mile out to sea, we heard a horrible sound. The engine sputtered to a halt. Suddenly the boat started taking on water. There is nothing more humbling than the imminent threat of death when you are in the middle of the Atlantic Ocean, surrounded by angry waves!

The fisherman turned to us and said: "Stay calm! Everything will be fine!" Ironically, a soothing silence took over for a moment. But in the history of maritime disasters, when has the saying "everything will be fine," ever been true? Yeah, I am sure that's what folks on the Titanic were told upon hitting the iceberg.

We passed around a single bucket, racing to keep the water out while trying not to make any sudden moves. God forbid we mess up the strategic distribution of bodies orchestrated by a mathematically inclined fisherman.

All eyes were on the driver as he tried to restart the engine. He wrapped a rope around the engine gear and pulled. Nothing! He pulled again. The engine backfired while spewing black smoke! Still nothing.

Everyone, including my mother, was either freaking out or praying. I was praying too in all the languages I could think off; Arabic, French, English, Wolof, Pular, Hassanya—as if God wouldn't understand. The man pulled the cord again and this time the engine started.

When the boat finally hit land, it was immediately weighed down and could not get all the way out of the water. We had to pay an extra 50 cents to get piggy-back rides to the beach. My mom squabbled again with the fishermen. She thought that the extra 50 cents was opportunistic and akin to highway robbery. I wanted to tell her: "Mom, pay the man already! We are alive, aren't we?" But I kept quiet.

This was one of a handful of moments in my life when I felt the wondrous power of nature. In the grand scheme of things, we are but a minute speck in the amazing fabric of nature. Every minute in this life could be our last. Today, whenever I find myself in Senegal, I make an effort to go to the Gambia. My mother, who is now an octogenarian, seldom travels to the Gambia. As I ride the official ferry to cross the infamous stretch of ocean, I lose myself in the memories that this personal pilgrimage has afforded me over the years. I smile and wish that more people would experience the many wonders of the world that are waiting to be travelled.

Question and Answers

1. What compelled you to set out on your pilgrimage?
This pilgrimage is more of ritual that grew out of my parents insisting that I work as an apprentice every summer. One of the apprenticeships was working as a jeweler at my uncle's shop. The trip always took an entire day and was exhausting in hindsight. But as I got older, the trip became a pilgrimage.

2. Is there a book, song, poem, or movie that inspired your quest?
Not so much. It was more from a need to maintain family ties and be exposed to extended family members and gain a strong work ethic.

3. Where is your sacred place and why did you choose it?
The place is Gambia, specifically the stretch of ocean between Senegal and Gambia. The country is a former English colony in the south of Senegal. It was a place where two of my uncles lived with their families. One of them had four wives, which made my visits very interesting.

4. How did your pilgrimage change your life or not?
Travelling to the Gambia at an early age allowed me to trust myself and to be open to travel. It also taught me that there is a lot to see out there. That is probably why I ended up leaving my native Senegal for the United States.

5. What is the most important piece of advice that you have received in your life? Do you have advice to share from your experiences?
Always look on the bright side, especially when it comes to travel. Put yourself in others' shoes, it allows you to be compassionate.

Photograph courtesy of Oumar Dieng.

Biography

Oumar Dieng is a self-published author, storyteller and entrepreneur. An eternal optimist, he writes and speaks about positivity and ways of overcoming life's various obstacles. He lives in Minnesota with his wife and three children.

Website: http://oumardieng.com
Podcast: https://www.facebook.com/MotivationalVoicePodcast
Facebook: https://www.facebook.com/GriotTales
Twitter: https://twitter.com/odieng

"Twenty years from now you will be more disappointed by the things that you didn't do than by the ones you did do. So throw off the bowlines. Sail away from the safe harbor. Catch the trade winds in your sails. Explore. Dream. Discover."
~Mark Twain

Photograph by George Hardeen.

Steven Wesley Law

Rise free from care at dawn and seek adventures.
~Henry David Thoreau

Dress Rehearsal
In which, the author spends ten days in the wilderness
preparing for his upcoming pilgrimage

*E*very time I have spent quality time (anything over three days) out in the canyons or forests or mountains I have found something amazing or I've witnessed or experienced something quite miraculous. Not *most of the time*, not *once in a while,* but *every time.* And I always come back home with a new insight or two about myself as well. So when I go for a period without being alone with nature I get antsy and anxious. I grow increasingly restless.

Knowing that something spectacular and wondrous occurs every time I go out there, I know that I'm missing something by staying at home. Standing in line at the grocery store I can't help wondering, what amazing thing would have happened to me today if I would have spent it wandering in the backcountry of the Colorado Plateau, Yellowstone, Montana, Patagonia? What should I call the miracle that could have happened to me today, but didn't, because I wasn't there?

I am feeling an almost desperate need to get back out there. And spend some time in the laboratory of me.

The dawn canyon was as cool as an October hayloft. The grass sparkled with sequins of dew. The canyon's silence was actually made stronger (or perhaps just more noticeable), by the occasional buzzing of insect wings, the distant caw of a raven, the wind-stir of leaves.

Few things are finer than the desert in the morning. That's one of the nice things about being in the bottom of a deep, shadowy canyon: that morning coolness goes into extra innings. Though it was mid-May in southern Utah my thermometer registered a soothing 61 degrees F.

What I felt like doing was lingering in camp. I wanted to heat some water for tea and sit cross-legged on my mattress of leaves warm in my sweatshirt, while I watched the sun rays work their way down the western cliff walls. But nine miles of difficult desert terrain still separated me from my next campsite, and the next fresh water, and I knew from long experience that it was best to take advantage of the cool morning and lay down some miles before the heat burned away the enjoyment of the hike.

So instead of making a cup of tea I put a Clif bar in my pocket for later. I hoisted Annabelle, my dear backpack, onto my knee and from there onto my back. I walked down the manzanita covered dune on which I'd made camp and reconnected with the trail.

The trail, any trail, is a long isthmus, and today it's surrounded by a sea of sand, cliff walls, wonders and delights that connects last night's camp to tonight's camp. In this stretch of Grand Gulch the trail and the dry streambed slithered around each other like courting snakes, or a transverse wave seducing a sine wave. And damn! What a beautiful day it was. The morning light chorused off the canyon walls as if reflecting off the walls of Cibola.

The place where I intended to make that night's camp was the spot where Sheik's Canyon joins Grand Gulch, because that's where I'd find the next reliable spring with clean, flowing water.

It was May 1998. I was taking a ten day backpacking trip through Grand Gulch, which is located in the southeast corner of Utah, at the very heart of the Colorado Plateau. Grand Gulch now lies inside the boundaries of the newly created Bear's Ears National Monument. My ten day journey through Grand Gulch was an experiment for a 40 day pilgrimage I intended to take two years later in Dark Canyon. Dark Canyon is only 50 or 60 miles north of Grand Gulch and the two share identical terrain and climate. I approached my journey through Grand Gulch as a dress rehearsal of the larger one to follow. The objectives of my dress rehearsal trip through Grand Gulch were to determine what I should bring and what I could safely leave behind during my 40 day trip. It came down to a matter of comfort and sacrifice, and as I learned during my trip through Grand Gulch, the comforts of the trail and the comforts of camp are two very different things.

The terrain was an encore of yesterday's terrain. Hilly with a sandy trail stealing through grass that was as tall my elbow. I also passed through cottonwoods, tamarisks, willows, scrub oak, prickly pear, rabbitbrush and sagebrush. A few wildflowers bloomed here and there. In the very bottom of the canyon lay a parched, sand and gravel streambed that was about twelve to fifteen feet wide. The sandy trail repeatedly dropped into the dry streambed and reappeared on the other side where it climbed up a sand dune hill.

I kept a map of Grand Gulch in one of the side pockets of my shorts and I pulled it out and consulted it from time to time to maintain my bearings and progress. I passed Todie Canyon on my left a short time after leaving camp and a short time after that noticed more Anasazi ruins tucked under a cliff. I almost didn't see them. I walked over to them. For the most part they were still intact and in good shape. I entered the ruins and looked around until my curiosity had been satisfied.

I left the ruin, once again brought Annabelle onto my back and continued down the trail. It felt good to be back on the trail again. To once again feel the familiar, solid weight of the backpack, the sand trail under foot, extracting from me a modest tribute of strength and energy with each step. I was more than happy to pay it. I enjoyed the whisper of spider webs across my forehead and face as I walked along.

The sun had risen over the canyon rim while I was exploring the ruins, and it was surprisingly hot for mid-May. The first half hour that it fell upon my back it felt wonderful. And, Oh! those beautiful canyon walls! I hadn't seen enough of them in the last year and a half. To once again enter the winding redrock hallway, surrounded by them. To once again see the familiar jagged silhouette of the cliff's rim. I felt hidden. I felt welcome. I felt content. Except for one thing: water.

Water was my biggest concern. A constant worry, a simmering pan I was unable to remove from the burner at the back of my mind. The ranger at the Kane Gulch ranger station—Grand Gulch's trailhead—with whom I had consulted before starting the hike, looked at me grimly and sighed when I asked him about the water situation. "There is very little water available in the upper section of Grand Gulch," he said. "It's mostly old potholes filled with nasty water you won't want to drink, and the good springs are few and far between."

"Okay," I said, spreading my maps out across the table in his office. "Can you show me where the reliable water is?"

"You won't find any till you get to Fortress Canyon. There's a pretty deep pool of it there but it's muddy and stagnant."

"That's alright," I said. "And beyond that?"

"The last report we got from hikers about a week ago is that there's still water at the Pour-off, but it's also stagnant, muddy, full of dead bugs, dead birds, that sort of thing."

I located it on my map, and marked it with a red X with my sharpie.

"And below the Pour-off," he continued, "the only known water is at Sheik's Canyon. But beyond that hikers have reported that it's quite abundant."

So after leaving the ruins below Todie Canyon I kept an eye out for the Pour-off, the next reliable source of water. About a mile after leaving the ruins I met a man with two dogs on his way out of the canyon. His dogs were suspiciously wet. I asked him what he knew about the water situation farther inside the canyon and he confirmed what the ranger had told me: there was water at the Pour-off, and up Sheik's Canyon. "The water at the Pour-off is pretty nasty stuff though," he warned me. He saw me staring at his wet dogs and confirmed my fears. "And I'm afraid my dogs took a swim in it too."

He looked like he wanted to laugh when he told me this. I must have looked like I wanted to punch him (and I did, and very badly!), because that's where he ended the conversation. I was still standing there watching him in disbelief as he and his wet dogs walked up the canyon.

There are ethics to desert travel and this man had broken the most cardinal one: don't foul the water! Don't bathe in it. Don't wash your face in it. Don't wring out your bandanna in it. And don't let your stupid dogs bathe in it! Especially when there are only two watering holes over the course of 16 miles.

Even though I had two sources saying there was water at the Pour-off I was still concerned that I'd miss it, even though they told me the trail went right by it. "Impossible to miss," the wanker with the wet dogs had told me. But I was still concerned. I have done the impossible before. I reached the Pour-off about 45 minutes later. The gravel-bottomed streambed which I had been following all morning then opened onto scoured limestone rock that abruptly ended at a drop off. The Pour-off.

The Pour-off was a large plunge pool lying about 20 feet below it. And yes, it would have been nearly impossible to miss. I walked to the edge of the cliff and looked down at what appeared to be a suppurating, infected sore on the canyon's floor. It was the color of amber ale. If I dug under this plunge pool I wouldn't have been surprised to find that its source was really a backed-up septic tank. The mud around it was ringed with dog tracks. I sighed.

I walked down to it and found that its surface looked like it was covered with a sheet of tracing paper. I walked to its edge, scraped the debris away with my hand.

"Are you feeling hungover," I asked my water bottle, "because if you are, I'll get you some hair of the dog." Am I hilarious or I have I just been alone in the desert for too long?

I dipped in the bottle, filled it and held it up to the light for inspection. Yeah, it was cloudy as an octogenarian's eye but I had captured only a couple bugs and bug skeletons, and surprisingly no dog hair. I placed the bottle on a flat spot and filled the second bottle and inspected it. I dropped two iodine tablets into the open mouths of each bottle like a priest giving communion.

"Make thyself pure," I said, again laughing to myself, and screwed the lids back on.

The area surrounding the Pour-off was wide and open. Above me I could see the sky was heartbreak blue, the surrounding scenery set on stun. Immediately beyond the open area the canyon floor again returned to a jungle of tamarisk, white oak, cottonwoods and willows. I adjusted my backpack and plunged back into the jungle's catacombs, pushing the dense branches aside like a stage actor parting an endless mass of curtains. Grass, rabbitbrush and tamarisk lined the trail thicker and cheerier than Tour de France fans. Bandoliers of vines and ivy drooped between the cottonwoods, across the trail.

I hiked about another hour and arrived at another group of Anasazi ruins, listed on my map as Split-Level ruin, and spent about 45 minutes exploring their rooms. I then sat down under the shade of some tamarisks, in the center of the ruins, and took my first real rest of the day.

From my vantage at the center of the second level of the ruins I looked out upon the area in front of the ruins. You would have to be a complete dullard to sit amongst these ruins while looking out on the canyon and not try to imagine what life was like for the Anasazi who looked out upon this same view. The canyon floor, circa 1998, was covered quite densely with cottonwoods and white oak. What did the Anasazi see? Did they too see cottonwoods and white oaks, or did they have corn and bean fields planted there? Were domesticated turkeys pecking about for acorns? Was water more plentiful then or was it a source of anxiety like it was now for me? Did the sounds of laughter, of flute and drum echo and resonate among these cliff walls?

I licked my thumb, rolled it in the ancient dirt among the ruins and pressed it onto a page of my notebook, a small totem to connect myself with them.

After a 20 minute rest I heaved Annabelle back onto my back and once again pressed into the paparazzi of tamarisks, vines, cottonwoods and willows. Morning glory vines adorned the cottonwoods like filigree. In many places the vegetation on the right side of the trail reached across to the left side of the trail and vice-versa that formed a tight, arboreal tunnel through which I walked. Inside the jungle the air was heavy and muggy, a sweater knit from humidity that stuck to me like Naugahyde. Viewing the scenery behind the dense trees and vines was like viewing the world through the holes of a piano player's music roll as is scrolled by. I got a small glimpse of ochre cliff walls and a jagged pot shard of sky. And then the trail would climb up out of the jungle onto a sun-scorched dune where the vegetation receded to sagebrush and Brigham tea casting their castellated shadows on parched grass and sun-scorched, pissed-off prickly pears. Up on the dunes I had a much better view of the surrounding scenery, but up on the dunes, out of the shade, it was 97 degrees F and my appreciation of the view was elbowed out of the way by my greater appreciation to get back to the shade.

After six hours on the trail I was in pain. Particularly my right shoulder where the backpack strap rested. To take some of the weight off my shoulders I hoisted up my backpack and cinched the belt strap up to the "Elizabethan Corset" level. I was hot and I was getting tired. I was breathing so hard I could have blown up my Therma-rest in two breaths. My sweat glands were impersonating a popcorn popper. My quadriceps felt like something out of a Salvador Dali painting.

I was in pain. I was hot, tired, thirsty. A bit lonely. Sometime around this part of the hike you ask yourself, "Why am I out here? What is it about this that I find enjoyable?"

As someone who has spent a lot of time backpacking, I have spent a lot of time thinking about comfort and discomfort.

The main purpose of my journey through Grand Gulch in 1998 was to help me determine what gear I would need and what gear I could leave behind when I took my longer, more intensive, more immersive 40 day trip two years later. Essentially it boiled down to if I wanted to be more comfortable on the trail while hiking during the day, or more comfortable in camp after I had completed the day's hike.

This morning was a perfect example. It would have been nice to sleep in an hour, then relax in the cool canyon while reading some Wyslawa Szymborska and drinking some tea, but that would have meant hiking two hours during the hottest part of the day.

Of course, many of the items I brought to make my stay in camp more comfortable add weight to my backpack that make the day's journey that much more uncomfortable.

The comfort I found most indispensable was my peace of mind, and many of the items I carried with me I carried for that purpose. For instance, I really enjoy having a tent to sleep in at the end of the day, even if the forecast calls for clears skies for the duration of my hike. During the ten days I'd be backpacking through Grand Gulch the forecast called for no rain for the first seven days, and that time of year I knew it wasn't likely to rain after that, so I certainly could have left my tent at home and made my backpack five pounds lighter. But I didn't sleep in a tent to protect me from rain. I slept in a tent to shield me from mice. Mice freak me out! They're potential carriers of Hantavirus, rabies and who knows what else. There have been several occasions when I have opted to sleep out under the stars and have been awakened by the touch of little mice feet scampering across my body. One time, sleeping on a sand bar in Zion's Narrows I was awakened by a mouse scampering around *inside* my sleeping bag. I was out of that sleeping bag quicker than Sunday clothes. I unzipped my sleeping bag and shook it out. I slept barely a wink the rest of the night afraid the mouse—or one of its relatives—would find its way back inside my bag. Carrying my five-pound tent is worth a good night's sleep.

One of the greatest contributors to a heavy backpack is food. And, of course, there's the dilemma of how much food to bring. It's nice to eat quality food and to have a few snacks when I'm kicking back at camp, but again, if l bring too much food its weight just makes the hiking portion of the trip that much more miserable. And yet a wise backpacker prepares for the worst by bringing a couple days extra food just in case something goes wrong and they get stuck out there longer than they originally planned. Again, it's a peace of mind issue. The comfort of my peace of mind outweighs the discomfort of carrying the extra food.

One of the most uncomfortable things to carry is water because it weighs so much. But out here it's more comforting to carry some extra water, and lugging all that extra weight, than only carrying a little water and the whole time worrying that I'm going to run out before I find more. Again, I do it for the peace of mind.

This is why I filled up all my water bottles at the Pour-off. Sheik's Canyon—and a potential spring—was only six miles farther down the trail but it was still a chance I know better than to take out here. What if I had an accident and my progress was slowed down? Then I'd be very glad I had it. And speaking of water, I used purification tablets rather than a water purifier because I don't want its added bulk or weight, even though it's minimal. I also carry a big, stout knife with me. I very seldom use it. I bring it with me in case something goes very wrong out there and things shift into survival mode. If that should ever happen, a good stout knife is the first piece of equipment I want to have in my possession.

I also like to bring a camera with me when I go backpacking. In 1998 it was an SLR. It used film. It weighed 2.8 pounds. It didn't add any comfort to my trip on the trail or in camp, but it brought me a lot of satisfaction later when those pictures and memories were hanging on my studio wall. Interestingly enough, when I look at these pictures, some of the most memorable and even the fondest memories were the trips when things went wrong and things became very uncomfortable. Hmm.

It seems to me, the more familiar I become with comfort and discomfort, that the backbone of comfort is sacrifice. During the summer of 1997 I spent two weeks at the Boulder Outdoor Survival School. During those two weeks I hiked through the deserts of the Grand Staircase Escalante with a minimum of comforts and had the time of my life. We had no tents, only ponchos. For warmth we had only a wool blanket. We ate only two small meals a day. We got rained on. We were sunburned. We endured numerous discomforts. Yet through it all we learned how to build a shelter, make a fire using a bow and drill, how to build a bow and drill, how to find water, which plants are edible, which are medicinal, how to read a map and use a compass. We endured many discomforts but it was very comforting, at the end of the two weeks, knowing I was then better prepared to survive in the desert. I have carried that comfort with me on every hike since. And it doesn't weigh an ounce.

I usually bring a book or two to read in camp. Books are heavy but they're always worth the extra weight. I have never asked myself, is this book worth its weight?

My ten day trip in 1998 was basically a dress rehearsal for the 40 day trip I would take in 2000. Besides finding a balance between trail and camp comforts there were several other things I was figuring out during that trip. During my 40 day pilgrimage into Dark Canyon I wanted to bring all 40 days' worth of food with me for the simple reason that I wanted the freedom to wake up every morning and be free to travel wherever I felt like going. My pack would obviously weigh much less if I visited Dark Canyon ahead of time and cached some food, but that would also be pre-selecting my route, and I didn't want to do that. So the plan for my 40 day pilgrimage into Dark Canyon was to eat two Clif bars, a granola bar and a packet of rice per day. So during my ten day dress rehearsal trip through Grand Gulch I also ate only two Clif bars, a granola bar and a packet of rice per day. I wanted to determine if such a meager diet would provide me with enough nutrition and calories to see me through. Would I lose weight? And if so, would it be an unhealthy amount?

There were other important questions too. High up on that list was the question of solitude and loneliness. My 40 day journey into Dark Canyon would include high amounts of both. Could I handle it? My ten day trip through Grand Gulch would help me find out.

And there was also this to consider: in our modern world we live under a practical anesthesia of comfort. We are so swaddled in it that it's quite enjoyable to leave those comforts behind for a while and experience the rawness and realness of the wilderness. No filters. No insulation. No barriers. That rawness, that authentic experience, was and still is one of the reasons I love backpacking in a deep wilderness setting.

There is nothing in the world I enjoy more than exploring, and I have always preferred to do it on foot. I love backpacking because everything I need—or the tools I need to make it—is all on my back. Backpacking is my preferred method of travel. When backpacking I travel through country that is beautiful, full of new discoveries, and I'm able to move through it at a pace slow enough to best notice and appreciate that beauty, and to make those discoveries. When backpacking I really enjoy stretching out my hands and letting the tall grass tickle my hands and forearms as I walk through it. When I get tired I pause beneath a juniper and appreciate its shade. When I find a new variety of flower I have time to stop and smell it. When the sandy trail rises to a vista I can stand there and take in the great view. I feel the wind in my hair, the sunburn on my shoulders, the fatigue in my muscles, the crush of my backpack, the pain in my knee, the weight of loneliness in my heart. But being present to experience the day's wonders, mysteries, insights, knowing that I'm not missing the miracle is the greatest comfort of all.

An hour after leaving Split-level Ruin I found a shady spot beneath a juniper and sat down for another rest. I couldn't help noticing the deep canyon's wonderful silence. It was a heavy silence. Silence-after-a-quarrel kind of silence. Except for me, breathing like Phidippides at mile 25. While sitting there I pulled the map out of my pocket and determined that I was probably about an hour away from that night's camp.

After a fifteen minute break I huffed Annabelle back onto my back with a spontaneous groan of fatigue and started down the last leg of the trail. That section of Grand Gulch was a series of hills. Where the trail plunged into the streambed it was a jungle of tamarisk, willow, cottonwood, white oak and green grass that grew up to my armpits, dripping with vines that I had to breaststroke through. While up on the dune, the vegetation was prickly pear, sagebrush, Brigham tea, dead grass only six inches tall, and dusty as a Texas science book. When I was up on the dune tops with an unobstructed view of the cliff walls that bordered me I scanned them for pareidolia, a hobby as fun as looking for shapes in the clouds. Along that section of trail the cliff walls looked as if archaeologists began excavating into the cliff wall until they came upon a cubist sculpture. The cliff walls were a collage of Roman noses, hipbones of Ethiopian cattle, the belly of a woman six months pregnant, muffin tops. An eyebrow over here, a Mongolian cheekbone clear over there on the opposite cliff wall. Up there was a hole in a salesman's shoe. Over there an homage to the crack in the Liberty Bell. And up there, built into a horizontal seam located more than a hundred feet up on the cliff wall was an Anasazi granary, or perhaps the former residence of an Anasazi Rapunzel.

While keeping one eye open for cliff wall pareidolia, I kept the second open to spot the next obvious landmark which, according to the map in my hand, should be the Thumb. From the Thumb it was only another half mile to Sheik's Canyon. And camp. And rest. And spring water. Hopefully.

After a few more bends in the canyon I came upon the Thumb: a low peninsula extended out into the canyon floor away from the main cliff wall at the end of which protruded a stubby obelisk of sandstone. It indeed looked like a huge thumb pointing skyward. A petrological Ebert giving his review of the day's cloud shapes. It gave me the impression that this particular section of cliff wall had enough of this simple canyon life and was intent on hitch-hiking to Hollywood to be in a Western.

Forty-five minutes after passing the Thumb I pushed my way through the last of the day's tamarisks, with their long strands of blossoms hanging down like purple dreadlocks. The trail climbed out of the jungle onto another barren dune top and from there I could see the mouth of Sheik's Canyon just ahead on my left. I left the main trail and followed a secondary trail that veered toward Sheik's Canyon. I followed it to a spot right at the place where the two canyons merged. It was a pleasant little spot nestled among shady tamarisks and cottonwoods.

With a thankful plunk of my backpack I declared the spot to be camp. My sigh ruptured into an exclamation. "Wooh!" which the cliffs echoed back to me. If I had a football I would have spiked it!

Of course, before I could truly be comfortable I had to know the situation of the Sheik's Canyon spring. Without resting, I carried my two empty water bottles up the canyon to find it. Without having to carry the weight of a backpack my legs no longer felt weary.

After hiking up the canyon about a quarter mile I came to a spot where water trickled over bare sandstone, where it rapidly evaporated in the heat.

I continued farther up the canyon and the trickle widened. When I reached the canyon's more shadowy depths, the rock was covered with blackish-green algae. Next came grass, then flowers, then an eruption of dense willows.

I found the trickle's source hidden, nearly exiled, in a little pocket behind a jealous screen of reeds, willows and white flowers, that hovered eight inches off the ground like a scrim of fog. The last eight feet of ground was swampy. I balanced across a few rocks as I pushed through the reeds and willows and stepped through onto a round rock the size of a car tire that was situated right next to the spring. The spring was only the size of a grade schooler's desk and nearly its entire surface was covered with a thick papier-mache cream of algae. It looked like cud soup. Like something thrown up by a bulimic cow. Though it may have looked disgusting to a desert greenhorn, the green shag carpet that covered the spring was actually a good sign. It showed that the water was well-oxygenated and pure.

The resident water skeeters, who spent more time walking across algae clots that skating over open water, made a run/skate for it when they saw my big hand approaching them. I pushed aside a curtain of algae to have a look at the water beneath it. Phlegmy green veils of algae hung down to the spring's base, like thrum from a wool mitten. I cleared some of this out of the way to reveal clear, deep water. Startled water beetles rowed desperately for the spring's shadowed, hidden depths. I filled both of my bottles with its cool, clear water. No iodine tablets necessary.

This little side canyon was a picturesque little Eden, well shaded and cool. Beautiful cottonwoods, willows, ferns, wildfowers. Dragonflies. Canyon walls. I sat down on a delightfully cool sandstone ledge, and with a little water intake and some rest in the shade, exorcised the excess body heat built up from my day's exertions.

Eventually, I made my way back down to camp where I crawled under a tamarisk and spent the rest of the afternoon below the sun's radar.

As afternoon cooled to evening I noticed that it brought with it an ethereal cologne. A pungent base note of peat moss and decaying forest bed material that aproned out from the trees under which I'd pitched my tent. Above that I detected a middle note of green willows and warm mucky mud, and above that a top note of earthy rain and the ozone of spent lightning. Storm's coming.

Bats and crickets were the buskers of the desert evening. The bats were, of course, swooping around chasing insects, but they flew with such grace and mobility that it appeared they were showing off. About the same time the bats emerged, the crickets rosined their bows and began playing, which, when I listened to it closely, sounded like they were trilling their Ts the same as Spaniards roll their Rs.

I watched the bats for a while and then made the final preparations to the tent and my sleeping arrangements, after which I read until it was too dark to read anymore. And nevermind the dark; my head was drooping like an August sunflower. I lied back on the cool sand beside my tent and watched the first of the galactic freckles appear. And I was very aware that I was not missing the miracle.

And I took great comfort in that.

Questions and Answers

1. What compelled you to set out on your pilgrimage?
I've always loved exploring the outdoors. When I was 18 I started going out in the deserts and woods alone and I discovered that anytime I spent three or four days out there I'd catch little glimpses of my inner self. Any explorer knows what I'm referring to when I say that. So I thought, if I'm able to explore my inner self when I don't set out to do it, what would happen if I intentionally set out to explore my inner self? I wanted to see what was in there. And map it!

2. Is there a book, song, poem, or movie that inspired your quest?
Two books. Henry David Thoreau's *Walden*, and Robert Pirsig's *Zen and the Art of Motorcycle Maintenance*. Both of these men embarked on transformational journeys and both wrote about their experiences beautifully.

3. Where is your sacred place and why did you choose it?
My sacred place is Dark Canyon. It's a large canyon system in southern Utah, deep in the heart of the Colorado Plateau. I wanted to go on a 40 day transformational journey. I needed someplace isolated with challenging terrain, lots of solitude and silence. Ultimately I chose Dark Canyon from a H.D. Thoreau quote, which says, "Humility, like darkness, reveals the heavenly lights. The shadows of poverty and meanness gather around us, and lo! the creation widens to our view." And I thought, where better to see the light than from the bottom of a dark canyon.

4. How did your pilgrimage change your life or not?
I set out to explore my inner self and I was successful in doing just that. During my 40 day pilgrimage in Dark Canyon I ground the lens through which I now view life.

5. What is the most important piece of advice that you have received in your life? Do you have advice to share from your experiences?
Probably one of the best pieces of advice I've received came from my dad the day I left for college. He told me, "Don't let your classes get in the way of your education." I took it to heart, probably more than he meant me to, and have applied it to my life beyond college.

My advice to others would be to explore more. Explore the world. Read more books. Be spontaneous. Be brave. Take chances. Learn to make peace with failure so you can do it often and spectacularly.

Biography

Steven Wesley Law is an award-winning feature writer and columnist for the *Lake Powell Chronicle*, where along with the news he also pens a travel column about adventures and travels called "Gone." He's the author of *Polished*, a book of poetry about exploring the Colorado Plateau by boot and by raft. He's a Contributing Writer for *Panorama: the Journal of Intelligent Travel*, a British travel magazine. He's a four time recipient of the *Travelers' Tales* Solas Awards for best travel writing. He lives in northern Arizona with his wife and daughter.

http://curiosity101.com

"Wandering re-establishes the original harmony that once existed between humans and the universe."
~Anatole France

Photograph by Johan Reinhard.

"We have what we seek, it is there all the time, and if we give it time, it will make itself known to us."

~Thomas Merton

"There is no moment of delight in any pilgrimage like the beginning of it."
~Charles Dudley Warner

Walking Meditaion at Plum Village. *Photograph by Joy Thierry Llewellyn.*

Joy Thierry Llewellyn

I would love to live like a river flows, carried by the surprise of its own unfolding.
~Irish poet John O'Donohue

Plum Village Lightning

*M*y mother was struck by lightning. One evening in 1947, when my newlywed parents were living at an isolated Hudson's Bay Post in northern Quebec, she had been standing near the two-way radio during a summer storm. A bolt of lightning traveled down the radio wire, exploding the battery-powered short-wave radio, spraying acid onto the nearby lace curtains and tossing her across the living room. The current continued, jumping from one nail in the linoleum to the next, burning a long line of black button-like marks onto her body when she landed on the floor. The acid didn't touch her, one more sign the cup that measured her life was half-full. She had a heart-deep faith in the rejuvenating power of prayer and a hot cup of tea.

Many years later and early one morning, I leave the drafty France farmhouse I now call home, the air thick with darkness. I travel in silence on an unlit country road, but once I'm on the E8 AutoRoute I pass signs for Nimes and Montpellier and the challenges begin. Drivers race up behind me and flash their lights because my 130 kilometers is too slow, even in the blustery, rain-racked weather.

I clench the steering wheel, already regretting what I've done. Signing up for a meditation retreat when I feel so restless, when anything that involves movement appeals to me, seems like a particularly stupid idea. I am an efficient and intense multi-tasker. The idea of spending days breathing (mindfully) while putting one foot in front of the other is terrifying. What if I fail and run screaming through the vineyard-filled countryside?

Here is the problem. December holds both my mother's birthday and the day she died. This year I am too far away from British Columbia to visit my father. There will be no weekend with him re-telling family myths, or the two of us strolling along the ocean where my mother loved to walk. I have learned not to talk about her. Fifty-seven years of marriage has left a gap hard to fill. Yesterday, I entered into forbidden land during a phone call; I asked my father outright how he was doing. He mentioned his new double-pane windows and how much warmer the living room is now.

Avoidance works for my father, but I yearn for more. A pilgrimage to Zen Buddhist monk Thích Nhất Hạnh's home in exile, Plum Village near Bordeaux, will be a chance to mourn and reflect. "Pilgrimage" may seem a grandiose word for this trip but it fits my definition of that ancient word: "a journey to a sacred place, usually with difficulties, but with the possibility of a transformation at the end." I miss my mother. And I want to transform that ache.

Six hours later, I turn off the highway and drive down country lanes where the locals consider signposts and road rules an unnecessary distraction. Only when I see brown robes hanging from laundry lines do I know I have found New Hamlet, one of four residential monasteries that make up Plum Village. Fifty women live here: a Vietnamese Abbess, 39 Vietnamese, French, and American Buddhist nuns, novices, and 10 lay visitors. I will be staying in a 19th century stone manor house where my sparse and shared room has two clothing hooks per person and a sloping roof over two single beds. It looks like even our room reflects Thích Nhất Hạnh's belief that "Our actions are our only true belongings."

Even though I am in southern France, everything reminds me of a northern winter. The old-fashioned dining room hearth may crackle invitingly but it barely warms the bench in front of it. The larger *Zendo* or Meditation Hall is heated only enough to take off the chill during our meditation times. I put on every piece of clothing I have brought.

The monastery's routine is quickly learned. A bell wakes us at 5 am and by 5:30 we have all gathered in the *Zendo* for our first session of sitting and walking meditation. The day progresses with mindfulness work periods, dharma talks (discourses on Buddhism), and three delicious meals. At 3 pm, we meet for a Community Gathering in the Dining Hall where everyone turns up layered with sweaters, coats, hats, and gloves. The hour is a mixture of Buddhist chants and covering community business involving schedule changes and misplaced van keys. If a nun speaks in Vietnamese, another one quietly steps up behind those of us who don't speak that language and translates into English, French, or German as needed. If a French nun speaks, someone else takes up the translating duties. This distracting background murmur ensures that in this international community everyone receives the same information. The only pause in the hum of conversations is when the phone rings or the kitchen clock chimes and we all stop to take three breaths of gratitude.

My mother would have liked it here. I imagine her sitting on a bench under one of the plum trees that give this place its name, listening to young homesick nuns. People found her easy to talk to, and you knew she was actually listening when you were with her.

Dinner is a vegetarian meal of pasta and tomato sauce, or *cháo* (spiced rice soup). There are several kinds of fresh green salads and a variety of cooked and raw vegetables. Most people have a small bowl they fill to the brim. Sitting beside me is an elderly Vietnamese nun who carefully picks up a few grains of rice at a time with her chopsticks. She eats oh-so-slowly, providing yet another lesson in mindfulness. It takes her 30 minutes to finish her dinner. By then, I'm itchy all over from sitting that long in silent stillness and I'm not sure I'm going to make it through to breakfast, let along to the end of the retreat.

Evening meditation is next. Moving from the bright dining room into the pitch black of the front yard makes the walk to the Meditation Hall a challenge of stubbed toes and blind faith. After sitting down on a purple meditation cushion, I learn my body is not as flexible as I had assumed. I don't have a regular meditation practice and quickly become aware of my aching back, sore knees, and the shooting pains in my hips and thighs. I shift. And shift again. I want to apologize to the nuns around me who settle into a full lotus and stay that way for hours. My mother's laughing voice echoes in my head: "Stop fidgeting!"

It will take me 48 hours to start slowing down what Buddhists call "monkey mind," that critical, chatty head noise that keeps us company all day long: "Will Alyd remember to tell his father the football practice field had been changed this week? I'm hungry. I bet the figs are finally ripe. I should have watered the houseplants before I left. I wonder how the sick horse is? I'm cold." Stop! Breathe in. Breathe out.

Sister Bamboo, an elderly Vietnamese nun, patiently answers my questions. She glows and laughs often. She obviously doesn't have any monkey mind problems. One afternoon she takes a group of us on a walking meditation in the rain. She glides down the country road, each step the exact distance as the last. We all follow this small beacon of serenity. Close behind her are two nuns and a novice. One of them is wearing a Vietnamese bamboo hat and another is carrying a bright yellow umbrella. It could be a painting titled *"Chapeau de bamboo en marche"* [bamboo hat walking] or *"Parapluie jaune sous la pluie"* [yellow umbrella in the rain].

Suddenly, three gunshots shatter the calm. A yelling group of hunters point toward a corner of the nearby field. Sister Bamboo doesn't pause; she just keeps gliding. There is a fourth, then a fifth shot, this time accompanied by the sound of a hunting horn. Dogs are howling with excitement. The hunters shoot again. The men shout excitedly to each other and the dogs yelp at the scent of blood.

In the family photo album of those years my parents lived at the isolated Waswanipi Hudson's Bay Post, there is a black and white picture of my tiny mother heading into the stunted black spruce bush. It is a cold winter's day. She is on snowshoes, a .22-calibre rifle in her hand, and the hood of her HBC wool coat hiding her face.

"I wasn't a good hunter," she said, staring at the photograph during one of my last visits. "The first time I shot a grouse I cried, but we only received a few food orders a year and we needed to add game and fish to our meals. I didn't like hunting, but I did like getting away on my own. There was only your father and his young clerk for company, and sometimes the solitude was a nice break from the men." I imagined her lifting her left snowshoe slightly and gliding it over the inner edge of the right one, and then repeating the motion with the opposite foot. We refilled our teacups. "The only thing you can't do with snowshoes is walk backward," she said.

Sister Bamboo stops, turns, bows to us, and together, we continue our walking meditation home to New Hamlet. She glides while the rest of us stumble into ragged order behind her.

That afternoon we are assigned work meditation. My roommate, Karen, and I are to help three young, giggling Vietnamese nuns clean the windows of the Entrance Room. It turns out I am good at this chore. Karen, who has never done housework before, is not happy doing manual labor. Her windows are streaked. She looks over at my almost invisible glass panes and snorts.

"I'm not being very Buddhist in my window-pride," I laugh, "but at least I'm warm for the first time in hours." She shrugs and makes another haphazard streaking motion.

Washing the windows gives me time to think about my attraction to multi-tasking, something that is surely an alien concept in Plum Village. A mindfulness practice is having awareness of each moment as we experience it, and to do so without judgment.

Karen is providing me with many chances to practice compassion and non-judgment. She has come "to check the little guy out." She slams doors, stomps down the hall, and talks incessantly. In a booming voice, she demands answers, not bothering with a polite preamble.

"How do you shave your head?" she asks Sister Pine.

"With a Mach Three razor," Sister Pine replies with a smile, "once a week."

Early one morning Sister Ann, a mid-40s, tall African-American woman who describes herself as a baby nun because she was only ordained three months ago, drives eight of us to Lower Hamlet. Three hundred people congregate in the Assembly of Stars Meditation Hall. When we enter, Thích Nhất Hạnh or *Thay* ("teacher" in Vietnamese) is already meditating on a slightly raised platform at the front. He is small and looks much younger than his 82 years. I sit and focus on my breath but am distracted by a woman coughing in the corner. I again focus on my breathing but even wearing a long sleeve shirt and two sweaters it is freezing in here. Eventually, I relax and can concentrate on my breath and not on the noises around me. By the time Thay stands up 60 minutes later, my brain is quiet. He begins leading us in simple Qigong exercises and my body becomes looser, stretched in all the right places.

Several nuns adjust Thay's microphone, reposition the white board, and set down a tea tray. I cannot imagine how many of these dharma talks he has given. He has been a monk since he was 16. He tells us in a hypnotically soft voice about mindfulness and compassion, and how we are seeds that need a healthy ground for growing. "Walk as if you are kissing the Earth with your feet," he says. He draws on the white board and makes jokes. I had not expected to laugh. His language is simple; the translation by an enthusiastic Vietnamese nun is flawless in my headphones. When he is finished, he smiles, turns, and walks slowly out of the room. Our group laughter triggered a memory. I saw my 95-pound mother holding a broom in her hand. She is laughing and bouncing on the bed, banging the broom handle against the cabin wall in an attempt to encourage the porcupine hiding in the darkened back corner to leave. You would have thought she was ten-years-old.

I go outside and stand by the flagpole. It is bitterly cold, the freezing wind blowing through every buttonhole and open space, nipping at wrists, ankles, and my throat. People have wrapped blankets around their shoulders—no one is worried about fashion. Thay suddenly appears, along with a French nun carrying an umbrella that flops about and is not doing much to shelter him from the drizzling rain.

I am near the front of our walking meditation. Within seconds, there is a *National Geographic* photograph opportunity when Thay glides by me and passes the large peace bell hanging in an open pagoda. I hesitate. Pulling out a camera is just too crass. Then it is too late. He has passed the bell, but there is still the lotus pond, the bare vineyards in the background, and 300 people walking slowly behind him...stop! I shush my monkey mind and walk slowly, repeating "Breathe in calm, breathe out peace."

I look for Karen but can't find her in the crowd. I'm not sure what I want to say. I still don't like her but her presence has been a constant reminder to me of how quickly I can get impatient with people, and of my own judgments, which I consider the "right" ones, unlike Karen's, which are "wrong" of course. In my twenties and thirties, I remember feeling impatient with my mother's constant calm sweetness. Didn't she ever get mad? Or want to lash out? I had never thought to wonder—or ask—what she did with her anger and frustration. My father was not always the easiest of men to live with. What was her monkey mind like?

This mindfulness path is not easy.

When I return to our village of Beaurecueil, Evan welcomes me with a glass of tart, local wine. Alyd, our long-legged teenage son, grunts "hello." I pause, taking three breaths of gratitude. In my home, a grunt is as good as the sound of a bell. In that moment of loving silence—and without any sign of a lightning bolt—I am struck by three thoughts. My mother would be happy with the life I have made. She is with me no matter where I am. And for a woman who had never heard of "mindfulness," she practiced it for 84 years.

Breathing in slowly, I hear her tell me during a moment of tearful, teenage angst: "Just take it one step at a time, Joy. That's all you have to do."

Here's my hand. Walk with me.

Questions and Answers

1. What compelled you to set out on your pilgrimage?
When I struggle with an issue or person I can usually find an answer—or at least some peace—if I go outside and walk. Until I was 17-years-old, my family experienced an annual spring and fall migration, leaving Ottawa, Canada, in June and flying, via a series of progressively smaller planes, into our isolated, family-run, tourist fishing camps on the Kaniapiskau River in northern Quebec. My childhood summers were spent without electricity or flush toilets, and doing chores from filling woodstove boxes and washing dishes to cleaning guest cabins. There were also hours of playtime for fishing, hiking, and reading by lantern light at night. It was a glorious childhood of freedom. That annual migration—into the bush in June and back to the city in early September—put movement into my soul, I think, and always results in my heading out "to kiss the Earth" when I need to resolve something.

2. Is there a book, song, poem, or movie that inspired your quest?
I had just seen an episode of *Absolutely Fabulous*, where screenwriter and actor Jennifer Saunders says to her daughter, "Sweetie, you wouldn't say that if you knew how much we owe to my chanting, darling.... In Buddhist, obviously, darling, not in English, when I do it properly." It made me laugh, but also led to me researching Buddhist retreats in France. Isn't it wonderful when one moment leads so serendipitously to another?

3. Where is your sacred place and why did you choose it?
I have hiked the Santiago de Compostela a number of times and can't seem to get it out of my system. There is something about those long days of walking in rain and heat, combined with evenings of camaraderie—snorers and all—that continues to call my name, even though it is getting so busy. The first time, Evan and I walked 1,600km from Le Puy, France to Santiago, Spain, and after 72 days found ourselves in Finisterre with our knees, feet, and marriage not only intact but strengthened. Who could ask for more?

4. How did your pilgrimage change your life or not?
I don't think we North Americans are very comfortable dealing with grief. Spending time in that spiritual community—in particular, my interactions with the funny, wise, and kind Buddhist nuns I lived, worked, and meditated with—reminded me of the healing power of acceptance.

5. What is the most important piece of advice that you have received in your life? Do you have advice to share from your experiences?
I lived in an intentional community where Zen poet Paul Reps spent the last

year of his life. He used to say, "How you drink your tea is how you live your life." Do you buy the cheapest, no-name brand of teabags or only organic loose leaf? Do you drink from a stained mug? Do you let your tea get cold because you are so busy with other things? I believe Rep's statement was a reminder that the attention we give to preparing and drinking our tea is probably the same attention we give to our relationships, work, play, and health. I forget that sometimes. Being an accomplished multi-tasker means I can get a lot done in a day, but there are negatives attached, in particular tiredness and impatience. These days, I drink my morning coffee and afternoon tea from a beautiful patterned China cup my sister-in-law gave me.

Photograph courtesy of Joy Thierry Llewellyn.

Biography

Joy Thierry Llewellyn's attraction to storytelling and working with writers fuels her love of travel and results in a feeling of kinship with genre writers and Bohemians. She has lived in isolated bush camps in Canada, worked on sheep stations in Australia, spent a fun-filled 1970s winter in Mexico, lived in France and Germany, taught screenwriting in India and China, and visited 30 countries. One of her favorite adventures was backpacking around the world for a year with her husband and two children. She and her family lived in Southern France while she wrote her Master's thesis, *The Act of Pilgrimage*. In 2010, she lived in a Tibetan Buddhist Monastery outside Kathmandu, Nepal to research the resident Rinpoche and his family. A retired film and TV screenwriter and story editor, her creative non-fiction essays have been on the radio and in national magazines and newspapers. With their children now out on their own, Joy and her husband Evan live on a small island a 2 ½-hour ferry ride from Vancouver, Canada. Their travels involve long distance hiking.

www.joythierryllewellyn.com, Facebook, LinkedIn, Twitter:@JoyTLJourney, WeChat: JoyfromPenderIsland

"Promise me you'll always remember: You're braver than you believe, and stronger than you seem, and smarter than you think."
~Winnie the Pooh (A. A. Milne)

Echoes of Adobe

Painting by Pierre Delattre.

Pierre Delattre

Echoes of Adobe

*J*ung wrote about *Modern Man In Search of a Soul*. Perhaps that kind of search is the essence of our adult pilgrimage: our inward psychic journey toward self-realization. Yet I've found that the inward journey is not the pilgrimage young people most often yearn for. Something in us during our youth backs away from too eager a search for 'modernity', for presuming to be avant-garde, for exploring the question "Who Am I?" before experiencing the deeper connection to "Who were We?"

Having to break new ground can make us feel fraudulent—and rightly so—when we haven't yet connected physically, to what I would call old ground, old earth, to what gave and can still give resonance to our souls.

While we are still in our teens, an unconscious yearning, an instinct, calls on some of us to leave home, hit the road and go in search of a spot where we can literally 'sit' upon, or even live for a time within the very ground of our being; where we can enjoy finally being connected with the natural materials that awaken ancient resonance within us.

We go looking. But, of course, we don't know what we're looking for until we've found it.

For me at sixteen, this meant leaving home and hitting the road. That home of mine had been built of metals, pressed wood, plywood, concrete, plaster, tar, stylishly 'modern' plastic furniture. I couldn't have known that my soul was yearning for an immersion in different materials than these: my soul had been searching for an earth-made dwelling.

I got dropped off at one point in Taos, New Mexico and for reasons I no longer remember found myself being taken in by an artist couple, Beatrice Mandelman and Louis Ribak. They introduced me to houses made of thick adobe bricks with 'vigas' and 'latillas' supporting the packed earth roofs. Rugs woven by local native people were on the floors and on couches. Their artistry decorated their bodies, walls, mantels, fireplaces. Something quickened inside of me. I knew my soul had come home. I heard the drumbeat from the pueblos, watched the deer decked out in juniper come dance with the corn maidens as they emerged from the underground kivas. I could feel the guardian presences of the ancient ones.

All the time I was living in different cities, different countries, I could hear and feel the echoes of adobe calling me, felt in my veins that need to stay physically connected to our ancient history. My wife Nancy Ortenstone and I eventually built our house in northern New Mexico on a hundred and fifty year old adobe ruin on Picuris Indian Reservation land with the

Acequia Madre, the mother ditch, flowing through our back yard. Many of my paintings are made entirely of earth on canvas. Many of Nancy's express the mystery of living between two worlds.

Finally we became what we had always wished to be, consciously ancient people who need no longer go in search of their souls.

Jung eventually found his soul spot in Switzerland, built his famous tower of local stones, enclosed himself therein with ancient symbols, painted mandalas and ended his days as a very old man whose soul had evolved into something not so modern after all.

Wellspring
Painting by Nancy Ortenstone.

Nancy Ortenstone

Tell me, what is it you plan to do with your one wild and precious life?
~Mary Oliver

My Pilgrimage to Becoming a Painter

*I*n 1977 I was a single mother raising two daughters, teaching school, writing poetry and performing with a small theatre.

On an icy February night in Minneapolis, I drove across town to an artists' party a friend insisted I attend because she said I had to meet Alvaro Cardona-Hine and his wife, Barbara, new to St. Paul from LA. She also intended for me to meet Pierre Delattre. At the time, I had no idea how profoundly these two men would influence my future.

Pierre and I were immediately attracted to one another and it didn't take us long to realize we had found our soul mate. Forty years later we are still happily together, sharing our creative lives.

Alvaro was a composer, writer and painter. That night I saw for the first time his light-filled work which resonated deeply with me. My first husband was a painter whose work had been filled with angst. While witnessing his creative struggle, it never occurred to me that I would ever want to paint. Looking at Alvaro's work, however, I could see a whole other creative experience.

Soon after we all met, Alvaro hired Pierre and I to work with him at the Minnesota Museum of Art where he was Director of the Hispanic Program. We invented games that taught the elements of art to the school children who came to visit the museum. And Alvaro taught them how to paint. Often I would sit in one of the children's easel chairs and join in the fun. That's when my pilgrimage began.

During that time we attended salons at Alvaro and Barbara's house and became great friends. I felt as though I had found my "tribe."

Pierre and I went to all of Alvaro's exhibits. It was a delight to witness his joy towards creating—even as he painted in the basement—and to see his new paintings as he created them.

The next year Pierre had the opportunity to teach at the Instituto in San Miguel de Allende, Mexico. We left with my two daughters to live there for the next 5 years. We wrote our books and I earned my MFA. The brilliant colors of Mexico permeated my soul and Pierre often made the comment that my poems were color-full like paintings.

In 1983, after my eldest daughter went off to college, we returned to Minnesota where my youngest could finish high school. Pierre and I created a program for the Minnesota Chautauqua and we performed throughout the state on weekends.

Pierre taught creative writing at the university and I worked for Poets in the Schools, a program that also hired Alvaro. We all continued with our own creative lives, and held salons where we shared our work.

Throughout my life, my dreams have helped me see where I should travel next. I've learned to pay attention and follow the ones that are guideposts.

During this time I dreamt that a goddess-like woman on horseback rode up to wake me as I slept in an emerald forest. She led me to a cottage that had an easel and several blank canvases. 'Oh what a perfect place to paint,' I thought but then realized that I wasn't a painter.

In 1986 we moved to northern New Mexico to a community filled with friends we had known in San Miguel. As the silence embraced me and the wide-open skies made me feel like anything was creatively possible, I knew that I had finally "come home."

Pierre and I wrote our books and taught at the community college. After I started working in a Santa Fe Gallery, I had the following dream: As I swiveled my desk chair around 180 degrees, I saw eight bassinettes with babies in them. 'Oh those are my paintings,' I thought. But I didn't paint.

One day while writing in my journal I asked, 'if I were to die soon, what would I regret not having done?' To my surprise, my hand wrote 'painting.'

Soon Alvaro and Barbara also moved to New Mexico and started a gallery in a mountain town about 30 minutes away from us. It was here that Pierre first sold his painted rocks.

On my birthday, Alvaro and I were walking to his studio when he asked, "What birthday is this?" "My 43rd," I said. "Oh that's how old I was when I first began painting."

Hearing this gave me permission to begin. I asked Alvaro if he would teach me. "I can't teach you to paint," he insisted. "But you can come paint with me once a week in my studio." I did, even though I didn't know how to use a brush or what questions to ask.

I watched him create beautiful images, and then quickly obliterate them to move on to something totally different. His playfulness was palpable. I soon discovered that I intuitively knew color and realized I could learn the rest from Alvaro by watching him paint and listening to his comments about my work. From the very first painting I did, I knew I had finally found my soul's expression.

After several months of painting with Alvaro, I dreamt that the birdcage covering my head was giving me a terrible migraine. I hiked the highway over the mountain to Alvaro's studio and when he saw me, he said, "oh do you need some help?" As he began sawing on one of the birdcage bars, the sound was intolerable. I reached into my pocket and pulled out a key. "Here, would you like this?" I asked. I hadn't even known I had the key. Could the message be more clear? I discovered the key to my own cage after Alvaro offered his help.

Soon after that dream, I quit painting with him to work on my own, but I continued to follow his advice: "Paint every brushstroke with love. Have fun. Play."

Whenever I felt critical of my work, I would repeat a quote by Thoreau: "If I am not myself, who will be?"

The floodgates opened. I painted eight to ten hours a day as often as possible. My inspiration came from the New Mexico light and colors, the skies and landscape. Whenever I traveled anywhere else, the painter didn't come with me.

Pierre began painting on canvas also and soon opened his own gallery in Truchas. I loved hearing about the people he met who bought his work. At the same time he continued to write his books.

In 1990 I applied to Helen Frankenthaler's Master Class at the Santa Fe Institute of Art. She chose 10 students from all over the world. I was #11, the alternate. Of course I was disappointed when all 10 showed up. I consoled myself with the thought that because I was just discovering my voice, maybe it wasn't the right time to have such a strong influence.

Very quickly my work began selling. Within the next year, I was able to make my living as a full time painter.

In 1994, I was accepted into Nathan Oliveira's Master Class and I still remember his sage advice: "Don't always paint large, you won't know where you are. Painting is about so much more than expressing."

I was seduced by color. Whenever I attempted to resolve a painting, I would reach for yet another color. Oliveira helped me discover a limited palette. I began to understand that the process of painting is complicating and simplifying over and over again.

During the 90's I was working all the time and loving it.

I couldn't stop painting. My best selling gallery was in Santa Fe on Canyon Road. I also worked with several other galleries and art consultants across the country. I painted two solo shows a year. It was a glorious time until an unscrupulous art dealer and one of my galleries royally ripped me off. I worked for 2 months painting a large commission for which I was never paid.

I had been so driven with my painting that I didn't have time for anything or anybody else. In 1995 I had three solo shows within six months. When I fell onto the pavement and sprained my ankle, I knew my body was no longer asking me to slow down and take a rest. It demanded that I stop. That night I had a dream that told me I must shift from obsession with my art to devotion to my art. I understood that obsession meant I was working in a way that almost felt possessed. It was like having blinders on, always forging ahead.

When I crossed over from obsession to devotion, I had much more insight into my work. I felt as though I was finally painting from a place of effortlessness. I felt more connected to the people who would eventually see and live with my art.

In the beginning, each time I entered the studio it was as though a different person stood before the easel holding the brush. I didn't yet know the new painter or how she painted from this place of devotion.

It took a while but gradually I relaxed into a grace-filled space.

In 1999, after my first decade of painting, I excitedly looked back at my work and could clearly see how my paintings had evolved. Now my paintings were more about light than about color. I continue to paint abstractly because that is my natural visual orientation.

In the year 2000 all my stars lined up again—like they did on the night when I first met Pierre and Alvaro. While my sold out show was hanging in Santa Fe, an agent came to town looking for artists to be represented by her publishing company. During these past 17 years, they have printed more than 100 of my images, and have shown my work in 60 countries. Because of this, people have sought me out to purchase my originals.

In 2006 I opened my own gallery in Taos, New Mexico.

I wanted to hear how people responded to my paintings and I delighted in the freedom to explore new territory whenever I felt like it. It was a prosperous time until the economic crash in 2008.

In 2009 Pierre closed his gallery and we joined forces to open a gallery together in Taos which continues today as Ortenstone Delattre Fine Art.

During the next couple of years, my focus began to shift toward friends and family. A dear friend lost her life to breast cancer, Pierre had open-heart surgery and my mother died.

In 2013 one of my closest friends was diagnosed with ovarian cancer and I wanted to be there for her. She had come to all of my shows over the years and made many visits to my studio to help me see and appreciate my own work. I trusted her aesthetic. Two years later she died.

Soon my paintings became mostly calming, comforting space. Not always though. My operatic voice appears at times but usually it is the introvert, the quiet one who hums the tune on the canvas.

In 2016 Alvaro died. His last words to me were, "Paint up a storm."

I promised I would. I feel so grateful that I had the chance to thank him one last time for being my mentor.

"Oh it was always there, I just brought it out," he said.

"Yes, but even so, what if I had lived my whole life and nobody helped bring it out? That could have just as easily happened."

There has been so much loss to process but the deepest grief has taught me how to embrace the smallest delights.

Pierre and I continue to maintain our gallery in Taos, meeting people who resonate with our work, some choosing to live with it. At the same time, we happily create our paintings and write our books while feeling blessed that we live in beautiful New Mexico, the place that has embraced our psyches and nurtured our souls for more than 31 years now.

Life *is* a pilgrimage toward the full realization of our gift. Along the way, we are always asking, 'which path will lead me home?'

Question and Answers

1. What compelled you to set out on your pilgrimage?
I was compelled to set forth on my pilgrimage in an attempt to discover the mystery of my own soul.

2. Is there a book, song, poem, or movie that inspired your quest?
My dreams inspired my quest and helped lead the way.

3. Where is your sacred place and why did you choose it?
My sacred place is in the northern New Mexico landscape because here I feel as if anything is creatively possible.

4. How did your pilgrimage change your life or not?
By becoming a painter, I feel as though I am living my purpose in life. Through my paintings I can offer the viewer a place of reverie where they can experience a calm and comforting world.

5. What is the most important piece of advice that you have received in your life? Do you have advice to share from your experiences?
I think Nelson Mandela offers the best advice: "There is no passion to be found playing small—in settling for a life that is less than the one you are capable of living." My advice from what I learned: Paint with devotion to beauty and love.

Photograph courtesy of Nancy Ortenstone.

Biography

Nancy Ortenstone lives in the Northern New Mexico Mountains with her husband, Pierre Delattre. Their shared gallery is in Taos: Ortenstone Delattre Fine Art. Nancy received her MFA from the University of Guanajuato in Mexico. She is the author of a non-fiction book, *Because of Birds*, available from Amazon. Her paintings have been collected nationally and abroad. Many of her images have been published by McGaw Graphics.

www.ortenstonedelattre.com Social Media: FB and Instagram

Pierre Delattre recently published his fifth book, *Korrigan's Shadow*, a fictional journey about a young man and woman's journey toward artistic self-completion. He took his graduate degree in Sacred Arts at the University of Chicago, and since then has made the art life one of sacred explorations, both in creative solitude and in merging his life with 'bohemian' communities where new visual and literary expressions are conceived. During the Beat era he ran a spiritual coffee house in San Francisco's North Beach, spent eighteen years writing and painting while exploring his theme in Mexico and Puerto Rico, has been living in the northern New Mexico countryside since 1986 while running an art gallery in Taos, New Mexico with his wife Nancy and daughter Carla, both fine artists. At 86 he continues to hit the trail almost every day, regarding art as a way of hunting, gathering and bringing home new vision.

www.ortenstonedelattre.com

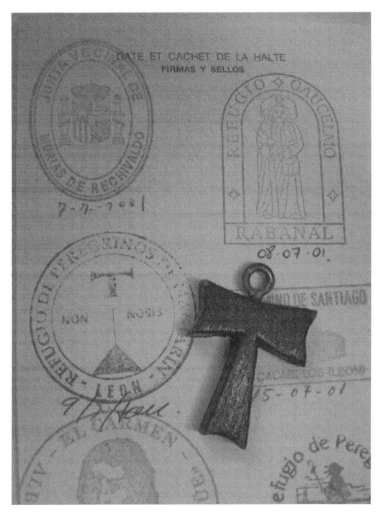

Photograph by Mony Dojeiji.

Mony Dojeiji

A Journey of Initiation

I arrived in Murias de Rechivaldo, hot and tired from the day's long walk. I'm not sure why I didn't stay in Astorga, a must on every pilgrim's itinerary, four kilometers back. My feet seemed to have a life of their own, carrying me forward as my mind replayed words I had overheard only days earlier:

"Every individual on a journey of personal transformation must walk three paths. On the Camino to Santiago de Compostela, you walk the Way of the Sword, battling your personal demons and claiming your courage. On the Way of the Heart, you walk to Rome, exploring the meaning of love in all its facets, from the human to the Divine. Finally, on the Way of the Soul, you walk to Jerusalem, towards the most sacred within you, to touch its brilliance and offer its gifts to the world."

Steps that were now leading me to Santiago began to hint at steps long forgotten that led to more ancient lands. The mere mention of Jerusalem— *Yeru Shalom*, City of Peace—stirred my imagination. Perhaps it was my Lebanese roots, or the soul connection I longed for, or the peace my heart craved; but at that moment Jerusalem and the promises she held conjured a powerful elixir that began to magnetically draw me to her.

The statues of two eagles—my totem—greeted my arrival at the Murias municipal albergue, adding to my anticipation. The place was modest, and offered the magnificent gift of a single bed, not a bunk bed, upon which I triumphantly placed my sleeping bag. By evening, every space was taken.

I settled into my bed, and began my daily ritual of updating my diary, trying once again to bring order to the latest round of emotions and stirrings that the word Jerusalem had wrought. I looked up, and noticed a man standing in the doorway of the albergue, casually glancing about. He appeared to be in his fifties, with salt and pepper hair and beard. He wore thick, dark-rimmed glasses and sported white pants with a matching waist-length tunic. An air of the eccentric hovered about him.

I smiled at the array of characters that made up the pilgrims I was meeting on this Camino, and continued writing. When I chanced to again look up, the man was standing by my bedside. He smiled at me with affection and spoke in a rapid-fire Spanish I could not understand. I returned his smile and nodded, not so much at the words spoken, but at the feeling of care and encouragement he transmitted.

In the setting sun, a ray of light momentarily flashed off a large medallion that hung around his neck. In that flicker, I saw emblazoned one word: Jerusalem. Every hair on my body stood on end, but before I could react or find a way to communicate with him, my mystery man moved on to other people in the albergue and left soon after.

I leaned back in my bed, trembling. *Who was that man? Why did he come straight to me? And that medallion—what does it mean? Surely, he is a connection to my Jerusalem omen. I must find him.*

Those were the only thoughts that accompanied me the following days, as I moved higher into the mountains of Galicia. I passed Foncebadon and the iconic *Cruz de Ferro*, and was rounding a corner on that majestic day when, suddenly, the sound of classical music filled the air. I stopped, just to make sure I wasn't hearing things. This was, after all, the Camino and all manner of the unexpected was to be expected. The music played on and as I continued ahead, I began to make out the occasional toll of a bell. I hurried my steps.

Around a bend and down the hill I rushed until I found the source of all those sounds: a hobbled-together shelter bustling with pilgrims, sharing space with white geese wholly unperturbed by their presence. A hand-painted sign indicated that I was a mere 222 kilometers from Santiago, 2475 kilometers from Rome, and, to my shock, 5000 kilometers from Jerusalem.

Finally, I saw him. My mystery man, dressed in white pants, a white tunic with a large Crusader-like cross stitched across the chest and a flowing white cape, and wielding a sword.

I was in Manjarin, and the enigmatic man was Tomas, the Knight Templar who ran this shelter for pilgrims.

With barely-contained enthusiasm, I approached Tomas to introduce myself; but he hurried past me, leading a small group of pilgrims to a large, wooden cross near the entrance. I wasn't sure what was happening, but joined the small group that now enfolded him. He spoke in solemn, confident tones, and with the few words that I recognized—*ángeles, paz, Jerusalén*—understood that he was praying for peace in Jerusalem. Tears filled my eyes. I had found my next steps.

But Tomas left shortly after and never returned, leaving me alone with the million questions that I had for him. With no other option but to walk, I continued towards Santiago, knowing that Tomas held the answers to my quest and that I would somehow find a way to connect with him.

I finished my Camino a few weeks later in Finisterre, more confident than ever in the signs that were leading me to walk the Way of the Soul. Determined to get my answers, I decided to return to Manjarin to work as a *hospitalera*, serving the pilgrims on their journeys, and to build my Spanish in an attempt to communicate with the mercurial Tomas.

Tomas gave me a knowing smile when he saw me and, in his warm embrace, only said that he was expecting me.

The days and nights passed quickly. The rustic setting, with no electricity, toilets or running water was challenging, but I found pleasure in the simplicity of welcoming pilgrims, making conversation, and helping to prepare and clean up the morning and evening meals. It was physically tiring because of the large number of pilgrims in August, and emotionally intense. At the daily prayers that Tomas held, I would often find myself weeping, my fears of walking alone to Jerusalem completely overwhelming me. Tomas would continually come over and reassure me, telling me to have faith and courage for the journey ahead. He encouraged me to meditate in the energy circle he had on the property, and to gather my strength. I did just that and, along with my yoga, found myself receptive in ways that I had never been before.

One day, Tomas asked me to help him with the new cape he had received, as he was having difficulty tying the knot around his neck. Standing before the wall-sized print of a Templar Knight praying before the city of Jerusalem, and preparing Tomas for his habitual ceremonial prayers, I truly felt as if I was in another time and place, very far indeed from the serious business woman named Mony.

As I smoothed out the knot, Tomas suddenly went very still. His eyes seemed to look past me and a smile of recognition crossed his lips. He began to speak, so I hurriedly asked one of my companions there to translate for me.

"You and I knew each other in Phoenicia (modern day Lebanon). You were a Sufi warrior and I a Christian knight. Your name was Yasser ibn Tubal. We had a deep bond and, together, fought for good and justice in that land. You were also with me when I died in Nazareth in 1270, and were the last person to tie my cape before I was buried. Your final words to me were that we would meet again, and that I would recognize you by the light in your eyes."

He held me in a warm embrace and I thought, "Finally, I can ask all my questions!" But he released me just as quickly and proceeded to the daily prayers without uttering another word or speaking of it ever again. Such was my time with Tomas, marked by one fly-by encounter after another that only added to my questions.

As the only Arab woman in the group, I was affectionately called *la sarracena*, a term referring to the Saracens, the Muslims who ruled most of Spain for 500 years. When one of the men there, named Andres, was to be initiated into the Order of the Knights Templar, I was invited to attend this typically secret ceremony and asked to stand as a Saracen, to symbolically unite Muslims and Christians in their common goals of brotherhood and peace. I couldn't be more thrilled, or honored. Donning a scarf that covered the lower part of my face, with flowing pants and shirt, I looked very much the part, especially with my tanned skin and darker features.

The late night air was fresh as we drove the winding, dirt roads that led us high into the mountains of Galicia. I had no idea where we were. At one of the highest points, we finally stopped and got out. The wind howled at those heights, and darkness blanketed the valleys below. Only the stars lent their light.

I followed the small group into what I was told were the ruins of a Templar church, not knowing what to expect, only that the magical awaited. Inside a small temple, shielded by ancient stones, an altar had been erected and several candles lit there. The white robes and polished swords of the Knights gleamed in their soft light. The smell of incense and soulful chanting of Ave Maria added to the holy and mystical of that moment.

We formed a circle around Andres, as Tomas spoke words in a language I could not understand, or perhaps not meant to understand. His voice ebbed and flowed, at times not even sounding like his own, heightening the aura of mystery that engulfed us. The energy was palpable, moving among us, sharing its presence, its love and ancient wisdom. When the ceremony ended, I felt as if I too had received a blessing for my journey ahead, and that it was time to leave.

On my last day, Tomas gifted me a red Tau pendant that he had carved and painted. He explained that it symbolized friendship, protection and the union of the spiritual and material worlds. Placing it under a portrait of the Archangel Michael, he prayed for my safe arrival and that I may always have the courage, strength, truth and integrity to walk this Way of the Soul to Jerusalem. I would wear the Tau from that day onwards until I arrived in Jerusalem.

Tomas also presented me with a letter, written in Spanish and sealed with the Knights Templar stamp, asking those who read it to help me on my journey.

I felt prepared physically, mentally, emotionally and, now, spiritually.

In the end, I did not choose pilgrimage. It chose me, weaving a web of improbable synchronicities to reveal to me the guiding steps of my life. I would learn to flow with those synchronicities and to trust their wisdom in ways that my logical mind couldn't always comprehend. Pilgrimage—the act of walking outwardly to an inner, sacred destination—opened up a way of being in the world that would never have been possible had I stayed in the comfort and predictability of my routine life or had I listened to logic alone. Pilgrimage offered me the great opportunity to open my heart, and to trust its whispers and gentle guidance.

That remains its greatest gift and lesson to this day.

Questions and Answers

1. What compelled you to set out on your pilgrimage?
I had just abandoned a corporate career and was looking for clarity and direction. I thought it was a long walk, and didn't yet appreciate how sacred pilgrimage truly is and how it connects you to what is sacred within you and around you. Once on the Camino, I received an inspiration to walk the Way of the Soul to Jerusalem, and looked upon it as my opportunity to understand my own soul's calling. I started in Rome, on what would become a 5000-km, 13-month walking pilgrimage.

2. Is there a book, song, poem, or movie that inspired your quest?
It was Shirley MacLaine's book *The Camino: A Journey of the Spirit* that inflamed my imagination. As soon as I saw the cover—the profile of a woman walking with a backpack and walking stick—I instinctively connected with it. Reading about her experiences cemented my decision to explore pilgrimage for myself.

3. Where is your sacred place and why did you choose it?
At the beginning of my journeys, I believed that the sacred sites held some kind of magical elixir that answered all the questions of my life. So, I chased them, waiting for them to reveal some grand secrets. I've come to appreciate that the most sacred location is inner, in that small, still place within the heart that I now journey to more frequently than any outer site.

4. How did your pilgrimage change your life or not?
Pilgrimage became my laboratory to put into practice all the spiritual teachings I had read about. As the great Morpheus of the movie *The Matrix* proclaims: "There's a difference between knowing the path and walking the path." I had gained a great deal of knowledge, but the experiences I had during pilgrimage made them my wisdom. From them, I emerged more confident in the kind of person I wish to be in the world: open, trusting, engaged, curious, and above all else, loving.

5. What is the most important piece of advice that you have received in your life? Do you have advice to share from your experiences?
I was encouraged to let the path lead me, and to let go of the need to control every aspect of it. It seemed impossibly difficult, but ever so slowly, I saw how surrendering a little bit each day brought me all manner of unexpected delights—what pilgrims often refer to as magic. I realized that magic is around me all the time, a beautiful loving flow that awaits my connection to it.

That is my biggest piece of advice to others: let go, and allow the path to bring you more marvels than you can conceive. It is Love, and it is with you in every moment.

Photograph courtesy of Mony Dojeiji.

Biography

Mony Dojeiji is a modern pilgrim and storyteller. Together with her pilgrim husband Alberto Agraso, they are the multiple award-winning authors of *Walking for Peace, an inner journey*, memoir of their 5000-km, 13-month pilgrimage for peace along the Way of the Soul from Rome to Jerusalem. Look for them on all social media outlets and their website.

http://walkingforpeace.com

Tibetan musicians, Gompo Dhundup and Jamyang Yeshi, in Banff, 2005.
Photograph by Karen McDiarmid.

"Across faiths and denominations, down the green lanes of England, along the dusty roads of Spain, up the cobbled streets of Alpine towns, through the marl deserts of Israel and the West Bank, around the sacred peaks of the Himalayas, over the frozen lakes of Russia and along the holy rivers of India, millions of pilgrims are on the move: bearing crosses, palm branches, flaming torches, flower garlands, prayer flags and over-stuffed rucksacks, clutching scuffed wooden staffs or shiny trekking poles, and tramping, prostrating, hobbling, begging and believing their ways onwards, travelling by aeroplane, car, bus, horseback and bicycle, but most often on foot and over considerable distances—for physical hardship remains a definitive aspect of most pilgrimage: arduous passage through the outer landscape prompting subtle exploration of the inner."
~Robert Macfarlane

Photograph by Tom Fakler.

Anita Lee Breland

This magical, marvelous food on our plate, this sustenance we absorb, has a story to tell. It has a journey.
~Joel Slatin

In search of Cambodia's 'Lost Continent' of flavors

*I*t is a steamy May afternoon on my last day in Cambodia, and I am spending it with former street children in a Phnom Penh restaurant kitchen. Donning a service cap and freshly pressed green cook's apron, I head in to meet the crew, lined up to greet my husband and I. The youths—boys and girls ranging in age from ten to 18—perform a *sampeah* of welcome. Palms together at mouth level, they bow politely. I may be an 'older person', and 'higher ranking' but I feel silly in my green cap, unsure how to respond. When my little speech of introduction is translated, though, I feel a rush of acceptance.

My taste memories from two months of traveling around Cambodia are mixed. The sweet perfume of ripe jackfruit mingled with the stench of rotten fish. In Phnom Penh's Orsay market, a vendor's swirl of her knife around a fresh pineapple, simultaneously cutting out the eyes and carving the fruit into geometric shapes. A ripe mango, musky with a slight tang, peeled and handed to me on the pointed tip of a farmer's knife in a Kampot pepper field under a blazing sun. The mad dash to a farmer's market in Siem Reap on the back of a French chef's motorcycle, hanging on for dear life. The discovery of *prahok*, that rotten fish I'd whiffed, in gourmet format at that same French chef's restaurant. His preparation put *prahok's* intense, savory qualities on show and it was love, plain and simple. All this offset by my recurring disappointment at the insipid rice bowls I tasted at street-side restaurants, and with the food on tourist menus. There were some good meals, for sure, but not nearly as many as I had expected from the succulence of the fresh produce all around.

And then, shortly before my trip was to end, Tom and I ate at Romdeng, Cambodian fine-dining in a magnificent colonial house on a side street not far from our apartment. Just after sunset beside a reflecting pool in a tropical garden, we clinked glasses of the crisp Riesling suggested by our waiter—one of the few times we ordered wine in Cambodia. Under the twinkle from lights strung through the branches overhead, we tucked into a salad of rice noodles in coconut and lime vinaigrette. A burst of citrus, followed by the back-of-the-mouth smoothness of coconut took us back to the seaside and Kampot province. This was more like it! A *prahok* appetizer catered to my newly minted love for stinky fish. And although we had not made it to Kampong Speu province, the main course, a galangal-perfumed fish stew from the central Cambodia region, made me want to go there.

Now, on my very last day in the country, we are at Romdeng, invited to go behind the scenes for an afternoon. The restaurant is run by Mith Samlanh, a non-governmental organization (NGO) serving marginalized communities in Cambodia and elsewhere. Mith Samlanh, whose name is 'Friends' in Khmer, began its work with street children in Phnom Penh in 1994. Romdeng served its first customers 11 years later. Gustav Auer, the NGO's hospitality coordinator, is our host.

The restaurant had its origins in a different, much rougher country than the Cambodia Tom and I have experienced. Nearly a fourth of the country's population—1.7 million people—perished during the 1970s rule of the Khmer Rouge, and in the mid-1990s, remnants of the regime were still active in the provinces. Phnom Penh was a dangerous place then, plagued with energy blackouts and water shortages. To make matters worse, much of the country's culture, especially around food, had been virtually annihilated during the Khmer Rouge years. Many victims of the gangs roaming Phnom Penh were children, who themselves landed on the streets for a variety of reasons.

Fast-forward to the current century. More than a decade in, Phnom Penh still has a large population of vulnerable or abandoned children. Friends offers them a range of vocational training courses to impart skills toward rewarding employment and a fulfilling life, and one of these skills is cooking. As the NGO's intermediate level training restaurant, Romdeng is a laboratory operating in full view of a paying clientele. Here, in a beautiful building furnished with locally made furniture and decorated with vivid paintings by the children of Friends, students learn to make and serve exciting dishes from the Cambodian provinces. In the process, both they and their teachers rediscover an important aspect of their culture: food.

Gustav introduces me to sous chef Sok Socheat, who tours me around the kitchen while Tom joins a group of ten or so staffers on the dining terrace. The group clusters around teak tables for math drills and vocabulary exercises. Nearby, others are learning new recipes on the break between shifts. These young people have missed out on formal schooling to varying degrees, so, as they train in the kitchen, they are also catching up in all the standard subjects.

The restaurant's kitchen workers have already been through introductory training, serving lunch each day to more than 1,000 students in the Friends training and education center in Phnom Penh. With the help of an English-speaking colleague, Sok Socheat describes the topics each student must master, from preparing all the restaurant's recipes to food hygiene and the exacting details of customer service: filling water glasses, setting tables with cutlery, flowers, candles and more. The staff also learn English along with kitchen techniques. In a few hours, they will work in pairs to explain menus and take orders, newbies alongside their more senior colleagues. The most experienced will pour wine and help kitchen workers pace order placement and delivery of dishes to the tables.

On any given afternoon, two cooking sessions run in parallel. Several members of the team make a healthy meal for staff, while others prepare for the restaurant's dinner service. I've been asked to help with the staff meal, cooking up an enormous batch of *khor sach ko,* beef stew in a tomato sauce developed around stir-fried whole shallots and cloves of garlic, chunks of onion and fire-roasted galangal, and enriched with crushed lemongrass, kaffir lime leaves, and hand-pounded chili paste. This is pure comfort food, not on the restaurant menu, but with a homely elegance that would make any Cambodian grandmother proud.

Across the room at the kitchen's central stations, dinner preparation is in full swing, in anticipation of up to 160 guests. Specials are white-boarded and studied. Sauces, condiments, and *mises en place* for menu orders are set. The bustle is professional, steady, and as the time for opening the doors to the public nears, picks up in pace and volume.

Romdeng's menu reflects the diversity of provincial Cambodian cookery, the seasons of Southeast Asia, and important traditions such as wedding celebrations and lunar festivals. Palm sugar sweetens the Khmer Muslim beef curry that is served at both Buddhist and Muslim weddings. Vinaigrettes are made with wild honey from Rattanakiri and Kratie provinces in Cambodia's northeast. A fine soup of baby pork ribs soured with *slack knang* leaves comes from Battambang province, Cambodia's 'rice bowl', also known for its oranges, pomelos, and sweet corn. *Ambok*, a young, partially ripened rice, is pounded into flakes for crispy dumplings with bananas and palm sugar syrup. Diners in search of more exotic fare can try crispy tarantulas with lime and Kampot black pepper dip. This is an elegant leap from the arachnids sold by street vendors and in the Kampong Cham Province village of Skuon, famous for 'spider tourism'.

Most dishes feature *prahok*, the fermented fish paste beloved of Cambodians and the cornerstone of the country's cuisine. The paste comes in varying levels of potency and is served both as a dish with fresh vegetables and as a condiment. It is made from cleaned and descaled river fish that are crushed, sun-dried for a day, then salted and fermented for at least three weeks and up to three years. *Prahok* is protein-rich and urgently *umami*. Since that first taste in Siem Reap, I have developed quite a taste for its bold, cheesy flavor and back-of-the-nose kick. Romdeng's *prahok* sampler—steamed, fried with lemon grass or mixed with coconut cream—is a food explorer's delight. I learn that the chef will ask servers, "Cambodian or foreigner?" and for Cambodian guests, add more *prahok*—a lot more.

Vegetables are central to Cambodian cooking, and the sous chef sets me to my first task—vegetable 'butcher' under the supervision of a student chef, one of two young women in the kitchen on the day of our visit. I chop carrots and radishes into tidy heaps and crush lemongrass to her exacting—albeit unspoken—instructions, the citrusy bits fairly bouncing off my knife. Satisfied with my contribution, my companion at the cutting table turns her attention to preparing and icing vegetable garnishes and after that is done, cleaning and trimming banana leaves. They will provide an elegant backdrop for every plate that leaves the kitchen this evening.

Before long, it is time to temper the spices and stir-fry six kilos of beef for the *khor sach ko*, and Sok Socheat assigns a student chef to help me power-stir the wok. The steady hands and attention to detail of my co-workers would be commendable in any professional kitchen, but I can't help but think how remarkable this tableau is. I've been wielding a chef's knife and am about to stir a pot under the tutelage of two teenagers who, until not all that long ago, had scraped their own meals from the discards of others. Until they came into the Friends orbit, these street kids had never set a fancy table or garnished a plate with artful curls. Now, they are showing me the ropes.

Romdeng is Khmer for galangal, the ginger-like root that figures so prominently in Cambodian dishes. Sok Socheat shows me how to fire-roast galangal and asks me to temper garlic, peppercorns, shallots, and lemongrass before we add onions, tomatoes, broth and finally six kilos of cubed beef and the rest of the spices. Heady aromas swirl above the wok, wafting a delicious pungency that deepens with the addition of fish sauce and rice wine vinegar. The sauce darkens and thickens as I stir, and when the beef goes in, my stirring of the enormous wok's contents turns hapless. The sous chef offers gentle correction: "Dig deep, scrape up the best bits..." I know, I know, but I am wrangling a very big spoon, and enough beef to feed a crowd! My assistant, who looks younger than his sixteen years, steps up to the wok with a charming display of energy and good humor, ready to double down on his stirring assistance. I hand over the spoon with relief, my back stiff and 'wok arm' throbbing.

Sok Socheat finally pronounces the stew done. Soup bowls are ready, a bundle of dried wheat noodles in each one. Nearby, spinach and salad leaves, Thai basil, 'rice paddy herb' and slivers of spring onion are laid out for dressing the bowls to individual taste. As each staffer presents a bowl, the chef ladles sauce over the noodles, sprinkles coriander leaves liberally on top, and hands the bowl back with a slight bow. After a few minutes, Sok Socheat smiles at me and motions that I should take over. Ladle, sprinkle, bow. Repeat.

Meanwhile, preparations for a busy Saturday evening eddy all around. Several younger boys squat beside the dining tables on the terrace preparing mosquito coils, industriously and with an occasional giggle. When coils are in place under each table, napkins folded, and orchids neatly arrayed in small vases, the boys file into the kitchen and grab their bowls.

At 5:00 pm it is time for staff dinner on a side terrace of the restaurant.

My kitchen cohorts look pleased when Tom and I ask if we can join them, so we ladle up a couple of bowls of stew and pile on the leafy extras. A couple of very welcome chairs materialize at the long table as fans whir above us, lifting the fronds of potted palms. The cooks and servers of Romdeng slip into their seats and pick up chopsticks, then swivel to face our end of the table. All eyes are on Tom and me as we take aim at our bowls of brothy noodles. We manage to maneuver a small portion of the food into our mouths to nods of approval and, in a display of chopstick competence, our companions dive into their stew. We do our best to keep up.

After a few minutes, a boy of about twelve fidgets with his chopsticks then lays them aside. Taking a deep breath, he exclaims "I am very happy to eat noodles with you!" Another boy, this one a bit younger, asks "Do you like Cambodian food?" I've been the object of shy curiosity all afternoon, and these two have worked up their courage to attempt conversation in English. What bravery! My heart melts. The table is quiet except for contented slurping and the soft whoosh of ceiling fans. When the bowls are empty, the students clear the table, and someone brings us a fruit shake made of winter melon, longan and jackfruit. It is a (very) sweet Cambodian after-dinner tradition Tom and I are happy to share.

When we visited the killing fields at Choeung Ek and the Tuol Sleng Genocide Museum, formerly the notorious S21 Prison, my husband and I came away saddened at the inhumanity documented in these places, and at the reality of so many Cambodian lives cut short. Today, as I prepare to leave the country, the message is a very different one. Our time with these young people has replaced gruesome statistics and stories with images of calm, confident youth taking charge of their futures.

The restaurant's menu of creative Cambodian fare began with the recipes of a woman who had been a cook prior to the dark days of the Khmer Rouge. It was a discovery that Friends founder Sébastien Marot has called 'a lost continent of taste and dishes'. Romdeng chefs sought inspiration from provincial cooks and gave their recipes a modern twist. The recipes—from ethnic Khmer cooks and more broadly defined Cambodian traditions with influences from India, Thailand, Vietnam and China—will live on in the individual collections the students are building for use when they become chefs. Some students will not complete the Friends training program, but not because they fail. Instead, they will join professional kitchens or open their own neighborhood restaurants or *bancho* stalls, serving up vegetable-filled Cambodian pancakes with the flair they've developed here.

Several years ago, Chefs Gustav Auer and Sok Chhong co-authored a cookbook, *Spiders to Water Lilies: Creative Cambodian Cooking with Friends,* and each of the 36 staffers at Romdeng signs my copy. Huddled over the book, they work out what they want to write. This may well be the first time they have written anything in English other than schoolwork, and several find that chewing on a pencil helps with concentration.

Food was lovely and I am happy to see you learn Khmer food.
I hope everything is going great with you.
I wish all the best to all of you!
I love you.

The rediscovery of Cambodian cuisine is a key building block to the pride that these young people now take in their heritage. The budding chefs of Romdeng have shown us its culinary future.

Questions and Answers

1. What compelled you to set out on your pilgrimage?
To me, food travel is part of a pilgrimage that never really ends. It's always about traveling via one's stomach in some form or other and gaining cultural understanding through the experience.

I've been doing this since I first crossed the Texas border into Mexico and got a whiff of corn tortillas fresh off the griddle. From early on, I was eager to try the local fare, meet the grandmothers who were passing along a family recipe, and especially important to me, join locals and other travelers at table. I only realized how important food—and making food memories—is to me, much later, after I made a career move to the Philippines. There, I found myself a member of 'the hot and spicy gang', a group of colleagues who went out for lunch once a week, the only constant from one meal to the next being a hefty side of chilies and hot sauce.

2. Is there a book, song, poem, or movie that inspired your quest?
I have a food travel blog, begun after a meal with my neighbors in Switzerland and inspired in part by the film *Babette's Feast*. In that movie, the main character is a strong woman, a trained chef whose culinary gifts break down distrust and superstitions in an isolated Danish community. In the space of a single meal, old wrongs are forgotten, ancient loves are rekindled, and a mystical redemption of the human spirit settles over the table. Why not aspire to that?

3. Where is your sacred place and why did you choose it?
I don't really have a place. Rather, it is connecting with people through food that makes a destination worthwhile—perhaps even sacred—for me. The setting and attitude around a food experience can be multi-dimensional and transformative, whether the act involved is feeding the homeless or sharing the food of a sacramental ritual. I experienced this when sharing the devotional foods of a Sherpa funeral and as a participant in a Hindu puja before embarking on a journey. I experienced it too when breaking the fast with Moroccan friends during Ramadan. And I felt I'd food-traveled full circle when my husband and I attended church and dinner on the ground in rural Mississippi, a tradition for generations of my own family.

4. How did your pilgrimage change your life or not?
I try to travel with intention when it comes to food. I have found that experiencing local food ways and flavors always bring me closer to the culture I am exploring, even my own. Experiential food travel has greatly enhanced my understanding of the cultural traditions in the places I have visited and especially, the places I have lived around the globe. The language

of food is transcendent and I never tire of meeting makers, artisanal producers, and winemakers who are passionate about their life's work. I traveled extensively during my corporate years, and travel experiences centered around food and wine have made my second career as a traveler and writer a fulfilling one.

5. What is the most important piece of advice that you have received in your life? Do you have advice to share from your experiences?

I'll be travel-specific here. Some years ago, when I applied for educational leave from my post as a corporate library strategist, a leading university library director advised me, a non-academic, to put in for a position teaching in post-Ceausescu Romania, rather than more traditionally recognized places like the British Library. He said it would be more challenging and interesting, and was he ever right! I took his advice, and became IBM's first-ever Fulbrighter.

My stint in Romania set me on a course toward a career in international development. It also introduced me to food traditions in a country where social norms had been upended and the economy de-stabilized. Standing in bread lines with locals, sharing rationed foodstuffs, and joining family gatherings with my Romanian colleagues gave me a sense of 'living local' that has served me well in unfamiliar environments ever since.

When it comes to travel, I think it is helpful to ditch the bucket list and to think opportunity—for personal growth and to cultivate delight in the unexpected. I would also advise any traveler to slow down and revel in the moment.

Photograph by Tom Fakler.

Biography

Anita Breland is an American who has lived, traveled and eaten well on five continents. She is on a never-ending pilgrimage into cultural understanding through authentic food and wine experiences at home and abroad. She blogs at *Anita's Feast* and has contributed to several anthologies of food writing. She and her husband currently indulge a shared passion for travel from their base in Porto, Portugal.

www.anitasfeast.com, anitasfeast on Instagram, Twitter and Facebook.

Francis O'Donnell and Denis Belliveau.
Photograph courtesy of Francis O'Donnell.

Francis O'Donnell

I haven't told you even half of what I have seen.
~Marco Polo

The Accidental Pilgrims

A sea of black spread out before me, it undulated in mournful waves. An ocean of heartbroken, yet joy-filled tears flowed down from the surrounding rooftops flooding the jam-packed square. An eerie silence could be heard, only to be broken by a whimper or wail. Speckles of color dotted the crowd, woven in the subdued, red embroidery decorating the vestments donned by Coptic monks or the blazing, yellow silken robes adorning Ethiopian holy men from head to foot. Greek and Armenian priests dressed in black comforted the worshipers lining the barricades. Tens of thousands of pilgrims from throughout the Eastern Orthodox Church had journeyed to Jerusalem. Here at 'The Church of the Holy Sepulchre' the faithful believe Jesus Christ died, was buried, and was resurrected; it is the most sacred site in all of Christendom. Tomorrow would be Easter, but today 'Holy Saturday' the supplicants had gathered to witness the miracle of 'The Holy Fire'.

Several days earlier the Patriarch, His Holiness Diodoros I, explained the event to us saying,

Within these walls, Christ completed his passion play, up these steps, is the Triportico, the site of Golgotha, the Hill of Calvary, where Jesus of Nazareth was crucified. Come with me into this small building in the middle of the rotunda, it encloses the tomb we Greeks call the Kouvouklion. Behind us here is the 'Martyrium' the site of the burial and resurrection of Our Lord. This stone is the spot where Jesus' body was anointed after the crucifixion. It is from here, once a year, during Easter, the Holy Fire emanates and keeps the lamps above eternally lit with his sacred power.

I stopped him there and asked, "Is it true, really true, your Holiness, the power of the oil and the sacred lamps, does fire really spontaneously ignite, do these things really cause other miracles to happen?"

He looked at me directly and answered,

My son, in my official capacity as the Advocatus Sancti Sepulchri Protector or Defender of the Holy Sepulchre, I can only tell you what I have seen with my own eyes over my fifteen years of service. Many hundreds of sick and ill have been healed by the miraculous power of the Holy oil. I have seen the crippled walk and the blind see, and every year when I enter the tomb this is what I have experienced.

Through the darkness I find my way toward the inner chamber; I fall on my knees in supplication. Then I recite ancient prayers that have been handed down through the centuries from the time of the first Patriarch,

James the Just. Once I am finished, I wait in silence. Sometimes it may be just a few minutes, but normally the miracle happens immediately. From the very core of the stone on which Jesus lay, an indefinable light pours forth. It is usually blue in nature but the color varies and changes, taking on many different hues. It cannot be described in human terms as it is unlike any fire I have seen on earth!

The Holy Light rises out of the stone as mist at first; it covers the surface of the stone. The fog then gathers, and rises up imbued with the power and spirit of the Holy Ghost. The light begins to swirl around in a funnel, whipping around the small space wildly; the whole interior of the sepulcher becomes illuminated with a blinding light, so much so that the faithful who wait outside can often see the glow emanating from the tomb! The thirty-three candles I hold, one for each year of our Savior's life on earth, are miraculously lit. Having received the Holy Fire, I share it with my brothers, the Patriarchs of the Armenian and Coptic Churches, who share it with the masses of people. Then within seconds, the entire Basilica looks as if it has been set on fire! But the fire does not burn, I have never been burnt by it in all my years of having performed this sacred rite.

He procured a vial of Holy Oil for our expedition, and for good measure blessed it again. As he handed it to me he said, "Here take this and go in peace, my friends. May it keep you both safe on your journey to Xanadu and the land of the Tartars, 'In the Footsteps of Marco Polo'."

Finally, after hours and hours, the doors of the mighty church opened and the faithful streamed in. Each person jockeyed for position, trying to be the closest to the entrance of the tomb. I stood there gazing at the crowd of people, many who had saved and struggled their entire lives for this moment. I thought, how odd, a few short months ago I had no idea this entire ceremony even existed, now, because of Marco Polo I have been afforded a front row seat. How lucky am I?

* * *

Our first stop was Venice, Polo's hometown. The flight from NYC would be the first and last until the expedition was complete. This was our self-imposed prerequisite: no flying, no matter what. Anyone can fly in and out of a place. This is one of the areas where other expeditions had failed. What does it mean to retrace a route? Our plan was to use Marco's book as a guide, the way others use *Lonely Planet* or *Frommers*. We would travel overland in chronological order, visiting the places he described in his book: *The Travels of Marco Polo*, and seek out the things he observed and wrote about more than seven hundred years earlier.

As we descended the steps of the Biblioteca Nazionale Marciana in Venice, we again had to turn to one another and say, "We will show them. Two years from now they will offer up Polo's last will and testament to us on a silver platter." Having given us the run around for several days, then eventually acquiescing, the director had turned down our request to view the document. A document we know Marco saw; he dictated and signed it on his deathbed. The will is the most tangible evidence of his life. We were nobodies with no status. It was not the first time we were so ignominiously treated, it would not be the last.

* * *

With Israel, Jerusalem, the Holy Sepulchre, and its myriad of pilgrimage sites behind us, such as the Wailing Wall and the Temple Mount, it was on to Turkey, the beginning of our overland journey along the fabled Silk Road. In the city of Konya, the great Sufi poet, Mevlana Jalal ad-Din Rumi, lived and is buried. The turquoise colored, Persian tiled dome of his tomb ablaze in the midday sun floats above the rooftops and beckons his followers from far and wide. Mevlana was a contemporary of Polo's, although there is no proof they ever met I would like to think otherwise. Marco did visit Konya in 1271 while Rumi was preaching interfaith tolerance and sharing his poetry of brotherly love and spiritual ecstasy in communion with God. His writings represent some of the most mystical in Islamic thought. This was during the Crusades, a period of extreme religious conflict, and is a great lesson for us all today.

As novices, we along with other pilgrims were allowed to sit in on a practice session of the 'Sema', a Sufi ceremony which induces a spiritual trance, a journey of ascent through the mind to a union with the perfect one. The dance takes place in the 'Cemevi' where the seekers gather together to start their adventure. The outfits worn have deep meaning: the white gown symbolizes death and purity, the wide black cloak represents the grave, and the tall, funny looking, brown wool hat signifies the tombstone.

Together we entered the room in a stately procession. We walked along in single file and formed ourselves into inner and outer circles. Next, we all bowed to each other as bowing represents our breath. Those of us in the circles were the Moon and stars. Our master, as the sun, took his place in the center. The dance started with a song, in a remembrance of God, and praising the Prophet Muhammad, Peace be upon Him. The ney then took over proclaiming our separation from above; the reed flute started off softly, at first, silently, imperceptibly, building to a crescendo. The dancers began to spin, thinking all the time, "I shall return to Him." Music, poetry, and dance are the pathways to God. Music helps the devotee focus their whole being on the divine. My heart filled with love and joy as I stretched my right arm out and up reaching high for the cosmos. Spinning around and around, my right foot was the axis, my right palm faced upwards toward God in heaven and my left hand faced downwards connected me to the earth, so I would not spin off into the universe. We danced on like this for hours, lost in love's reflection, but it seemed like seconds, spinning toward the truth abandoning our egos. I returned to the center a more mature seeker. One who had gained the wisdom to love, and one who will be of greater service to the whole of creation, regardless of race, class, or nation without judgment or discrimination. This is how I took my first baby steps with the Whirling Dervish.

* * *

Days turned to weeks and weeks to months; we put thousands of arduous travel miles behind us on the *Ipekyolu*, Turkish for Silk Road. The countries of Central Asia, Turkmenistan, Uzbekistan, Tajikistan, and Kyrgyzstan were exotic and wide open. The Soviet Union had collapsed only a few years earlier and there was an atmosphere of anything goes. People who had been forbidden, for seventy years, were once again beginning to visit and worship in their holy places. In Afghanistan, we had traveled the northern length of the country with a contingent of heavily armed Mujaheddin bodyguards, often by jeep, but horses, camels, and yaks came in handy in the mountains and deserts. In Mazar-I-Sharif we survived a firefight and capture at the hands of a rival faction. This happened in the shadow of the Hazrat Ali Shrine, the most sacred site in the entire country. It amazed me that even in the midst of all the bloodshed and heartache, brought about by twenty years of constant turmoil and war, that pilgrims continued to flood in, not just from Afghanistan and Iran, but from across the entire Shia world.

* * *

The Wakhan Corridor is a lost and all but forgotten secret passage into the back door of China. The town of Ishkashim is split and divided by a branch of the Oxus River. I stood in its floodplain looking out at the spires guarding the entrance to the corridor. To the south lies the Hindu Kush and to the north the mighty Pamirs, the Bam-i-Dunya, the Roof of the World. Marked on the map I had plotted at home, the Wakhan was one of the obstacles, if crossed, I knew would separate us from all the failed attempts before ours. While there, I contemplated the Universe, asking: "Why, why me?" I had what could only be called a religious experience. "Why am I being so blessed?" knowing, soon, I along with Denis would traverse that mythic corridor becoming the first Westerners in a generation to do so. It was the location, we knew before we left home, that would be the crowning jewel of our expedition.

Other obstacles, too, were soon at hand, for instance, traversing the entire southern route of the Silk Road around the Taklamakan Desert, at that time closed and off limits to foreigners. Its name translates to: "You go in but you don't come out alive." The Taklamakan is about the size of Germany and is the world's second largest sand-shifting desert. By far, our biggest challenge, as Americans, was obtaining visas and gaining access into the Islamic Republic of Iran; however, barely surviving the Afghan civil war and traversing the Wakhan would do for now!

* * *

Dunhuang lies at the eastern convergence of the northern and southern Silk Road near the Taklamakan. For caravans lucky enough to have made it out of the ocean of sand to the oasis, it is today, for the traveler, very much what it has always been, the twin of Kashgar, a place one can rest up, resupply, and ready themselves for the long journey yet to come. Here, one can get anything they so desire, for a price, especially salvation, Dunhuang's number one commodity.

For a millennium, pilgrims numbering in the tens of thousands journeyed to, stopped, and stayed at the Mogao Caves. There were hundreds of chambers cut into the living rock, cave altars, in which idols were erected honoring the many manifestations of the Buddha. The chambers varied greatly in size, some were so small that only one man, maybe two, could enter; others were carved out so grandly that many hundreds of people might gather within and worship. I imagined a constant stream of monks and other attendants going to and fro casting spells and chanting various incantations while envisioning others bringing incense, lighting candles, and placing offerings which they dedicated to various incarnations.

The size, shape, disposition, and temperament of these idols was confounding. Many had the countenance of the devil and seemed to be tortured souls living in some type of purgatory or perdition itself. Others were very tranquil and happy, in a thousand different poses of rest and repose. Here, in the Dunhuang's Grottoes, one will find masterpieces of art that span the entire history of Chinese Shakyamuni Buddhism. Caves from just about every period and dynasty can be found.

These caverns not only contained idols but the walls and ceilings, too, were richly decorated with murals and paintings in the most vivid of colors. Images of great beauty and craftsmanship, but bewildering in their message and meaning, some representing different scenes of Shakyamuni's life, and yet others were lessons from his teachings. It is as if the whole canon of the religion was written in pictures on the walls, for the ignorant, uneducated, or uninitiated to read! In several caves there were paintings of the seated Buddha. This likeness was repeated over and over again. The whole wall was covered with thousands of little Shakyamuni. These effigies were for those followers who came to meditate and chant; they would focus on each depiction then repeat their prayers, praising their god and his saintliness, over and over and again, then move to the next representation, in this way, they attained increased merit.

Dunhuang was a repository of sacred knowledge, and pilgrims traveled hundreds, often thousands, of miles to get there, study, and give offerings. In 1921, Swedish Explorer, Sven Hedin discovered a treasure trove in the back of one such cave. There he found thousands of written texts, in the form of books, scrolls, and tablets, which were inscribed with every conceivable language, and were comprised of different mantras, stories, proverbs, and lessons. It is said that many other caves had once also contained collections such as this, in fact, many were grander and more vast.

* * *

Unlike Dunhuang, we didn't have to fantasize about pilgrims of the ancient past, here the ancient past came to life before our eyes. We risked this sidetrack in our expedition because a great festival was about to take place and thousands of pilgrims from all over Tibet would be conjoining. It was our intention to witness and document the festivities and to seek out trade goods such as coral, amber, silver, gold, and other precious gems, which according to Marco Polo's account of the region 700 years prior: "With which the Tibetans decorate their women and idols." Soon in the distance, we could see the golden rooftops and whitewashed walls of the great Labrang Gompa peeking out from behind the trees. The smell of pine and cedar was everywhere as breakfast fires filled the air. Even at this early hour, the path was packed with thousands of Tibetan pilgrims performing parikrama as they paraded proudly past, dressed in their Sunday-going-to-festival-best. Families, tall and proud, walked hand-in-hand toward the town. Fathers wore fox fur hats of great height, bodies wrapped in inverted sheepskin cloaks, tied tight at the waist, with colorful silken sashes, fastened with gem-encrusted brooches. A mighty pommel in his hand, dagger sheathed, the patriarch led his clan. A father's swagger, he did sway, as the growing crowd parted way. His wife and children scurried close behind happily, their frostbitten cheeks grinning from ear-to-ear. They were here to share in this annual Festival of Losar. The thousands of pilgrims in attendance believe that their mere presence increases their Karma. By obeying Dharma and commemorating Gautama's spiritual victory over the forces of ignorance, greed, fear, and anger they can accrue good fortune for themselves in the New Year. So, it is a kind of renewal. This act, too, may help one attain merit on their path to enlightenment.

We came to stay in a chamber run by the monastery. Our cell was small and dark with shutters shut tight; a profusion of oil lamps lit the space. It was freezing cold, in late January, in what was once Amdo Provence. Over the next few days we explored the town and made ourselves known. With still two weeks before the main festivities, we had a chance to make friends with many of the monks. We spent time with them kicking a soccer ball around in front of the main temple. We cut the line joining the never-ending stream of pilgrims who walked the circuit around the sacred precinct, and spun the many thousands of prayer wheels which lined the way. We too chanted Om Mani Padme Hum "The Jewel is in the Lotus." Labrang Gompa is a renowned center for Buddhist thought and Tibetan cultural heritage. It contains eighteen prayer halls, six institutes of higher learning. The central house of prayer contains a golden statue of the Buddha, more than fifty feet high, with a relic of the Lord Buddha contained within. The main purpose of the Great Prayer Festival, or Monlam Chenmo, is to pray for the long life of holy Gurus of all traditions, for the survival and spreading of the Dharma in the minds of all sentient beings, and for world peace. The Monks have much to do during this period. Each student is required to study the canon of Buddhist scriptures. During Monlam, they must participate in examinations for advanced degrees and debate. These debates kick off the activities, next comes the Cham Dance itself, followed by the revealing of a huge sacred Thangka painting, closing with the ritual offering and burning of the Tormas cake and elaborate butter sculptures. Lastly, there is the circumambulation of the entire Gompa complex one hundred and eight times. They carry images of the Lord Buddha with them in prayer.

The big day arrived at sunrise, supplicants started to venture toward the main plaza and the festival grounds where the Cham Dance was to take place. The ground was frozen when we got there and packed with thousands of pilgrims and crimson-clad Lamas. The Monlam Cham Dance would take place in front of the Gompa's main temple. Finally, after hours of sitting on the freezing cold earth, dancers who had donned majestic silken robes, and wore the most demonic masks ever to be seen, slowly and methodically emerged from behind a hidden screen. One at first was crouching and bending, swirling, and shaking, waving his arms about casting incantations with sacred amulets and symbols of Karmic powers. He called forth his cousins, who gladly appeared, scowling devils with faces twin to his. All joined his evil romp, stomping around together; this act hallowed the sacred ground. Fierce countenance was so profound as to scare the sources of bad luck and evil away from the town. Now, in a more frenzied fashion, they moved, faster, and faster until coming to completion, full saturation. Their secret message sent again, and again, and again, on, and on it went, 'til every soul present was spent. Hour after hour, we endured the mesmerizing haunt of drums and bones. Horns in repetition blew, the thunderous symbol crashed too. Upon their demon heads, they wore a crown of skulls, grinning at the hypnotized crowd, lost in meditation. Each and every one of us was proud to have been witness to this sacred troupe's operatic ballet, ensuring happiness and good fortune throughout the land. Happy Losar to one and all.

The time had come, our fantasy over, soon we would catch the bus, our caravan for the four-hour ride back to Lanzhou, the capital of Gansu Province. We stood on a hillside overlooking the monastery, nestled in the Daxia River Valley below, as the last pilgrims melted back into the steppe. Smoke rose up to the heavens and we could hear the soul-stirring song of nomadic tribesmen echoing on the wind and off the mountains that surrounded us. We communicated in silence, each understanding the profound experience we had and knowing we had been changed. Not daring to speak so as not to break the spell, a tear rolled down my cheek for having to leave. Shangri-la may not exist in this world, except in the world of our hearts and minds. This was my 'Lost Horizon' and it extends on forever.

Our journey did extend on like that, forever, and does so now eternally. Marco Polo was a merchant and often described for his readers the best places to find the choicest goods and commodities. Most scholars will tell you his biggest contribution to the world is in that of geography. There is no question he was extremely curious about the world around him and had a great eye for detail. His contribution in other disciplines is monumental, as in the case of zoology. Marco described for science several species of flora and fauna for the very first time. Every day for those two years we did our job; we sought out relevant examples, quotes, and passages from Marco Polo's book. Often they jumped off the pages and came to life before our very eyes. What in many ways seemed to be an outward, material journey was anything but. It became an inward spiritual journey of self-discovery, and compassion because the truth is our tour guide. Marco Polo was the world's first ethnographic anthropologist and the quintessential pilgrim. He took one along on a kaleidoscopic odyssey of the world's great religions in all their various forms and introduced the reader and the traveler in his footsteps to the greater face of humanity. He delivered grandly on the promise set forth in the prologue of his book, which reads:

"Emperors and kings, dukes, marquises, counts, knights, and townsfolk and all people who wish to know about the various races of men and the peculiarities of the various regions of the world, take this book and have it read to you. Here you will find all the great wonders and curiosities of Greater Armenia and Persia, the land of the Tartars and of India, and of many other territories."

In doing so he led us to hundreds of sacred sites, where we became immersed in an endless sea of pilgrims seeking the answer to the mystery of life itself on a never-ending variety of pilgrimages. In doing so we became *Accidental Pilgrims.*

Our epiphany came bright and early one morning as we set up our video camera at the base of Adam's Peak in Sri Lanka. Polo described Sri Lanka as the most beautiful island of its size in the world, he also goes on to describe the life of the Buddha in great detail. At two a.m. we had joined the trickle of pilgrims that continually climbed the sacred peak. Pilgrims from various religions believe there is a footprint on the summit that was left by their respective deity. Buddhists who make the pilgrimage believe the footprint is that of the Buddha; the Hindus: Shiva; the Muslims: Mohammad; and of course, the Christians believe that it is the footprint of Adam, as Marco put it: "Our first parent." With the camera rolling, we started our ad lib discourse describing for posterity where we were, what we were doing, and why. More than a year and a half into the expedition we were tired and began to recount some of what we had been through. We spoke of this pilgrimage site specifically and others we had visited when almost simultaneously it came spilling out of both of our mouths, "The truth is the reason we are out here, doing what we are doing, we, too, are on a pilgrimage. That is what it has been, a pilgrimage of Marco Polo."

Questions and Answers

1. What compelled you to set out on your pilgrimage?
I had just turned thirty and wasn't living the life I wanted. I had a job I hated and was with a woman I shouldn't have been. Something had to change. Having just returned from my first trip to India and Nepal, I was high on life, and my soul was reeling. I was doing the cosmic dance of Shiva Nataraja. I knew I had to get back to Asia. This thought persisted day and night for months; it incubated in my subconscious. I had studied Asian art and culture to some degree, but now I started reading everything I could get my hands on. Then one day my mother gave me a dusty old atlas she found while foraging through one of the many antiquarian book stores and second-hand junk shops she frequented. It was from the end of the nineteenth century and was fertile ground. It contained a universe from which to fantasize. The atlas held the changing and shifting tides of world history since the beginning of recorded time.

Then there it was—a bi-fold map of Eurasia and the ancient trade routes from East to West. There were routes of great mariners; Henry the Navigator, Vasco De Gama, Magellan, but it was the Silk Road that fascinated me! I saw the route of Marco Polo, and my life has never been the same. A light bulb went off in my head—Marco Polo. "Look at the scope and breadth of his journey. Think of all those magical places with names like Bukhara, Samarkand, Isphan, Kashgar, Xian, and Xanadu! Think of the art one would see, the people, cultures, and religions one would meet." Then I took a closer look at the map, the trail Marco blazed was more than twenty-five thousand miles long. It took the traveler across the world's largest land mass and back; he would have to scale the world's tallest mountain ranges, traverse foreboding desert wastes and slog through steamy jungles dark and deep. I wondered if anyone had ever retraced Polo's route. I found through my subsequent research that there had been other attempts; all had failed for a variety of reasons. "That's for me," I thought, "A chance to make a mark in the world, to do something of meaning and bring life to life."

2. Is there a book, song, poem, or movie that inspired your quest?
Without question, popular culture had a huge influence on my psyche and inspired the path I was to take later in life. Of course, Polo's book was seminal, as was Mark Twain's, *Tom Sawyer, Huckleberry Finn* and a dozen others. The music of our age like *The Seeker* by the Who or *Ramblin Man* by the Allman Brothers band helped spark the fire, as did Bob Dylan's, *Like a Rolling Stone*, Lynard Skynard's, *Freebird*, Willie Nelson's, *On the Road Again, Roam* by the B52s, and *Katmandu* by Bob Seger, and a hundred others. However, Movies and TV were central to churning the fantasy mill. *Batman, Gilligan's Island, Bewitched, I Dream of Jeannie, Lost in Space,* and *Daniel Boone* were more than fertile ground for any imagination, as

were *Taras Bulba, Ben Hur,* and movies about the Vikings and other historical explorations, such as depicted in *North West Passage.*

3. Where is your sacred place and why did you choose it?
My Sacred Place is wherever I am. Since I learned Om Mani Padme Om, The Jewel is in the Lotus, there is no need for me to look outside myself for peace, happiness or fulfillment.

4. How did your pilgrimage change your life or not?
I had a fear of flying caused by my stint in the Marines with some crazy pilots, but magically this anxiety inexplicitly disappeared upon returning from my first pilgrimage to the East. I have no real answer for it except to say it must be the overall karmic lesson one learns from spending time in such cultures and seeing how people live and the hardships they endure on a daily basis. After all, what was I afraid of? Dying? I was holding on too hard to that which I did not control. Seeing the Wheel of Dharma spin before my eyes and observing lives lived out in crushing poverty and deprivation, and yet done so with dignity and joy, changed my perspective and gave me an insight into what is truly important in life: friends, family, and love. People in places like India understand this innately. These experiences taught me to be less attached to the material world. To let go and to be in the moment.

5. What is the most important piece of advice that you have received in your life? Do you have advice to share from your experiences?
On the eve of my first trip overseas, with my mother behind the wheel, we made an unexpected stop at her bank. She said "I have to run in for a minute," she returned with the gift that extended the length my journey considerably. And with that, she gave me an even greater gift, a lesson about life and myself that I have never forgotten. At first, I didn't understand exactly what she meant. "No one knows you in Europe; you can be whoever you want to be." The wisdom she was imparting was that every day is new and a fresh start; we need not be encumbered by our past. Isn't that the promise of life itself? No matter what our past mistakes, setbacks, sins or failures, we are allotted a do over with each sunrise. From my mother, I received this, the most important piece of advice concerning the ability to reinvent one's life.

My advice is to surround yourself with positive like-minded people and never take no for an answer. Believe in your hopes and dreams; if you don't, you can't expect others to. Ignore the little voice in your head that might crop up, saying "Why me?" or "I am not good enough, smart enough, rich or good looking enough." The only thing that counts cannot be taken away from you unless you let it. Lock it into your heart and mind. Will what want you want into existence, and it will appear. As Joseph Campbell would say "Follow your bliss."

Francis O'Donnell and Denis Belliveau on the route of Marco Polo.
Photograph courtesy of Francis O'Donnell.

Biography

Francis Daniel O'Donnell is an artist, author, poet, filmmaker, and explorer. He has lectured on his experiences throughout the United States at various colleges, schools, universities and organizations, clubs and libraries, and around the world as a guest speaker aboard 'Celebrity Cruise Line' ships. He is an alumnus of the School of Visual Arts in NYC where he earned a BFA in Media Arts and was studio assistant of world-renowned sculptor Joel Perlman. Francis contributed to the restoration of the Ludwig Mies van der Rohe house in Weston, Connecticut. A veteran of the US Marine Corps, he has run several NYC marathons. O'Donnell has traveled the world extensively, visiting over seventy countries, often participating in or leading research expeditions and archaeological digs. He is a member of the New York Explorers Club and the Adventurers Club of Chicago. His Emmy nominated PBS documentary, *In the Footsteps of Marco Polo* and companion book, were both co-produced and written by him. The film chronicles his historic two years, twenty-five thousand mile journey, retracing the Venetian merchant's 13th-century "Travels" along the fabled Silk Road.

He is a regular contributor to *The Heretic Magazine,* and the Scholarly blog *China Mongols and the Silk Road.* He has also contributed to *Ripcord Adventure Journal* among other journals, including the *Smithsonian Magazine—Marco Polo's Guide to Afghanistan.* Most recently his work has been featured in *The Walkabout Chronicles* an anthology published by Sacred World Explorations.

Currently, Mr. O'Donnell shows his art work around the country at various shows, most notably the ArtPrize Competition in Grand Rapids Michigan, and at The Crossroads and Art Works Galleries in Richmond, Virginia where he resides.

www.facebook.com/inthefootstepsofmarcopolo
www.artworksrichmond.com/FrancisODonnell.html
Macro Polo film: www.wliw.org/marcopolo

Photograph by Christian Martinez. Istock photo. Courtesy of Erin Byrne.

Erin Byrne

In the midst of the Iberian summer one glimpses a sharp, fleeting black form, one so full of passion it makes us shiver.
~Federico García Lorca, *The Poem of the Bull*

The Stance of the Toro Bravo

*T*he crowd's roar lulled into a hushed "Oooooooooh," and rolled over my head as I hunched over my notebook in Plaza de Toros de Las Ventas in Madrid one warm July evening. Teeth clenched, I shaded in a series of arches while stuffing imaginary cotton in my cochlea.

There had been only one other time in my life I had so fervently wished to be elsewhere.

Four months previously, while planning this trip to Spain, where my college-aged son Kellan would be studying for the summer, I had announced to my then husband John and him that under no circumstances would I go to Pamplona to watch their running asses grazed by horns.

"We'll go to the bullfight in Madrid instead," I pronounced, blithely unaware. In my reading about Spain, I had been mesmerized by poet Federico García Lorca's description of what he called the *duende*, the painful cry of longing that we all struggle with, the dark thread that runs through our lives. Lorca had said this was most impressive in traditional guitar music, flamenco, and the bullfight, which he called "the terrible play." I, like Lorca, was in search of *duende,* and had found it lurking in a cave in Peru, screaming out of a painting in the Louvre, and cowering in the crypt of a cathedral in Vienna. Now, I'd go straight to its source.

"Really? Okay." Kellan gaped, then quickly moved on to other plans: We'd watch the World Cup Tournament playoffs in a bar in Madrid, and then go to the Costa Brava, east of Barcelona. We could hang out on the beach ...

Ahhhh, *España*! Madrid's iron balconies presented its pastel buildings with a flourish, and the Prado and Reina Sofia museums rivaled any I'd visited—El Greco's paintings dripped with *duende*. The daily *siesta* inspired me to begin writing a screenplay. The evening of the *Corrida de Toros*, the Spanish Bullfight (literally "running of bulls"), as we approached the arena, I felt a spring in my step at the anticipation of learning more about the Spanish culture.

"You know they kill six bulls, right?" John asked, in falsetto.

I stopped. "What?"

"Come on Mom, you knew that," lied Kellan.

"You brought me here to see *death*? How dare you; how insensitive," I snarled, for since my sister had died three years previously, I had avoided all mention of death.

John and Kellan had failed to act as my protectors. But, I could see from their eyes that the only reason they had kept this from me was that they'd wanted me to come, and I was brushed by a feeling of foolishness.

Inside the arena, determined not to watch the barbaric ritual, I sketched. I could hear John's click of the camera, and ignored his attempts to get me to look up. Trumpets blared, applause rippled.

Kellan, a double major in English and Spanish, had studied up on the bullfight and gave me a whispered commentary.

"The matador's marching around with his toes pointed. The other name for him is *torero*. Now here come some guys with long lances called *banderilleros*, some more on padded, blindfolded horses, called *picadors*. Here's the *toro bravo*, the fighting bull."

I know now that there are three stages in a Spanish bullfight. During Stage 1, *Tercio de Varas* (the Lances Third), the torero watches the bull as it charges the banderilleros' capes, noting its weaknesses. They say that when the beast lowers his head and appears most threatening, he is, in fact, the least dangerous. It is when he seeks out and heads for his *querencia*, his turf, that the bull is most ferocious. In Spanish, this word describes a place from which one's strength of character is drawn, where one feels safe, or at home. It comes from the verb *quere*, which means to desire, to want.

"Now the matador's waving his cape. Whoa, that bull's mad!"

During this stage, the picadors stab the bull's neck, which induces the beast to attack the horses.

This Kellan described in gory detail, and would have been what caused the crowd's "Ooooooooooooohhhhhh."

Training my eye across the arena to the top without looking at the scene on the sand below, I examined the way the fading sunlight fell upon the ground beneath the arches. The crowd surged into another wave.

"God, this is really sick. I can't believe you didn't tell me they kill SIX bulls. We have to sit through this six times? You knew I'd hate this. Maybe I'll just go back to the hotel." I seethed, staring at my drawing through a curtain of curly hair.

"Did you see that, Kellan? They're stabbing him with those darts. Yeow!" John. Click, click.

Stage 2, *Tercio de Banderilleros*, was occurring then, in which three banderilleros ("little flags") plant darts in the bull's shoulders, causing blood to spurt, and spurring the bull to charge.

"That poor bull. No, I'm not *looking*." I twisted away from John's tap on my shoulder, wondering if the toro bravo felt alone and afraid.

The crowd exploded.

"The matador's back, he's got a sword," breathed Kellan, who, by age four had developed a lifelong fascination with swords, and had smacked everything from our shrubbery to his tricycle with his gray plastic weapon.

This is an odd part in the bullfight. The matador enters with his cape and a sword and teases the bull into making a few passes. But he is not yet going to use the sword; it is as if he's revealing what destiny has in store for the creature.

Stage 3, the "Death Third" of the Spanish bullfight, is *Tercio de Muerte*. This time the matador enters with a small red cape which hides the sword. He lures the bull into passing closer and closer to his body, demonstrating his control of the animal. The color is meant to hide the bloodstains that glob upon the fabric as the bull brushes against it.

The crowd began to chant *"Olé!"*—which I deduced from John's "Wow, that was close!" to mean they were thrilled with the proximity of the bull to the matador's side. I felt dizzy and angry, wishing I was in Pamplona after all, watching John and Kellan's backsides careen down a narrow alley.

In the final moments of the *Tercio de Muerte*, the matador maneuvers the bull into a position where he can plunge his sword between the bull's shoulder blades and into its heart. The only thing that can save the bull is if *El Presidente*, the President of the event, is particularly impressed with its fighting spirit and gives the signal to spare its life. It is intriguing to note that once a bull has been spared, it can never again enter the ring because it *knows*. It has learned the way of its fate in this scenario, and will now be wise to the ways of the bullfight.

"He's down."

"Blood everywhere, Mom, don't look."

"Don't worry, Kellan." I couldn't wait to get to Catalonia, the northern area of Spain, where they adamantly opposed this absurd tradition.

Cheers, clapping, accolades for the murderer. After the bull topples over, its heavy carcass is dragged out by a team of mules.

"Here comes the next one."

Another bull! I stared at my lap and realized I should have anticipated this killing when I had read Lorca's famous *Poem of the Bull*. I'd thought it a bit dramatic, but aren't all poems? Now I understood the real meaning of Lorca's *bellow of pain. . . it comes from the bullring, from an ancient temple, and it zigzags across the sky . . .*

How clueless I'd been. As the stomping thunder raged on, I was startled to discover that I had envisioned this event based on that beloved matador-and-bull scene I'd watched so many times over the years. One in which the triangular-shaped bull, ring in nose, puffs smoke, stomps the ground, and hurls himself at a thin, gray, floppy-eared matador in a turquoise *traje de luces*, and races into a TNT explosion. I'd fallen victim to Warner Brother's version, and had been ill-prepared for the reality.

The spectacle continued, the actions repeated (I gauged by the sound) two more times. The cacophony was a sinister moan from the dark, a chaotic anthem to *duende*, a concept I was beginning to loathe.

My artistic eye focused again on the top tier of seats, which were dotted with spectators. I wished I had more colors. How was I to endure? Time dragged on. We were toward the end of the third repetition, the *"Olé!"* chanting well underway, when I saw that my drawing was starting to resemble a real work of art. I held it up and squinted at it, examining my shading technique.

At that instant I saw, beyond the upper right hand corner of the white paper, the black bulk of the bull.

His side heaved as he breathed, shaking the long, red darts embedded in his flank, their tissue paper streamers fluttering. His tail switched. Scarlet streams trickled down his black mountain of a back. The creature's eyes glowered with a desperate gleam, but his lowered brow gave him a menacing mien. With nostrils flaring, he lowered his head almost to the ground, showing a startlingly strong instinct to fight with every cell in his body. This bull would not die easily.

Several feet in front of the bull, the late afternoon sun deepened the torero's fuchsia jacket, flashed on its gold curlicue design, and softened the jet black of his two-cornered hat with the little dip in the middle. His head was tilted down, chin on his chest, which curved out in the shape of a question mark. His tie was a line down the middle of a blindingly white shirt. A green sash was tied around his tiny waist and his legs were spread and straight all the way down pink knee-length socks to black ballet-style slippers.

The small red cape turned over and over in hypnotic waves, revealing the flashing point of the sword's blade.

The bull's stance straightened, his back a hulking mound, his hooves planted firmly on the ground. He teetered a fraction, then seemed to gather into his body every bit of dignity that existed in the world. So slowly the motion was almost imperceptible, he raised his magnificent head and looked at the torero, facing him head-on. All was still.

I saw this moment in the terrible play as if through a grainy haze, and it annihilated me. But the tears that ran down my cheeks were not for the bull.

Three years earlier, inside of a room with windows overlooking the jagged snow-capped peaks of Colorado's Rocky Mountains, I stood at the end of a bed in which lay my sister's 42-year-old body, a skeleton out of which her eyes blazed feverishly, registering nothing. My hands twisted a pink cashmere cap I'd brought because it was soft and her favorite color, and which I now knew was useless. Allison was beyond sensation.

A nurse beckoned me out into the hall, where Allison's husband Steve stood ruffling his hair absently, eyes wide, mouth grimaced.

"Her internal organs have shut down and are no longer working," the hospice nurse said. "She's been like this for a day and a half now. Technically, she should be gone, but she is resisting. We've never had a patient hang on so long in this state."

I wasn't surprised. My little sister had always been the sweet one, the red-haired girl who minded her manners, got good grades, and was considerate of the feelings of everyone from the handicapped girl across the street to our pet basset hound. I was the bossy, rebellious daughter.

During our outwardly idyllic childhood, I was the serious observer, brooding in my room writing stories, and she was naturally cheerful. Each Halloween, my carved pumpkin menaced, hers beamed. Between the two of us, we achieved a balance between light and dark, which made our days flow, as both are essential for grasping the sublime beauty of life. As years passed, radiance was plunged into gloom like high-speed landscape photography, but also the unlit was set alight by our connection.

We were inseparable, and she was my most ardent cheerleader. But when we tangled, she showed a stubbornness that startled me.

The time I sprayed Right Guard deodorant toward her head, she refused to speak to me for two whole days; I sneaked a late-night viewing of *Batman* without her, and she set up a courtroom drama in which my parents found me guilty; another time, when I yelled at her, she put tape across the floor of our shared room, barricading herself on the side away from the door for hours, staring at me above crossed arms. Allison was sweet, but she was feisty.

Every once in a while, in the middle of the night, at one of those moments when fear burns a path through dreams and ignites the body with terror, I would imagine a world without Allison in it. I'd grasp the size, the density, the capacity of this earth to hold people, and I'd feel the horror if it were minus one. The black would engulf me then. My eyes would stretch wide, my heart boiling. If Allison was not in the world, I did not want to be in it either. Eventually, I'd look across the room at her sleeping form, and discern, across the grainy gray, her small head of tangled hair upon a white pillow. Safety would seep into me, and I'd fall back to sleep.

Through the years we remained close—played tennis and went sailing together; were sorority sisters in college; when married, lived a half-hour apart; had our sons within months of each other—always intertwined. When she and her family moved to Colorado, we gabbed on the phone for hours, continuing to balance each other.

She'd endured, in her gentle, trying-to-be-good-natured way, two years of diagnoses that tumbled downhill from "most aggressive form of breast cancer" to "nothing more we can do"; chemo and radiation; discovering its metastasis to her brain the day of her 42nd birthday; the fear that she'd never see her son, Jack, graduate from high school. She had absorbed blow after blow.

She and I had said many goodbyes, for during her last six months—since our visit to M.D. Anderson Cancer Center in Houston—the two of us were the only ones who knew her dire prognosis.

By the time she ended up in the hospice, I knew that she was mostly out of this world, with dwindling moments of presence. One by one, I had seen her let go of each person she loved—our closest friends, our parents, and even Jack. Only Steve remained, and I knew Allison's stubborn streak had held out until she was ready to let go of him.

She died with silent dignity when and only when she was ready.

After my trip to Spain, I became a bullfighting aficionado with a new affinity for the *Corrida*. I told everyone that I had not grasped its significance until I'd seen it. The doomed bull's dignity had reminded me of my *sister*. The pageantry, the three stages that showed the inner workings of a creature as he faced his tormentors and killer, the wonderful idea of killing six bulls: another bull, another chance! I argued with animal-rights-activists, and urged anyone traveling to Spain to partake of the pantomime at Plaza de Toros de Las Ventas. As I am always anxious to spin a good story, this comparison between the stance of the bull and Allison's death begged to be written.

I could not write it.

One year passed, then another. I wrote a bullfighting scene in the *Siesta* screenplay, and a short story about a character who identifies with the anger of the bull, but my pen froze when I tried to write about Allison. I was not afraid to evoke a bit of *duende*, so I had no idea why this story stopped me in my tracks.

I had not yet grasped the second analogy of the toro bravo.

At times in life when I need help, books are the places I find strength. After Allison's death, I immersed myself in hopeful titles: *Healing Your Grieving Heart*, *A Journey Through Grief*, and *Five Stages of Grief*, but the only book that made sense to me was, oddly enough for a then-practicing Catholic, *When Things Fall Apart* by Pema Chödrön, a book which shares traditional Buddhist wisdom. I was particularly struck by the idea of embracing grief, of welcoming it, as the Buddha's teaching seemed to suggest.

In the months after Allison's death, I cancelled river rafting trips and weekends with friends and family, cultivating a bring-on-the grief bravado. I spent time alone sensing the pain, then zigzag out of it. I'd weep, then distract myself with a movie; look at an old photo album, then write some poetry about Leonard Cohen; reminisce, then make bruschetta. I appeared a normal, functioning adult who only privately lapsed into crying jags and barely said two words on each anniversary of Allison's death.

It was my secret that my world was black. I had not gone through all the stages of grief or arrived at the place of acceptance. I alone knew that I'd refused to contemplate the truth that my torch bearer was gone.

Still, I remained interested in this idea of embracing grief. One evening, I went to a talk by Dr. Mark Epstein, a psychiatrist who has written a number of books about Buddhism and psychotherapy.

Dr. Epstein read from his book, *The Trauma of Everyday Life*:

" The Buddha took a different approach, one that seems more realistic.

There need be no end of grief, he would say. While it is never static—it is not a single (or even a five-stage) thing—there is no reason to believe it will disappear for good and no need to judge oneself if it does not. Grief turns over and over. It is vibrant, surprising and alive, just as we are."

Grief is vibrant and alive, I thought. *And it holds a red cape under which hides a sword.*

Primitive feelings, Epstein went on, continue to be stirred. Understanding them does not turn them off. But we can cultivate what the Buddha called The Realistic View: examining feelings rather than running away from them, acknowledging rather than pretending normalcy. The Buddha, said Epstein, managed to make trauma tolerable by easing people into the burning nature of things.

Buddhist wisdom has been preserved in a collection of koans, which are paradoxical questions meant to challenge the mind as trauma does, asking us to make sense of the inconceivable and to explain the unexplainable, and to transform the way we orient ourselves in the world.

I began to see the moment in Plaza de Toros de Las Ventas as my own kind of koan, albeit one that would have appalled the Buddha, with his admonition against killing.

The tableau beyond the edge of my notebook had struck much closer to home than I'd realized. It had shown me that if I looked up, I'd face full-on the reality of a world without Allison in it: the shiny point of a blade aimed straight at my heart.

How pretty it would be to write that I am now a devout Buddhist, liberated from within, opening myself fearlessly and calmly to the tumult of the sublime, gathering all of the brightness in the world with abandon. But I still resist. When I travel I search for her, absurdly surprised that she is not in Brazil, or Ireland, or Africa. I look at old photos of us and hate the piercing pain that turns over and over inside my chest. I search out places to hide from it, and fight instinctively against it. Only one person would still admire me, even though I've skipped out on the stages of grief, broken down on the journey, and remain unhealed. I want my cheerleader back.

But every time I acknowledge this grief, I feel a little wiser in the ways of loss. In trying to embrace the burning nature of everything, the glow within the flames eases my vertigo, and I am changed slowly, almost imperceptibly, into a person who seeks less often to be spared. One who looks up.

The inconceivable terrible play continues. I remember the sharp, fleeting black form of the toro bravo, and I shiver.

Questions and Answers

Every man and every artist, whether he is Nietzsche or Cézanne, climbs each step in the ladder of his perfection by fighting his duende, not his angel, as has been said, nor his muse.
~Federico García Lorca, *In Search of Duende*

1. What compelled you to set out on your pilgrimage?
I had read *In Search of Duende* by Federico García Lorca, and became fascinated with this concept which he harnessed in his writing and offered as a creative inspiration.

2. Is there a book, song, poem, or movie that inspired your quest?
In Search of Duende by Federico García Lorca
The Poem of the Bull by Federico García Lorca

3. Where is your sacred place and why did you choose it?
I chose Spain, but feel that Plaza de Toros de Las Ventas chose me.

4. How did your pilgrimage change your life or not?
It changed my life incredibly. I experienced the meaning of Lorca's description of *duende*, which includes *arrows of gold being shot right into our hearts*, a struggle with something that *climbs up inside you, from the soles of the feet*, and the *precious stone of the sob*.

This experience changed my life in so many ways. I now go deeper until I know I have made all the connections between a place and myself before I even try to write about it, and I am able to better face life, death, grief, hardships, and challenges. I have more appreciation for sunlight and shadow, and feel a range of emotion that I didn't before this trip.

5. What is the most important piece of advice that you have received in your life? Do you have advice to share from your experiences?
Phil Cousineau once told me to write until I reach the truth of the vein pulsing in my neck. Now, I try to live from this place. I believe that when human beings respond to the call of any place on this earth, near or far, transformative gifts open inside them that are theirs to keep.

If what you are following, however, is your own true adventure, if it is something appropriate to your deep spiritual need or readiness, then magical guides will appear to help you. If you say, "Everyone's going on this trip this year, and I'm going too," then no guides will appear.

Your adventure has to be coming right out of your own interior. And if you are ready for it, then doors will open where there were no doors

before, and where there would not be doors for anyone else. And you must have courage. It's the call to adventure, which means there is no security, no rules.
~Joseph Campbell, *A Joseph Campbell Companion: Reflections on the Art of Living*

America's Cup qualifying races, San Francisco.
Photograph courtesy of Erin Byrne.

Biography

Erin Byrne is the author of *Wings: Gifts of Art, Life, and Travel in France*, winner of the Paris Book Festival Award and the Next Generation Indie Book Award, editor of *Vignettes & Postcards from Paris* and *Vignettes & Postcards from Morocco*, and writer of *The Storykeeper* film. Erin's travel essays, poetry, fiction and screenplays have won numerous awards including three Grand Prize Solas Awards for Travel Story of the Year, the Reader's Favorite Award, Foreword Indies Book of the Year, and an Accolade Award for film. She has taught writing at Shakespeare and Company Bookstore in Paris and on Deep Travel trips, and is host of the LitWings event series at Book Passage, Sausalito, which features writers, photographers, and film-makers. Her screenplay, *Siesta,* is in pre-production in Spain, and she is working on a novel set in the Paris Ritz during the occupation, *Illuminations.*

www.e-byrne.com

Boating to the Perfume Pagoda. *Photograph by Alison Ormsby.*

Alison Ormsby

Accepting the Invitation ... and Respecting the Sacred

*M*onday February 16, 1998. Vietnam.

What a day. We left early (again) for the Perfume Pagoda. It sounded like a tranquil trip—a boat ride and hike to a high temple.

In the late 1990s, I was backpacking around Thailand and Vietnam with two good friends who share a love of adventure traveling. These were intrepid women with whom I had served in the Peace Corps in West Africa several years before. In Vietnam, we visited a sacred mountain, home to the Perfume Pagoda. It was the kind of destination that appealed to us, involving multiple modes of travel (bus, boat, walking), and learning about the local culture. The Perfume Pagoda (Chùa Hương) is considered a primary pilgrimage destination in Vietnam.[i] This area of Vietnam has iconic limestone formations that contain numerous pagodas and Buddhist shrines carved into the karst cliffs of Huong Tich Mountain, about 75 kilometers from Hanoi.

My travel journal entry for that day continues:

But this time of the year, thousands of people make the trip, so it was very *crowded and trashy. I was feeling so bad that I stopped halfway and didn't go to the top—which was a good call. I went to the side 'human rights' temple and associated cave. My worst nightmare— slippery steep rocks and lots of people all day.*

At the time, I didn't realize the significance of the site and that we were entering a pilgrimage route. We were the typical oblivious tourists, not having done much previous research on the site and just picking a day trip based on how interesting it sounded; I have learned to be better since then! The journey started with our hiring a metal boat and paddler to take us up the river to the bottom of stone stairs leading up to the sacred mountain and Buddhist shrines in mountain caves. Crowds were already apparent at the dock as people jostled to hire boats. On the one-hour journey up the river, we passed between several beautiful karst limestone formations, small mountains rising above fields of rice.

We were shocked once we arrived at the steps leading up the mountain at both the large number of visitors, mostly Vietnamese Buddhists, and the scale of the vendors and number of stands and shops lining the steps all the way up the mountain. The stone steps were worn smooth (and therefore tricky for fear of slipping) from thousands of pilgrims over the years wearing down the route.

The path up the mountain to the Perfume Pagoda is two kilometers.

Along the stone step mountain pathway, lining both sides, are vendors selling trinkets, food, drinks, and offerings for the shrines in the caves in the mountain. Of course, the food and drinks contained wrappers and containers that became trash littering the path. During our visit, I was suffering from a stomach ailment, so only made it partway up the mountain before I decided to rest with a vendor on their mat and let my friends continue ahead without me. I stopped to relax and watched the crowds walk by and climb the stairs to the shrines.

We had happened to pick the busiest time of the year, as February to April is the most popular time to visit. Price gouging has been documented at the annual festival at the Perfume Pagoda.[ii] In our case, we were tourists, but we had happened to pick the pilgrimage time of year to visit. Nowadays, new development enables visitors to take a cable car up to the sacred site.

What is a pilgrimage? How are tourists different than pilgrims?

Since my experience in Vietnam, I have reflected on how I ended up at a pilgrimage site as a tourist. Going on a pilgrimage may mean different things to different people. What are pilgrims seeking? They may be on a religious or spiritual journey, following in the footsteps of others, or questing for a destination, perhaps entering a sacred landscape.

I am not a typical pilgrim; my ongoing search is more a curiosity and research quest about sacred forests. About 20 years ago, I lived in a small village in Sierra Leone, West Africa. Community members were primarily farmers. Most of the landscape was either rice fields or various intercropped fruits and vegetables—like pineapple, sweet potatoes, cassava, and peanuts. Still, small fragments of forest were left, very visible amidst the rice fields. One day, walking from our community to a neighboring area and passing by a small dense piece of forest, I asked my friend, "Why is this forest still here? Why has it not been cleared?" And he matter-of-factly replied, "Because it is a sacred forest." Ever since then, I have been fascinated by the idea of sacred forests. Over time, I have learned that these are areas protected by communities for a variety of reasons: religious or spiritual significance; the dwelling place of a spirit; the burial place of the ancestors; and sometimes containing a sacred spring.

Ever since my interest in sacred natural sites was sparked in Sierra Leone, I have done a great deal of reading about sacred sites, and have visited many. With my increased awareness of sacred natural places has come a deeper respect for the need to use care and caution when visiting sacred sites, and the need to do advance research to understand the cultural significance of pilgrimage sites that tourists might be drawn to casually visit. One issue I have seen in person and read about is the potential impacts of pilgrimages on places, especially sacred natural sites.

The reality is, pilgrims taking part in large-scale pilgrimages may love places to death. For example, the Huanglong Scenic and Historic Interest Area in Sichuan, China is a pilgrimage area that attracts followers from three different religions, receiving over 10,000 pilgrims each day during the peak summer season.[iii] Japan is also home to several pilgrimage routes. The Kii Mountains in Japan, which contain sacred sites and pilgrimage routes, is a pilgrimage destination for Shugendo followers (a combination of Buddhist and Shinto beliefs).[iv] And in southern India there is the annual pilgrimage to Sabarimala, the main temple of Ayyappa. In 2012, while I was visiting India with students, we were driving to visit Periyar National Park in the state of Kerala where the Ayyappa pilgrimage occurs. All along the road we passed men dressed in black clothing on the Sabarimala pilgrimage. I admired their tenacity and commitment to walk the long distance to the Ayyappa temple in the heat. Starting in mid-November, millions of pilgrims from southern India visit each year within a period of only about 60 days.[v]

Some people are on modern quests to achieve certain destinations or goals. These may not be strictly religious pilgrimages. Uluru in Australia and Mato Tipila in the United States are two examples of quest sites for rock climbers. Pilgrimage or quest locations may be "contested sites"—where there are conflicts over matters of site access and use.[vi] These sites may attract both pilgrims and general tourists (like my experience in Vietnam), as well as recreational users. Contested sites are "sacred locations where there is a contest over access and usage by any number of groups or individuals who have an interest in being able to freely enter and move around the site."[vii]

For example, Uluru in Australia is both a sacred and contested site. The area is also referred to as Ayers Rock, a name given to the site in the late 1800s in honor of the Chief Secretary of South Australia, Sir Henry Ayers. The area was declared Uluru-Kata Tjuta National Park in 1958. Although the rock monolith at Uluru is sacred to the indigenous Anangu people, "in the 50s, the Northern Territory government evicted Aborigines from the areas in the vicinity of the Rock."[viii] In 1985, "the Australian government returned Uluru-Kata Tjuta National Park to [the Anangu] as traditional owners, and the Anangu, in turn, leased it back to the government in a joint management arrangement."[ix] Uluru was designated a UNESCO World Heritage Site in 1987. Sacred sites at Uluru are now marked and signed. Climbing of Uluru is a controversial topic. The traditional Anangu owners prefer that visitors do not climb Uluru, and instead walk around the base of the sacred landform. A voluntary climbing ban has been put into place by Parks Australia, although many visitors are unaware of the controversy surrounding climbing this sacred place.[x]

A similar controversy exists at Mato Tipila or Bear's Lodge in the United States, also known as Devil's Tower National Monument, in the state of Wyoming. This is both a sacred site to numerous Native American groups and also a sought-after site for rock climbers.[xi] Like Uluru, visitors to Mato

Tipila are asked to observe a climbing ban, although this is a temporary voluntary ban specific to the month of June when most sacred ceremonies are conducted.*xii* As I have reflected on pilgrimage sites, I wonder about the roles and responsibilities of tourists visiting these sites.

Conclusion

Having visited many sacred natural sites and ecological tourist destinations, and observing the impacts of visitors to these sites, has made me think about the motivations of travelers as well as the responsibilities of those people who manage natural sites—whether they be park managers, committees of elders, community groups, or individuals. I am so grateful to the people who have accompanied me to visit sacred forests, when appropriate, and have answered my questions about how plants are used in the sites, as well as when and where ceremonies are conducted. It is key that visitors to natural and pilgrimage sites show respect, and do research ahead of time to honor the cultural history and significance of the place.

The speed or pace of pilgrimage has changed over time, and the volumes of tourists have increased significantly. Places previously only accessible on foot are now accessible by road or even helicopter. The Perfume Pagoda in Vietnam that took me hours to reach by bus, boat, and walking can now be accessed by a cable car.

One question that arises is, should there be limits on the number of tourists or pilgrims to certain sites? It would be useful to try to anticipate possible conflicts between pilgrims and tourists, and recognize that their objectives for visiting a site may not be the same. Some sites are under pressure from hundreds or even thousands of pilgrims, needing resources like firewood, food, and there is also the matter of waste disposal. Tourists add to the pressures. This raises the question of how to manage the site to maintain its integrity. It may be necessary to have voluntary bans or even permanent limits on activities or number of visitors, and mandatory bans on access to certain areas.

Part of what makes sacred spaces special is that they have associated taboos on activities that can be done there, who can access the sites, and when.*xiii* For example, some sacred forests have a taboo on hunting certain species of animal, like monkeys at Tafi Atome sacred grove in Ghana, and many communities forbid hunting and farming in their sacred forest. We should learn about and respect these special place-based meanings and requirements.

Twenty years after I lived in Sierra Leone as a Peace Corps Volunteer, I returned to conduct research on sacred forests. The forests associated with women's groups are called Bundo and the men's forests are Poro. Cotton trees (*Ceiba pentrandra*) are especially sacred. As I looked back through my research and interview notes, this passage stood out:

The village was tucked in on a dirt road off the main gravel and dirt road. All groves were near the center of the village. The chiefs and Bundo bush were near the house where we conducted the interview. The Poro bush was on the other side of the village, and we observed large cotton trees in it, including one cotton tree with a large wild beehive on it. We observed turacos and hornbills flying near the forest during the interview. The forests still seemed to have large trees in them.

It may be that active community management of pilgrimage sites, like the community management of these sacred forests in Sierra Leone, is crucial to their future preservation.

Notes

[i] Lauser, A. 2015. *Traveling to Yên Tử (North Vietnam): Religious Resurgence, Cultural Nationalism and Touristic Heritage in the Shaping of a Pilgrimage Landscape.* In: DORISEA Working Paper Series, No. 20.

[ii] McElroy, J.L., P. Tarlow, and K. Carlisle. (2007). Tourist harassment: review of the literature and destination responses. *International Journal of Culture, Tourism and Hospitality Research* 1(4): 305-314.

[iii] Kang, X. 2009. Two temples, three religions, and a tourist attraction: contesting sacred space on China's ethnic frontier. *Modern China* 35(3): 227-255.

[iv] Bernbaum, E. and N. Inaba. 2016. Mountains divided: Kii mountain range. *World Heritage* 78: 21-25. http://whc.unesco.org/en/list/1142

[v] Osella, F. and C. Osella. 2003. 'Ayyappan Saranam': Masculinity and the Sabarimala pilgrimage in Kerala. *The Journal of the Royal Anthropological Institute* 9(4): 729-754.

[vi] Digance, J. 2003. Pilgrimage at contested sites. *Annals of Tourism Research* 30(1): 143-159.

[vii] Digance, J. 2003. p.144.

[viii] Digance, J. 2003. P. 151.

[ix] Sarmiento, F., Bernbaum, E., Brown, J, Lennon, J. and Feary, S. 2014. Managing cultural features and uses. In G.L. Worboys, M. Lockwood, A. Kothari, S. Feary and I Pulsford (eds.). *Protected Area Governance and Management*, p. 685-714. ANU Press, Canberra.

[x] https://parksaustralia.gov.au/uluru/do/we-dont-climb.html

[xi] https://www.nps.gov/deto/learn/historyculture/sacredsite.htm

[xii] Zeppel, H. 2010. Managing cultural values in sustainable tourism: conflicts in protected areas. *Tourism and Hospitality Research* 10(2): 93-104.

[xiii] Colding, J. and Folke, C. 2001. Social Taboos: "Invisible" Systems of Local Resource Management and Biological Conservation. *Ecological Applications,* 11, 584-600.

Questions and Answers

1. What compelled you to set out on your pilgrimage?
My fascination with sacred natural sites, which started in Sierra Leone, has created a lifelong personal quest to visit and understand these sites in a variety of contexts and locations. So far, my journeys have taken me to Ghana, India, and back to Sierra Leone.

2. Is there a book, song, poem, or movie that inspired your quest?
Nothing specific, but most travel writing piques my curiosity.

3. Where is your sacred place and why did you choose it?
Not one in particular. I am interested in sacred natural sites everywhere. Personally, my own special place would be the creek at my grandparents' house that I enjoyed every summer. An especially memorable and moving experience was seeing hornbills near numerous sacred groves in Sierra Leone.

4. How did your pilgrimage change your life or not?
Each place I visit influences me and stimulates my thinking and understanding.

5. What is the most important piece of advice that you have received in your life? Do you have advice to share from your experiences?
My main piece of advice, and what is often most memorable about traveling, is to be friendly and to accept spontaneous opportunities that arise, like being invited to tea or for a meal—we should both accept and offer hospitality. If you are offered a canoe ride, go.

Photograph courtesy of Alison Ormsby.

Biography

Alison Ormsby teaches Environmental Studies, Humanities, and Environmental Art at the University of North Carolina, Asheville. She is a human ecologist and is interested in the connections between people and conservation of natural areas. She has conducted research at sacred forests in Ghana, India, and Sierra Leone. She has published numerous articles about her work, as well as chapters in the books *Sacred Species and Sites: Advances in Biocultural Conservation* (2012, Cambridge University Press) and *Sacred Natural Sites: Conserving Nature and Culture* (2010, Earthscan).

"The quest for certainty blocks the search for meaning. Uncertainty is the very condition to impel man to unfold his powers."
~Erich Fromm

Photograph by Lonnie Dupre.

"Thousands of tired, nerve-shaken, over-civilized people are beginning to find out going to the mountains is going home; that wilderness is a necessity..."
~ John Muir

"We travel, some of us forever, to seek other states, other lives, other souls."
~Anaïs Nin

Ernest White II

To the Dungeon: A Nighttime Walk in São Paulo

*F*austão arrived at my hotel around eleven at night and waited in the lobby, since visitors weren't allowed in the room without first registering with the front desk. He greeted me with a hug and a pat on the back, his broad and muscular body stretching the fabric of his red, sleeveless tee.

"Brother, how are you, good?" he asked and I nodded yes, still unsure of what exactly we were about to get into. We had met earlier at the gym down the street from the hotel. Faustão had overheard me struggling with Portuguese and with a halting, endearing English he learned at a language school and from watching American movies, he helped me decipher the kilo-to-pound conversion of the weights. We talked for a long while, cutting our respective workouts short and comparing musculature in the locker room. I told him I had been a fat teenager—360 lbs when I graduated high school fifteen years before—and he stared incredulously. "No, brother. Your body good," he said, and I stared incredulously. I needed him, or someone like him, to like me, and he seemed to. He invited me to meet his friends who were working as go-go dancers at a gay club that night.

The night air of São Paulo was chillier than I had anticipated, and I felt goosebumps forming on my arms. "Aren't you cold?" I asked.

"No, not cold. Fresh."

"Fresh? You mean cool?"

"Yes, cool. Yes. We walk fast because we need be there before twelve. And I hate bus."

Faustão and I walked briskly down the hill, legions of punk rockers, yuppies, and prostitutes streaming up and down both sides of Rua Augusta. We had to walk single file and Faustão led, the perfect Y of his body a constant reminder of my own imperfections and failures. We passed the Blue Night strip club and the be-suited man standing out front spoke to me in English, "My friend, come in. Girls!" to which Faustão barked back in Portuguese, "Trankweeloocaralyou." I tried to walk with Faustão's confidence, like I knew exactly where we were going, and I tried not to stare at passersbys. But from the corner of my eye, I saw pale fluorescent skin, piercings in noses and lips and eyebrows and cheeks, and a rainbow of unnatural hair colors. The existence of a punk scene amazed me, considering all I knew of Brazil before that night was samba, soccer, and porn, dominated by a demographic without pallor, piercings, or pink hair. The crowd on the street was loud and boisterous, laughing and talking in the rounded sounds of Portuguese; the only stores open at that hour were sex shops, video stores, a couple of beauty salons, and 24-hour lanchonetes, which, with their white tile walls and shiny lunch counters, shimmered like lighthouses in the decadent darkness.

The Pussycat, another strip club, glowed persistently ahead of us with red and pink and blue neon. The other establishments had names in strange English like Night House and Love Love, and some even had a few women in hot pants lolling about in front, chatting and laughing with the black-suited security guards. We passed a group of young women in working-girl attire: brightly-colored tube dresses and extra-high heels, obviously-fake hair, and I soon realized they were transgender prostitutes. They stared at Faustão and I as we walked through their cloud of marijuana smoke and too much imposter perfume, their blue and green contact lenses looking wicked and unearthly and even beautiful against their tanned, heavily made-up faces.

"Travestis," Faustão turned and said, sensing my curiosity.

"Transsexuals?" I clarified.

"Yes," Faustão nodded without further comment. We walked another few blocks as the crowd on the sidewalk thinned but the traffic—buses packed with late-night commuters and tricked-out Fiats bumping Rihanna at Miami-bass decibels—coursed steadily and in single file in each direction, climbing or descending the semi-steep incline of Rua Augusta. I thought, at that moment, of the Colombian who had broken my heart in the months before that trip; I hoped to have it mended in Brazil, by Brazil, by some heretofore-unknown Brazilian who liked me enough to make the first date a second one. Certainly, Faustão had already ruled himself out when he mentioned his girlfriend, and despite the intended destination and his overt affability. "Me, girls only," he had said earlier at the gym. "But no problem, brother. I many gay friends."

Soon, we reached a viaduct and I shivered in the chilly air as traffic streamed at high speed beneath us, the freeway exploding up and out from a tunnel under our feet and framed by buildings, countless concrete blocks with countless glass eyes lighting the urban darkness. I suddenly felt warm as the city engulfed me, the pulse of the metal and concrete that cradled twenty million other people.

"Ven ca," Faustão said in a beckoning tone and I followed as we crossed Rua Augusta and headed down a dark street, dark even under the orange wash of the streetlights. Apartment and office towers loomed overhead, and the signs at street-level advertised goods and services peddled during business hours, but now closed-off behind metal, roll-down barriers. Ahead was a cylindrical-shaped building behind the spire of a church, the cylinder white and slick, as much a temple to the future and modernity as the church was an intricate nod to history and tradition. The street was empty except for me, Faustão, and a stray dog, and as we walked past the church, I started to ask Faustão where we were going, but before I even got the chance to speak, Faustão raised his finger to his mouth and said, "No talk English here."

We turned more corners, past the ornate stone facades and columns of São Paulo's true and original downtown, for there were several across that massive agglomeration. The necessary silence became obvious when we saw several dirt-caked, unwashed homeless men, wandering aimlessly in tattered clothes and often without shoes. They walked slowly, like zombies, and I sensed that they had probably taken something to dull the pain of, well, everything. I realized that the hotel shuttle bus had passed through that same area earlier in the day, when the streets swarmed with people interacting, transacting, buzzing productively under a warm winter sun. At night, the place was a ghost town, the dark streets haunted by the undesirables of society—the homeless who may or may not suffer from a mental disability, drug addicts who would just as soon rob you as offer you a blow job for ten reais—and random assortments of street kids, late-night fast food vendors, and city sanitation workers. At that moment, that particular city block became the same block in any big city in the world. The trash always gets thrown downtown.

We turned the corner onto a street lined with a few hole-in-the-wall bars, bouncers perched on stools next to metal doors lit by neon signs that read "Open" in English. The tight shirts and jeans and careful, stylish coiffures of the men—and the relative absence of women—let me know that we'd reached a gay area of town. We approached, then walked past a long line of guys, some thin and wiry and femme, others buff and butch with extra-long sideburns intimating their sexuality, all staring and commenting as Faustão and I went by. We reached the door of The Dungeon, the club where Faustão's friends danced, and he greeted a heavy-set drag queen in a yellow frock and platinum blonde wig, a vague imitation of Marilyn or Mamie or Mae. Faustão kissed her on the cheek, said something in Portuguese in a rather seductive manner, and the drag queen laughed. She looked at me, said something to Faustão, who responded and she extended her bejewelled hand to me: "Bengvindooamigoojeewashingtoe."

I took this as a greeting and shook her hand, delicate in appearance but with a strong grip. "This Mariana," Faustão said. "Owner girlfriend." Mariana had allowed us to skip the queue. Faustão had juice, it seemed.

I nodded, not knowing what else to say, and Faustão said, almost sweetly, "Ven ca." I followed this heretofore-unknown Brazilian, hopefully and willingly, into The Dungeon.

Questions and Answers

1. What compelled you to set out on your pilgrimage?
I think I was drawn into my pilgrimage more than compelled to make the leap of my own volition. I've had a yearning to discover the world and all its ways of being since I was a small child walking around with a road atlas or almanac when other kids my age were playing sports or with toys. It was inevitable that I'd set out for something, somewhere.

2. Is there a book, song, poem, or movie that inspired your quest?
The song *Samba do Gringo Paulista*, by the late Serbian-born producer Suba, warmed me up for an lifelong love affair with Brazil's largest city. Suba's album *São Paulo Confessions* really captured the ethos of a massive city being crushed under an oppressive past, an urgent present, and a future just out of reach. The title of this particular song speaks to those of us from other places, like Suba, who felt an unexplained and magnetic kinship with that chaotic assemblage of humanity called São Paulo.

3. Where is your sacred place and why did you choose it?
My sacred place is in music. Certain songs, by virtue of the sensual world they create, offer me a place of escape, of contemplation, of safety, of love. Some songs make me want to live inside them, if that makes any sense.

4. How did your pilgrimage change your life or not?
I think my particular pilgrimage will last my entire life, but I can without a doubt see where my journeys in and through Brazil brought me a better understanding of my own humanity as it relates to other people. There is such sensual energy in Brazil—and I include the food, the music, the friendships, the joys and pains of life as much as I include the stereotyped sexuality of the place—that you really get the space to learn how to manage yourself as a being in the world. Because of that, I have a deep, abiding love for Brazil.

5. What is the most important piece of advice that you have received in your life? Do you have advice to share from your experiences?
Allow everything and everyone—including yourself—the opportunity to be new every day.

Photograph courtesy of Ernest White II.

Biography

Ernest White II is a storyteller, explorer, and proponent of reasonable recklessness who has circumnavigated the globe five times. He is the producer and host of global reality-travel television series *Fly Brother*, host of the travel—and culture—focused Fly Brother Radio Show, and publisher of multicultural travel portal FlyBrother.net. Ernest's writing includes fiction, literary essay, and travel narrative, having been featured in *Time Out London, USA Today, Getaway, Ebony, The Manifest-Station, Sinking City, Lakeview Journal, Matador Network, National Geographic Traveler's Brazil* and *Bradt's Tajikistan* guidebooks, and at TravelChannel.com. He is also nonfiction editor at literary travel journal *Panorama*, former assistant editor at *Time Out São Paulo*, and founding editor of digital men's magazine *Abernathy*.

Appearing on the Travel Channel television series *Destination Showdown* and *Jamaica: Bared*, as well as in the 2013 documentary film about the dangers of mass tourism, *Gringo Trails*, Ernest also works as a voice over artist for radio, film and television, audiobooks, and educational materials, and speaks to youth and adult audiences about the incomparable magic of international travel.

A Florida native, Ernest's obsessions include Indian curry, the city of São Paulo, and Rita Hayworth.
www.ernestwhite2.com

Hickling Broad. *Photograph by Jack Moscrop.*

Jack Moscrop

Nature does not hurry, yet everything is accomplished.
~Lao Tzu

Norfolk Booming

Part I – Beginnings

*T*he cathedral organ screeched at the hands of the tuning technician as he wrestled it into pitch. On my knees before the altar, I continued praying for love. Stained glass windows haloed the crucifix in a rainbow of light. I repeated the word "Hope" and dropped my clasped palms to the altar rail. That was the Father taken care of. And I'm not even a Christian.

I pushed myself to my feet and adjusted my heavy rucksack. *Had I been ruthless enough with the contents?* Tent, sleeping bag and mat, one change of clothes, camera, binoculars, map and torch. Not even a stove, book or bowl. Yep, there was no spare fat in the bag at least.

Once I established a manageable centre of gravity, I walked outside to the labyrinth stones set in the cloister's lawn.

'Labyrinth Closed–Grass Growing' read the sign cordoning off an area meant to afford moments of personal reflection. A sunflower seed in my pocket demanded that I step over the rope and plant it as the offering to Mother Earth I'd intended. And I'm not even a Pagan.

I wondered if the date of my walk would be enough for the Mother. Tonight would be the first full moon after the Pagan-celebrated spring equinox, the same moon which triggers the Christian Easter the following Sunday. This moon is the bridge of light between the darkness which can too easily entrench opposing views. To my mind, spring and Easter are the same: renewal and resurrection. What better time for a pilgrimage?

Without the projected tower of the sunflower to imagine, I was forced to regard Norwich Cathedral's soaring steeple. Within it, I saw the strength of the collective: humanity's capabilities when it works together. Near the top, a box jutted from a window ledge. Peregrine falcons nested there. A bold and fearless raptor—the opposite of the bird I sought.

The sunflower seed fidgeted in my hand. I could have hurled it into the labyrinth and still achieved my plan, but that felt more like floral vandalism than a spiritual offering. I zipped the seed back into my rucksack, left the Cathedral's peace, and walked towards the River Wensum.

The Wensum would be the first of five rivers which might lead me to the object of my pilgrimage. I desired to hear the booming call of a bittern, a bird made extinct in Britain in 1885. It returned from Europe of its own accord in 1900, breeding in 1911. As a child of twelve, its dappled, striped, bulbous brown body tapering to a long beak captured my imagination. It looked more like Pacific island exotica than a native of the Norfolk fens. I had only ever seen them stuffed in museums.

In 2015, East Anglia boasted eighty males. I hoped to hear one at Hickling Broad, fifty-six miles and four days' walk from Norwich, following the Wherryman's and Weavers' Ways. My desire to hear a bittern boom was a pilgrimage to find something fragile and transient which I could not control, was of no practical use, and utilised a sense other than sight.

The Wensum led me to The Great Broad at Whitlingham Country Park. Boys raced towards the banks in sailing dinghies, tacking at last minute with feigned cries of disaster. A primary school group stopped to watch swans hissing at a golden retriever. Joggers overtook chatting and laughing mums with prams and dachshunds. Pockets of midges filled the air, and an Orange-tip butterfly fluttered along by my feet. It was a joy to be outdoors on a new quest where birdsong was louder than the city's police and ambulance sirens.

After Whitlingham I strolled through acres of rapeseed whose startling yellow flowers released a biting perfume. The fields butted into rustling woods, which provided welcome shade before I popped out at river number two, The Yare. At Bramerton moorings I ate sprouted beans and oat cakes for lunch while watching a kestrel hover to collect his toll of vole, and a pair of crested grebes dredged the river for weeds to build their nest. A pip alerted me to a kingfisher, a blue and red dart flashing by full of purpose.

Further down river, a much less focused pair of jackdaws took five minutes to add a single stick to their nest inside the flint tower of Surlingham Church.

At The Ferry House pub, I turned inland onto empty country lanes. At the head of a family outing, a teenage boy in tight jeans and a straw hat impressed a young girl with his modelling experiences. The mums tagging along behind talked about believing in God but not being Christian. I liked the contrast of committed vanity to noncommittal faith.

I turned a corner and startled a heron, a knight whose long legs and sleek body were mere counter-weights for its lance of a beak. On one side the wind whooshed in the woods, and on the other it whispered in the reeds. The sun caught in the fluff of their heads, sparkling like thousands of tiny mirrors sewn on torn flags.

At Coldham Hall, I walked through a mini-sailing club whose tilted dinghies half-slept waiting for their owners to come and play. I would have loved to take one for a jaunt down the river, but the trail turned inland past the Ted Ellis Nature Reserve. The reserve's scrappy tumble of trees and weeds gently opposed the GPS-guided furrows sculptured into the adjoining fields.

I reached water again at Rockland Staithe and snacked in a hide overlooking Rockland Broad. A gull rose from the reeds and spiralled up a thermal. The door jolted open and a birder stepped through, stooped over his binos. He stopped with a start.

"Sorry to disturb your peace," he said.

I invited him to sit. He did, but only long enough to be polite, then left to find his own peace.

Back alongside the River Yare, a sharp and constant wind whistled across the flatlands. Swans slept and grazed in the ditch-divided pastures. A train siren carried across the expanse, reminding me how crucial the river was to Norfolk's prosperity until rail replaced its wherries in the early twentieth century. Before becoming uneconomic, these twenty-five-ton-carrying, single-sailed, barge-like vessels hauled raw materials from Norfolk's premier port of Great Yarmouth to the county's capital of Norwich, returning with manufactured goods. Gradually pleasure wherries replaced the trading ones and today only eight vessels survive.

When I turned inland near the Beauchamp Arms, a flock of starlings lifted into the air, almost swirled into a murmuration, but fizzled out. I too was fizzling out. After passing the Norfolk Polo Club, where some well-appointed foals swished flies with uncommon grace, I arrived at Langley Dyke.

Narrow boats, yachts, and family cruisers lined the moorings. Rooks screeched in a nearby wood while I pitched overlooking the river. I watched a marsh harrier hunt back and forth across the reeds while the setting sun painted the clouds pink and peach. The rooks fell silent, and I passed out with them.

I woke at midnight and went outside to bask in the full moon's magnificence. The boats and riverbanks glowed. Their perfect reflections hovered above water which shone like patent leather. Owls hooted across the pastures. Foxes screeched from the woods. Geese chatted in the reedbeds. Fish plopped out of the water. I grabbed my sleeping bag and laid down, feeling a breeze whisper on my face as though it were the moon's lullaby.

The rooks roused me at dawn. I packed, but when I picked up my rucksack, it felt lighter than the previous day. I double-checked that nothing was lying around and then allowed myself a little note of satisfaction; this was getting easier. I would be able to complete the walk despite not having hiked twelve miles a day for many years. "Trust," I said as a prayer.

A pair of Canada geese splash-landed in the river, and I set off.

Jet-black slugs sparkled across the path. Tufted ducks whizzed by, peeping mayday-like calls before landing with precision. And the Cantley sugar factory sat alone and out of place on the far bank. Its mass of external piping hung to its side like disembowelled entrails glistening in the sun. I resented its intrusion on the countryside.

After walking around a gentle meander in the maturing river, I came upon a windmill. An industrial giant of the past, its gearing also hung out intrusively. But in its case, I was filled with wonder.

Further around, the river's meander afforded a view of the windmill and sugar factory side by side. I realised that my wonder at the windmill partly patronised its designers (amazing what those simple folk could achieve in those backward times). Now I saw the factory's pipes as a tumble of luxuriant hair.

I smiled. The river's looping path was presenting views of where I had been, offering chances to reassess harsh perceptions—exactly what I'd hoped to achieve in the cathedral's labyrinth.

I turned onto the River Che's banks and stopped to investigate hot-spots which had been building in my heels since yesterday afternoon. Peeling back my left sock revealed blisters spreading across the heel and onto the sole. The right foot was nearly as bad. I applied second-skin plasters and broke into the emergency sugar-free chocolate.

Further disappointment came when a trail repairs closure diverted the route inland away from the river just before Hardley Flood where I had looked forward to resting and watching the nature.

As I crunched along a stony farm track and more tarmac, two fighter jets repeatedly circled each other filling the sky with their roar. The noise fuelled the war going on inside my head: the war against myself for using new boots and socks without testing them. For the vanity of thinking it would be all right despite my lack of fitness. For having soft heels.

I ate more chocolate.

At Loddon, I left the river and recalled February just gone when I'd shredded my feet ski-touring in Chamonix. Those wounds had taken weeks to heal. I thought forward two weeks to my Portuguese surf trip. Torn feet would scupper that. These both seemed like valid reasons to stop my pilgrimage. But weren't they anchored in the past and the future? Shouldn't I focus on living in the now and just get on with it? Is pain the point of pilgrimage? Do I need a baptism of fire to achieve enlightenment? Was I weak? Or is self-harming actually not at all spiritual? Would continuing merely satisfy my ego?

Catkin blossom as fine as silk strands coated the path leading to Heckingham Church. A mass of wild flowers filled the churchyard with fragrance. The shade cast by the hexagonal tower and thatched roof made for a peaceful place to eat.

As I finished my cheese and nuts, I wondered why god, any god, wasn't supporting me on this pilgrimage.

When I set off, my feet felt better, but they deteriorated again by the time I reached the chain ferry at Reedham. The squeaking, clanking platform carried me to the north bank where I rested against a grass verge to remove my socks. The blisters had multiplied. Why did this have to happen now, just when I'd grown immersed in my walk?

But was I really still immersed? Hadn't I been ticking boxes for the last six miles? *Chedgrave, Loddon, Heckingham Church, Reedham Ferry.* If I carried on like this, hearing a bittern boom would be reduced to a mere formality.

I retreated to my morning prayer, "Love always protects, always trusts, always hopes, always perseveres." Yesterday morning I'd 'hoped' in the cathedral. This morning I'd 'trusted' at the campsite. So tonight, should I persevere or protect? I considered the timing of my walk: the full moon bridge between spring and Easter. Times of renewal and forgiveness, not destruction and recrimination. So I forgave myself for my poor preparation, called my girlfriend to collect me early, and vowed to return when my feet healed.

That's both protection and perseverance, Love answered.

Part II – Continuings

Six weeks later my friend Jason dropped me off at Reedham Ferry on a day when the moon would be a late waning crescent. I chose this day so that my pilgrimage would finish on a new moon—a pair to the full moon under which I had started, and a portentous opportunity to refresh dreams and desires. In particular, my wish to hear a bittern boom.

Jason and his greyhound Alfie walked with me for a while alongside the River Yare. We passed a converted windmill which had the cap removed and a glass balcony ringing it. *Stick a hot tub in the top and you've got a Hugh Hefner palace,* we joked. It seemed odd to be talking about Hugh Hefner at the start of a spiritual journey, but when Jason and Alfie turned around, I missed them. Leaving my girlfriend Emma in bed that morning had also been hard, especially after discussing doing more walks together following my previous attempt at this pilgrimage.

Gradually my steps settled into the rhythm of reeds, river, lapwings, tufted ducks on one side; and meadows, woods, songbirds, and pigeons on the other.

Then a 'Path Closed' sign blocked my way. Some trampled grass alongside a field led me to a confluence of wide but shallow looking ditches. I removed my boots, rolled up my leggings and stepped in. My leg slid up to my groin into methane-releasing mud, and I nearly toppled backwards into the fetid water. I extricated myself back to the bank—straight into a nettle patch. The other ditch was deeper but proved less muddy, and after crawling under a bramble bush, I reached Reedham village bedraggled and stinking of ditch. Not so Hugh Hefner now.

I squelched to the village moorings, graced with several 1930s traditional gaff-rigged yachts—beautiful visions of varnish, brass, wood, and canvas.

After a short walk between the river and buttercup-filled meadows, I spotted some dock leaves. Rubbing them on my legs soon relieved the bubbling nettle stings.

The occasional boat slapped by on the river and an egret glided from one meadow to the next, prospecting for a meal. The day was becoming a scorcher, and many of the grazing sheep and cattle had already laid down. From the raised riverbank I counted six windmills and windpumps dotted all the way to the far horizon. I checked my watch. I wanted to reach Berney Arms Mill by 12:30 p.m., Acle by 4:30 p.m., and camp by 7:00 p.m. at the Rivers Thurne and Bure confluence.

In truth, I wanted this whole damn walk done so I could get back to the real world.

The real world where, between stopping and restarting my pilgrimage, I'd been to a dear friend's funeral and my girlfriend's beloved uncle had died. On the yang side, I had set a publication date for a book about Patagonia, and I'd been to my first Hindu Holi spring festival. And I'm not even a Hindu. All these events were hard to put aside to walk alone in search of something which probably wouldn't happen and had no quantifiable significance.

I was walking in the manner of acquisition, not the spirit of openness. And I couldn't shake it.

Passing by Polkey's Mill, swallows swooped chitter-chattering from the barns to the river where they hurtled left and right, low and high, scooping up bugs.

Further down the river, prehistoric-looking cormorants stood on marker poles, their wings spread to dry. A bird rose and mewed in the meadows. I grew desperate to identify it. Why was knowing its name so important? Wasn't it beautiful enough in its own right? Why was rarity more exciting? Religions say god is in everything, including us. If so, is spirituality falling by the wayside because it's too commonplace for us to value it? It didn't feel like god was in me at all.

I chastised myself for being reliant on, and not letting go of, the outside world.

I missed my girlfriend.

At the Berney Arms Mill, I arrived at the junction with the Weavers' Way, two hours early. Top time acquisition marks for me.

The turn north started me cross-country towards the River Bure at Acle.

One meadow in, I saw three cygnets. The innocent balls of fluff waddled to cover in a column led by mum, with dad watching me from the rear. I finally broke my 'no phone' vow and called my girlfriend to say how much I would have enjoyed her company sauntering amongst the birdsong and buttercups.

Then I entered a field full of bullocks.

All of them stared at me. None moved out of my way. Some had horns.

I unclipped my walking pole from my rucksack and extended it, scant defence though it would be against thirty bullocks each weighing roughly the same as a bear. Those nearest closed ranks and followed me. Others charged in to join them until the whole herd was at my heels. "Good bullocks," I said, determined to maintain a steady pace. I hoped my ditch stink masked the smell of fear. I waved my pole to make myself bigger. "I don't eat steak, you know," I said. And I'm not even vegetarian.

The gate wasn't far now. Ten feet away, I yielded to the urge to run. The bullocks continued piling into it after me, squashing each other, until I was well across the next meadow.

There were many herds spread across these marsh pastures. A quad bike thumped around counting heads. The cowboy finished with one group and drove towards me. I was preparing to ask about cow attack procedures when the bike got close enough to see the driver was in fact a cowgirl, and a young one at that. Suddenly I was too embarrassed to raise the matter. At fifty years of age, I thought I was more mature than that.

An hour of self-recrimination later, I realised fear of judgement had driven me the wrong direction. I retraced my steps past a poor lapwing who once again had to scream and swoop to draw me away from its nest. At 2:00 p.m. I reached a signpost which I should have passed at 11:45 a.m. *Oops.* If I didn't relax soon, I wouldn't deserve to hear a bittern boom because hearing it wasn't the point. Being in a state to enjoy hearing it was the point, and then it wouldn't matter if I heard it or not.

The trail left the meadows, and I quickly ticked off Halvergate and Tunstall, after which the track was so overgrown that a pheasant had nested right on it. We pretended not to see each other.

Approaching Acle, I walked through shoulder-high cow parsley alive with common blue damselflies. Spiders scurried across the path. Snails clung to new growth reeds, and a murder of crows strutted about a field.

At Acle Dyke I stopped for a berry bar and to admire a river cruiser for sale, wondering: *could I become a river captain?*

Happy to have a river for company again, I walked along the Bure to the Acle Bridge Inn. Holidaymakers packed the beer garden, eating, drinking, and laughing. I didn't feel the slightest twinge of envy. At last, I'd transitioned from real world to walk world.

Just off the Acle Bridge, a congregation of starlings chattered on a grass bank. A tern plunged into the river and flew off with a fish. Near Clippesby Mill mown grass had clumped into little piles with round entrance-like holes in them, I assumed the work of rats, mice or voles. But when I nearly stepped on one, a wagtail hurtled out with a bug in its beak.

At the ruined Wiseman's Oby Mill, swallows and sparrows combined forces diving at a Kestrel, driving it away from their young. I sat for a while watching a pair of terns fishing, wondering if owls lived in the trees surrounding the mill. What started as a few irritating midges built into a swarm, so I moved on.

In a pale orange sunset, I pitched next to a secluded mooring and sleep came quickly. Not long after, a noisy duck began rousing me from sleep.

Eventually, I unzipped my tent, wondering how it could still be twilight.

The constellations' brightness shocked me, and I remembered a new moon's absence of light meant the stars stole the show. And in that moment of starlit wonder, I heard it. Or at least I think I heard it. The sound of air blown across a glass bottle mouth—a bittern's boom. I froze and waited.

There it was again.

Could bitterns be here? I was miles from Hickling Broad. I'd read of dawn and dusk booming but never night calls. I tip-toed back into bed. Maybe, just maybe I'd heard what I sought. I was excited for morning to come, to find someone to ask if it were possible.

A cuckoo woke me before sunrise to a faint mist hanging low on the meadows. While I packed, the sun rose into a lemon-yellow sky, and rooks greeted it with their jabbering squawks. I was still savouring the potential of success and relishing the prospect of discovering if I could believe my ears. There would be birdwatchers to consult in Hickling Broad.

I left the river and walked alongside a towering hedge. A curtain of spiders' webs hung across the path like nets cast to trawl in the clouds of insects. New leaves still unfolding, puffy and verdant, decorated the oak trees punctuating the hedgerows. In the fields, young crops pushed aside furrowed soil alongside land dense with barley already bent over by plump ears. In a farm paddock, I said good morning to a horse and scratched its forelock.

At the village of Thurne I joined my fifth and final river, the Thurne.

A warbler followed me along the river, his relentless stream of Morse code stutters an impressive contrast to the occasional blackbird's choral blasts.

On reaching the Repps and Heigham waterfronts, strips of eclectic holiday shacks pushed me along their backs. Their gates sported names like The Harbour and The Pilots Cabin. A mushroom-capped half-tower closely followed a thatched barn; then something materialised resembling a Buck Rogers' space station. I couldn't decide if the whole art deco flow effect with fifties flamboyance constituted stylistic genius, or more resembled an over-sized crazy golf course.

I soon left the riverside playground behind and entered some flood plains on the edge of Hickling Broad.

A short way ahead, I saw a group of birdwatchers.

I strolled up, nodded hello, and fished out my binoculars to legitimise my presence. My petrol station pocket binos were woefully small compared to their tripod telescopes and field glasses.

The fear of judgement will not win today, I told myself.

They talked about the fragile tern colony at Winterton and last weekend's sea eagle sightings near the broad. There was a pause. "Have you seen any bitterns?"

"A male, last week, flying over the Brecks at Lakenheath," one replied.

"I've seen them climbing the reeds in Minsmere," added another.

"They're here too," the last one said, who had wardened locally. "But they're easier to spot in the winter."

These were the people I needed. "Do bitterns boom at night?" I asked the warden.

"Yes."

Easy does this. "I thought I heard a bittern boom last night, near Oby Mill. Is that possible?"

"Bitterns do nest north of there. With the right wind, a boom could carry that far."

HALLELUJAH!

I wanted to run around with my shirt over my head, then slide to the ground on my knees and kiss Norfolk's hallowed soil. And I'm not even a football fan.

Instead I thanked them, shouldered my rucksack, and sauntered off grinning like an idiot.

Hallelujah.

Questions and Answers

1. What compelled you to set out on your pilgrimage?
I often overlook the beauty on my doorstep, only noticing when it is gone. Therefore, as a reminder to stop taking things for granted, I sought something local that had been destroyed but has now returned.

2. Is there a book, song, poem, or movie that inspired your quest?
Ordnance Survey maps and river courses inspired my route choice. The bird paintings of John J. Audubon (and all the artists who illustrated the bird books I loved as a boy) combined with my joy of the mysterious and the unlikely inspired the object of my quest.

3. Where is your sacred place and why did you choose it?
At one time, my answer would have been the mountains, any mountains. Recently though I have found a connection in lakes, rivers and the sea. So, my sacred place is more of a sensation than a place. Movement makes me feel spiritual. Trees make me feel good too.

4. How did your pilgrimage change your life or not?
It restored my connection to the wild. A connection I need to top-up to cope with the demands of modern living, which often overwhelm me and distort my perspective. I'm always a nicer person when I come back from a trip in nature.

5. What is the most important piece of advice that you have received in your life? Do you have advice to share from your experiences?
Life has so many stages, so I can't think of an all-encompassing piece of advice that I always rely on. 'You keep what got by giving it away' however, is one of the best pieces of advice I have received. I don't always apply it, but life is smoother and happier when I do.

Advice from my experience would be to try kindness, patience, and tolerance first in any situation. Again, I don't apply that approach enough, but when I do, either I get what I want, or it transpires that what I wanted wasn't what I needed—the latter is the usual outcome.

Photograph courtesy of Jack Moscrop.

Biography

Jack Moscrop grew up in England's East Anglia walking his beloved border collie around farm tracks and woods. He left home and moved north to stomp the hills and mountains of the English Peak and Lake Districts. Gradually ski touring took over his winters. The satisfaction of skinning uphill, akin to hiking, combined with the reward of exciting downhills opened the arenas of the European Alps and the Canadian Rockies. In the summers, he returned to the Scottish Munros and Welsh 3000s until dream treks called him to Patagonia, New Zealand and China. For the future, who knows, other than he hopes to follow his grandmother's example—an indomitable Cumbrian who hiked the hills to her last breath.

Website: jackmoscrop.com, Twitter: @jackmoscrop, instagram.com/jackmoscrop/, facebook.com/jackmoscrophome/, Pinterest: https://uk.pinterest.com/jackmoscrop/

Rimachi. *Photograph by Jacki Hill-Murphy.*

Jacki Hill-Murphy

Off the beaten track is the real world.

A Homage to Noise:
A Journey Down the Great River Amazon

A gentle plop into the water of the boatman's pole, its silent withdrawal; our boat glides effortlessly forward, scarlet macaws fly overhead, and all, it would seem, is well in the world of serene travel—well off the beaten track.

I was leading a small team in traversing the muddy waters of narrow tributaries of the Amazon by dug-out canoe, hoping to find it unchanged since the Spanish Conquistadors barged their way into the regions in the 16th century. Moments of equanimity like this did not last long—and in the weeks spent travelling the length of the Amazon, from a stream in Ecuador to the Atlantic Ocean, I found the sounds along the river one of the most dominant factors of my entire odyssey.

Firstly, the front boatman of the dug-out canoe, unlike his straw-hatted counterparts punting tourists through Cambridge, would soon get fed up with the slow progress effected by his pole pushed along the bottom of the river bed, with a nod of his head to boatmen number two and three at the stern, on would go the noisy two-stroke enine and we would whizz off. Unfortunately along with any wildlife that may have been snoozing along the bank.

As a pilgrim of Isabel Godin, not satisfied with retracing her fateful journey as far as the Peruvian border some years earlier—I wanted to go the entire way. To feel the pain of those 4,000 tedious miles with her, the inherent dangers, plus, would my eyes fall upon the same extraordinary sights as she had 260 years previously? They would and they did, but we experienced deprivations of differing natures. When Rudyard Kipling coined the word jungle in the 19th century, could he have imagined that within the century the serenity of its river banks would be very different?

Progressing slowly down the river, camping at night on sandbars that butted the forest to the sound of the lapping water, struggling through Amazonian days and nights hot and humid enough to strip gloss paint, her tragic story unfolded before me, along with the noisy backdrop. A monkey frog rattling its throat or a lone spectacled owl crying out its long deep call above my head... these natural sounds thrilled me—but sadly, the man-made ones would soon drown them out.

The night I slept in an open-sided, stilted-shelter as an invited guest of the Kichwa Indians on the Bobonaza River, there were families clustered around open fires in their straw kitchens below me, chatting and laughing.

Before dawn, as the throaty resonance of a bullfrog and the water-drop call of the yellow-tail bird danced in and out of the thatched roof, a baby cried in the dark and a male voice called out salutations to the new day. Shortly after, the village came alive with children and chickens and the echoes of chopping and pounding for breakfast, as wisps of smoke puffed, like dragons breath, through the trees.

I was losing myself from my cultural moorings, each day I felt further away from life as I knew it on earth. I was in the forgotten land of Isabel Godin, so close to where she lost herself in the deep, dark impenetrable forest I was surrounded by, so hot, so humid, so energy-sapping.

Time slipped by and days took on a new perspective, to the slow rhythm of villagers who live without calendars or fridges. A hand of finger-length bananas are eaten when naturally ripe, not forced; meat is eaten when it is available, not removed from a freezer, shrink-wrapped; if a child deserves a treat, dad will climb a cacao tree and throw down a pod and the seeds, covered in a sweet candy-like white coating; sucked with relish. Orphaned animals are family pets; I saw a pygmy marmoset on a string and a small monkey clutching at a small girl's T-shirt. Life here was organic, things happened when they needed to, and when life is this raw, humanity and love abound. Snakes moved in the grass, caiman lived in a metal barrel, tarantulas nested in the cracks of the schoolroom window, and the children ran freely in bare feet—laughing and shouting; safe in the knowledge that they would be swiftly scooped up from any inherent danger.

Back on the river, the noisy outboard engines on the metal canoes dominate, while the smaller wooden ones have modified generator engines, like grass strimmers, that sound like a sixteen year old lad flat out on his first moped as they wail and whine and herald their arrival from a distant meander down the river. Allowing my senses to come alive to the gentle sounds of the rainforest wasn't going to last, as the soft wind, allowing the smallest vestige of relief from the staggering heat, gave way to a journey edgier and noisier than I'd expected. The softer singing tone that came from the cloak of vicious manta blanca sand flies and mosquitos looking for my flesh was always there too; the ever-present bringer of mischief and misery .

Crossing from Ecuador into Peru we had to wait in a small border oil town for the Peruvian guide and his boat to arrive from Iquitos. After two days he still hadn't shown. My Kichwar boatmen had to leave; this was alien territory for them. The sun hit the bleak dusty square where dogs lay lifeless. I began to worry; this was no place to get stranded, in this heat and humidity. I was as beached as the canoes in the sand where the river had left them when it receded; as shipwrecked as the lost colourful bird looking for its logged forest roost. Men spat in the dirt that the chickens scratched noiselessly in, and a few boys played football with an improvised goal-post before giving in to the relentless heat. There was one place to stay, a series of rooms off a corridor, each with a foam mattress and a mosquito net, and a noisy mosquito of a different kind was operating in Room 2.

At six-o-clock the electricity came on and a television, high up on a roofless wall above tables and benches where food was served, played out, at full volume, fortunately obliterating the passion wagon—that was constantly engaged! Beers were drunk and this life seemed so normal to the people who wandered in and out. A little girl lay on her stomach on a cushion and watched a Spanish cartoon on the TV and a young man washed his clothes under a tap with a large bar of green soap. I mixed my beer with a 7-UP and attempted to teach some locals the word 'shandy'; which only led to Spanish hilarity with its innuendo, until nine o clock, when the electricity was shut off. I fumbled my way through the dark to my dirty room and slipped into my cool, clean sleeping bag.

And then, when all seemed peaceful and Room 2 had shut up shop, there was the town disco. A generator leaped into action and thumped out its funky beat until 5 am; I lay with my sleeping bag wrapped over my ears, listening to the same four Peruvian pop-songs, which would pop up, like bad pennies, for the entirety of my journey until morning.

Daybreak broke through a piece of wire mesh covering a small high window, and its lozenge of light exposed the cockroach, the size of a rat, near the head of my mattress. I had shared my room with him overnight. Out on the street, neat and scrubbed school children made their way cheerfully to school; how had they slept? How had anyone slept alongside that noisy disco? I was relieved when my guide finally arrived and we could leave this little whisky town behind.

The next night, on this darkly dangerous Pastaza River, we stopped to camp at a small Achuar Indian village, a tribe not known for their hospitality. As we scrambled ungainly up the muddy river bank after the boatman and guide, the tribespeople were lined up in the fading light, mutely watching us. There were no gentle sounds of the wind blowing through the palms here. The awkwardness of our presence, as we erected our tents under the high tin roof of the one-room school, was exacerbated by the disturbance of a water filtration plant cutting out all the ambient sound, jarring our senses as it clanged and plunged its steel hammer into the night. Then suddenly, when it got dark, it was shut off and all went quiet. Through this welcome silence, as we drifted into an uncomfortable sleep, came new sounds—large drops of water bouncing off the corrugated roof heralding a storm which turned into a torrential downpour, gushing and leaping onto the mud beside the school. It gathered in intensity, thunder crashed around the surrounding forest, and lightning flashed light through the unlocked doors that swung open and shut all night, bouncing off our flimsy tent canvas. I wrapped myself up into a cocoon in my sleeping bag, aware of an intruder, the ominous flip flop of a man's steps moving around our tents, I could hear him breathing between the spates of fork lightning and thunder crashes, there was a weak beam from a flashlight he held.

Our hearts beat fast to the precipitating dangers; I knew that if anything happened to any of us no one would come and look for us here. In the morning we clambered back onto our small craft and slipped noiselessly away on the fast flowing River Pastaza. It had been a wet, threatening and menacing night, we hadn't washed and we were hungry; but the experience was unforgettable, even if it was edgy and dangerous, this was exploration. I was gathering my stories about the lives of others, to recount and to cherish, and wondering if Madame Godin had similar ones, but she never spoke about her weeks being lost in the forest; the experience had been too traumatic and turned her hair white.

The Pastaza emptied onto the Marañón, which rose from the Andes northeast of Lima and now thundered on towards its Atlantic destination as the mighty Amazon. At Iquitos City, the capital city of Peru's Maynas Province and Loreto Region, the largest city in the world that cannot be reached by road, the dynamics of my journey changed once more. What was once a sleepy Colonial town, home of the rubber baron Fitzcarraldo, has been transformed by the constant presence of 40,000 auto rickshaws or moto-taxis that buzz like swarms of noisy flies along every narrow rutted street, and lurch at break-neck speed towards lone pedestrians, that may or not want to ride them.

No longer did my team have to erect tents on tribal lands or in pop-up oil settlements; now we took to the water on wooden, round-prowed boats that plied the pirate and drug-dealer-infested waters carrying their cargoes along the thousands of miles of Amazon River. As we slung our hammocks up on the first of many such open decked boats, another world was emerging on the lower decks, where teams of men, weather-beaten and as tough as the leather of their boots, constantly shifted multifarious consignments of cargo; bananas, huge open-mouthed pescada fish, crates of empty, or full, soda bottles, furniture, rice, motor bikes, tractors, livestock and even small boats, night and day, at settlements along the river.

Sleeping on a hammock boat could never be seen as a holiday—it's a necessity, but the experiences are shared with many men and women and children who, in the absence of roads, need to move up and down the river. Throughout the night, the cool air blows in black beetles that die on their backs in a flurry of waving legs amidst our baggage. While we attempt to sleep, the men below are at work, in the hot engine room, or fan out at the water's edge to load and unload alongside a throng of shouting passengers waiting to alight.

Still a hammock virgin, I awoke near Santa Rosa at 5 am, desperately trying to imagine what it was I could hear. Chunk, chink. Chuck, chunk, chink. These sounds were repeated over and over against authoritative shouts, and as I lay there in the fingers of first light, I decided that it probably was something far too culturally interesting to miss and I climbed blearily down to the open cargo deck at the prow to investigate. Amid an earth-moving machine, a grey horse, two donkeys and a pig and other anonymous looking heaps of cargo, were a pile of thousands of square bricks—and each one was being thrown from hand to hand onto waiting wooden canoes by a throng of men at an unpopulated bend in the river. As the piles in each canoe grew higher, so too did the franticness of the bucket baling as they took in water. I will never know if one sank on its homeward drift through shallow waters into their deforested scrubland village.

From the shriek of delight of a group of small children pulling a red-bellied piranha fish out of a net; the noisy hubbub of city ports; the stomp of feet as anti-narcotics police, carrying machine guns, raided our boat; the crying of the babies lying in hammocks; the strum of a traveller's guitar; the screech and flapping of the king vultures flying overhead; the slop of brown water against the hull, all these sounds are the sounds I shall remember. The sounds I associate with a long and memorable journey that was my dream—to recreate a journey, which took far longer in 1769, than it took me in 2016.

On reaching Belém, in Brazil, near to the eight mile-wide mouth of the Amazon, I had been traveling for nearly eight weeks. I stayed in a swanky hotel, walked around the city, and relaxed before flying out of its big international airport. In the cool of a well-known coffee-shop chain, a British pop song played in the background and I closed my eyes and sipped my latte. I had just experienced one of the hardest journeys of my life, I had worried about the safety of my team, we had travelled where disease was rife, tribes were hostile, along a dirty river with water as hot as a bath and where dangers lurked in its murky depths. But at that moment I could have been in Piccadilly Circus or on the Champs-Élysées; this modern city may have been locked into a jungle—but there are some things that are the same the world over, the taxis honked their horns outside, sirens wailed, orders were shouted to the barista, and I wondered what Rudyard Kipling would have thought of this noisy, tropical metropolis at the end of a the great, but noisy, Amazon River.

Questions and Answers

1. What compelled you to set out on your pilgrimage?
Recreating Isabela Godin's terrible journey down the length of the Amazon in 1769 has been a dream of mine for many years, but to make it happen I had to overcome my fears and set in place arrangements that made it possible to do it safely. It took a long time but I succeeded and am glad that the small team I put together and myself got through safe and well.

2. Is there a book, song, poem, or movie that inspired your quest?
Where the Trail Runs Out by John Blashford-Snell has gripped me since I was a teenager, particularly the part where he tries to get a land-Rover through the Darian Gap. Add any seventies rock music that will fuel the wild side of my personalty!

3. Where is your sacred place and why did you choose it?
I think it has to be Sarayaku village where the Kichwa tribe live on the River Bobonaza, as mentioned in my story. I have stayed with them twice now and find the richness of their lives living in the jungle quite fascinating. Their way of life is now in danger as the Ecuadorian Government have sold their land to a foreign oil company without telling them at the time. At any time the army can escort the oil workers in, if necessary using tanks and heavy weaponry. The villagers have continued to protest peacefully, through film, inviting in journalists and by kidnapping the oil men when they arrive, for a short while, to preach to them how their actions will destroy the environment and their way of life.

4. How did your pilgrimage change your life or not?
I have acquired a passion for the early female explorers and that passion has sent me on another wonderful journey—speaking, writing and filming their stories of adventure.

5. What is the most important piece of advice that you have received in your life? Do you have advice to share from your experiences?
Actually I have had to shun most of the advice I have ever been given in my life or I never would would have gone anywhere! Like, 'be sensible' or 'well you've got it out of your system now'. So my advice would be—follow your heart.

Photograph courtesy of Jacki Hill-Murphy.

Biography

Jacki Hill-Murphy has travelled to some of the most inhospitable places on earth to re-create the journeys of daring women adventurers from the past. In tracking valiant women who left inhibition at home and journeyed into the unknown, she pays tribute to their invincible spirits and achievements. She has followed in the footsteps of Victorian explorers Isabella Bird who travelled by yak across the Digar-La in Ladakh, India; Mary Kingsley, who pioneered the route to the 13,255 ft summit of Mount Cameroon; and Kate Marsden who trudged from Moscow to Siberia in search of a cure for leprosy. Jacki also braved piranha-infested waters in a dugout canoe to replicate the 1769 expedition of Isabel Godin, the only survivor of a 42-person, 4,200-mile expedition along the Amazon River. Jacki says: "We are all adventuresses who need to travel to be who we are and we are better people for it."

www.Jacki Hill-Murphy.com, twitter: @jackihillmurphy

"I am more and more convinced that our happiness or unhappiness depends more on the way we meet the events of life than on the nature of those events themselves."
~Alexander von Humboldt

Michael Warburton

Things of enduring value are difficult.
~Raymond Ogunade, Nigerian professor and poet

Finding Home amidst Rising Seas

*T*uesday's walk was in the hills. The swirling mists weren't dissolving over the Brower-Hus-Muir La. The fog was thick as ever. No peaks or hidden valleys would be revealed that day. I hadn't even reached the pass and my knee was in searing pain. It was frustrating to hurt so much after so little distance. My physical therapist had assured me I wouldn't be stupid if I "pushed" a little. But what sort of yardsticks was she using for her measure of "pushing" and "stupid?" I had, after all, a record that could appear to others as a long and repeatedly embarrassing history of forcing my body well beyond its design constraints.

Admittedly, one time, I had drifted into a five day coma with high altitude cerebral edema in the Himalayas before realizing that I was in any danger. But that was decades ago and by this time my family and friends all hoped any important lessons had been indelibly inscribed onto my routine judgment. But what if they hadn't? There are always nagging doubts, especially when I begin to feel enthusiastic...

Today's walk certainly had the feel of a pilgrimage. I was consciously observing my thinking to be sure to be open to any important signal that might emerge along the way. The pain in my knee had a high likelihood of being a "message." I knew this was a mental journey as well as a physical one, and my mental history included its share of instances where I had been absolutely "sure" of something, only to discover much later that my actual circumstances were quite different from those I thought I was dealing with. It evoked the same sort of feeling I had when thinking about the great wilderness explorer Davey Crockett saying, "No. I've never gotten lost. But I have been a might bewildered for a few days."

The "real" journey I was reconnoitering was certainly a big one. This walk was more for preparing my mind for understanding the parallel transformations from "here" to "there," in a much larger sphere, without ever losing my understanding of "here" and "now." Somewhere, I'd learned that was a key part of the toolkit of every "real pilgrim." But now I couldn't even remember where I'd heard or read that.

I had meekly turned around and limped home that Tuesday without reaching the pass. In fact, I hadn't reached it since my health crisis several months before when I coughed up 45% of my circulating blood supply. My doctors told me that my own close scrape with death was a common occurrence for people who take anti-coagulants for long periods and start bleeding internally. After all, the medicine had the same chemical basis as the most popular rat poison. A blood clot had developed in my leg along with the cerebral edema I suffered in the Himalayas 37 years before, and the long term anti-coagulants were part of the price. The most recent saving grace was that the additional artery that burst this time did so at the doorstep of the hospital emergency room. My wife, Anne, took me there when I knew something wasn't quite right and she suggested I call the advice nurse.

Now I am more able to walk and think clearly (October 1, 2017). I'd make it at least as far as the pass today and I was thinking again about the "real journey" that would involve so many people moving away from shoreline communities as sea levels continue to rise along with the warming atmosphere and melting ice on our planet. There will be profound transformations in all of our lives that will be needed to reduce the human contributions to climate change. But even with those transformations, the greenhouse gases already released by historic industrialization will inevitably result in the submersion of parts or all of many coastal cities. This will force massive relocations of homes and urban infrastructure from shoreline settlements around the world. Even here in Berkeley, California, many people would have to move to higher ground

The options for the San Francisco Bay area are much clearer from a viewpoint higher up the ridge than the Brower-Hus-Muir La on my regular walking route. The lowland flats and hill features are obvious from higher vantage points. One such viewpoint is located very near the top of the very appropriately named "Hill Road." From here, both promising and futile plans for long term resistance to rising waters can be more easily compared. But the most likely routes toward a healthier way of life, would probably take many different forms. There will, most probably, be a diverse mix of individual and collective journeys that will ultimately create the cumulative effect.

It's easiest if our transformational journeys can be made with a background of peace and harmony rather than as desperate, grasping dashes. One is so much more vulnerable to temptations, and at greater risk of self-delusion and distraction, when in a desperate dash of a quest. While it's often quiet and uncrowded in the hills, most of Berkeley is buzzing with activity and rushing urban denizens. That's exactly why my best friends have always advised me to invest a lot of energy in attaining the "right" frame of mind, free from the most obvious prejudices, before starting out on any pilgrimage.

Since so much of my early life was devoted to rock climbing and then alpine mountaineering, I began thinking of climbing itself as my first experience with pilgrimage. For me, the act *was* the journey. I turned to the "holy" books, the great expedition narratives, as well as shorter, emerging literatures in anthologies and magazines. My own journeys eventually crossed with those of many involved in the adventures I read about, but most often, those actual meetings were years after I read about them.

Climbing is indeed serious. Many have lost their lives allowing their concentration to wander in dangerous places. But the entire activity is also so obviously absurd, so completely mentally constructed, and, of no plausible value if you do lose your life. And beneath all that, finding oneself part way up an enormous granite wall with a snowstorm brewing can only be the result of a deliberate choice made long before under "safe" conditions. The addictive pastime must have been "worth it" to me because it happened so often. But if I am completely honest with myself, the whole enterprise has become harder to explain with a straight face.

I am possibly the only one now thinking of the first pass on my Berkeley Hills walk as "The Brower-Hus-Muir La." Others might describe it as the place where John Muir Way leads East from Grizzly Peak Boulevard toward Wildcat Canyon. On the other side of the boulevard, just a little down Stevenson Avenue, is the house where David Brower, the legendary conservationist, settled and raised his family. Between that house and where Stevenson intersects with Grizzly Peak, the "Anne Brower Path," named for David's wife and longtime editor, heads downhill and straight west. It begins with a stunning view of the Golden Gate Bridge directly across the bay from Berkeley. A house on one side of the path and a tall hedge on the other narrowly crop the view, but on a clear day the Farallon Islands are clearly visible on the horizon.

Both Anne and David grew up and started working at U.C. Press in Berkeley before and during construction of that bridge. Dave was the first Executive Director of the Sierra Club, the venerable conservation organization founded by John Muir. Dave's commitment to preserving the beauty of wilderness made perfect sense to Anne Hus, but she was, after all, the granddaughter of John Hus, who had made his living selling goods derived from sheep herded in high Sierra meadows. And even though Muir himself had undertaken summer employment doing exactly this, he came to refer to sheep as "hoofed locusts" which threatened the very existence of his "temples not made by human hands." The Sierra Club has a long history of campaigning against sheep in the Sierra, but when Dave and Anne's daughter, Barbara, was becoming an academic geographer, she wrote her Master's thesis on Basque shepherds in the American West. She found that they were far more ecologically knowledgeable and sensitive than their American capitalist counterparts. In other words, it wasn't the sheep that should be blamed for the ecological destruction but rather the businesses which employed the unsustainable grazing practices.

Since my own experiences in the Himalayas, I've frequently fancied a mani wall draped with prayer flags to mark that transformation in land form and the progress in history and economics marked by crossing the "Brower-Hus-Muir La." There is no doubt that such a display would incur the wrath of most motorists intent on reaching their destinations via Grizzly Peak Boulevard. But maybe such a curious edifice might be worth any inconvenience suffered. Certainly the San Francisco Bay view that opens up near the top of the "Atlas Path" is enough to wake up any sleeping soul. The gleaming city with its "TransAmerica Pyramid" and new skyscraper-punctuated skyline across the eastern span of the Bay Bridge is certainly impressive from here. But in the Berkeley lowlands of the foreground, the parking lot-covered site of the first human habitation in the region stands just across 4th St. from the well-known Spenger's seafood restaurant.

Before any Egyptian Pharaoh even thought of building a pyramid, the Ohlone People fished and smashed shells and sang songs celebrating their lives here in their original villages. One of the most famous villages, along with its ancient graveyards and ceremonial sites, is directly beneath an Emeryville Shopping Mall and movie theatre complex. But the oldest one of all, the West Berkeley Shellmound, was officially designated long ago as a "Sacred Historical Landmark." But the present descendants of the initial inhabitants, along with the support of a fairly wide range of community organizations, have proposed a more respectful ceremonial open space park for the site. That would certainly be more consistent with the pilgrimage I was making today, in clear view of the very spot. And it would square far better with any lofty thoughts about continuing human migrations and other social and political theatrics destined to play out in this place.

Over the decades I've been walking these paths, more houses have been built and new trees and hedges have grown and been cleared. Fires and floods have come and gone in shaping the continually changing patterns of habitation by the full range of animal and plant species that call the area home. And I've continually been learning more about the people and events that shaped current appearances and various human appreciations of the area. My own range of "sacred spots" has been expanding as I've been learning more.

Just a few years ago, a friend of a friend was working on a documentary film about the legendary photographer Dorothea Lange, who seemingly singlehandedly shaped the soul of the Great Depression in the United States through her iconic images frequently accompanied with brief statements by her subjects. One of the scenes in the documentary was described as Lange's Berkeley home and studio that she shared with her economist husband, Paul Taylor. It looked immediately familiar, as I recognized it as the structure behind the graceful branches of a favorite old oak tree, above the steps built by a WPA crew during the New Deal on a section of my own path toward the Brower-Hus-Muir La. In a recent display of Lange's historical work at the Oakland Museum, a hand written letter from noted author, John Steinbeck, thanked her for the deeply moving human record she gave him with her photographs. Those images inspired his own classic writings depicting the period.

The same museum display alerted me to Lange's important role in documenting other human relocations in addition to the migration caused by the Dustbowl in America's midsection in the 1930's. She also documented the forced removal of Japanese-American citizens from their homes and farms along the west coast in the months following the Pearl Harbor bombing and their forced resettlement in fenced camps in often bleak and arid landscapes.

In Dorothea Lange's "Death of a Valley" collection, she documented the filling of California's Berryessa Valley with a new reservoir. The abandonment and loss of the town of Monticello was poignantly captured in her images of those intentionally flooded refugees. She had a wonderful talent for being able to capture both human pain and dignity as peoples' lives engaged with change. I wondered what photographs Dorothea Lange might take of Berkeley's residents and the structures we build for ourselves as our climate changes and the surface levels of the Pacific Ocean and San Francisco Bay inexorably rise.

One of my favorite spots on my walking path down from the top of the ridge above town is a grassy hillside just below the baseball field built into the reclaimed rock quarry that was made into "La Loma Park." From a tiny, double-humped rock outcrop on a grassy hillside, one can see Berkeley spread out below and San Francisco and the Golden Gate Bridge, and of course the sweep of the Marin Headlands up to Mt. Tamalpais on the western horizon. It's another great place to watch the sun set and I often meet other "pilgrims," some engaged in very similar journeys to my own, and some on different paths altogether.

When I continue down the winding path below the outcrop, I'm usually much more hopeful that we'll be able to manage this collective journey and take care of our spirits as we do it. We've certainly got a lot to learn from each other and the land and weather. We'll never all see it in the same way, but that's exactly what makes it so interesting.

Question and Answers

Things don't have value. People confer value on things.
~Michael Thompson, British anthropologist and mountaineer

1. What compelled you to set out on your pilgrimage?
I was curious about "here" and "now" and wanted to know as much as I need
to be who I am and do what I'm meant to.

2. Is there a book, song, poem, or movie that inspired your quest?
The poem that my wife, Anne, and I chose to read together at our wedding
has always been an inspiration: *The Law that Marries All Things* by
Wendell Berry.

1.
The cloud is free only
to go with the wind.

The rain is free
only in falling.

The water is free only
in its gathering together,

in its downward courses,
in its rising into the air.

2.
In law is rest
if you love the law,
if you enter, singing, into it
as water in its descent.

3.
Or song is truest law,
and you must enter singing;
it has no other entrance.

It is the great chorus
of parts. The only outlawry
is in division.

4.
Whatever is singing
is found, awaiting the return
of whatever is lost.

5.
Meet us in the air
over the water,
sing the swallows.

Meet me, meet me,
the redbird sings,
here here here here.

3. Where is your sacred place and why did you choose it?
My most sacred place is "here" and it is much more of an "agreement" than
any "choice" of mine. This is because it "chooses" me just as much as I could
ever "choose" it. But I also know that if I am living "right," I'll treasure *many*
"discoveries" of sacred places along my way.

4. How did your pilgrimage change your life or not?
It often feels like my life is a series of pilgrimages and wanderings that have
sometimes led to some awesome surprises as well as a collection of some
pretty mundane revelations.

*5. What is the most important piece of advice that you have received in
your life? Do you have advice to share from your experiences?*
The most important piece of advice I ever received was when Phyllis
Munday was worried enough about me to remark that, "No mountain is
worth losing your life for." I tend to think of myself in need of too much
supervision myself to venture giving other people "advice."

Photograph courtesy of Michael Warburton.

Biography

"Valuable knowledge is deeper appreciation of the processes by which people confer value on things." Michael Warburton

Michael Warburton is the Executive Director of the Public Trust Alliance where he helps defend Californian's environment. Michael earned his JD at Boalt Hall Law School, UC Berkeley, in 1992. He established the Community Water Rights Project and served on the founding Steering Committee of the Environmental Justice Coalition for Water. He assisted with the State of Alaska's litigation of the Exxon Valdez oil spill case. He was a member of the scientific staff at the International Institute for Applied Systems Analysis (IIASA) in Austria, where he worked with interdisciplinary scientists on solutions to environmental problems that cross national frontiers.

His mountaineering career includes the 1975, first Soviet-American ascent of the Salathe Wall of El Capitan in Yosemite; first ascent of North Ridge of Mt. Waddington, traverse of British Columbia Coast Range over its highest peak; 1976 Joint Soviet-American expedition to Central Asia and the Caucasus; 1977 American Peruvian Andes Expedition: first ascent of East Ridge of Pukajirka Central and ascents of Huascaran and Ranrapalca; 1978 Winter Expedition to the Alaska Range and ascents of Orizaba and Popocatepetl in Mexico; 1980 expedition to Makalu in the Himalayas. Michael's gratefulness to the mountain people who saved his life in several 'remote' locations has been a primary shaper of his career path and thinking.

www.publictrustalliance.org

Crossing party pays respects to Shackleton at his gravesite, Grytviken.
Photograph courtesy of Colin Monteath.

Colin Monteath

No Turning Back:
Crossing South Georgia on Shackleton's Route

*W*ind-worn, wet and with one team member seriously chilled, our mud-spattered party stumbled out from the mountains as nightfall clamped around South Georgia. Bone-weary, the eight of us trudged across soggy snowfields and knee-deep bogs on the last leg of our three day traverse from King Haakon fjord to the old Norwegian whaling station in Stromness Bay. Elephant seals belched from the ooze, king penguins gawked and moulting reindeer sniffed the wind, all indifferent to our passing.

Dodging a platoon of fur seal pups nimbly defending their territory, we entered the derelict manager's house, a welcome refuge from freezing rain. Drenched garments were stripped and steaming underwear hung from makeshift clotheslines, puddles spreading across the floor. Shivering, we huddled around the chugging primus, eager for tea. Though little was said as we sipped the scalding brew, our haggard faces beamed at the thrill of having made it across this wild Antarctic island. Befuddled by the need for sleep, we soon curled up on the floor, each of us with private thoughts of Sir Ernest Shackleton and a new appreciation for what is surely the greatest escape story of all time.

Shackleton's attempt to cross Antarctica from the Weddell Sea to the Ross Sea foundered when his ship *Endurance* was trapped in the maw of ice floes in the Weddell. Through the dark nagging fear of winter the inexorable grind of pack ice gradually pinched the wooden hull. Heartbroken at not being able to attempt his long-dreamed-of traverse of the continent, Shackleton took his Kiwi Captain Frank Worsley aside—"The ship can't live in this Skipper....what the ice gets, the ice keeps." Twenty eight ship's crew, Mrs Chippy—the ship's cat, and the soon-to-be-chopped-up-for-stew-barking-mad huskies—all stood forlornly on an ice floe and pondered their future. On 21 November 1915, *Endurance* sank.

So began an epic retreat to the north, at first man-hauling lifeboats across the sea ice, then, as another cruel winter gnawed at the tent flaps, it became obvious that survival lay with their three open boats. On 16 April 1916 they were finally launched into the Southern Ocean. Shackleton was desperate to reach land...any land, or he knew they were dead men. Fully 497 days since *Endurance* had set out from South Georgia, they fetched up in the South Shetland Islands, on a thin shingle beach at the base of a steep prow on Elephant Island—a precipitous ice-clad shard of rock now known as Point Wild, after Shackleton's second-in-command Frank Wild.

The Boss, as Shackleton was called by the crew, knew that there was only one chance to raise the alarm of their plight. A six-man party readied the 7-metre *James Caird* for what they knew would be a merciless 800-nautical mile passage to South Georgia. In an effort to make her more seaworthy they heightened the gunwales and covering the boat in with canvas and box-lids. With the all-too-familiar savagery of winter all-but upon them, the *Caird* was launched 24 April 1916.

With Shackleton gone, Frank Wild was now in full command; his leadership and care for the 21 men during the ensuing ordeal has always been greatly under-stated. Everyone huddled under two up-turned boats, in a dug out hovel of frigid squalor they named The Snuggery—surviving largely on penguins or seals battered to death on the beach. Conditions became so desperate that the 19-year-old Argentine stowaway Pierce Blackboro's frost-bitten toes were amputated with tin-snips. (When first discovered as a stowaway out of Buenos Aires, Shackleton threatened Blackboro that if the chips were down, then he would be eaten first.)

For 16 gruelling days the heavily-iced *Caird* wallowed northward, thrashed pitilessly by gigantic waves in the Scotia Sea. With one on the tiller, others bailed for their lives. Below decks they took it in turns to sit on a shifting ballast of boulders, with one cradling a kerosene primus between his legs while brewing a soupy mix of fat-rich Hoosh. Dehydration took its toll as fresh water supplies became contaminated by salt. Two precious reindeer skin sleeping bags became so saturated and heavy they were thrown overboard. Held tight by a crewman, 'Wuzzles' Worsley barely secured three sextant sun shots during the entire voyage. Wuzzles could not get his calculations wrong...miss the southern coast of South Georgia and they would perish, as would those left behind on Elephant Island.

Miraculously, the *Caird* hit King Haakon fjord right on the nose. Despite the rudder being ripped off at the last minute, they stumbled ashore in a tiny nook called Cave Cove at the southern tip of the 20 km-long fjord....to drink their fill of peaty-brown water, rest under a dripping rock overhang and kill albatross chicks for food. Days later, with a make-shift rudder attached to the *Caird*, they pushed off once more bound for the head of King Haakon...and as they did so, the original rudder, with all the Southern Ocean to roam in, somehow came floating towards them.

Shackleton left the weakest three with the *Caird* at a bleak beach they named Peggoty Camp. Tom Crean, Wuzzles and Shackleton had waited six agonising days to get a break in the weather and a full moon to guide them before heading inland on crisp early winter snow in their attempt to reach one of the whaling stations on the north coast. They had a crude outline map of South Georgia's coastline but the alpine nature of the interior was a complete unknown. Their only mountain equipment was a carpenter's adze to cut steps in ice, a short rope and had screws driven through the soles of their boots to act as crampons. They also had a primus with just enough fuel for a single meal of Hoosh. Failure was not an option.

***

I cut my polar teeth on Ross Island in October 1973 in what turned into ten summers working out of New Zealand's Scott Base. Like me, many Kiwis working in McMurdo Sound and in South Victoria land were inspired by Shackleton, his men, and their achievements especially during the 1907-09 Nimrod expedition that almost reached the Geographic South Pole.

I have been out on the Ross Ice Shelf with dogs, worked on the Polar Plateau and Transantarctic mountains and even climbed the active volcano Erebus by the same first ascent route from Cape Royds that Shackleton's men had taken in March 1908. So, in 1983, when I went freelance as a polar and mountain photographer, I finally had the privilege of venturing into the heart of the Weddell Sea on an icebreaker. Later, I was able to land on the forbidding Point Wild. But, the one place of pilgrimage I had not been to in Antarctica that was synonymous with the name Shackleton—was South Georgia.

The end of the 1983/84 season found me in The Falkland Islands witnessing the aftermath of the 1982 Argentine-British war. We then sailed eastward to South Georgia that was still reeling from what had been an ugly conflict. There was a fresh grave for an Argentine in the little whaler's cemetery at Grytviken where Shackleton is buried. On nearby King Edward Point, memorial crosses for British servicemen stood alongside fresh-faced soldiers in barbed-wire dugouts guarding the entrance to the harbour. With backpacks of detergent, British servicemen were spraying spilled oil in the harbour that had leaked after trigger-happy troops had holed old storage tanks. For the next 20 years Gurkha soldiers were in residence at Grytviken and as I made regular visits to the island each summer to act as a guide and to photograph the wildlife, they beamed when greeted with Namaste and talk of their distant homeland.

It took until 2001 before my old climbing buddy and fellow polar-nut Greg Mortimer and his Antarctic cruise company Aurora Expeditions (50 pax, four guides and 22 crew aboard Russian vessels) found the courage and created the opportunity to take a small group of clients across South Georgia on Shackleton's route. Despite modern clothing and equipment, and the Aurora team completing the journey a dozen or so times now, the full crossing remains a venture not to be taken lightly. (The Crean Glacier is no place to get stuck for there is almost zero chance of helicopter rescue on South Georgia.) I have successfully done the crossing twice, the third attempt ending ignominiously when three of us were hammered by a southerly wind-storm under Trident Ridge (impossible to pitch a tent in such wind or dig a cave in the icy surface). This storm forced a retreat back to Shackleton Gap then down to Possession Bay on the north coast where, amid an audience of 100s of wide-eyed elephant seals, Captain James Cook had declared possession of the Island for King George III on 17 January 1775.

It is an easy-angled climb up a glacier from Peggoty Camp to the jagged barrier of Trident Ridge. While modern parties reach here in the long daylight hours of summer, Shackleton's trio reached the ridge in the winter darkness of May. Despite flickering moonlight to guide them, it was no easy matter to decide which of the narrow rocky cols would be safe to cross. After several failures, fear and urgency forced their hand: "A fronte praecipitium, a tergo lupi—In front a precipice, and wolves behind." Shackleton sat down, linking legs and arms with his mates in front, and bumslid into the darkness down an icy slope of unknown length and steepness. There was no turning back.

Crean Glacier is heavily crevassed and drops off in frightening icefalls into the ocean on the north coast. Early season crossing parties ski the Crean but we were forced to crampon on hard ice, repeatedly jumping crevasses. In a full-on blizzard on my first crossing of Trident we were only confident we had found the right route when we spotted a Tibetan silk kata scarf under a small cairn of rocks, left there by Reinhold Messner, the year before. But even Messner had found the Crean hard going for he broke his foot while jumping over the icy edges of slots.

Camping on the eastern end of the Crean is quite an experience; a chance to rest, to brew up and to think about Shackleton's mindset when they plodded on and on in their imperative to somehow get down to sea level. Reluctantly, he allowed Wuzzles and Crean to nod off, then kicked them awake minutes later, telling them they had been asleep for an hour. Utterly exhausted, famished and dehydrated, they cranked up the primus for a final mouthful of Hoosh before discarding the stove and pushing on... In vain, all these years later, I have looked for that primus.

The descent of Fortuna Glacier to the bay below is now much harder than in Shackleton's day, due to glacier retreat that is happening all over South Georgia as the climate warms. But finally, leaving the ice behind and taking off crampons, our little party dropped down easy-angled scree slopes and rubbly ridges to Fortuna Bay. It was somewhere here that Wuzzles had looked at his watch while the others looked on in anticipation. (The accuracy of Worsley's watch had been crucial to his navigation while aboard *James Caird*.) Sure enough, at precisely 7 am, there came a shrill whistle, a call to work for the Norwegian whalers at Stromness; the first outside man-made sound the explorers had heard for two years. They pressed on...

We stopped for food in a large cave on the beach once used by sealers, then stripped to our underpants to wade a glacial stream under Fortuna Saddle, much to the amusement of strutting king penguins and reindeer grazing nearby in the tussock grass. (Reindeer, introduced to South Georgia as a food supply in the early 1900s by the Norwegians have, in recent years, all been shot or removed from the island. Norwegian ship rats that created havoc with defenceless nesting seabirds have also been eradicated.)

Standing on Fortuna Saddle and looking down onto the rusty remains of

Stromness it is hard to work out where the waterfall is located that had caused Shackleton's trio so much trouble; lowering each other down its iced-up face with their rope. But their minds were fuddled by lack of sleep, with shredded clothing and emaciated bodies in ruins....and yet, dogging them constantly, was the thought of the threesome they had left at Peggoty Camp and of course Wild and his men so far away on Elephant Island. (For the complete harrowing story of this escape from almost certain death and the eventual recovery of all the men, read Frank Worsley's account *Endurance*.)

The end-point of our little polar journey was the Stromness manager's house, the same building at which Shackleton had knocked on the door, much to the disbelief of the Norwegians inside who initially didn't recognise the men that they thought long-dead. After Shackleton gave the basics of his tale and initiated the recovery of the men at Peggoty, he asked if the war had ended...."No, it still rages, utter madness, millions killed."

Gingerly, the eight of us tip-toed up the rotten, wooden staircase to where the explorers had stripped ragged clothing and taken their first bath. (Imagine the greasy black ring around the bath when they finished.) In homage to these great men, we all piled into that same bath, laughing and joking as only those can who have struck out on an adventure where the outcome was uncertain. Later, at Grytviken, we downed a tot of whiskey beside Shackleton's tall granite headstone. (On 5 January 1922, at only 47, Shackleton died of heart attack on another polar expedition aboard *Quest*. In 2011, Frank Wild was disinterred from his resting place in South Africa and reburied beside his beloved Boss. His headstone reads: "Frank Wild 1873–1939, Shackleton's right-hand man.")

For me, a pilgrimage that had started in 1973, on the far side of Antarctica southwards from my home in New Zealand, was now complete as I raised that whiskey glass in the darkness beside the Boss's grave. I felt enriched and rewarded beyond measure. Shackleton summed up his feelings more succinctly "We had reached the naked soul of man."

Questions and Answers

Colin is off on an expedition. His answers should be found within the essay.
Tor

Hammered by wind...it takes over 20 minutes to get crampons on.
Exhausted....scared. *Photograph courtesy of Colin Monteath.*

Biography

Colin Monteath is New Zealand's most widely published photographer and writer of polar, mountain travel and wilderness material. Colin has authored ten books and contributed imagery for many others. Colin spent 31 seasons in the Antarctic, four in the Arctic, and 22 expeditons to the Himalaya. Colin's images have been widely used in magazines such as *GEO*, *National Geographic*, and *Time*. Colin is an Honorary member of the New Zealand Institute of Professional Photographers and a Life member of the New Zealand Alpine Club. He has taken part in mountain journeys and climbing expeditions all over the world, including 21 expeditions in the Himalaya. Colin's most recent expeditions have been four journeys in remote parts of Mongolia: climbing Mongolia's highest peak, a bitterly-cold traverse riding reindeer through taiga forest and mountains close to the Siberian border and a camel journey across part of the Gobi desert. Colin runs the Christchurch Hedgehog House New Zealand polar & mountain reference book & image library.

www.hedgehoghouse.com
www.colinmonteath.com

Photograph by Quynh-Loan Pham.

No one really knows
The nature of birth
Nor the true dwelling place.
We return to the source
And turn to dust.

Many paths lead from the foot of the mountain,
But at the peak
We all gaze at the
Single bright moon.

If at the end of our journey
There is no final
Resting place,
Then we need not fear
Losing our Way.

No beginning,
No end.
Our mind
is born and dies:
The emptiness of emptiness!

~Ikkyu–Crazy Cloud

Iron bridge near Tawang, India. *Photograph by Michael Buckley.*

Michael Buckley

We build too many walls and not enough bridges.
~attributed to Isaac Newton

Tinker, Innovator, Engineer, Guru
A tale of suspension bridges, Tibetan pilgrims—and Herculean endeavours

"Would you like to stop at the temple with the iron bridge?" asks Pema, my guide. We are motoring along the road from Paro to Thimphu. The iron bridge rings a few bells. An internal radar starts scanning my brain to determine which bells.

"Who built the temple?"

"Tangtong Gyalpo, the great master from Tibet."

Eureka! The mad yogi from Tibet. The highly elusive guru. I have come across traces of his presence on extensive travels in Tibet. But very few of his temples and bridges have survived there. I have seen iron bridge links in museums, but never an intact bridge.

In medieval Tibet, there were no maps as Europeans knew them. The closest thing to a map was a painting depicting major temples or palaces, set in a mountainous landscape. These places were the object of devout pilgrimages. Traders journeyed across Tibet in yak and mule caravans, but the main reason for travel was pilgrimage. You would be hard-pressed to find a place on the planet more preoccupied with prayers and pilgrimage than Tibet. Even under current repressive Chinese rule, this devotion continues, despite severe restrictions. Tibetans strive to reach sacred temples, peaks and lakes to pay homage and accrue merit. Top of the pilgrim's wish-list is the sacred city of Lhasa. And the most sacred peak in all Asia, Mount Kailash.

Pilgrimage in Tibet is arduous—seen as a test of resolve, designed to build character. In centuries past, pilgrims encountered numerous obstacles along the way—from rapacious bandits to unexpected snowfalls—and perilous river crossings. At high altitude, rivers are freezing cold. More to the point, pilgrims could not swim. On the slow-flowing rivers of central Tibet, they would launch across the waters in a yak-hide coracle, made from yak-skins stretched over a wooden frame. Pilgrims would crouch down, praying the vessel would not capsize. But if the crossing was via a narrow precipitous gorge with a raging river below, this could only be done by bridging the precipitous gap. At some points, pilgrims had to winch themselves upside-

341

down across the river on a long yak-hair rope. Or embark on a kind of early zipline: a terrifying pulley ride via rope across the river. Occasionally, there were primitive rope bridges made from plant fibres, or thick bamboo poles lashed together to make a bridge, but these did not last long. Tangtong Gyalpo's iron-chain bridges were built to last. He built the bridges to smooth the pilgrim's passage to sacred sites.

And here, right in front of me, in the highlands of Bhutan, is an intact iron bridge, built by the man himself. Well, not quite. The bridge dates back to the 15th century. It was demolished at one point by rival religious sects and rebuilt. In 1969, it was washed away by high waters. A new cable suspension bridge was built alongside it—constructed wider for cattle to cross. Then in 2005, the original iron-chain bridge was rebuilt next to it as a living museum piece, using the same iron links. But today, the bridge cannot be crossed as it is deemed unsafe while still undergoing repairs.

Two stone towers—one on each river bank—anchor the iron-chain suspension. Thick flattened iron links form four lengthy chains. According to Pema, in the original design, yak-hair ropes formed cross-struts every metre or so—supporting a narrow wooden walkway. But that has been replaced with wire mesh and thin wire cables so a person can't fall through the gaps.

Inside a tower that anchors the suspension is the guru himself—at least, a fresco of him. He is depicted holding iron-chain links in his right hand, and the vase of longevity in his left hand. The guru sports a top-knot, long locks flowing onto his shoulders, full beard, pot belly. With his intense gaze, he is one weird-looking dude. So weird that at a ferry crossing near Lhasa, in his younger days, it is said he was hit over the head with an oar and thrown into the river due to his unkempt appearance. Tangtong Gyalpo's engineering feats were apparently inspired by this incident. Maybe being banged on the head by the oar sparked the insight. Or the indignity. Whatever the case, he found his true vocation in life: building bridges and ferry points, intended to link remote villages, promote pilgrimage, and propagate the Buddhist faith. Pious Tibetans engage in building temples, funding the construction of statues, or performing other good deeds to gain merit. Tangtong Gyalpo did all that, but his special way of accruing merit was to build bridges.

His sons carried on with his legacy, repairing bridges and building new ones. Across this bridge lies Tamchog Temple, started by Tangtong Gyalpo—but completed by his descendants. He acquired a consort in Bhutan, called Drubthob Zangmo, and fathered several sons. In the period from 1430 to 1460, he embarked on a building splurge. He is credited with building 58 iron suspension bridges, an equal number of wooden bridges, and establishing over 100 ferry crossings all over the Himalayas. He constructed innumerable shrines and temples. Mad yogi, mystic, scholar, civil engineer, visionary, sculptor, painter, poet, composer of song and dance, architect, physician who devised longevity pills—Tangtong Gyalpo is the Tibetan version of Leonardo Da Vinci.

In fact, Tangtong Gyalpo is credited with building the world's first durable suspension bridges. There may well have been iron-chain suspension bridges pre-dating him, but they have vanished. Iron-chain bridge designs appeared in China, such as the 103-metre bridge at Luding, in Sichuan—built in 1706 and still standing. But this form of engineering was completely unknown in Europe and America. In 1726, a book published in Germany described a Tibetan iron-chain bridge as 'a bridge was built into the free air and can be viewed at with astonishment.' Iron-chain bridges only started to appear in Europe after this and other descriptions were published. But it was not until 1820 that an iron-chain bridge built in England was able to match Tangtong Gyalpo's longest suspension bridges, reckoned to have a span of over 100 metres. And not until 1849 that a 200-metre iron-chain bridge built over the Danube in Budapest eclipsed the guru's great technical feats. Later, when iron links were replaced with wire cables, the spans grew much longer. Odd to think that the engineering marvel of San Francisco's Golden Gate Bridge, with a span of 1,280 metres, owes much to the visions of Tangtong Gyalpo.

The bridge-building guru was an eccentric anomaly—the sole civil engineer in Tibet, a land of zero engineering. Advances like the wheel were known, but reserved exclusively for sacred use, such as prayer wheels or the dharma wheel. Here's a civilisation that knew about the wheel, knew what it could do, but declined to use it for any practical purposes. Everything was carried on animal backs or the backs of humans. Which makes Tangtong Gyalpo's achievements all the more remarkable. Paro, I discover, was a prime source of iron. He not only built here and in other parts of Bhutan, but had 7,000 chain links manufactured by blacksmiths in Paro. And arranged for 1,400 mule-loads of iron to be transported back to Tibet, traversing precipitous trails that climbed into the Himalayas.

Making this even more of a Herculean task are religious taboos against mining in Tibet. Ancient animist Bon beliefs in Tibet held that important deities resided in mountains, lakes, rivers—and in the earth. And were not to be disturbed, as this could cause major disaster. Mining was thought to scar the surface of the earth. The smelting of gold, silver, copper and iron was, however, mastered by Tibetan craftsmen for making statuary in temples. In other words, if it had a spiritual purpose, it was permitted. Tangtong Gyalpo's spin on this was that he was creating iron-bridge pathways to enlightenment.

Tibet's conservative religious taboos will explain why blacksmiths were looked down upon—occupying the lowest rungs on the hierarchy of old Tibet—and were hard to find. Tangtong Gyalpo needed a small army of blacksmiths. To get them going, he composed rhythmic work songs—still sung while carrying out construction tasks and daily chores in Tibet and Bhutan today. Building an iron-chain bridge cost a small fortune, both in materials and labour. Undaunted, Tangtong Gyalpo came up with his own form of crowdfunding. He devised Tibetan opera as entertainment, and used the proceeds to fund bridges. Ache Lhamo Opera started with a troupe of seven sisters, who also worked on the bridges. This popular form of opera is performed to this day in Tibetan realms.

Tangtong Gyalpo travelled widely across the Himalayas, from Ladakh in the west to Arunachal Pradesh in the east, in search or iron ore, and to continue his life mission to build bridges to bring people together, remove isolation—and promote pilgrimage to sacred places. His masterpiece was Chaksam Gompa, the temple of the iron bridge. 'Chaksam' is Tibetan for 'iron bridge.' The foot-bridge, estimated to be around 135 metres long, spanned the mighty Yarlung Tsangpo in central Tibet, and led straight into the temple, with the monks collecting a toll to use it. At the time it was built, in 1430, there were no suspension bridges anywhere else in the world. The bridge fell into disrepair by the 1930s; both temple and bridge were completely destroyed in the Cultural Revolution in the 1960s. The same fate befell all of Tangtong Gyalpo's iron bridges across Tibet.

Outside of Tibet, the chances of finding an intact bridge are better. There are two iron bridges still standing in Bhutan, plus iron-chain links preserved in museums. At one museum, I come across an exhibit that tries to unravel the mystery of why the iron links miraculously do not corrode. They apparently have a high arsenic content and are in fact more closely matched to steel. That presents a technical challenge, as steel-like metals have a very high melting point for forging. The same exhibit identifies an intact iron bridge near Tawang, just across the border in Arunachal Pradesh, India. Although it is just next door to Sakteng, my furthest point east in Bhutan, foreigners not permitted to cross on foot here.

After a bone-shaking trip in a series of jeeps going all the way south to exit Bhutan, then turning the corner in India and heading all the way north again, driving over high passes, I finally reach Tawang, where I am faced with a terrible quandary: how to pay for food and lodging. Just a week before, the Indian government had decided, without warning, to withdraw all 1,000 and 500-rupee notes from circulation—in an effort to stymie blackmarket hoarders of these notes—and has replaced them with brand-new 2,000-rupee and 500-rupee notes. You are only allowed to draw a single 2,000 note per day at the ATM. I have been caught up in a serious currency crisis, with huge line-ups at ATM machines across the country, and banks refusing to exchange American dollars. Though rich by local standards, I have suddenly been reduced to the status of a beggar. And since everyone else has become beggars too, I am not likely to find anybody sympathetic to my plight. Salvation arrives via the manager of my humble hotel, who is heading out to go surfing in Bali soon. He desperately needs foreign currency, and I have an emergency stash of two 500-Euro bills. Somehow, this wheeler and dealer manages to come up with the equivalent exchange in a stack of newly minted 2,000-rupee bills. I am solvent again, able to pay the driver whose jeep brought me on the final stretch of road here. The manager invites me out to dinner—a repast that consists of yak-meat in a soup with chillies and very stinky fermented yak-cheese. And now I can pay for luxuries like this.

On the streets of Tawang, I spot groups of Bhutanese wandering around. The men are easy to spot from their plaid-patterned robes and Argyll socks. I ask a group how they got there. They tell me they have hiked for days over mountain passes. Why? They point to a large poster on a wall: the Karmapa is coming to town.

I think at this point, if I took a selfie, you would see my face creased into a huge smile. This is a once-in-a-century thing. More like four centuries. My timing is impeccable. For complex geopolitical reasons, this is the first time in four centuries that the leader of the Kagyu sect of Tibetan Buddhism has shown up in Tawang. And the whole town has turned out to see him. HH Gyalwang Karmapa is the 17th lineage holder in a tradition that stretches back as far as the 10th century. Bhutanese men in tartan-patterned robes, Brokpas with serge-red vests and yak-hair caps, Monpas with elaborate hand-embroidered dress, Tibetan refugees in graceful gowns, and burgundy-robed monks from the temples of Tawang throng open-air High Altitude Arena, seeking the blessings of the Karmapa. A crowd of over 20,000 shiny-eyed devotees, all bearing white scarves and incense as offerings.

The Karmapa shows up—steps out of a car surrounded by guards, who rebuff anyone attempting to get closer for photography, like myself. He takes his place on the throne provided, and launches into a long monologue about the ties of his lineage to Tawang, followed by a teaching. After he blesses the site, entertainment is stepped up. A huge hairy yak rampages into the crowd—well, actually, this is a yak-dance, performed by two dancers inside a yak-skin, with a deity riding on top. Then three snow lions magically appear, prancing around in costume—hairy white body, lengthy green mane, lion head with big rows of teeth. Male, female and baby versions dancing. Mythical snow lions are highly auspicious figures in Tibet, showing up on the Tibetan flag as protectors of the realm. Loud drumming adds to the excitement: the performers have to be careful not to step on seated monks crowding the venue. This is followed by singing troupes, a monastic masked dance, and snippets of Tibetan opera—the same opera devised by Tangtong Gyalpo many centuries ago.

Ceremonies and festivities over, it is time to feed those who have made the long pilgrimage here—from as far afield as Bhutan. From the elevated throne area, sponsors rain down packets of chips, sweets, fruit and assorted food items on the devotees, who gleefully tussle over the offerings. An exuberant end to an extraordinary event—which will remain etched in my mind.

The following day, I hire a driver to tour sacred sites around Tawang. Striking among these is the tiny temple of the Sixth Dalai Lama, who was born here—a renegade who was never fully ordained as a monk and who is famed for composing songs celebrating his dalliances with the beautiful women of Lhasa. He died young under mysterious circumstances, most likely assassinated, but prophesied that he would return to Tawang. And in 1959, he did return to Tawang—in the incarnation of the 14th Dalai Lama, escaping from Tibet.

But on to the mad yogi. By late afternoon, we reach a waterfall site 25 kilometres from Tawang. The falls cascade into a greenish glacial pool—a magnificent landscape. Close by is a small hydropower plant, built by Indian engineers to harness the river and supply power to Tawang. Nehru called dams the new temples of India. Time will tell if they are in fact the destroyers of riverine ecosystems.

Along the same powerful river, a short distance away, lies a small shrine. And next to that, a stone structure housing a wooden water paddle, run by a stream, that turns a huge prayer wheel embossed with sacred mantras. This is the extent of Tibetan engineering—harnessing the river to send prayers to the heavens. Well, there is another piece of engineering. To get to the shrine and prayer wheel, there's an iron bridge. An original iron bridge, as constructed by Tangtong Gyalpo: intact, festooned with prayer flags. A bridge to nowhere. Nearby is a wider wooden bridge, which I stroll across to photograph the iron bridge.

Time to test the iron bridge. How safe can a 600-year-old bridge be? Hopefully, it has been maintained and repaired over time. The walkway has been reset with matting and wire mesh, but everything comes down to the strength of those ancient iron links. The wind picks up. I am wobbling across. Can see the rapids swirling around rocks far below. Praying that the bridge doesn't snap and send me crashing into the raging river.

Everything seems to slow down, reduced to slow motion—the few minutes it takes to cross the swaying bridge seem to stretch into a much longer span of time—during which I find myself in the mindset of a 15th century pilgrim. A multitude of things going through my head. Reflecting on all the useless things I have done in my life. Reflecting on all the great and useful things I should be doing with my life. Trying not to stare at the thundering river below. In past centuries, this bridge would lie on a pilgrim trail to reach Tawang. Pilgrims would shoulder their humble possessions for the journey, making the balancing act of crossing this bridge even more tricky. But how on earth would a pack horse or mule be persuaded to cross? They must have blindfolded the poor animal to stop it panicking in the middle of the bridge. Horses are notoriously skittish on unstable ground.

At mid-bridge, a thought flashes into my head: there is a uniquely spiritual quality to the guru's iron bridge. Because when you cross this bridge, you *pray*. You pray fervently. You call on all the deities you know—

even ones you don't know—and pray for good luck to make the passage. And when you reach the other side, you feel renewed, alive. Ready to take on the world.

Questions and Answers

1. What compelled you to set out on your pilgrimage?
Fascination with one man's vision, dedicated to helping pilgrims by building bridges—a vision that impacted civil engineering hundreds of years later.

2. Is there a book, song, poem, or movie that inspired your quest?
The source was intriguing one-liners or two or three tantalizing sentences buried in books. Those snippets inspired me to find out more, much more.

3. Where is your sacred place and why did you choose it?
Shrines devoted to sacred waters are magical places. There are miraculous healing waters like the bubbling hotsprings at Bath, in the UK, where the Celts and the Romans invoked the worship of Sulis-Minerva. Or, as in my piece about Tangtong Gyalpo, the water-driven prayer-wheel shrines encountered in Bhutan and Arunachal Pradesh.

4. How did your pilgrimage change your life or not?
It changed my life this way: the realisation that from a tiny nugget of information, you can take a wild journey that leads to great discoveries. Another key insight is that we keep losing precious knowledge through war and neglect, and then re-discovering it. Tangtong Gyalpo's many bridges in Tibet are gone—but you can discover them again in Bhutan and Arunachal Pradesh. The finest example of lost and found cultural facets has to be hieroglyphics. The meaning of the writing was lost for over a thousand years until the discovery of the Rosetta Stone in 1799, which enabled us to decipher Egyptian temple art again.

5. What is the most important piece of advice that you have received in your life? Do you have advice to share from your experiences?
"If we are facing the right direction, all we have to do is keep on walking." (attributed as a Buddhist saying)

When you come to a fork in the road, always choose the tougher option, because that will ultimately be more rewarding.

Photograph courtesy of Michael Buckley.

Biography

Michael Buckley is a writer and photographer who specialises in Tibet and the Himalayan regions. He is author of a number of books, including: *Meltdown in Tibet*, an expose about destruction of ecosystems in Tibet and beyond; *Tibet, Disrupted*, a multimedia photobook; and *Eccentric Explorers*, about ten foreign travellers to Tibet.

www.himmies.com
www.WildYakFilms.com
www.FB.com/MeltdowninTibet

"Say it, reader. Say the word 'quest' out loud. It is an extraordinary word, isn't it? So small and yet so full of wonder, so full of hope."
~Kate DiCamillo

Amy Gigi Alexander

She promised herself she would see the world, and so she did.
~Virginia Woolf

Climbing the Milky Way

*G*rownups can run away from home, just like children—and sometimes, they should. Sometimes, that's what it takes, to live the life you were meant to live.

Fifteen years ago, I ran away from my very 'every day' sort of life to hike down the Grand Canyon alone. At that time, I was not a hiker, and in fact, the only time I went outside was to walk my dog around the block! I was a grownup of a particular breed: that sort of woman who prefers the mall. Air conditioning, pantyhose, lip gloss, blow dryers, the Chanel counter: those were the things that appeared to make my heart sing. However, I had a secret side, once. When I was younger, prompted by stories by writers like Jack London, and characters like Pippi Longstocking, I had wanted a more adventurous life. All I had dreamt of was to be a girl who could go anywhere and see anything.

As a kid, I got to sometimes leave the flat Sacramento Valley, that green to burnet brown landscape of California where I grew up. On one of those trips, I went to Colorado, where my grandparents lived in a worn-out suburb outside of Denver—and while it wasn't an outdoor adventure, they allowed me and a neighbor child to explore their house, which was full of treasures. One afternoon we discovered a box of books about the Grand Canyon: the original pioneers, photographs of that serpentine emerald snake, the Colorado river; and a fold out picture postcard album of the Canyon, a place which appeared, to my young mind, like a cut-glass salad bowl, made of rust colored rock: I'd never seen anything like that in my small town, which had no view but alfalfa fields, sunflowers, tomatoes.

That afternoon in the basement, surrounded by postcards and pictures of the orange rock walls set something off in me, made me think differently about the world. I wanted to see where life had begun, and for me, that was the Canyon herself.

It was a private obsession, the Grand Canyon, something I kept hidden, taking it out when I needed an escape from my life. Even though I never had the chance to visit it, I found other ways to get there: I filled sketch books with an imaginary journey, which included a hike that would take me from the North to South Rim, up and down trails with wonderful names like 'Thunder River' 'Bright Angel' and 'Tonto.' I pictured myself walking down to the river with a burro, living on canned baked beans, and pitching an army green woolen tent. In those daydreams, I collected wild berries, met up with cowboys, miners, and Navajo; tracked wild animals, made tea from weeds, never wore a dress and was happily covered in the red dust of the Canyon. I pictured all sorts of things at the bottom of the Canyon walls: aliens picnicking alongside their spaceships; lost boys who lived on the river in homemade boats; a dome to see the stars, alongside a resident astronomer; the daughters of the original pioneers, showing me their worn scrapbooks.

But it wasn't until fifteen years ago that I finally had the courage to hike the Canyon on my own. I'd almost forgotten about those notebooks, when an old school friend called me to tell me she'd found a Christmas tin, wrapped in plastic, with my name on it, buried in her parents' backyard while digging out overgrown rosebushes. She and I had buried lots of things in that backyard, things we were supposed to come back for, but I'd forgotten about them and so had she. I drove over to her house and we opened the tin together at her kitchen table: out came the Grand Canyon sketchbooks, the bits of survival lore, and a handmade map of the route I'd hoped I would take someday, alongside a letter I'd written to myself.

I opened the letter and it contained a single line, written carefully in perfect cursive: "Dear Amy, I do not know if you will get this letter, but if you do it is because you did not go—I hope you change your mind. Signed, Amy, 12."

My friend and I sat at that table until late that night, talking about our lost dreams. You do not realize you have failed your younger self until you have had the luxury of getting a letter from her that bluntly points it out. As a child, reason had not been important to me: it was likely I had believed that this letter would magically reach me, if I wanted it to—and so it had. Reasonable arguments as to why I had not made it to the Canyon now somehow felt feeble and ridiculous, and I knew I needed to go.

It took another year to get the vacation time, and then I set off, driving across the Southwest, with a backpack heavily loaded. The army green tent of my imagined childhood journey had been replaced with a practical lightweight backpacking tent; the sketchbook had been upgraded to a proper map; but I had been unwilling to give up the cans of baked beans, and planned on hiking down to the bottom with them and a can opener in tow.

I arrived a few days later at the North Rim when it was dark, and spent several hours setting up my tent, declining all offers of assistance, my pride convincing me that the way it sagged inwards and leaned helplessly on one side was the way it was supposed to be. Once inside the tent, my dimestore flashlight blinked on and off as I opened the first can of baked beans and ate them, trying to guess what the North Kaibab Trail would be like. The beans were terrible, and the map? I had no idea what I was looking at. Turned out, while I was very good at making imaginary maps, I did not know how to use a real one.

It was the start of July, and hot, so I set my alarm for 5 and after a poor night's sleep spent sitting up to keep the tent from falling in, wondering if I should just forget about the whole adventure and go to a hotel, I woke up in the dark, stuffed the tent into a sack, filled a water bottle, and got to the trailhead. According to the map, I had about 7 and a half kilometers before I made it to Roaring Springs. Seven and a half kilometers: piece of cake in my brand new hiking boots I hadn't broken in yet and my 75 pound bag.

It was clear after the first kilometer my feet were on fire. I forgot entirely about that twelve year old kid and her dreams, and instead wondered why I had not asked what 'breaking in' meant at the outdoor store. I had wanted to appear like I knew what I was doing, and now each step felt like hot asphalt was being poured on my toes. But I kept going.

The trail had a few places that seemed to have fallen in. A man who was galloping by at seemingly breakneck speed noticed me gingerly stepping around a missing part of the trail and gaily called out, "Oh, that's where tourists occasionally fall down into the Canyon." I looked down and realized, I was going to die here. Why had I not told anyone where I was going? The truth is I'd been afraid I wouldn't go thru with it, and I didn't want to have to tell anyone that, so I'd just disappeared. If I fell down into the Canyon, no one would even know I was there. I pictured my bones being picked clean by vultures, and then baked in the sun for ten years before they were found.

By the time I got to Roaring Springs, I was crying, both from the pain of my blisters and my stupidity for undertaking a hike when I knew absolutely nothing. I sat on a rock and sobbed, until I was rescued by a family hiking down with numerous toddlers strapped to their backs, whose no-nonsense matriarch told me to wear multiple socks, drink more water, and pull myself together.

The next stretch was to Cottonwood Camp, another 11 kilometers. It took me the rest of the day and more than two dozen breaks. Sometimes I pulled the letter from my twelve year old self out of my bag to read to keep me going. I was nothing like that girl now: I was fat, and out of shape; it was hot, and I was whiny and longed for a fan; I was soaked with sweat and my hair and clothes stuck on my skin, causing me to break out in a rash. I could hardly even look up at the Canyon walls: I missed everything because I was so uncomfortable, barely able to watch my steps on the path. I could have been anywhere on Earth, and all I kept thinking about with each step was that I was actually going down, and I was eventually going to have to come back out. I set up my tent somewhere before Cottonwood, because I couldn't drag myself another step, and passed out in the tent after eating another can of baked beans, which on night two, was the most delicious thing I had ever eaten. All I walked that day was about 15 miles, and it had taken me over 12 hours.

The next morning I woke up early, and something had changed: me. I was different after that first night in the Canyon, and in the early light I was seeing it for the first time, up close: the wildly bright rusts, reds, roses of the rock, the variations of green, from mustard yellow to frothy spined seafoam; the small lizards and birds that moved slowly, warming themselves in the new sun; the sky, which was airbrushed bright tangerine and robin's egg blue, with clouds like marsh mellows packed and puffed in between. Packing my tent, I ate another can of baked beans, and set off for the place I had read about as a girl: 'Bright Angel' Campground.

That single day was the day that changed me from being a woman who loved the mall, to a woman who preferred to be outside. The entire Canyon seemed to be putting on a show for just me those precious hours. There was not a single view that was not perfect; nor any step that did not have some small flower, stone, or pattern I needed to take note of. The colors of the rock changed by the hour, and even the sky altered, from faded to so bright it was electric. Ribbon Falls was the green of Chinese Jade, and I still recall standing beneath it and feeling joined to my younger self at last. True, I did not see any lost boys, pioneers, miners, or Navajo, but I did not feel disappointed, for I carried all those stories with me and I walked the same path as they had, in my mind. In some ways, the journey was not a pilgrimage for me right now: it was, instead, a journey to the storyteller I'd been at twelve, a thank you to climb down into the Canyon for the kid who knew elsewhere was out there, something I'd forgotten.

Finally I arrived at Bright Angel, and the rock was violet from the evening light, huge steely gray sheets of it soaring up on one side. The landscape shifted in the light, making the cliffs appear to move. Trees lit up by the stars went from shadow leaves to acidic yellow; small scrub rolled silver and lazy on the sand and dust. I had just finished setting up my tent and eating yet another can of baked beans, when I heard a man call out from one of the other tents, and I went over to see him.

He was old, with hair that was the same steely gray color as the cliffs that surrounded us—he seemed like part of the landscape, and I felt he had been waiting there just for me. We sat on a boulder and talked about the stars, and he took out a small telescope. I had found my Canyon astronomer that I had wished for at twelve after all! Thru the lens, I could see the Milky Way shining brighter and brighter, until it was a day glow ribbon across the Canyon, and it was as though we were climbing up into the sky alongside it, walking in that milky haze. It was so close it felt like we had left earth long ago, and that our boulder had detached itself from the other rock and floated up with us. We stayed up there for hours, while he told me star-stories, and in the middle of the night, we came down again, into the familiar womb of the Canyon.

The Grand Canyon. It was she who showed me I was made for a life of adventure after all, and that my dreams would not end up buried in a tin until I found them again.

I'll never stop climbing.

Questions and Answers

Be regular and orderly in your life,
so that you may be violent and original in your work.
~Gustave Flaubert

1. What compelled you to set out on your pilgrimage?
I think often, as grown-ups, we forget who we were going to be and the things we were going to do. I was living a life that was quite different than I had thought I would live, and when I discovered this was optional, I set out to go to the first place that had meaning for me as a kid, the Grand Canyon.

2. Is there a book, song, poem, or movie that inspired your quest?
No.

3. Where is your sacred place and why did you choose it?
My sacred place was—and is—the Grand Canyon in the United States. As a kid, I used to see photos of it and think it was not real, and I wanted to see it for myself. It took on more meaning when I realized the importance of it to my child-self, the daydreamer, the girl who thought everything was possible: going meant it was. I've always seen the Canyon as not just a place for story-tellers, but the landscape of God. It's a holy place, whether you simply see photos of it, stand on a cliff looking down at it, or touch the green of the Colorado River at the bottom. It's sanctuary.

4. How did your pilgrimage change your life or not?
When I decided to go hike the Grand Canyon alone, I'd never been an outdoorsy person. I had no idea what I was doing, and I'm surprised still that I managed to do it. Completing the hike changed my life because I realized I could be whatever I wanted, including a completely different person. Maybe I could be outdoorsy. Maybe I could travel the world. Maybe I could do lots of things. I think fulfilling quests does that to a person: gives one courage and the audacity to believe they can do it again.

5. What is the most important piece of advice that you have received in your life? Do you have advice to share from your experiences?
"Fear is good. If you're not afraid, it's not important enough to you."
~Tim Cahill (He told me this at a time when I was very afraid.)

Photograph courtesy of Amy Gigi Alexander.

Biography

Amy is a writer, editor, publisher, and geocultural explorer with an emphasis on travel writing, landscapes imagined and real, memoir, and lyrical magical realism paired with psychogeography. She is the Editor-in-Chief of the British literary journal with a modern approach to travel literature, *Panorama: the Journal of Intelligent Travel,* and has taught travel and landscape writing around the world, most recently in Rwanda, Uganda, Tanzania, and Kenya. Her award winning travel writing has appeared in many publications and anthologies, from *National Geographic Traveler* to *BBC Travel,* from *Lonely Planet* to multiple editions of *Best Travel Writing,* as well as many literary journals. Her upcoming mountain themed writing appears in *Alpinist* and *Waymaking,* among others.

Her current projects include a collection of short stories on place, and a guidebook on imaginary mountains, published in partnership with Imaginary Mountains Surveyors. It is both a bible on the history of mountains, as well as a sort of *Zen and the Art of Motorcycle Maintenance* take on the mountainscape—and our relationship to it.

www.panoramajournal.org

Ian with Mishmis' on porch. *Photograph courtesty of Ian Baker.*

Ian Baker

I live in hazard and infinity. The cosmos stretches around me, meadow on meadow of galaxies, reach on reach of dark space, steppes of stars, oceanic darkness and light. There is no god in it, no particular concern or particular mercy. Yet everywhere I see a living balance, a rippling tension, an enormous yet mysterious simplicity, an endless breathing of light.
~John Fowles, *The Aristos*

Passage to Paradise: A Journey up Tibet's Secret River

*A*n ancient, silver-haired woman festooned in flowers sat in trance on the floorboards of her palm-thatched hut. Coils of incense rose from a stone censer, wreathing shelves filled with multi-armed idols and nearly obscuring a rattan tray that lay between us, teeming with restless, long-legged spiders.

I had heard of arachnomancy, or divination based on the symbolic behavior of spiders, but had never encountered it first hand. Ancient Incan priests and shamans in Western Africa have been known to interpret the movements of often-deadly arachnids (spiders, scorpions, and mites) to divine past and future events. Here in the dense rainforests of northeastern India, female oracles called *jomo* continue the practice, offering, through their spirit allies, answers to any question.

I settled onto the floor. The hand-hewn boards groaned beneath my weight, and the jomo gazed at me coolly. For ten days, we'd wound our way up India's Brahamputra River, alternately on boats and in jeeps, to arrive in the village of Tuting in the easternmost Himalaya. We'd followed maps and a recently constructed road to get here. By the following day, these conveniences would disappear and we would have only legend, visions, and cryptic texts to guide us.

Tibetan Buddhist prophecies dating back to the eighth-century tell of a place called *Chimé Yangsang Né*, literally the 'Immortal Ultimately Secret Place'. Manuscripts, written in an intentionally obscure 'twilight language', describe it as an earthly paradise akin to Shangri-La. Tibetan pilgrims have sought this Promised Land for centuries, placing it near the headwaters of a tributary of the Brahamaputra called Yangsang Chu, the 'Ultimately Secret River', in one of the most impenetrable tangles of mountains and jungles on the planet. During the first half of the twentieth-century, a succession of lamas blazed a route to the very threshold of Chimé Yangsang Né, but the malarial jungles and vexing terrain ultimately thwarted all attempts to reach it. We were determined to go where they could not, taking guidance wherever it was offered.

After a lengthy invocation, the jomo stretched her pale hands into the tray of spiders and selected a particularly menacing looking specimen. She bid me to lean forward and, without warning, placed it on the crown of my head. I sat immobilized as the spider crawled through my hair and over my scalp. She and other villagers who had gathered in the hut watched intently as the spider descended on to my right shoulder and, from there, down onto the adze-cut floor, its ciphered movements responding to my query about the way ahead.

"Follow the Secret River to where it becomes a waterfall," the jomo interpreted. "Climb above it to where a crystal stream issues from a cleft in the rock. Drink this water together with the berries of the *Tsakuntuzangpo* plant and, if your karma is pure, you will find the way to the Ultimate Secret Place."

Although Shangri-la is firmly mapped in human belief, its geographical coordinates are strongly contested. Pakistan proclaims the Hunza Valley as the original location of the Himalayan eutopia, while Bhutan, Nepal, and Sikkim each make counter claims. Some researchers hold that Shangri-La was the ancient city of Tsaparang near Tibet's Mount Kailash or the oasis of Dunhuang in China's modern-day Gansu province. In 2001, Zhongdian County in northern Yunnan took matters into its own hands and rebranded itself as Shangri-La.

Most Buddhists believe Shangri-La to be a derivation of Shambhala, a mystical kingdom described in various ancient texts as a source of wisdom that will lead the world from a period of impending chaos. Others view both Shangri-La and Shambhala as allegories for a transcendent reality attainable through spiritual disciplines. Chimé Yangsang Né is not as easily dismissed. The Dalai Lama insists on its geographic reality as do many other prominent Tibetan lamas. They also claim that a time of great material and spiritual bounty will begin when the door to the Ultimate Secret Place is opened. A range of Tibetan texts describe it in vivid detail as the womb of a Tantric Goddess, *Varja Varahi*, whose supine body forms a 'hidden-land' that extends along the Tsangpo-Brahmaputra River Gorge—the Earth's deepest chasm—straddling the border between Tibet and India.

During the 1990s I made eight expeditions into the Tibetan reaches of the Tsangpo gorge, which led to the discovery of a 108-foot high waterfall considered a portal into the Ultimate Secret Place. The goal of the quest had been to locate the long-sought waterfall and pass beyond it into the innermost realms of the hidden land. But sheer cliffs and seething whitewater prevented us from reaching the apocryphal gate. Paradise would have to wait.

I later learned that the principal entrance to the Ultimate Secret Place lies in the far north of Arunachal Pradesh, 'Land of the Dawn-Lit Mountains', a little-known state in northeastern India. Tibet ceded this territory to British

India in 1914, but the area remained effectively off-limits for most of the century due to the inhospitable terrain and the local tribes' penchant for severing and collecting heads. Even today, the Government of India exerts little control over much of the area. Any meaningful governance is left up to the local tribes, many of which are still deeply hostile to outsiders.

The sheer remoteness and inaccessibility of much of Arunachal Pradesh has limited the advance of globalization. Its forests still teem with hoolock gibbon and red panda, Bengal tiger, and king cobra. Many of its tribes are still deeply traditional and much of its landscape completely unexplored. If there were still a region on this Google'd Earth that Shangri-La could exist, Arunachal Pradesh would be it. But for how long? The inevitable rumors of roads are rife and, with them, potential timber concessions and mining claims, enterprises fatal not only to indigenous knowledge and myth, but to one of the Earth's last remaining pristine ecosystems.

In 2006, a friend named Yeshi Choden helped procure a Restricted Area Permit so that we could explore northern Arunachal Pradesh before change wound its way up its valleys. In the early years of the twentieth-century, Yeshi's grandfather, a renowned Tibetan lama, had set out for the Ultimate Secret Place guided by an eighth-century scroll that he had unearthed from a cave in eastern Tibet. Mishmi tribesmen armed with spears and poison-tipped arrows had cut short her grandfather's quest. Yeshi wanted to finish what he'd begun.

Days before our intended departure, Yeshi boarded a helicopter in eastern Nepal bound for Kathmandu. Within minutes of taking off in heavy fog, it crashed into a mountain ridge killing everyone on board. A year later, I had come to complete our objective of determining, to whatever degree was possible, the coordinates of the Ultimate Secret Place.

To help reach that goal, Yeshi's colleague, Amchi Sherab, a traditional doctor from Bhutan and a specialist in medicinal plants, had agreed to join me. I'd also recruited Dorje Tenzing, the son of one of the area's most revered lamas and an expert on the Tibetan texts describing the Ultimate Secret Place. After our visit to the jomo, we returned to a raised wooden bungalow where we had stored our provisions; including bamboo baskets filled with dried mithun meat and jute sacks of rice and desiccated coconut. A crowd of prospective porters with 18-inch *daos* slung across their shoulders in rattan and bearskin sheaths had gathered on the porch, sizing up the loads. The headwaters of the Yangsang Chu were unknown to all of us, and the porters were wary. They grew even more uneasy when Dorje told them of our ultimate goal; an elusive sanctuary that no one had ever successfully reached. Still, work was work, and they agreed to meet us at dawn the following day.

A pair of giant hornbills lapped through the morning mists as we crossed a swaying footbridge and entered the valley of the Yangsang Chu. The river—a daunting torrent of jade green water—was smaller than the Brahmaputra and, for the first several days, we would follow its eastward course through land traditionally inhabited by the Adi tribe. As we climbed higher, we would eventually reach a Tibetan settlement that had historically served as a staging point in the search for the Ultimate Secret Place.

Sherab, Dorje, and I labored up a precipitous, muddy track, followed by our porters. Tree ferns, bamboo, and lianas overhung what was often a streambed, forming a shadowy corridor worn smooth by generations of bare-footed tribesmen. We had just begun to hit a rhythm when our fifteen porters set down their loads in a small clearing and refused to proceed.

"They want higher wages," Dorje said. "Otherwise they won't go any farther."

The porters sat stone-faced on their loads. Dorje remained unperturbed beneath his woven bamboo hat. He had grown up in this area and, besides completing a three-year meditation retreat in the jungle, he had worked in the local government. He brought his considerable authority to bear, broached matters of pride and respect, then upped the daily rate. The porters hoisted their loads and resumed walking.

Word of our presence had preceded us. At the outskirts of the first Adi village we were met by two Adi *gam*, or headmen, crowned with cane helmets fringed with hornbill feathers and the tusks of wild boar. Women draped in beads and silver, stood behind them holding bamboo flasks filled with *apong*, a potent brew made from local hill rice. They poured the apong into porcelain bowls and, following a custom ubiquitous throughout the Himalayas, kept them relentlessly filled to the brim.

During the British Raj, the Adi were known by their Assamese name, Abor, meaning 'those who will not submit'. Days before, we had passed a stone marker indicating the spot where two British officers had been hacked to death with war axes and wide, sharp-edged knives called *daos*. The British had launched a punitive expedition, replete with elephant-drawn howitzers, but were still no match for the Adi warriors who ambushed them using stone-chutes and intricate spring traps that sprayed the track with volleys of poison arrows.

Times had changed, and the Adi greeted Dorje heartily. They had known him for years. Led by a nimble, sword-wielding priestess, we were swept into a traditional welcome dance that, fueled by seemingly endless rounds of apong, morphed into an inebriated exchange of songs. My own repertoire was sadly lacking.

The following morning, I asked Dorje how we should deal with our contentious porters. "Don't worry," he said, "We'll find better ones up the river. Tibetans will go for less money; for them it will be a pilgrimage."

"Will we send back all the Adi porters?" I asked. "No, not all," he qualified.

While Dorje was known for his mastery of Buddhist philosophy and his dedication to his family, he was also known as a bit of a Casanova, a holdover, he claimed, from his younger years in Kathmandu where I had met him in the 1970s. In Tuting he had negotiated suspiciously hard for a beguiling group of five female porters who had eventually joined our ranks.

"What about the Adi girls?" I asked. "They're carrying only carry half the weight as that of the men."

Dorje looked at me seriously and said: "The texts say that, to ensure success, you must bring young women on the pilgrimage." He further added that five was an auspicious number, also indicated in the scriptures, and that what they would lack in terms of their load-carrying capacity they would make up for in terms of morale. I had no argument.

Although the concept of Shangri-la is as old as humanity's longing for a perfect world, the word first appeared in James Hilton's 1933 novel *Lost Horizon*. The primary source for Hilton's book was an earlier work by an obscure British writer named Talbot Mundy entitled *Om: The Secret of the Abor Valley*. In the early 1900's Mundy traveled up the Brahmaputra River into Adi territory in quest of ivory and, although he could proceed no closer to the Tibetan border due to the threat of headhunters, he heard rumors of a paradisiacal valley that inspired his fictional account of a monastic sanctuary perched against a 'sheer wall of crags' and protected by Adi tribesmen who watch over the hidden land 'as cobras guard ancient ruins'.

A few days trek from the Adi village we reached a place very much like what Mundy had described. A steep-walled limestone island, enveloped by luxuriant jungle, rose out of the Yangsang Chu, crowned by a timber-framed temple called Devikota, 'The Citadel of the Goddess'. To reach it, we crossed the Yangsang Chu on a tubular bridge woven from rattan and split bamboo and hauled our way up through a tangle of bamboo and rhododendron. Where the slope steepened we scaled notched logs that had been laid against the cliffs. As we climbed higher, the sonorous beats of a ritual drum drifted down through the trees.

Tibetans first reached Devikota in the middle of the eighteenth-century, following prophecies laid down a thousand years earlier by Tibet's 'Lotus Born' patron saint, Padmasambhava. His accounts of the valley, recorded thousands of miles away, ensured Tibetans that they would find a lasting refuge here from the wars and strife that would descend on Tibet in subsequent centuries. The prophecies further stated that, following a future Armageddon, the human race would originate from here anew.

The first pilgrims arrived at Devikota after the Mongol invasions of Tibet in the seventeenth and eighteenth-centuries. More followed in the wake of the Chinese Revolution of 1913 and still more after the Maoist invasion of Tibet in 1959 that sent the Dalai Lama into exile. Occasionally, Tibetans from India and Nepal visit the isolated valley to practice meditation and to venerate the Goddess Vajra Varahi. Many collect vermillion-colored mercuric sulfide from the surrounding caves that they hold to be her menstrual blood, a powerful talisman on the Tantric path.

Inside the temple, an elderly lama with dark grey hair pulled back into a topknot, sat cross-legged in front of a latticed window while beating rhythmically on a carved wooden drum. We stepped through the massive front doors and sat quietly on the floor.

"He's invoking one of the area's protector spirits," Sherab whispered. I reflected that placating local nature spirits was a good thing in northern Arunachal Pradesh: The epicenter of the largest earthquake ever recorded was a mere thirty miles to the north of us. When we told the lama of our mission, his eyes widened in bemusement.

"When so many great lamas have failed to find Chimé Yangsang Né, what makes you think you will be successful?" he asked.

"Even if the Ultimate Secret Place does not actually exist," I ventured. "We want to explore the landscape that gave rise to the legend."

The lama looked at me quizzically. "Don't think that it's just an imaginary place," he cautioned. He pointed to the large three-dimensional mandala representing the Buddhist cosmos that filled the center of the room. "Just like our own enlightened nature, the Ultimate Secret Place is fully present, even if hidden to our view."

Although the lama had never physically tried to reach Chimé Yangsang Né—his work, he said, was at Devikota—he spoke of it in intimate detail: ancient route descriptions, rites to perform and, most of all, the obstacles that we would encounter the closer we came to its door. As clouds billowed up from the gorge below and enveloped the temple, the lama spoke of hidden precipices, venomous snakes, and clouds of insects that would plague our way. And those were the least of our concerns. Citing the case of Yeshi's grandfather, Jedrung Rinpoche, he mimed the drawing back of a long bow and spoke about the un-predictable nature of the Mishmi tribesmen who inhabit the cloud forests further up the valley and who had habitually preyed on pilgrims with arrows dipped in poisonous concoctions of aconite and deadly nightshade.

"I don't think he wants us to continue," Sherab said.

In the two days since we'd left Devikota Dorje had been uncharac-teristically quiet. We were fast approaching Mishmi territory, one of the least known regions in an already little known part of the world. There was no certainty that we would be well received. As a British Intelligence Officer reported in 1911, the Mishmi "regarded strangers as welcome only as possible victims of extortion by pacific or violent means, or as allies from whom they might obtain weapons with which they could massacre their neighbours more efficiently than with their simple implements of death."

The last known incident of ritual headhunting had occurred half a century earlier, and I was hoping for at least a neutral reception. Finally,

Dorje admitted to what had been troubling him. "The Mishmi are angry with me," he said.

The Ultimate Secret Place, he clarified, lies within the Mishmis' ancestral hunting grounds. "Hunting in a sacred place goes against Buddhist teachings. So I petitioned the state government of Arunachal to protect the area. The Mishmi did not like this. They kill and eat anything that moves."

That prompted the obvious question: "So how will they receive us?" Dorje just shrugged his shoulders. "I guess we'll see how upset they really are."

As the trail steepened we climbed over buttressed tree roots, shafts of sunlight filtering down through the canopy and the air bright with butterflies. We had taken on new porters at the Tibetan settlement below Devikota, as Dorje had recommended, who were now strung out over several miles of footpath. Dorje usually took the lead with the porters. I stayed back with Sherab in his search for rare medicinal plants with names like Adamantine Serpent Tamer, Grass of Miracles, or the All-Beneficent Herb. Sometimes we'd fall so far behind that Dorje would send the five female Adi porters back to look for us, as if to prove their absolute necessity. As the number five related to the five elements of Buddhist cosmology, we began to refer to them, respectively, as 'Earth', 'Water', 'Fire', 'Wind', and 'Space'.

We saw our first Mishmi longhouse from a distance. Almost immediately, three hunters slipped soundlessly out of the bamboo to greet us. They were dressed in loincloths and cane helmets with bamboo bows slung over their shoulders. I looked at Dorje warily. He nodded and said something in Mishmi and they began leading us towards their small settlement.

In the largest longhouse, old headhunting swords and rattan back packs hung on the walls along with rows of smoke-blackened animal skulls including those of mithun, bear, leopard, wild boar, deer, and monkey. Apart from a Brittany Spears T-shirt that had filtered its way up from the bazaars of Calcutta, the only overt sign of the 21st century was an unused and unconnected solar panel that Dorje said had been sent in by the Indian Government.

If there was tension between Dorje and the Mishmi, I didn't feel it. Instead, our arrival presented the perfect opportunity for a party. Our chief host seated us at the central fire pit then went off to notify the neighbors. We were, he said, the first outsiders ever to visit their community.

As we waited for him to return, more Mishmis piled into the raised dwelling. Women kept their children at a sensible distance. Pigs wallowed beneath the floor that threatened to collapse under the increasing weight.

Amidst the unaccustomed activity our chief host reappeared at the top of the notched pole ladder leading into the longhouse, his earrings of beaten gold glittering in the backlight. "So you want to find the Tibetans' Ultimate Secret Place?" he asked through Dorje. "You'll need to eat well first!"

Though the Mishmi hunt a number of threatened animals from clouded leopard to takin, their favored delicacy is a distinctly unendangered species of Himalayan field rat that they stew with bones and fur. In one hand our host held his bow and arrows and, in the other, a rack of plump and glistening rats that his wife promptly added to the communal pot.

A woman with hair cropped closely beneath her ears soon arrived at the longhouse with two male attendants. She was the local Mishmi shaman, or *igu*, and, after a few rounds of apong, she drew a great rack of tigers' teeth from a cloth sack and slipped it over her shoulder. She then fastened a red panda tail around her waist and a bandeau of feathers and cowrie shells around her head. She'd been told of our destination and insisted on performing a ceremony to strengthen our life force and ensure our safe return. "If something happens to you or you die," she said, "the Indian Government will blame us."

She and her two male attendants began an extraordinary ritual; beating on drums, blowing on antler horns, and rattling swords which they periodically drove into the wooden floorboards with forceful incantations. Through Dorje, I asked the igu if she had ever visited the Ultimate Secret Place. In spirit only, she said. The Tibetans' Ultimate Secret Place was the same location as the Mishmi land of the dead, she said, and it was her duty to guide souls there after death. Eager to get more precise directions than those offered in the Tibetan texts I asked if she could describe the route.

Dismissing the rough map that I had sketched in my journal, the igu began to lay out strips of bamboo on the longhouse floor, explaining that they represented the series of streams and razorback ridges that the deceased person must cross to reach the door to the afterworld. The door, she said, was situated above a shimmering cascade at the heart of their ancestral lands. This echoed not only the jomo's account, but a passage from the *Darkness-Dispelling Lantern*, one of our primary texts, that described the doorway as lying above a 'Crystal Mirror' of falling water.

Like the lama at Devikota, the igu ran through a long list of dangers that await those seeking the Mishmi Valhalla, including snakes that drop out of the trees and a predatory tiger that, not long before, had reputedly killed the majority of a Mishmi hunting party that had ventured into the vicinity in search of musk deer.

"If you try to go there before you are dead," the igu stated, "you could easily die on the way." A disturbing theme seemed to be developing.

It was the moment a porter slipped through a hole in the earth that I fully realized why so few have actively sought out the Ultimate Secret Place. We had left the Yangsang Chu valley, and had been climbing almost straight up for two days. Using hands as much as our legs, we grabbed onto roots, rock outcrops, and curling lianas to haul ourselves up muddy, eroding slopes. In places, sheared bamboo, thrust into the sides of ravines, offered footholds to keep us from plunging down into a green abyss. Sherab cleared the route as best he could with his machete, reciting mantras to take his mind off the predations of rattan thorns and the ubiquitous leeches.

One of the greatest hazards was the moss. Northern Arunachal Pradesh, where moisture-laden air from the Bay of Bengal collides headlong into the Himalaya, receives some of the heaviest rainfall on the planet. One of its effects is to produce a rampant carpeting of moss that covers the roots of trees, creating an illusion of solid ground. An incautious step and one can plummet downward through a latticework of moss-encrusted roots. This is exactly what happened to the porter walking in front of me. In an instant, he broke through the spongy surface until he hung suspended from his armpits fifteen feet beneath the trail, his bamboo pack basket ricocheting downward into a morass of vertiginous jungle.

Establishing camp was an ordeal in such multi-leveled terrain. The porters usually holed up beneath overhanging rocks where they could start a fire. Where there were no shelters, they slept on sapling pole platforms covered in combinations of tree bark, plantain leaves, and plastic lashed together with rattan vines. Dorje, Sherab, and I would set up our tents away from trees that, in the event of a storm, could shower us with dead branches. I couldn't help but wonder if the Ultimate Secret Place just didn't want to be found.

A single thought had preoccupied me for days: How—if the jomo, the lama, and the igu had never physically searched for the Ultimate Secret Place—did they seemingly know firsthand details about the route? How could the igu lay out a ridge-by-ridge map of the area with bamboo sticks? And how could the Tibetan texts—if they were written a thousand years before any Tibetan had ever reached this place—describe detailed physical features of this labyrinth of dark ravines and valleys?

In the eighth-century scroll *Clear Light*, the author describes a series of five lakes spread across an undulating plateau high above the Yangsang Chu. Pilgrims seeking the Ultimate Secret Place needed to perform a series of purificatory rites at these lakes before proceeding to the portal. The lakes were the reason that Dorje had led us out of the Yangsang Chu basin. They were also the reason that our tents now leaked like sieves through their perforated floors and that we had almost lost one of our porters. And though they were well known enough now, it was still baffling to me when we arrived at their shores. How could the author of *Clear Light* have known that such lakes existed? I asked Dorje whose dismissive answer was that Padmasambhava was a living Buddha and thus omniscient.

Almost immediately upon our arrival at the first of the five lakes, it began to rain. For the next three days we sheltered in a small pine wood shelter perched on a knoll above the 12,000-foot high lake. With dwindling food supplies, we lived largely on buckwheat and coconut gruel as rain and hail lashed the walls. Sherab sorted through his plant collection and reviewed the Tibetan texts for further clues. Dorje spent most of his time in his oversized Korean-made tent that, ostensibly for their own protection, he shared with all five of the female porters.

After three days, with no sign of a let up in the rain, we began the customary circumambulation around the five lakes, each separated from the other by waterfalls and vegetated cliffs. The lakes vaguely conform to specific shapes—square, crescent moon, triangle, and circle—corresponding to specific Tantric empowerments as well as to the five chakras, or psychic energy centers, associated with the endocrine system of the human body. Pilgrims who drink the waters of each of the lakes reputedly absorb their respective qualities, removing obstacles on the path to enlightenment. Sherab and Dorje conducted simple rituals at each lake, preparing us for the final leg of our journey and the descent to the sources of the Yangsang Chu.

The climb down through the trackless, moss-drenched forest was more treacherous than our ascent. Sherab nearly disappeared over an escarpment while reaching for a rare plant specimen, saved by an exposed tree root and barbed vines that left his hands streaked with blood. I nearly plunged into a rock-filled ravine when a log bridge, hastily erected by our porters, collapsed beneath my greater weight. The lama at Devikota had said that the dangers would only increase the closer we got to the Ultimate Secret Place. By this measure we were right on track.

One threat kept me mindful to the subtlest movement in the underbrush. On our way through Calcutta, I had tried to purchase vials of freeze-dried polyvalent antivenin made from cobra, common krait, Russell's viper, and saw-scaled viper, in anticipation of northern Arunachal's unusual density of snakes, but the regional supplier was out of stock. Lacking alternatives, we had adopted the local custom of wearing protective amulets made from the saber-like tusks of Himalayan musk deer and black sachets of aromatic herbs. Apart from the startling sight of tree snakes that launch themselves from branches, most worrying was the notoriously aggressive Russell's viper that hones in on its prey through built-in heat sensors located in a cavity between its nostrils and its eyes.

Even if one survives the uncontrollable hemorrhaging of organs and tissues that results from envenomation, the bite of the Russell's viper wreaks havoc on the pituitary gland that regulates the flow of sex hormones. Victims begin a process of reverse puberty, losing facial and pubic hair and secondary sexual characteristics leading ultimately to impotence and sterility. As Dorje noted, few survive, or even want to survive, to demonstrate the sobering array of symptoms.

After two days of bushwhacking through rain and gnat-infested jungle, and aided significantly by gravity, we gained the upper reaches of the Yangsang Chu. We camped by rapids that hurtled through a dark precipitous gorge. If the texts were correct, we would find the Crystal Mirror in the following days. Would it be there? With their stores of rice nearly finished, the porters had taken to eating succulent fern tendrils and lightly roasted frogs. That night they built a great fire by the edge of the river. As the Adi girls danced, their bare feet rose and fell on the Earth like primal offerings, and their singing seemed to quell the rain. Hand in hand, they continued their dance around the glowing embers; guardians and revealers of an ancient world.

The following morning we moved silently through bands of light. The river narrowed; tree branches from the opposite banks met overhead to form a twisting passageway through the primeval rainforest. Sherab wore a characteristic circlet of ferns wrapped around his head. Dorje forged ahead with his bamboo staff, the rooted end of which he had carved into the horned head of a mithun. "Keep your voice low," he cautioned. "This is a place of spirits. If we disturb them they will send bad weather and block our way."

As we made our way upstream, we could hear the roar of a cataract. My heart quickened in anticipation. As we rounded a bend in the river, the mists parted and a waterfall came suddenly into view between moss-strung trees. A dazzling curtain of water, perhaps two hundred feet high, cleaved the mists. Just as the igu had said, the falls was double sided with two cascades tumbling on either side of a white quartzite buttress. The perpetual, pounding waters had smoothed the slabs so that they shimmered in the light. The Crystal Mirror.

Dorje knew from his father that we needed to ascend the cascade on the right. We crossed the base of the falls and, drenched in spray, began free climbing up a fault line, clinging to exposed roots and stripping the rock of moss in search of holds. We had accidentally left our climbing rope behind as we'd lightened our loads for the final stage of our journey, but continued without it. Dorje took the lead, his Indian-made rubber boots offering better traction against the water polished rock than my vibram-soled climbing boots. Where a torrent coursed through a shallow defile, Dorje lowered a dubious-looking branch to help Sherab and me across. Gazing down at the falls crashing on the rocks far below us, I realized that we were in mortal danger, yet felt unaccountably at ease, as if some benign protective force was guiding us deeper into the unknown.

We eventually hauled ourselves up to a sloping ledge and climbed to a cave that opened near the top of the falls. This was the Cave of Magical Daggers, so named because of the small triangular shaped rocks that covered the floor along with mounds of bat guano. Dorje and Sherab performed a short ceremony to appease whatever entities might be lurking there and then continued. To reach the door to the Ultimate Secret Place, we would have to climb through the Cave of Magical Daggers onto the steep, forested slopes above. I remained behind at the cave, thinking about Yeshi who, for all I knew, had passed this way before us. I left a small offering for her in the depths of the cavern and then surfaced to confront an overhanging wall of rock with a slimy 20-foot notched log placed precariously against it. It was saturated and half rotten but, assuming that Sherab and Dorje had already climbed it, I started up without hesitation. As I neared the top, the log dissolved beneath me, leaving me hanging onto a thin birch sapling. There was no turning back.

According to the jomo's account, the door to the Ultimate Secret Place lay at the base of an overhanging cliff where the womb waters of the Goddess Vajra Varahi issue from the rock. As I approached a sheer rock face of dripping limestone, I could see a moss-lined fissure, too narrow it seemed to enter, opening near the base of the cliff. Below the cleft, a thin stream of water poured from a lone white stalactite in a recess in the rock. How had the jomo known? Footprints in the mud showed that Dorje and Sherab had already been here. But where were they now? Had they somehow entered the cave or found another larger entrance higher up? The limestone walls were embossed with strange wave like markings.

I thought of Yeshi and her grandfather whose quest had lured me to this very spot. I unwrapped the red seeds of the tsakuntuzangpo plant that Sherab had given me and swallowed them with the translucent water dripping from the smooth stalactite. I waited in the stillness and then, without bothering to take out my headlight, I headed through the fissure in the rock.

The darkness was almost total. I felt the walls of the fissure tighten around me as I ran my hands along the thick wet moss, half imagining that they would graze upon a hidden lever that would reveal the uncharted sanctuary. It was not to be. About twenty yards in, the passage narrowed too much for me to continue. I turned and felt my way back into the light.

After trying for years to reach this fabled place, after weeks of struggling through treacherous jungle and over high passes, I'd imagined that I'd feel disappointed if I failed to find something tangible. But, on the contrary, I felt enveloped by consoling mysteries.

A powerful current runs through our everyday lives. Although we don't normally attend to it, still less credit its existence, this 'secret river' of ephemeral signs, omens, and latent possibilities is our innermost nature. It seemed no coincidence that the Tibetan scriptures, the jomo, the igu, and the lama had all pointed to this same geographical location. Somehow they had seen without seeing, known without knowing. And while I couldn't comprehend their mode of perception—its mechanics are in all likelihood ungraspable by the mind—I could not deny its reality. I may have been shut out from the immortal realm invoked in the ancient Tibetan texts, but I'd been shown a richer way of living in this one.

It was twilight by the time I started to look for camp. I could not return the way I had come. That route had closed with the collapsing log, and I needed to find another way down. Sherab and Dorje were nowhere to be found. I was alone in the jungle. Out of the corner of my eye, I saw a spider poised in a gossamer web. It was gold and black, similar to the one the jomo had placed on my head, and when it saw me, it darted off to my left in an incandescent blur. I smiled and, turning in the same direction, began my descent back to the headwaters of the Yangsang Chu.

Questions and Answers

*I have leaped and thrown reeds and balanced sharpened twigs, I have
lived on roots in a wood and held a queen in my arms.*
~Beroul, *The Romance of Tristan*, 12th c.

1. What compelled you to set out on your pilgrimage?
I first learned of Tibet's 'Hidden-Land of Pemako' (Beyul Pemako) from a
Tibetan lama in Nepal. The lama described an earthly paradise that seemed
too good to be true. At the same time, I began preparing myself for a
pilgrimage that I knew would be life changing, whether Pemako existed in
the ways it had been described to me or not. It reminded me of the
compelling account by René Daumal of Mount Analogue—a place that exists
simply because it must exist.

2. Is there a book, song, poem, or movie that inspired your quest?
Tibetans' oral accounts of Beyul Pemako, 'Hidden-Land Arrayed Like a
Lotus', inspired me to search for this realm where the spiritual and physical
worlds are said to intersect and where humanity and nature flourish in
harmony. I began reading Tibetan manuscripts that elaborated on Pemako's
'outer, inner, secret, and innermost secret' topography. Based on these
writings, Pemako seemed to be the geographical source of the story of
Shangri-La that James Hilton had invoked in his 1932 novel *Lost Horizon*,
and which Frank Capra transformed into a classic Hollywood film of a
Himalayan sanctuary where the best of East and West has been preserved
for posterity.

3. Where is your sacred place and why did you choose it?
Beyul Pemako, 'Hidden-Land Arrayed Like A Lotus' is located in contested
territory in the borderlands of southern Tibet and northeastern India, at the
easternmost edge of the Himalayan Range. I have made more than ten
journeys into Pemako, seeking out its innermost realms. The journey
described here was a quest for Chimé Yangsang Né, the 'deathless innermost
secret place' at the center of Pemako. According to ancient Tibetan texts, to
enter this hidden dimension is to discover the innermost reaches of the
human psyche. I wanted to experience firsthand the geographical analogue
of this compelling Himalayan myth.

4. How did your pilgrimage change your life or not?
To seek out a place as exalted as the 'deathless innermost secret place'
demands sympathetic imagination and openness to improbability. My
pilgrimages to Pemako have thus involved extreme challenges, not only on a
physical level but also psychologically. The journey in search of Chimé

Yangsang Né, described here, continues to shape my orientation towards life in general, opening me to the hidden possibilities within all experience.

5. What is the most important piece of advice that you have received in your life? Do you have advice to share from your experiences?
Sir Alistair Cooke told me when I was twenty-one to "avoid small securities and give success a chance." That advice has influenced all my subsequent decisions. I continue to pass on that dictum, as well as my own advice to challenge inherited beliefs so as to open the world to larger possibilities and change it for the better.

Biography

Ian studied art history, literature, and comparative religion at Middlebury College, Oxford University, and Columbia University and Medical Anthropology at University College London. He is an international fellow of the Explorers Club and was honored by National Geographic Society as one of six 'Explorers for the Millennium' for his ethnographic and geographical field research in Tibet's Tsangpo gorges and his team's discovery of a waterfall that had been the source of myth and geographic speculation for more than a century.

Ian is the author of seven critically acclaimed books on Himalayan and Tibetan cultural history, environment, art, and medicine including *The Heart of the World: A Journey to the Last Secret Place*, *Celestial Gallery*, *The Tibetan of Art of Healing*, and *The Dalai Lama's Secret Temple*, a collaborative work with His Holiness The Dalai Lama that illuminates Tantric Buddhist meditation practices. Ian has also written for *National Geographic Magazine* and has contributed to academic journals in the fields of Tibetan yoga and physical culture in Vajrayāna Buddhism.

https://ianbakerjourneys.com

Lundang Nunnery, Nepal. *Photograph by Tor Torkildson.*

Photograph by Tom Fakler.

"Something opens our wings. Something makes boredom and hurt disappear. Someone fills the cup in front of us: We taste only sacredness."
~Rumi

A Special Tribute

We would like to pay special tribute to these inspirational seekers and pilgrims who have inspired us along our own quests.

Jelaluddin Rumi was a 13th-century mystic, and one of the most passionate and profound poets in history. Today his presence still remains strong, due in part to how his words seem to drip of the divine, and startle a profound remembrance that links back to the Soul-Essence. He has the ability to describe the Indescribable, Ineffable-God.

"You were born with wings, why prefer to crawl through life?" ~Rumi.

Rumi.

Basho was a 17th-century Japanese haiku master born near Kyoto. His work, rooted in observation of the natural world as well as in historical and literary concerns, engages themes of stillness and movement in a voice that is self-questioning, wry, and oracular. In aproximately 1682, Basho began the months-long journeys on foot that would become the material for the new poetic form he created, called haibun. Haibun imagery follows two paths: the external images observed en route, and the internal images that move through traveler's minds during the journey.

"Do not seek to follow in the footsteps of the wise; seek what they sought." ~Basho.

Basho.

John Muir was an influential naturalist and conservationist. Through his own example and the books that he wrote, Muir taught people the importance of experiencing and protecting our natural world. His words have heightened our perception of nature. Muir is an inspiration for environmental activists and lovers of nature around the world.

"Everything is flowing...going somewhere, animals and so-called lifeless rocks as well as water. Thus, the snow flows fast or slow in grand beauty-making glaciers and avalanches; the air in majestic floods carrying minerals, plant leaves, seeds, spores, with streams of music and fragrance; water streams carrying rocks...the stars go streaming through space pulsed on and on forever like blood...in natures warm heart." ~John Muir

John Muir.

Alexandra David-Néel was a French explorer and Buddhist who was the first Western woman to visit Llasa in Tibet in 1923, at the age of 55. She lived in Tibet for 14 years, meditated for a year in an isolated cave, and throughout her life visited much of Asia. She went on to write *Magic and Mystery in Tibet* her most popular book, as well as numerous other books and articles about Tibet. She adopted a young Tibetan, whom she had traveled with, Lama Aphur Yongden, and he returned with her to France.

"...I consider as the happiest in my life those days, when, with a load on my back, I wandered as one of the countless tribe of Thibetan beggar pilgrims." ~Alexander David- Néel

Alexandra David-Néel.

Peace Pilgrim completed the Appalachian Trail in 1952, the first woman to do so in one season. After this walk she felt the need to walk for peace and gave up her possessions, other than the clothing on her back. Peace walked with a t-shirt that read 'Peace Pilgrim' on the front and '25,000 Miles on Foot for Peace' on the back of her shirt in order to bring attention to peace. She walked for 28 years (1952-1981) meandering across the United States seven times, into every state, and Mexico and Canada until her death at age 72. She was a great orator, and spoke at churches, universities and with the media to promote the message of Peace.

"I am a pilgrim, a wanderer. I shall remain a wanderer until mankind has learned the way of peace, walking until I am given shelter and fasting until I am given food." ~Peace Pilgrim

Peace Pilgrim.

John Trudell was a Santee Dakota activist, artist, actor, and poet, who led a life dedicated to indigenous human rights, land and language issues. He helped spark a spoken word movement that is a continuation of Native American oral traditions. Trudell was on a quest to bring about critical awareness when he walked on at age 69.

"Sometimes when it rains, it's not that simple, when the sky has reasons to cry." ~John Trudell

John Trudell.

Reinhold Messner is one of the great seekers of extreme WILD. He is one of the most impressive mountaineers and explorers of the 20th century. He was the first person, along with partner Peter Habler, to climb Mount Everest without supplemental oxygen in 1978. He also was the first person to solo ascend Mount Everest and the first to climb all fourteen 8,000-meter peaks, the world highest mountains. He has led expeditions to the north and south poles, crossed the Gobi Desert in central Asia on foot: and researched and wrote a book about the infamous Yeti. Messner has pushed the limits of the human potential.

"I always take the same perspective with each new adventure. I put myself in the position of being at the end of my life and looking back. Then I ask myself if what I am doing is important to me." ~Rienhold Messner

Reinhold Messner.

Clinton Pryor recently walked across Australia from Perth to Canberra as a pilgrimage to learn about Aboriginal concerns by visiting communities along the route, with the goal of bringing awareness of these issues to the Australian Prime Minister in the hopes of making change. As he visited communities he gave talks to inspire people to have dreams and hope.

Clinton, who earned the term "Spirit Walker" while walking, is a Wajuk Balardung, Kija and a Yulparitja man from Perth, and followed the songlines and roads along the way. As a school administrator who took off a year to walk, he became concerned when the Australian government started forced closures of Aboriginal communities, including the one he grew up in. When his father died, Clinton promised him he would help his people and keep his culture alive.

"I just wanted to make a difference and bring out the truth." ~Clinton Pryor

Clinton Pryor.

His Holiness, Tenzin Gyatso, 14th Dalai Lama — The greatest Pilgrim of all.

"Happiness is determined more by one's state of mind than by external events." ~Dalai Lama XIV

The Dalai Lama, XIV.

Afterward

Publishing, *The Walkabout Chronicles: Epic Journeys by Foot,* last year was a growing experience for Tor and I. We gained valuable insights about the publishing process and keep trying to improve. With the decision to carry on with the Chronicles Series we knew how time-consuming it would be, however, we also knew the joys of embarking on a labor of love and the friendships that would transpire as a result. We were willing to lose another summer to create *The Pilgrimage Chronicles: Embrace the Quest.* Tor jumped in with his networking and social media skills, and I carried out the editing and formatting work. There have been many long days working side by side hammering out another large-format book with 33 essays.

We are honored to include new and old friends in this anthology, some from, *The Walkabout Chronicles*, and others new to the Tribe. This Tribe includes people from all walks of life, from explorers to pilgrims, writers, and researchers, with quests that span the globe.

We have included photographs from talented friends to accompany quotes. Our hope is that the stories and photographs will inspire the reader to travel out on their own quest with wide open eyes. Everyone involved in this project has been kind, considerate, appreciative, supportive, and inspirational. It has been a pleasure to work with such an enthusiastic and encouraging group of people. It is with great joy that we share these essays and photographs with the world. I am fortunate to have a husband and a business partner that is easy to work with and fun. There is nothing as exciting as sharing a glass of wine together and creating a new book or dreaming of our next quest.

Siffy Torkildson

Sacred World Explorations
Alaska

Sacred World Explorations is a small publishing company. We publish articles on adventure travel, the environment, spirituality, food and wine, sacredness, and far flung journeys around the world. Guiding and consulting upon request.

Our destination is, in a sense, sacred, with the belief that certain voyages out, might become voyages in. Think of it as a sort of geo-poetic quest; the glint of an outer light reflected or of an inner light revealed. Through our memory maps, we will navigate the sacred world, creating a web of connections from everywhere to everywhere.

"Wandering re-establishes the original harmony that once existed between humans and the universe" Anatole France.

Books from Sacred World Explorations:

The Pilgrimage Chronicles: Embrace the Quest anthology with Tor and Siffy
The Walkabout Chronicles: Epic Journeys by Foot anthology with Tor and Siffy
Korrigan's Shadow by Pierre Delattre
Agadir Dreaming by Tor Torkildson
A Wild Hare: Finding the Life I Imagined by Siffy Torkildson
Cloud Wanderer:A Peripatetic Quest to Live the Life I Imagined by Tor Torkildson

We are thrilled to bring you the Chronicle Series:
Volume I- *The Walkabout Chronicles: Epic Journeys by Foot*
Volume II- *The Pilgrimage Chronicles: Embrace the Quest*

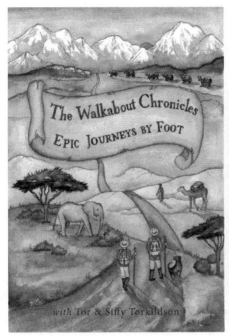 

Sacred World Explorations
Alaska

Made in the USA
Columbia, SC
18 December 2017